In Passing: A Book About Death

Concept and Design: Todd Herman
Design and Layout: Scott Idleman/Blink
                        www.blinkdesign.com

Printed in Canada

ISBN: 0-9765086-0-5

The Dancing Tree
Publishing and Distributing
San Francisco, California
www.thedancingtree.org

In Passing, a traveling exhibit, premiered
at the San Francisco Arts Commission Gallery,
401 Van Ness Avenue, San Francisco, CA 94102,
on April 20–June 11, 2005.

Cover photograph by Marilyn Michlin Herman

Endpapers
© 2002 Courtesy Stanley B. Burns, MD / The Burns Archive

In Passing

a book about death

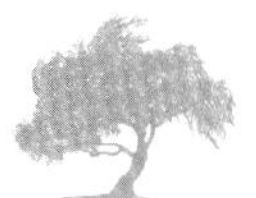

The Dancing Tree
Publishing and Distributing
www.thedancingtree.org

Contents

For
Irving Ira Herman
January 29, 1914–July 3, 2003

Preface

by Todd Herman

In June of 2003, I received a call that my father was dying. Some time after arriving at my parent's home, I took out my camera, as I always do in order to understand, and quietly began to document the time spent at my father's deathbed. Three days passed. My father silently waited for his family to assemble, for the camera to be put away, and for us all to go to sleep so he could die alone.

As I began sharing my experience of my father's last days with friends and colleagues, I was surprised at what I heard. There were those who spoke candidly of a lasting desire to have said more to, or to have done more for their loved ones before they died. Many others were clearly uncomfortable with the subject, offering verbal tonics to accelerate grieving or stories about how other cultures deal with death. All well intended. There were, of course, others who didn't know death.

I listened to their regrets, denials, joys, and pains that were much different from mine, some clearly articulated, while other stories advanced with ineffable poetry. *In Passing: A Book About Death* developed from these conversations and explores our complicated interactions with the artifacts, images, and memories of death.

Some of the work in this book speaks from places of healing, while others languish in the expansive quality of time dictated by grief. Some works are commemorative, some left over from ritual, others darkly humorous, and still others conjure mythic understandings borne from watching a life pass into ancestry.

In Passing includes work by artists, writers, photographers—professional and non-professionals—and touches on aspects of the very substance and frailty of human life as it passes, while exploring both the diversity as well as the common threads in our experiences of death.

It is my hope that within this book, readers might recognize some of their own struggles, questions, and fears around death. That through such reflection they will take whatever time they need to remember, to prepare for, or to pass through to that place of clarity on the other side of grief, loss, and longing.

Introduction

by Jay Ruby

Attitudes toward death in American society have had a complex history. In the nineteenth century it was a common topic of polite discussion. Mourning was a normal part of the public life of most adults. Widowhood was a primary lifelong social role for many women. Cemeteries were designed to be used as recreational sites. And then it all changed. From the beginning of the twentieth century until the 1970s, death became a forbidden subject among the Americanized middle class. The slightest sign of distress at the death of a family member was regarded as pathological.

Recently, some progress has been made in reintegrating death into the lives of people living in the United States. Certainly the popularity of Jessica Mitford's and Elisabeth Kubler-Ross's works signal a shift in popular attitude. Grief counseling has become more common and accessible. Death education is offered with greater frequency in the public schools. And the work of people such as Philippe Aries has legitimized death as an acceptable topic for research and discussion.

While pictures of death may be an acceptable part of our media fare, some Americans are less comfortable with the idea of producing similar pictures for private use. Photographic memorial cards and tombstones, posthumous commemorative paintings, or living video wills are somewhat unusual but not considered morbid or pathological. Other remembrances are viewed more negatively. People who wish to obtain postmortem or funeral photographs face a personal conflict and potential public disapproval if they take pictures or commission someone to do so. They appear to be trapped between contradictory cultural norms—using photography to memorialize important experiences and the belief that material remembrances of death prolong grief, and are therefore morbid and unhealthy for the mourner. Because images of those we love who have died form a significant part of the grieving process, we make and use photographic representations of the dead whether our society approves or not. We need to gain a better understanding of our private need to remember through photography.

There is no mystery as to why people take pictures of deceased loved ones. They feel the need for a last visual remembrance. If the deceased was a child, particularly a very young child, it may be the only photograph they possess. In the nineteenth century, people used corpse and funeral pictures in the same way they used other photographs—that is, mounted and hung in parlors, bedrooms, and living rooms, glued in albums, mailed to relatives, placed on top of mantels, carried in wallets, and so on. In contrast to the twentieth century, there was no attempt to hide these images. Anyone who was privy to your family photographs could see them.

In the twenty-first century, the uses of death-related photographs are more guarded. They are absent from all of the recent family albums I have examined. Those who do possess death-related family pictures regard them as very private pictures to be shown only to selected people. A rural Pennsylvania funeral director told me that the photograph he took of his young daughter upon her death was only for him and his wife, and that he had not even shown it to his other children. On the other hand, he sometimes notices that when he gives a family member a Polaroid postmortem they requested him to take, the family members pass it among themselves and any friends who happen to be around—much in the manner one passes around any newly acquired Polaroid.

I have interviewed families who keep postmortem pictures in their family Bible or with other important family documents such as birth certificates and property deeds. Based on my ethnographic studies, I conclude that postmortem photographs taken since World War II are not likely to be in the family album or deposited in other places where the family keeps their photographs, but rather kept in a special place of more limited access and privacy.

Perhaps it is not the photographs in and of themselves that are a sign of pathology or health, but rather how they are used by the mourner. We are only now coming to terms with the notion that normal grief is a long process with discernable stages—shock, preoccupation with the deceased, and resolution. How long each stage lasts varies from individual to individual as well as from culture to culture. Once our society accepts the fact that mourners have to work through these stages at their own pace, the use of photographs as an aide-mémoire may become more publicly accepted.

In the nineteenth century, the personal desire for a corpse or funeral photograph was socially appropriate and the behavior was supported by the culture. One could publicly display the photographs without fear of being regarded as pathological. Personal needs and society's expectation of what constitutes a normal response to loss were not in conflict. This is not true in the twenty-first century. Yet in spite of the social disapprobation, many, many people continue the practice. Americans have spent most of this century adoring youth and denying death. We have removed death, along with birth, from the everyday reality of our lives to institutions where strangers take charge of these crucial moments. We have shielded ourselves as much as possible from our species' beginnings and endings. We are slowly beginning to realize that pretending that death doesn't exist will not prevent it from intruding into our lives. As difficult as it has been, we are beginning to accept sadness and grief as a normal, even healthy, part of living.

We cannot prevent the loss of those we love, but we do sometimes mitigate the loss with an image. *In Passing* is a compilation of such imagery, offering the reader personal-idiosyncratic to sociopolitical accounts of one of life's most shared intimacies. Whether written years after a loved one's death, drawn to rekindle a fading connection to the deceased, or photographed during the moments when life passes from the body, the contributors of this book do not define, but preserve both the mystery and integrity of another's passing. They honor the ways that death lives among the living, the many efforts through which we are able to understand the contiguity of a human life.

References

Aries, Philippe. 1974. *Western Attitudes Toward Death: From the Middle Ages to the Present.* Baltimore, MD: Johns Hopkins University Press.
———1974. *Death in America.* Philadelphia: University of Pennsylvania Press
———1976. "The Reversal of Death: Changes in Attitudes Toward Death in Western Societies." *American Quarterly* 26:536–60.
———1981. *The Hour of Death.* New York: Knopf.
———1985. *Images of Man and Death.* Janet Lloyd, translator. Cambridge, MA: Harvard University Press.

Kubler-Ross, Elisabeth. 1969. *On Death and Dying.* New York: Macmillan.

Mitford, Jessica. 2000 (1963). *The American Way of Death Revisited.* New York: Vintage Books.

Stoudemire, Alan and Trig Brown. 1983. "Normal and Pathological Grief." *Journal of the American Medical Association* 1250:378–82.

Michael Bernard Loggins

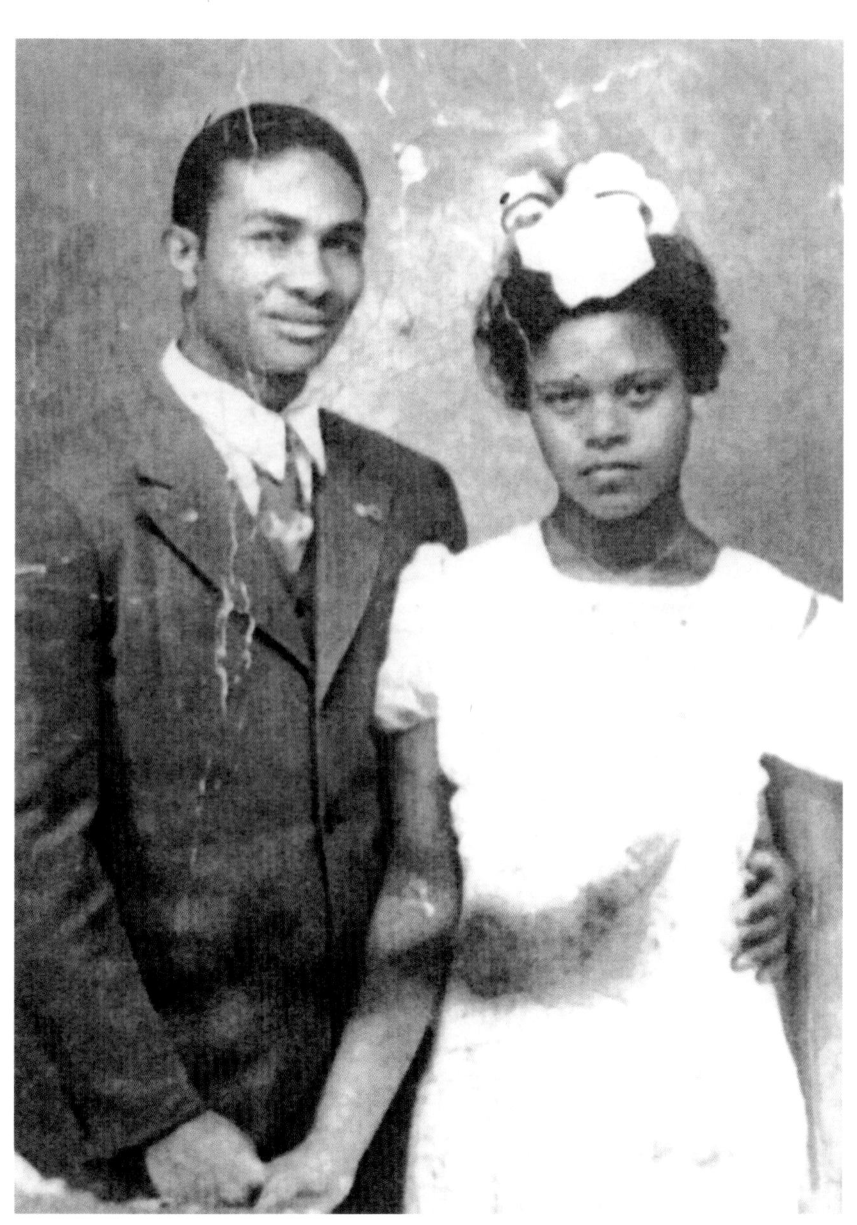

MY mother Died on
Monday October 29, 2001.

And My Father Died on
Wednesday March 27, 2002.

I May remember when My mother Cooked Beans and rice and she Used to Put Hot dogs in to my beans and rice to help it to taste Marvelous and Deliciously good Because she Cuts the Hot dogs up Into the Pot of Beans and Rice For our Dinner For the night.

We Enjoy Eating Beans and Rice and Hotdogs. Suppertime was the Best meal time of our Days of our Lives. But Life Left out of my mother's body.

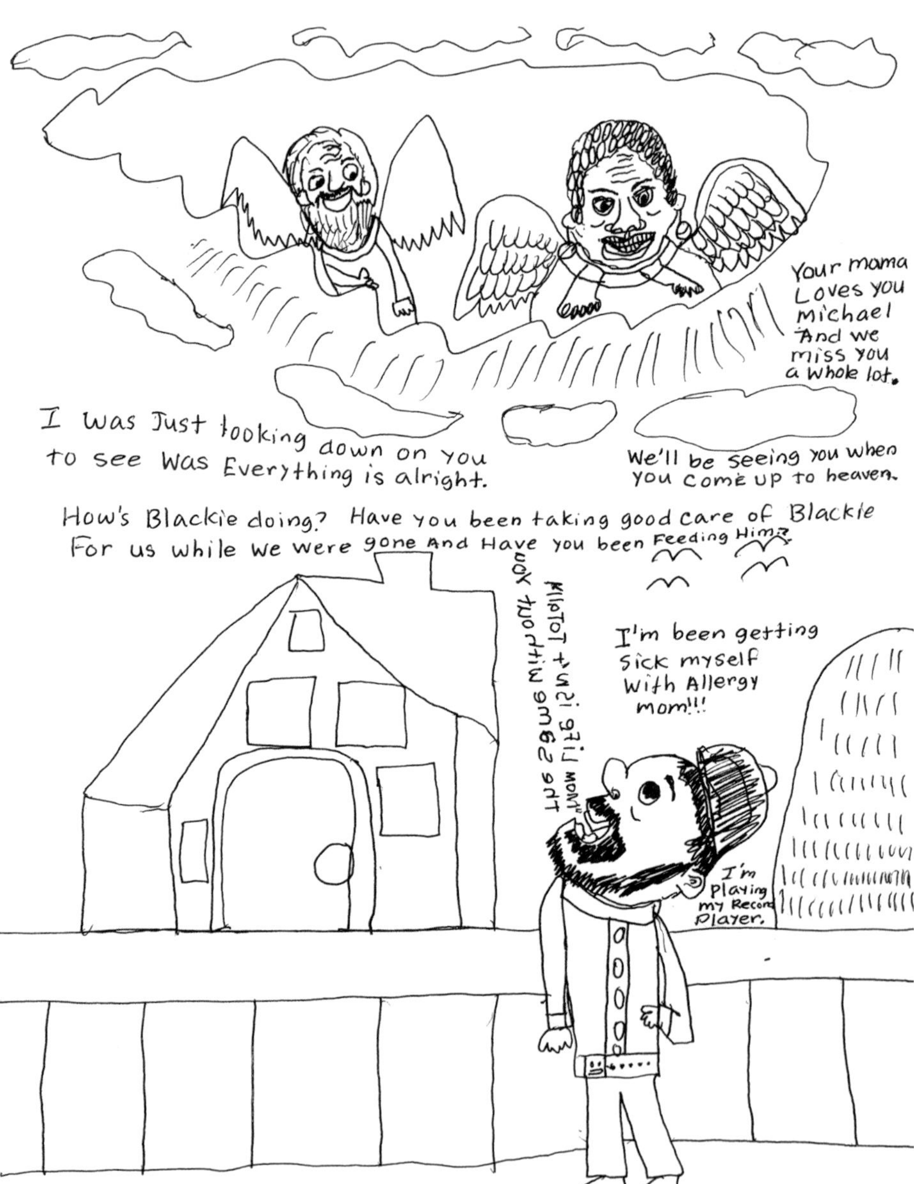

Your mama
Loves you
Michael
And we
miss you
a whole lot.
I was Just looking down on you
to see Was Everything is alright.
We'll be seeing you when
you come up to heaven.
How's Blackie doing? Have you been taking good care of Blackie
For us while we were gone And Have you been Feeding Him?
I'm been getting
Sick myself
With Allergy
mom!!!
the game isn't the same Without you
I'm
Playing
my Record
Player.

LiFE would never be totally the same when you come back Home to where your Parents once raise you in. But the memory of their Love still within your Heart even they are as if they were missing in Your Life, but they are watching Over you From Heaven.

A Life spent part of your morning sitting on a bench wondering what would you do without Your parents, and How is Life For me living Totally Alone in that great big old House when I wouldn't Know where the First thing to start to be brave and not be So Afraid. "Nah." I Feel really scared For the First time after we Loss our Parents. LiFe is a Cold and Scary Experience to go through.

In This Hard cold Freezing chilly season times is the worse times to ever want to live totally alone Scare As you can be after your Parents and Loved one's dies and LiFe can get very Freaky and cold cold and Scary.

is Living in Life is
Effecting you real bad
Now That Your Father Aren't
No Longer around Any
more to Look after You?

were your Father ever
taking You For a ride in
any of his Automobiles
Just You And him spent time
alone Just bonding close to
one another Having the time
of your LiFE Together being
LiFE long Pals back then As a
Son and Fatherhood Figures.?

Is Life without your
Father is a Lonesome
Living alone in physical
make you feel like if He
is missing in your Life
Like a orange without
an skin to cover it up
in order to make the orange
to be whole orange?

you aren't gonna go
Through Life as busy as you
can possibly be and not ever
keeping a written Journal to write about him?

LIFE MOMENTS
Shared With Family and GirlFriend and
Friends Through Hardship and Death
in the Living through tough times.

Tough times is sharing the Experiences
and Crying and Grief of A Dying
Family member crisis is happening.

Let your Crying of the Sorrow Hang on
out Let the Feelings come out Let it
Show so the people can understand
Just How Hurtful You are really Feeling
Over the Death of a Family Member
Ouch! Ouch! Ouch! I can Feel the Hurt

I only Need to Feel the Hurt
So Now I really Need to Focus
on my Hurting Crying Sorrow Crisis
right at this time of the hard
moment of my LIFE is Facing
Death in the LIFE AND MY Family
member Who has Pass away But Not
ON Purpose. "LIFE HAPPENS!"

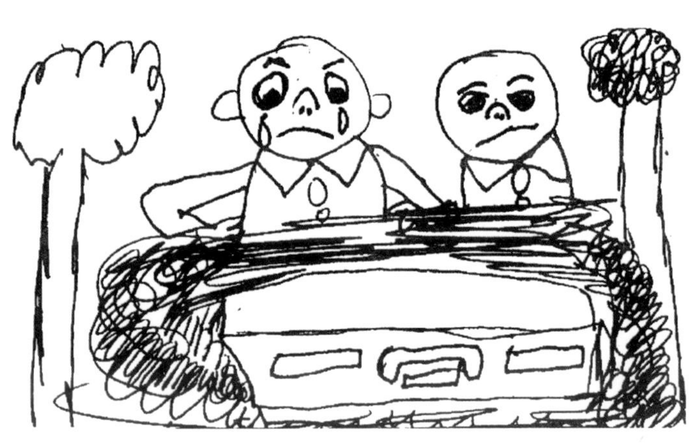

Letting You Know
What a Dead Person
Can't Do.

The Dead Person can't Harm You.
The Dead Person Just Be Dead.
The Dead Person can't wake up to see
You Standing up close to his / or her
Casket at All.

The Dead Person body isn't gonna
raise up To Hurt you or reach up
at You at all.

What Dies Must Die And what is Dead
is Dead and what is Dust Must Be Dust
The Dead Person can't not Hurt you or
Harm You ever, ever, ever again.

LIFE Left out OF your body.
That Dead Person Deceased gone into
Ashes what is Dead is Dead.

Can't come back to Harm Anyone.
Just like Ice Cream what goes up must
Come down what Dead is Dead.

When You go UP towards the Dead Person
Casket the Dead body Just be lying there.

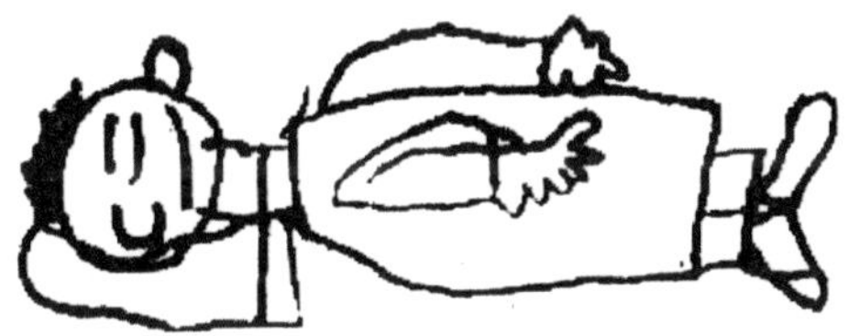

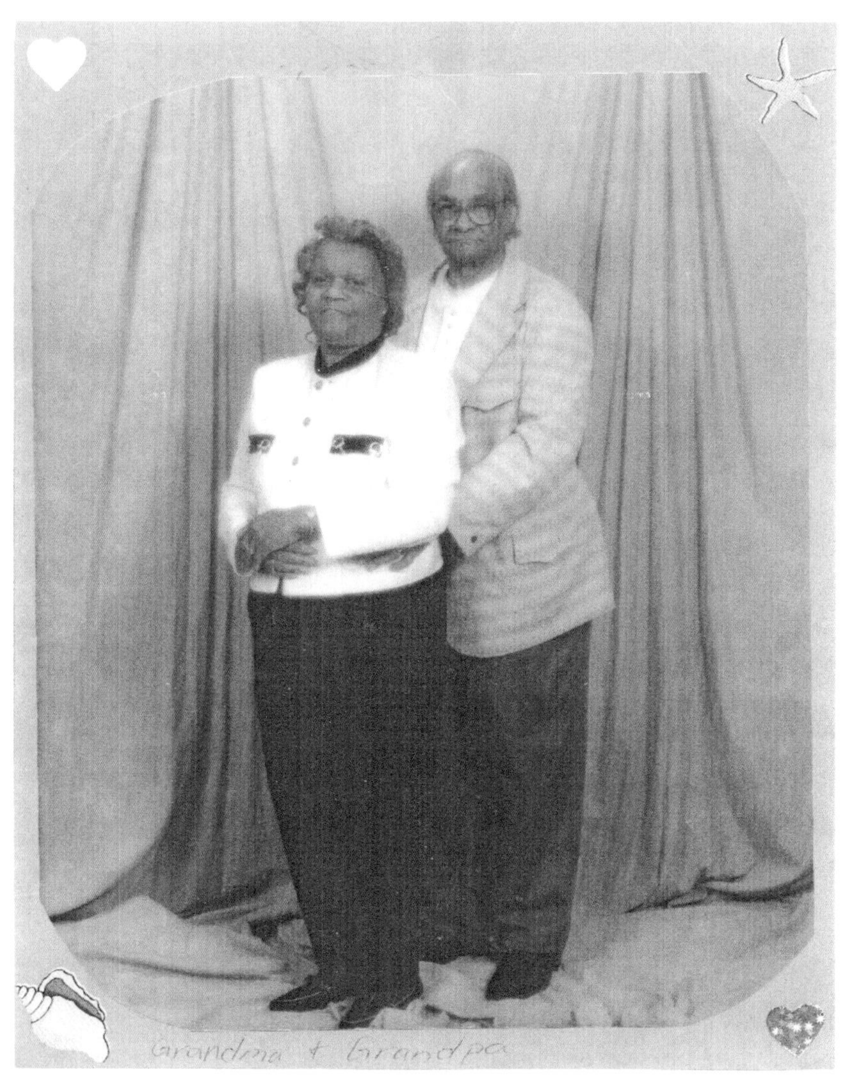

Together Again !!!

The Photo's kind of Help bring back the memory OF MY Mother and Father That I OncesEEn throughout my Living days or lives When they used to be here with us or me in Flesh and bodied.

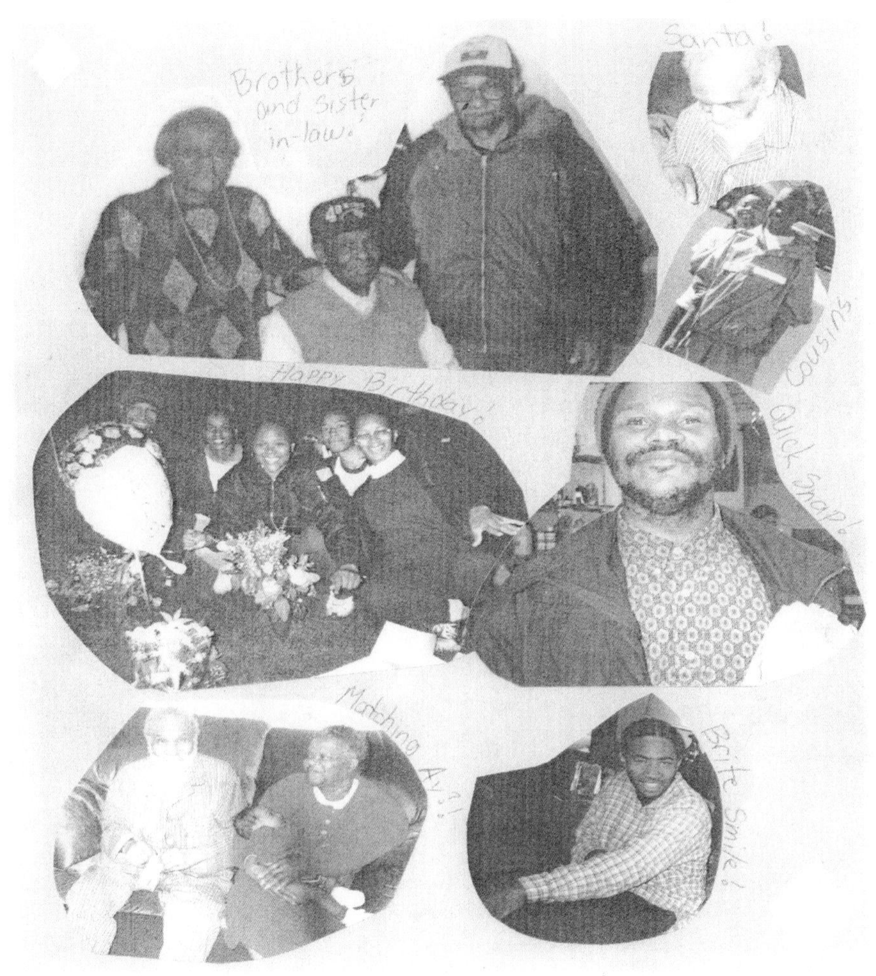

They Loved me and we used to go For a ride in our station wagon together a long time ago like going to Ocean Beach of Greathighway Doing things we would normally do when we go Places as Mother and Father and son should oFten do.

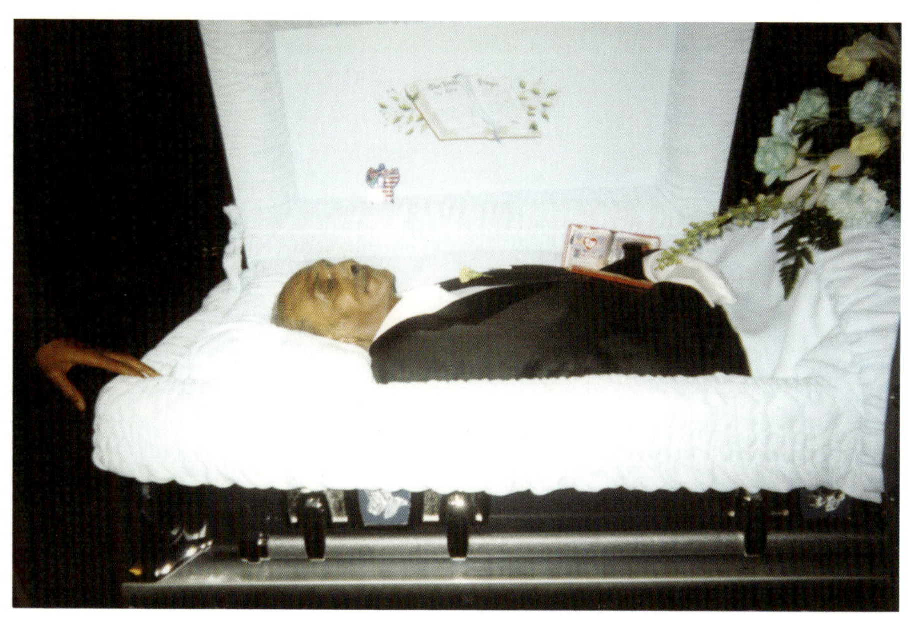

Yes I know That I can Face the Fact that my Mother and Father isn't coming back to Earth To where I'm at.

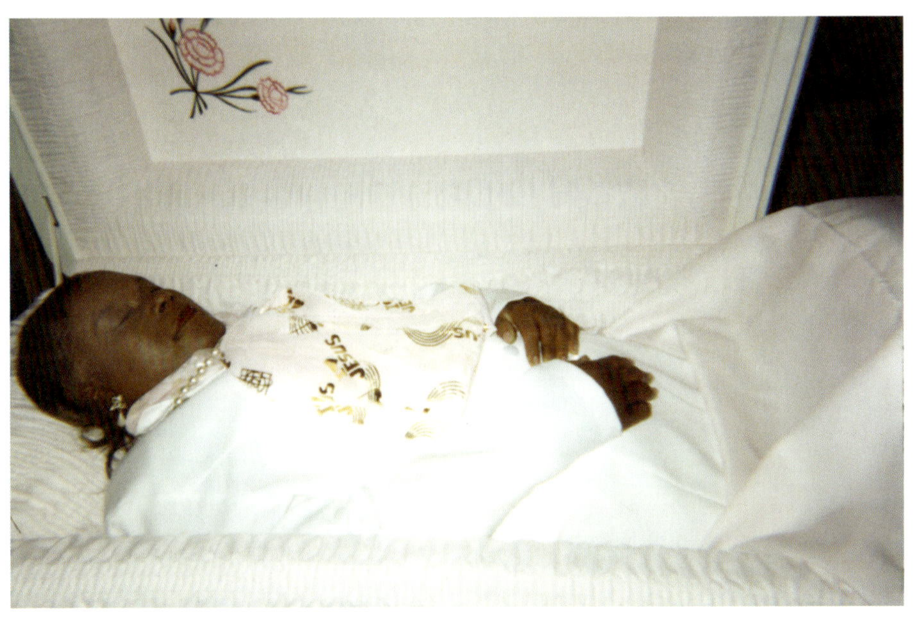

accept that Fact you won't be seeing your
Mother and Father anymore.

Jim Goldberg

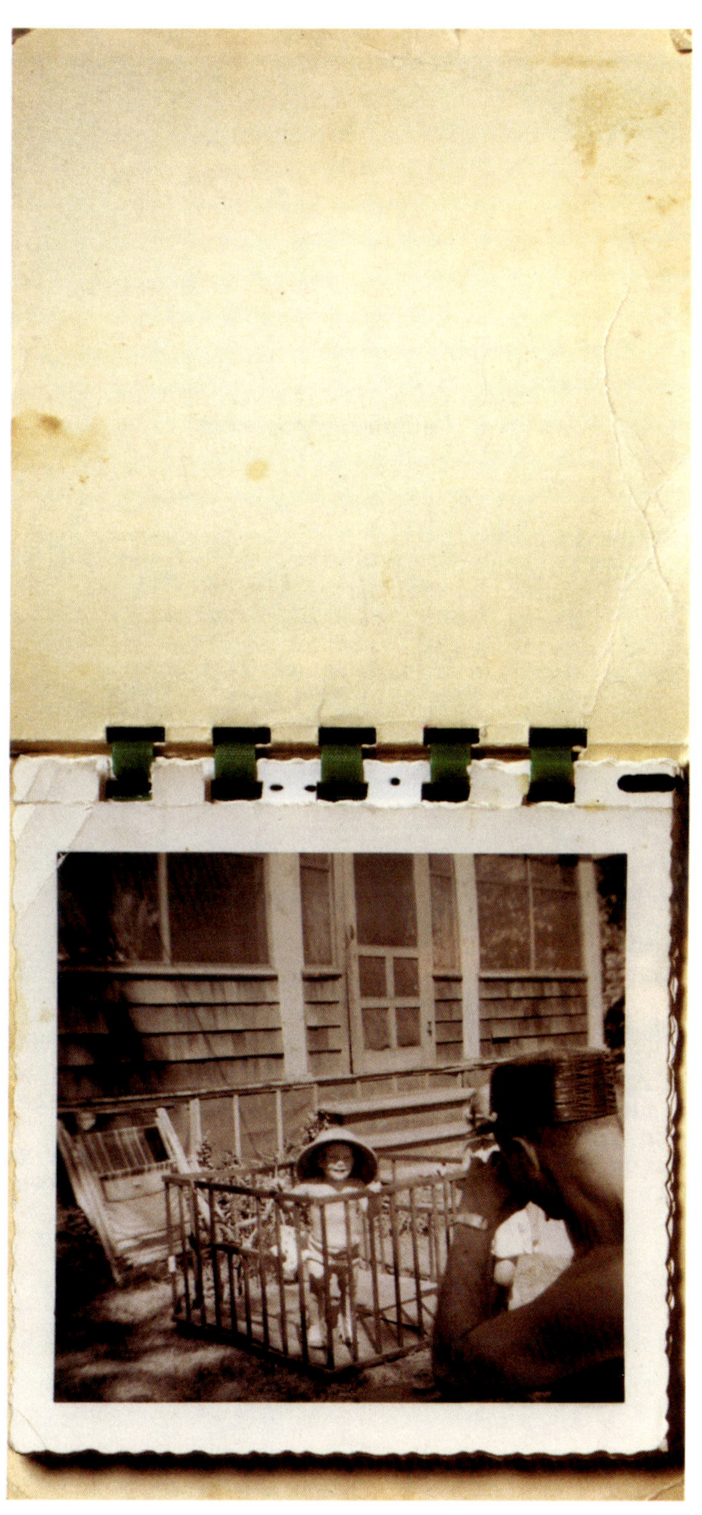

June, 1989

Dear Jim;

        I have decided to send you a letter containing things
I rememember about you and your young years. I remeber how
excited we were to have a beautiful tow-haired boy who was
spoiled by his brother & sister. How much fun we all had
trying to keep up with a veratible dynamo as you grew up.
How we had to rush you to the emergency room the night y u
ingested a bottle of baby aspirin and had to have your
stomach pumped and how you screamed. How I tried to get you
interested in playing basketball all to no avail and how you
fought against it.
        H w you at one of our anniversary parties insisted
that you must have lobster.
    How, after having your tonsils removed you insisted on
going on a trip with your buddies and how you had to return
in the middle of the night because you were hemmoraging.
        How you ran away to Rabbi Silver's house in Hartford
and how we had to beg you to come home.
        How you argued with me one night; how you ran out of
the house and I tried to catch you and you wound up in New
York at Glenn's.
        How you played hookey from school .
    How you got arrested for stealing a sign off a pole in
front of a policemans house and how we had to go to court
to get the charge squashed.
    How upset you were when I had a nervous breakdow n and
wound up in the hospital.
    How angry you were because we thou ht you were too young
to attend my mothers funeral
    Most of all, I remember one night walking with you and
your telling me all about the stars and planets when I
  realized that were indeed very bright and knowledgable
even though you fought reading.
You have made our life very interesting; we are very proud
of all that you have acc mplished and we love you very dearly.

                            Your loving father

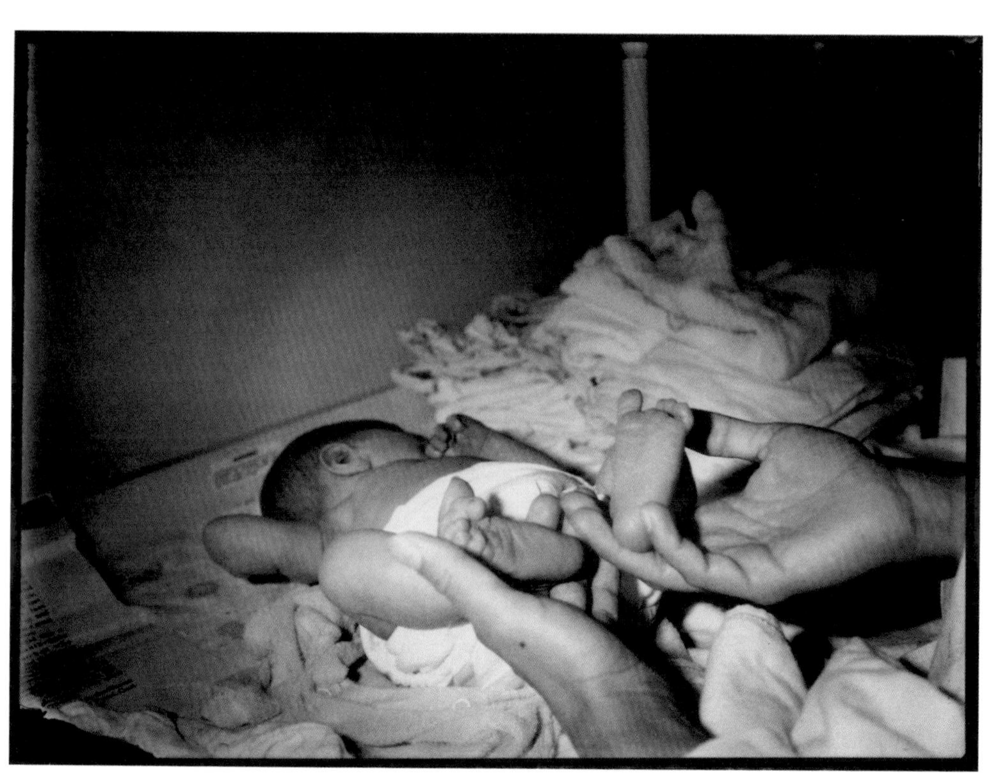

April 12, 1993

I am lying on the bed playing with Ruby Sophia, and there is this moment when we look into each other's eyes and she smiles at me and I swoon with memories of myself as a child looking into my father's eyes, doing the same thing. Then the phone rings and it's him, in his bed, weak-voiced. My daddy is dying.

April 17

This is Ruby's first plane flight. At the airport we find my mom at the bottom of the escalator, waiting impatiently for us to discover her more wrinkled face. "It's not so easy taking care of your father anymore," she says. I think she was trying to make a joke. My father is outside in the front passenger seat of their big pale-yellow car. We hug and I can hardly feel his grip on me. I smell his piss bottle hidden in a plastic bag somewhere below his legs. Dad doesn't look sick. His face is full, not wrinkled like Mom's. She sits in the back seat with Susan and tries to play with Ruby. Dad isn't saying much. I drive and try to make conversation and jokes. They become empty one-liners. There is silence, except for Ruby-girl, who is too young to know better.

The Disease

In 1943, during his physical for the draft, my father was diagnosed with a rare degenerative muscle disease. The doctors told him that the syringomyelia would cripple and kill him within a few years. Since then, Dad has lived in defiance of his worsening disability. He was never willing to let others know about his handicap. He used to tell me people thought he was a drunk because of the funny way he walked.

In 1984 my father was diagnosed with colon cancer. Six years later, the cancer had spread to his lungs. For as long as I could remember, Aunt Freda always said, "It's a miracle that Herbie has weathered such an awful storm. I mean look at the man. You would never know he was so sick." She usually said this loudly, behind my father's back.

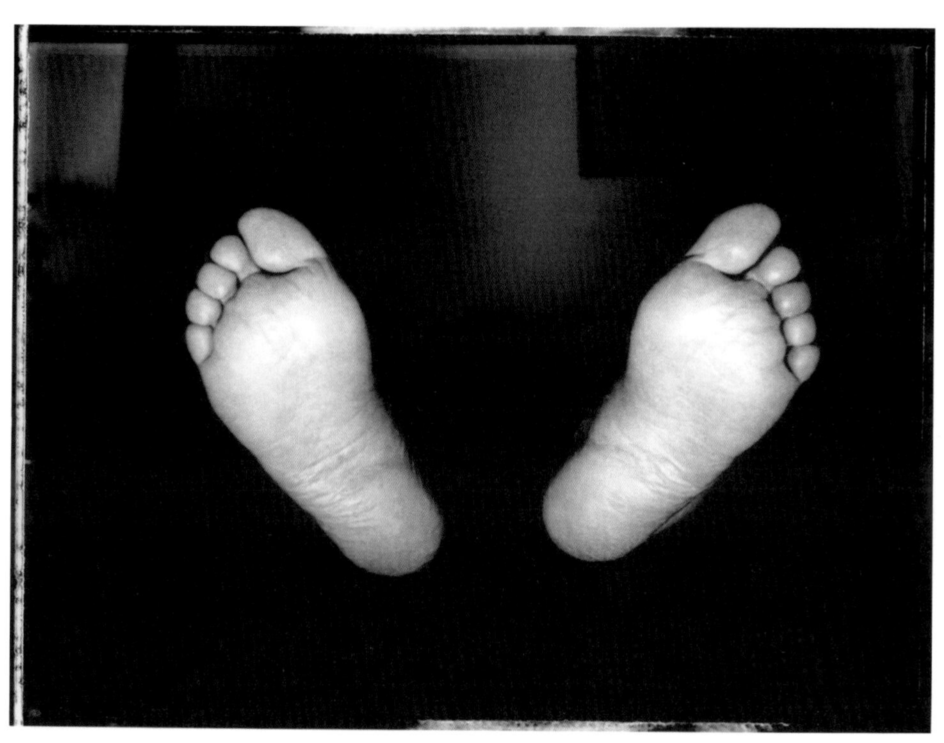

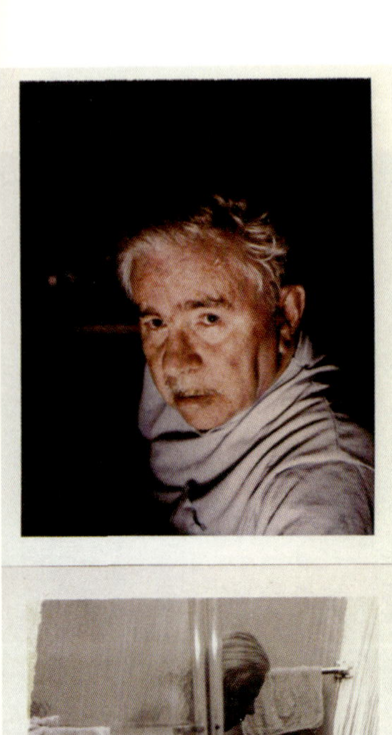
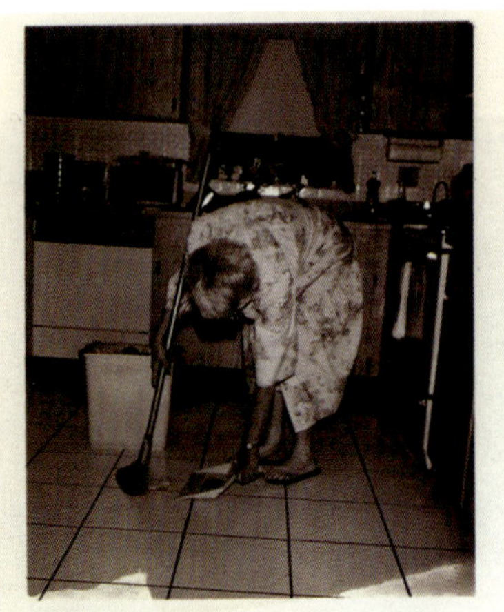

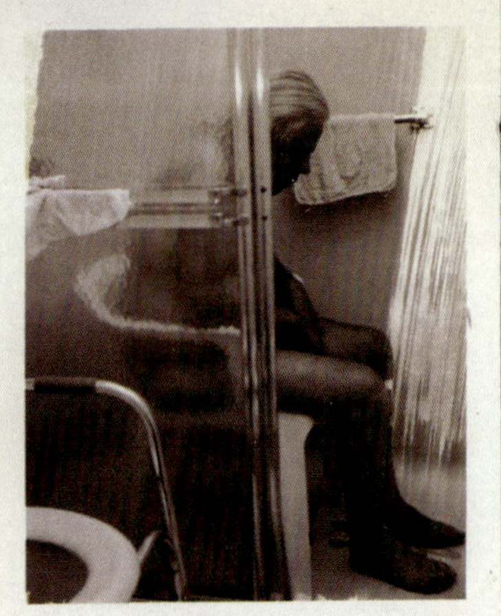
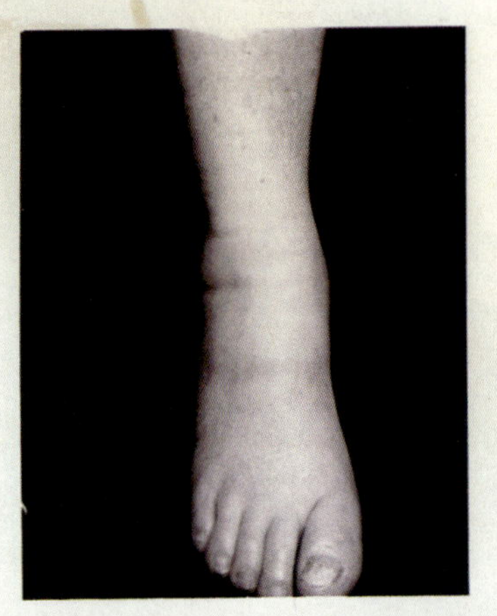
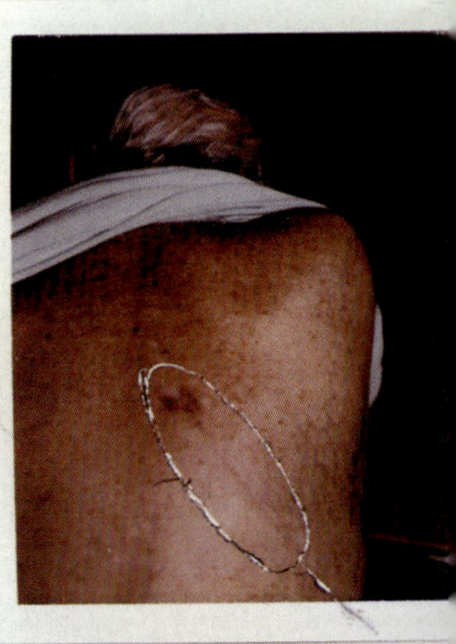
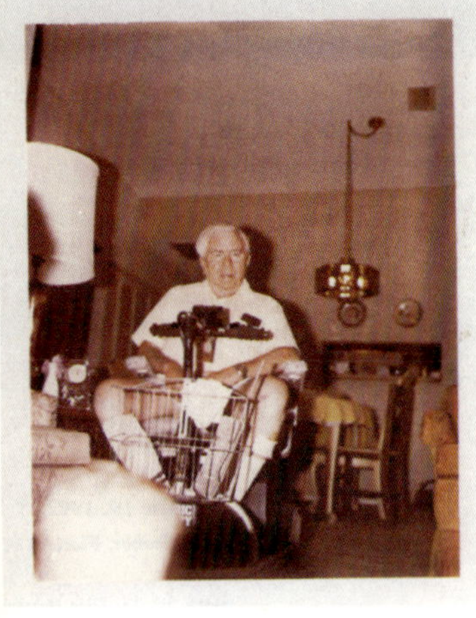
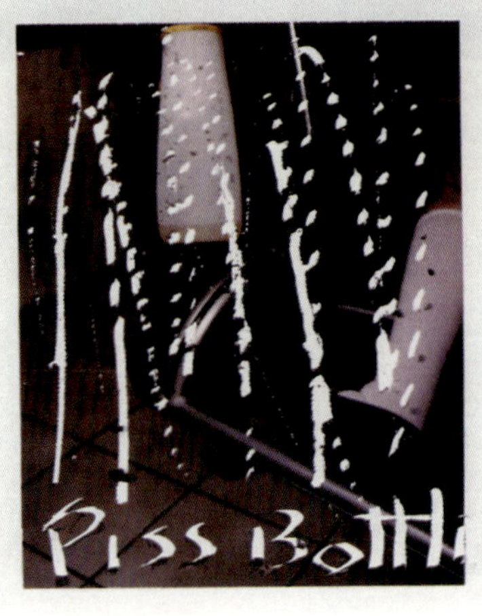
Piss Bottle
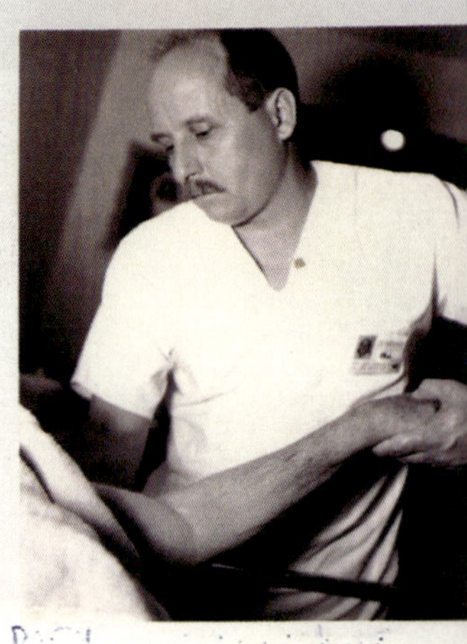

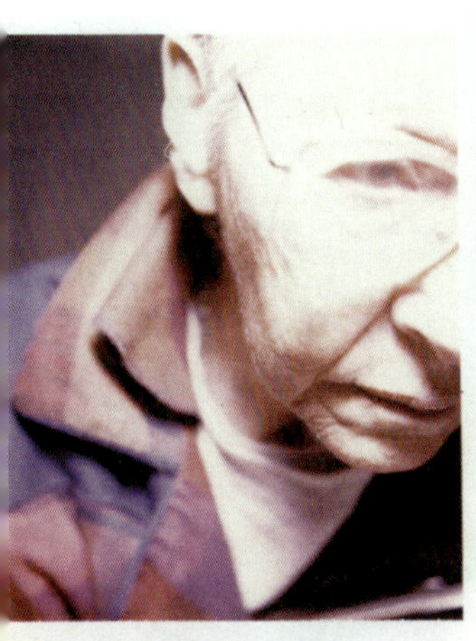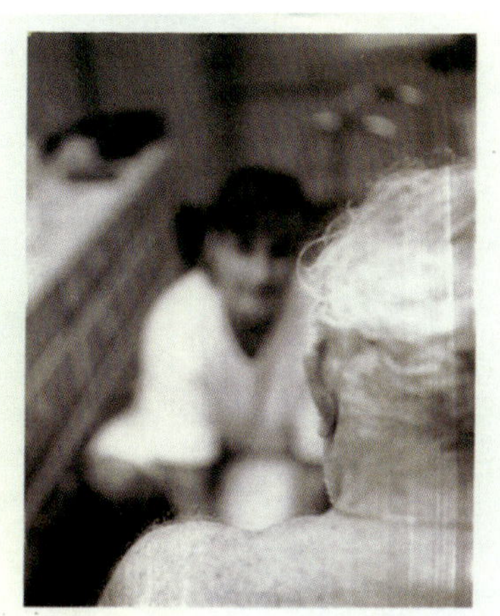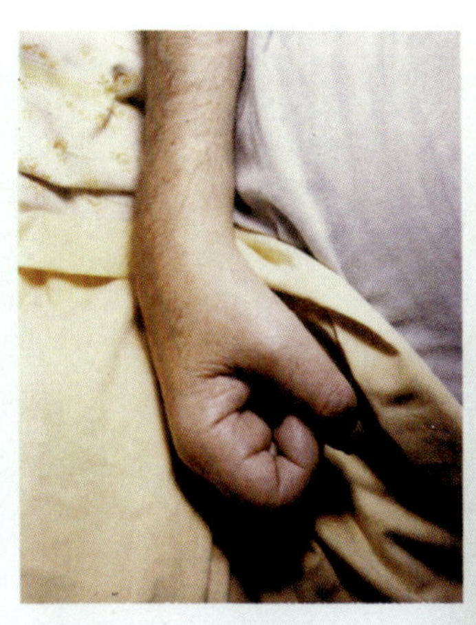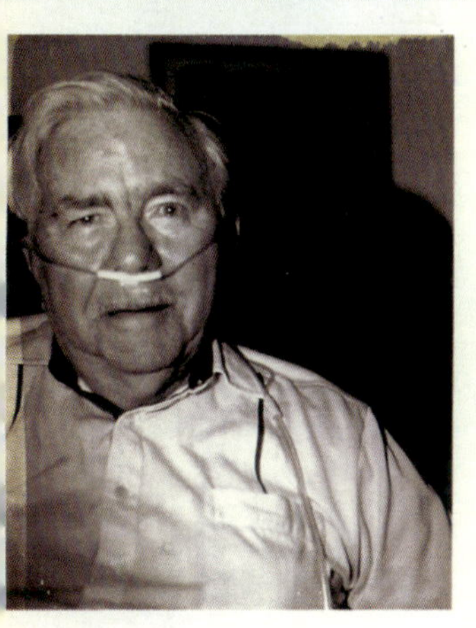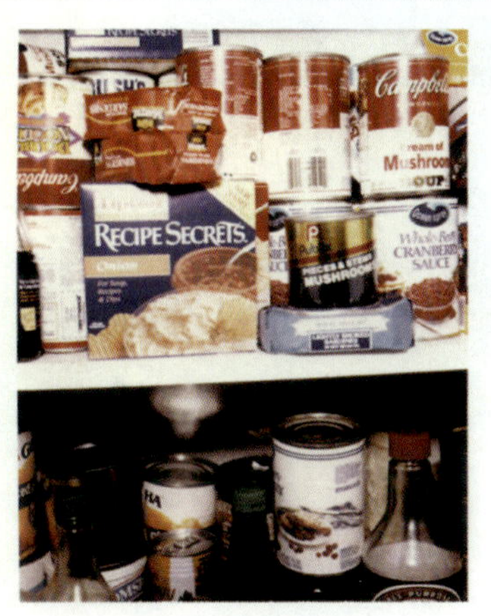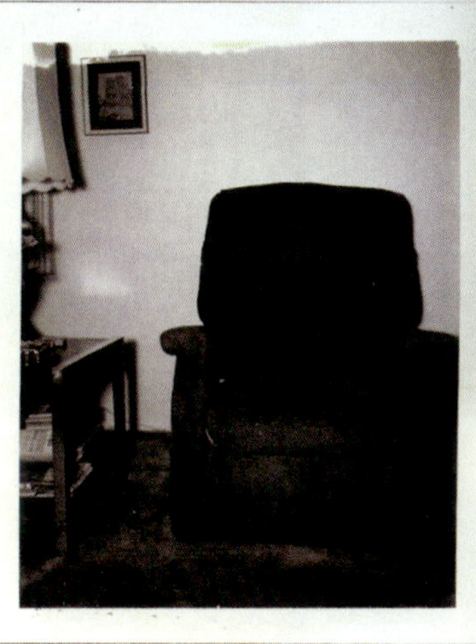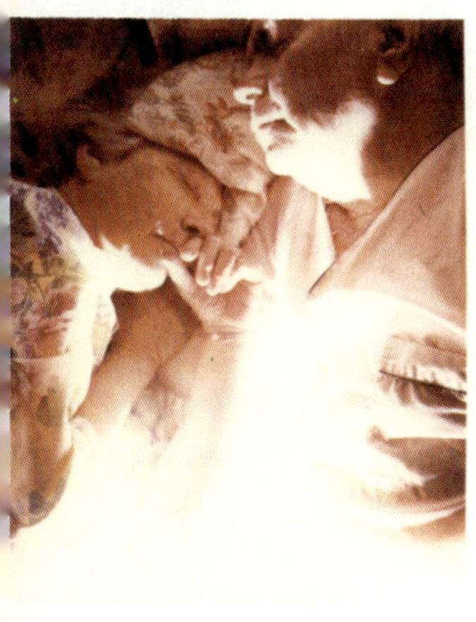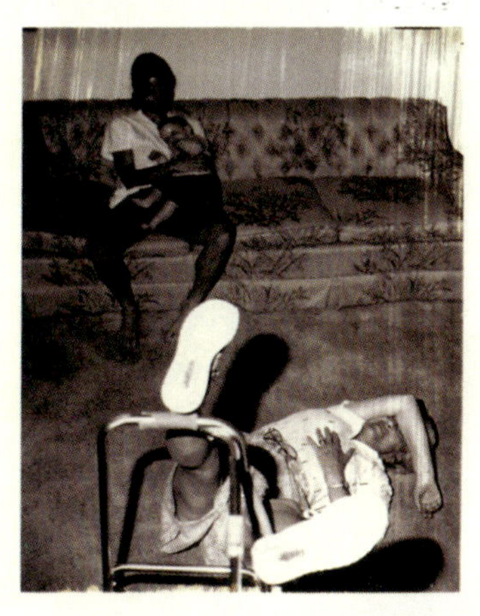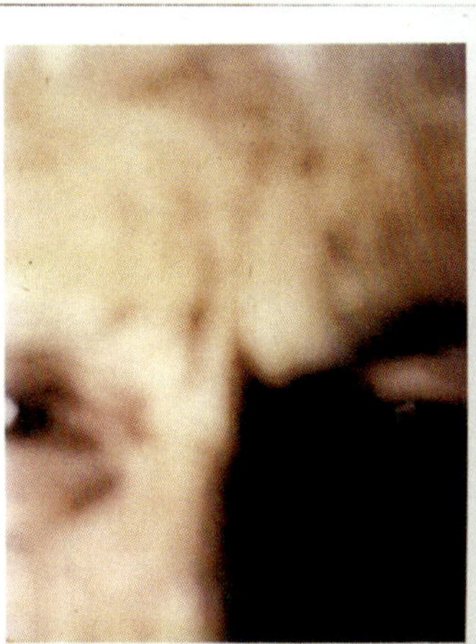

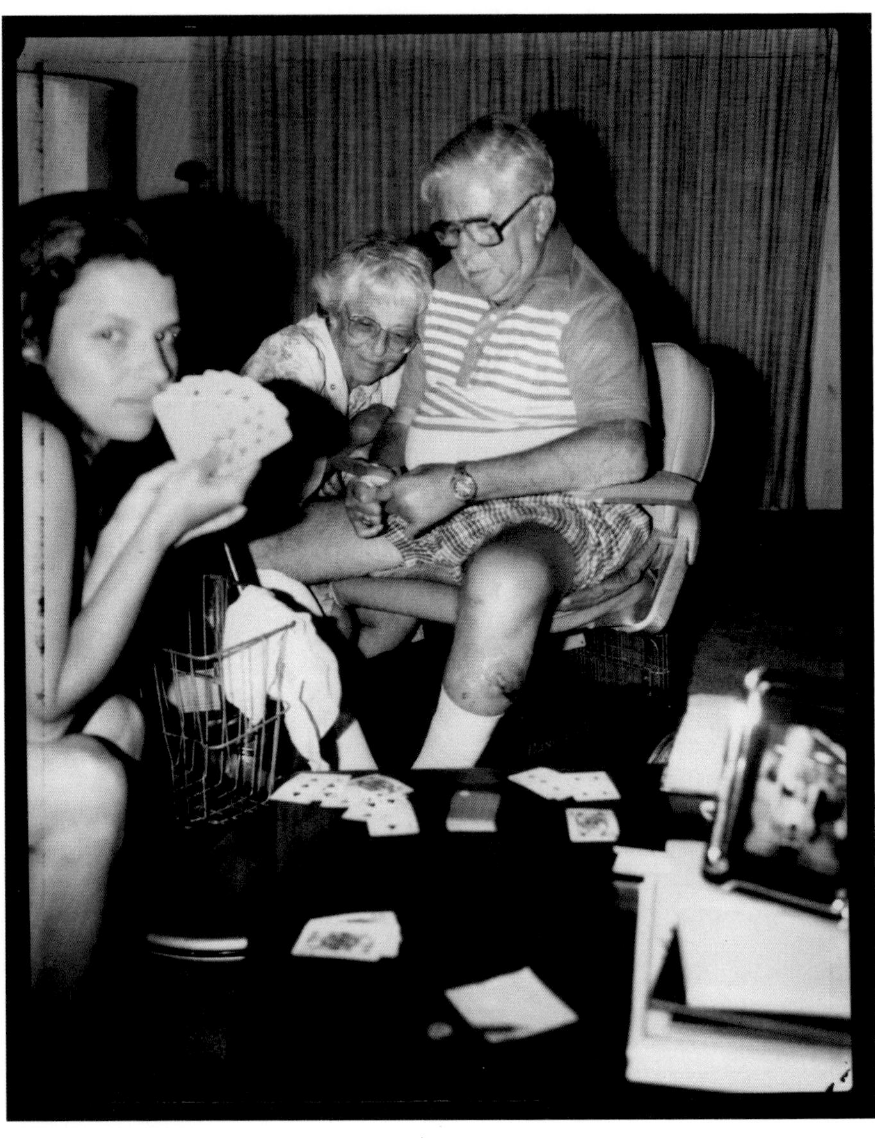

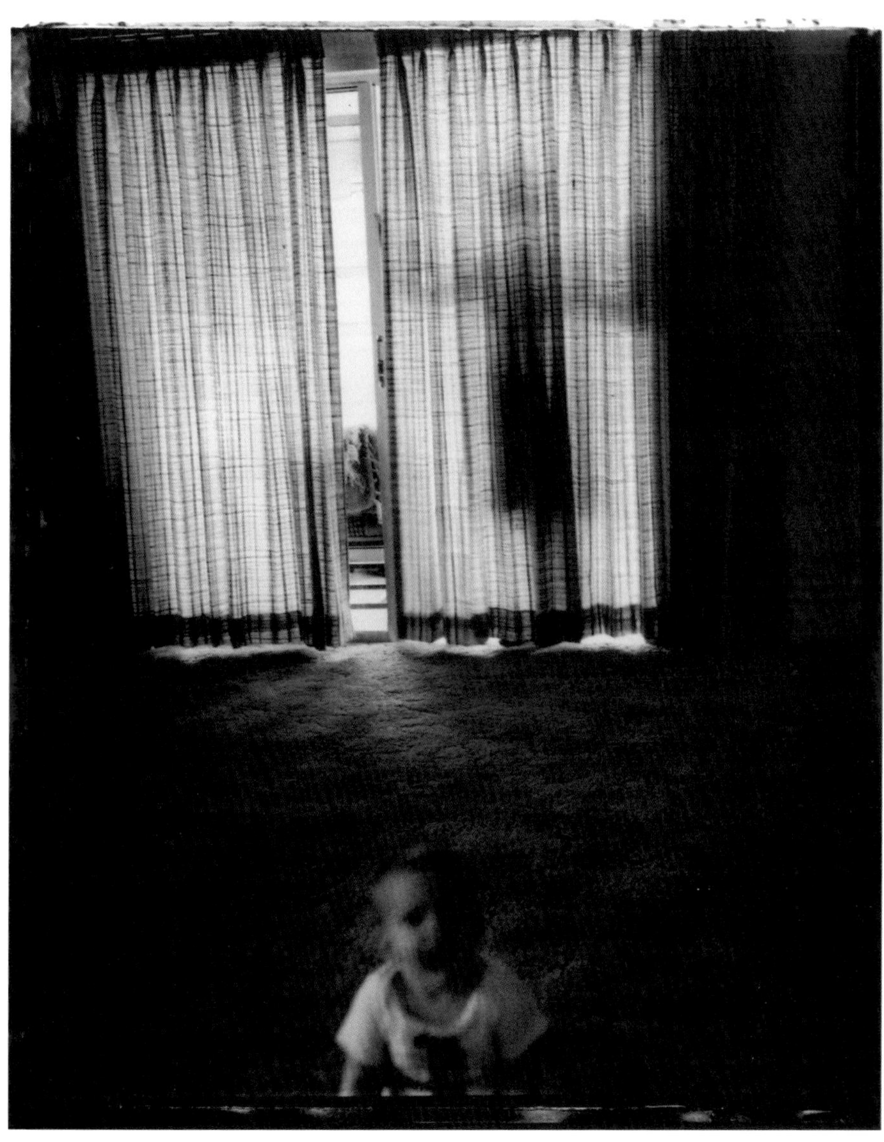

August 17 - Early Morning
Dad has trouble getting back onto his motorized cart. He becomes defeated and self-pitying. Fran, the hospice aide, puts her arms around him and hugs him hard, reminding him in the most unsappy way that hospice is "about living to the fullest and comfortably to the end." My father smiles at her and replies, "Bullshit." She gently rubs lotion on his arms and legs and dresses him. All the while, he gives her driving directions and advice on love and VCR programming.

After Fran leaves, Dad drives his cart to the kitchen table to eat his breakfast, read the paper, and do the crossword puzzle. Dad loves bacon. Mom microwaves it months before it will be served, then freezes it. She microwaves the bacon again to defrost it, then fries it a bit. Sometimes this process happens twice over before it reaches the table. She says she does this "to make sure it's cooked just right, just like your father likes it." Because today is their fifty-second wedding anniversary, Mom has made a mound of bacon. She says, teasingly, "All for my sweetheart, so don't touch any, Jimmy. Okay?"

Dad asks if I want to photograph him with his oxygen, as if the camera is an excuse to play a game of make-believe between father and son. He is obviously out of breath.

The oxygen is kicking in, and his voice becomes stronger. He becomes aware of the camera and vainly attempts to pull his stomach muscles in. But he has no muscles left. Dad says, "You know, Jim, I used to be even skinnier than you when I was a singer. Yes sir, I was a real looker. Do you know what I really want to do now? I want to smoke a cigarette and sing in a karaoke bar."

My father's dreams of a singing career were halted by several things: his marriage, the syringomyelia, his subsequent 4-F draft status, the war, and his decision to take over the family candy business. I first discovered he could lie when I found out that he actually wasn't a secretary on a submarine with Ernest Borgnine.

I ask Dad what he thinks of hospice. "They are very nice people, but it's not me who needs them. It's your mother," he says.

That Afternoon - It's Hot.
In the kitchen, Mom defrosts some sandwich meat for lunch. She mumbles, "Your father keeps saying, 'I'm dying. I'm dying.'" She looks down and confesses, "He won't allow me to talk to anybody about his 'condition.' No one knows about hospice. I have to take care of him twenty-four hours a day, and who is going to take care of me if I get sick? I have no one to complain to except hospice. If it weren't for them, I wouldn't have any relief. I don't know if I can take much more, Jimmy. I often think that I want your father to die peacefully—but soon! I know it's normal to feel this way, but still I feel like an awful person having these thoughts."

TV
At night we watch TV. We're all thirsty. I make cold drinks. The freezer compartment is so jammed that it's possible something will fall out and crush my toe. It smells like a luncheonette, but I'm hot, so I forget that the ice in my drink will taste like onions.

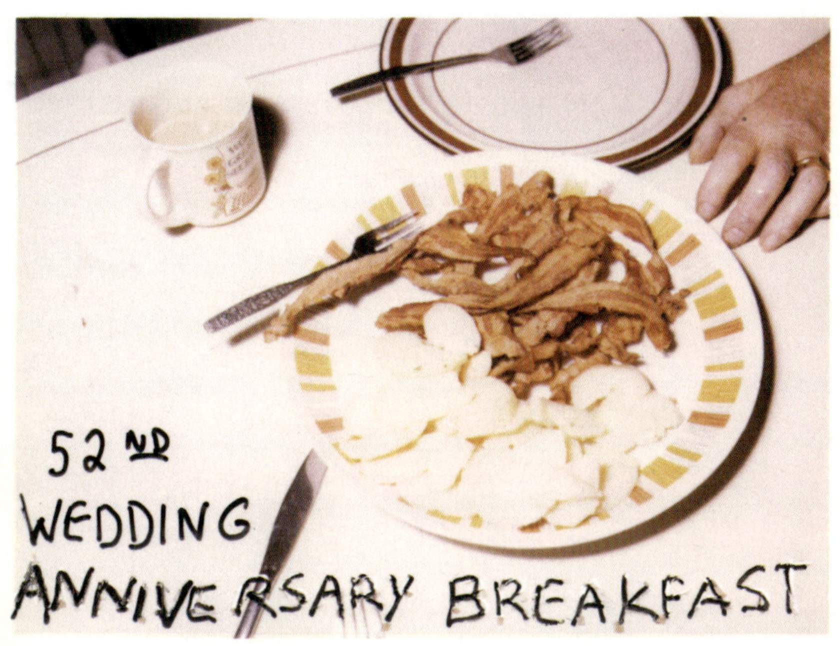
52 ND
WEDDING
ANNIVERSARY BREAKFAST

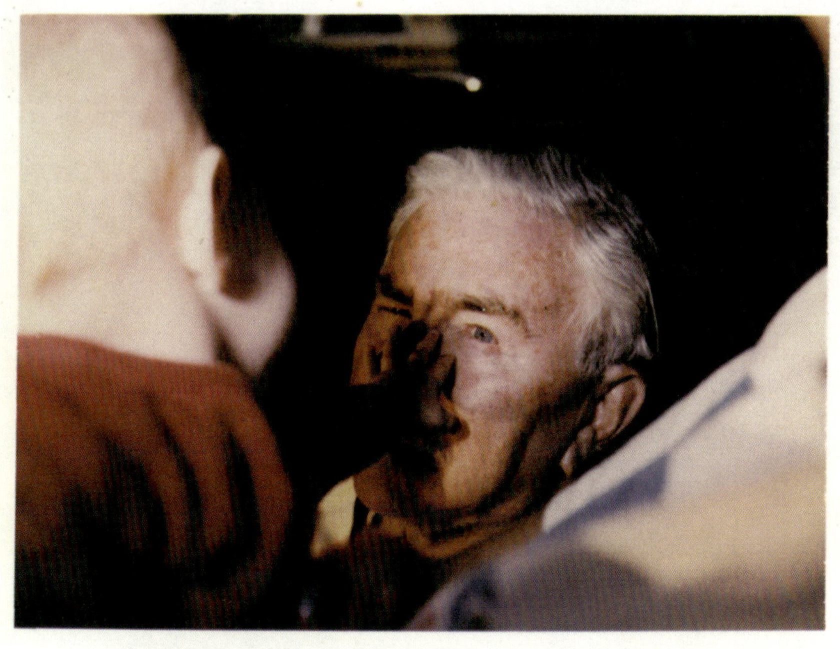

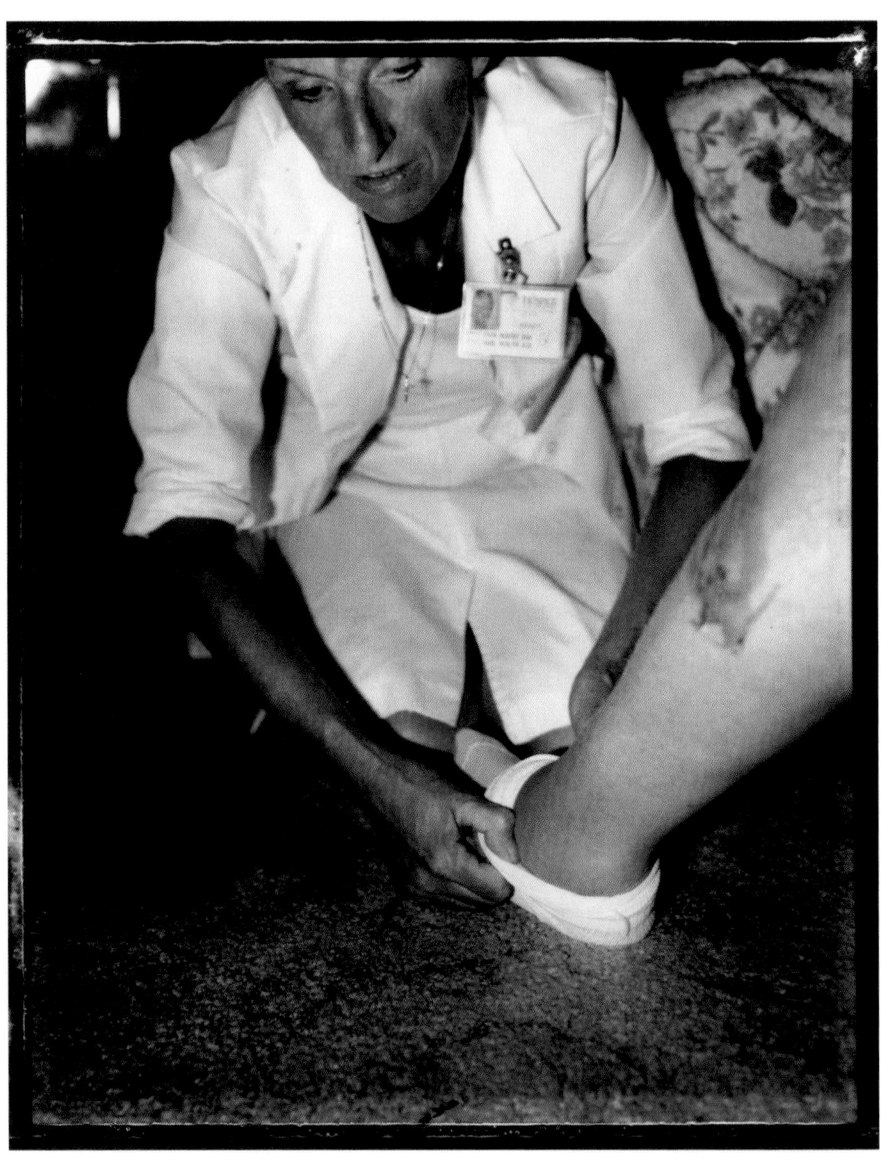

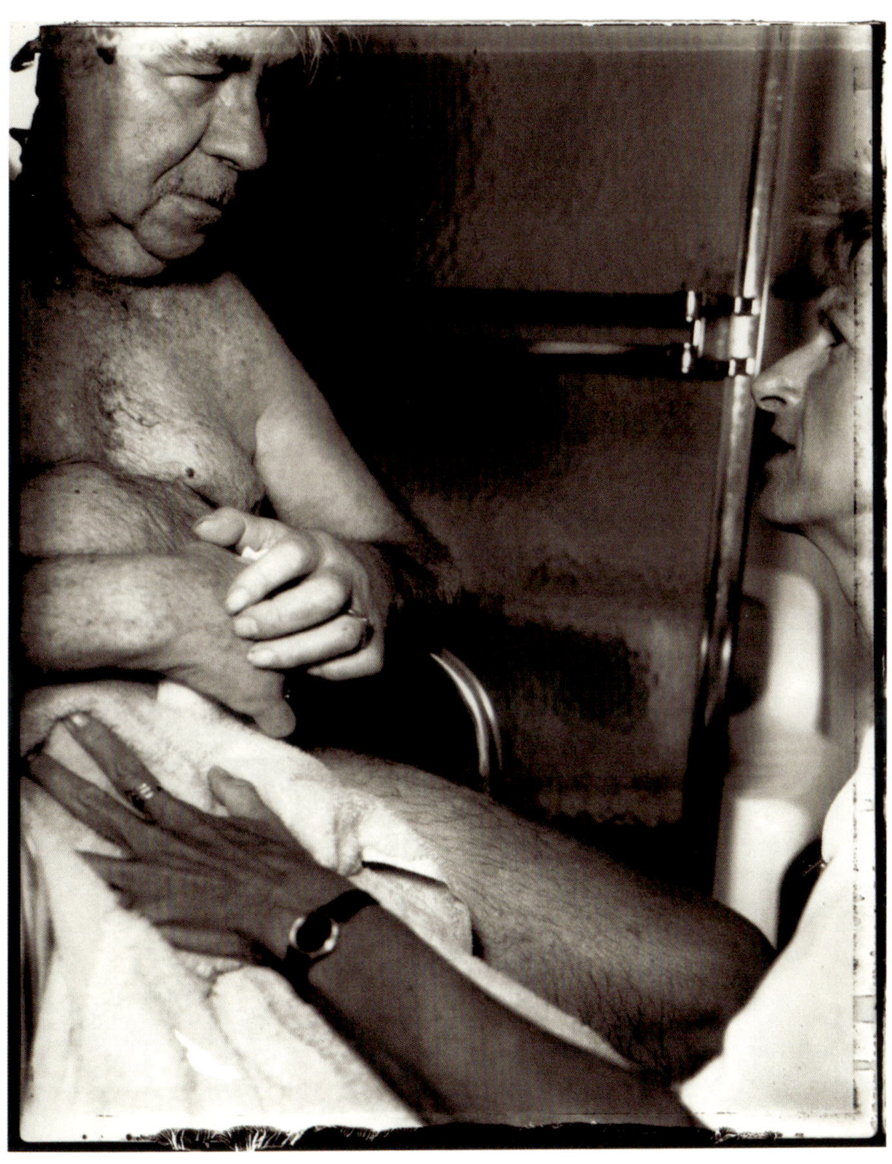

5.

Carol called
Dr. Ellis & Dr ordered thru Hospice
an evaluation Therapist for Dad -
The man called last night. He's
coming this afternoon - The Therapist
came, nice gentleman but couldn't
help Dad. He suggested exercise but
Dad said exercise tires him out -
Too bad, but we'll work on Therapy
idea when Carol comes next week -
Everyone from Hospice try to help us -
This afternoon they came (without
our calling) to check the oxygen
machine. Making sure it's working
properly - They left us bottles and
tube replacements - I don't know who
called Carol, or Hospice office to
have the machine checked - They
are something.!!

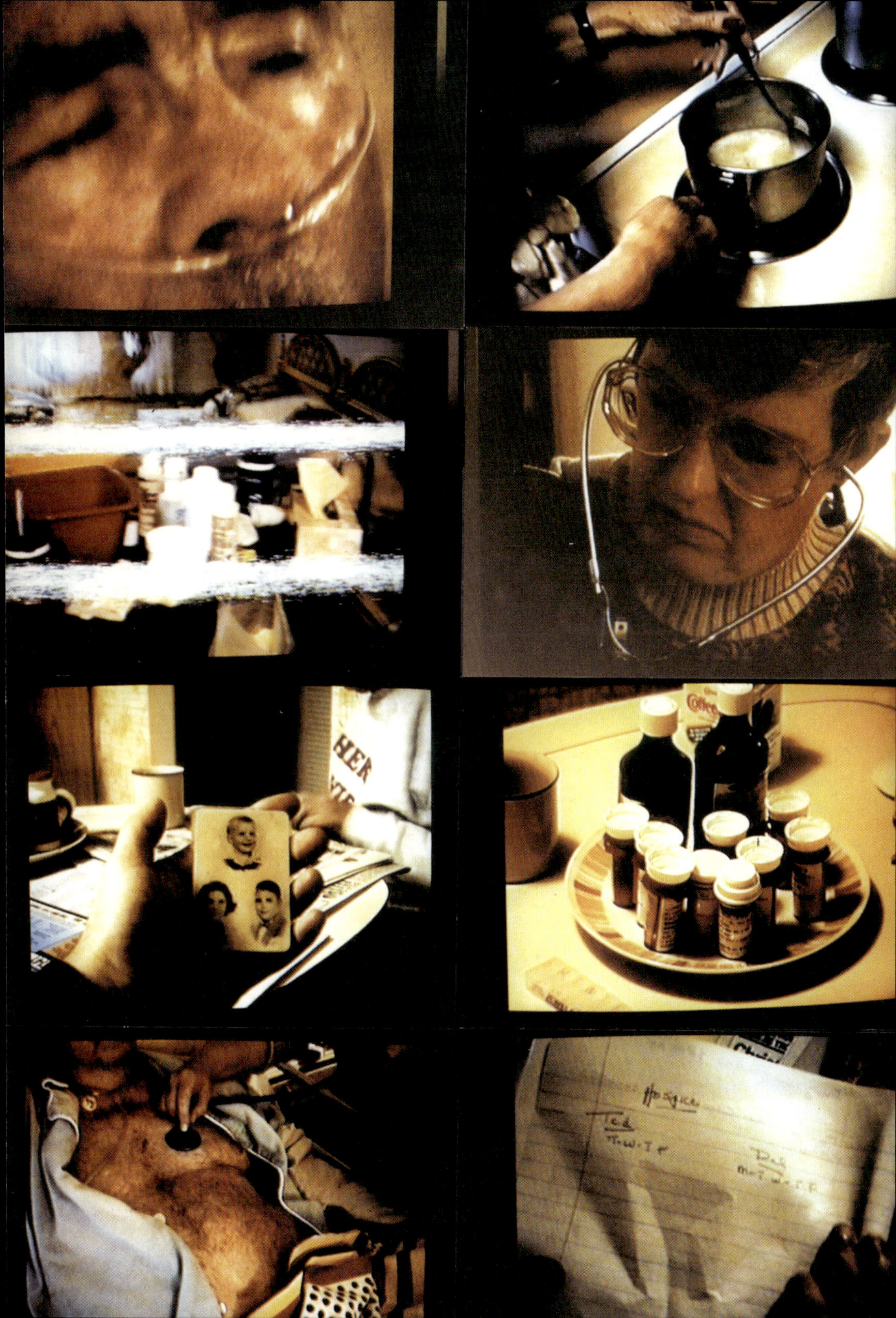

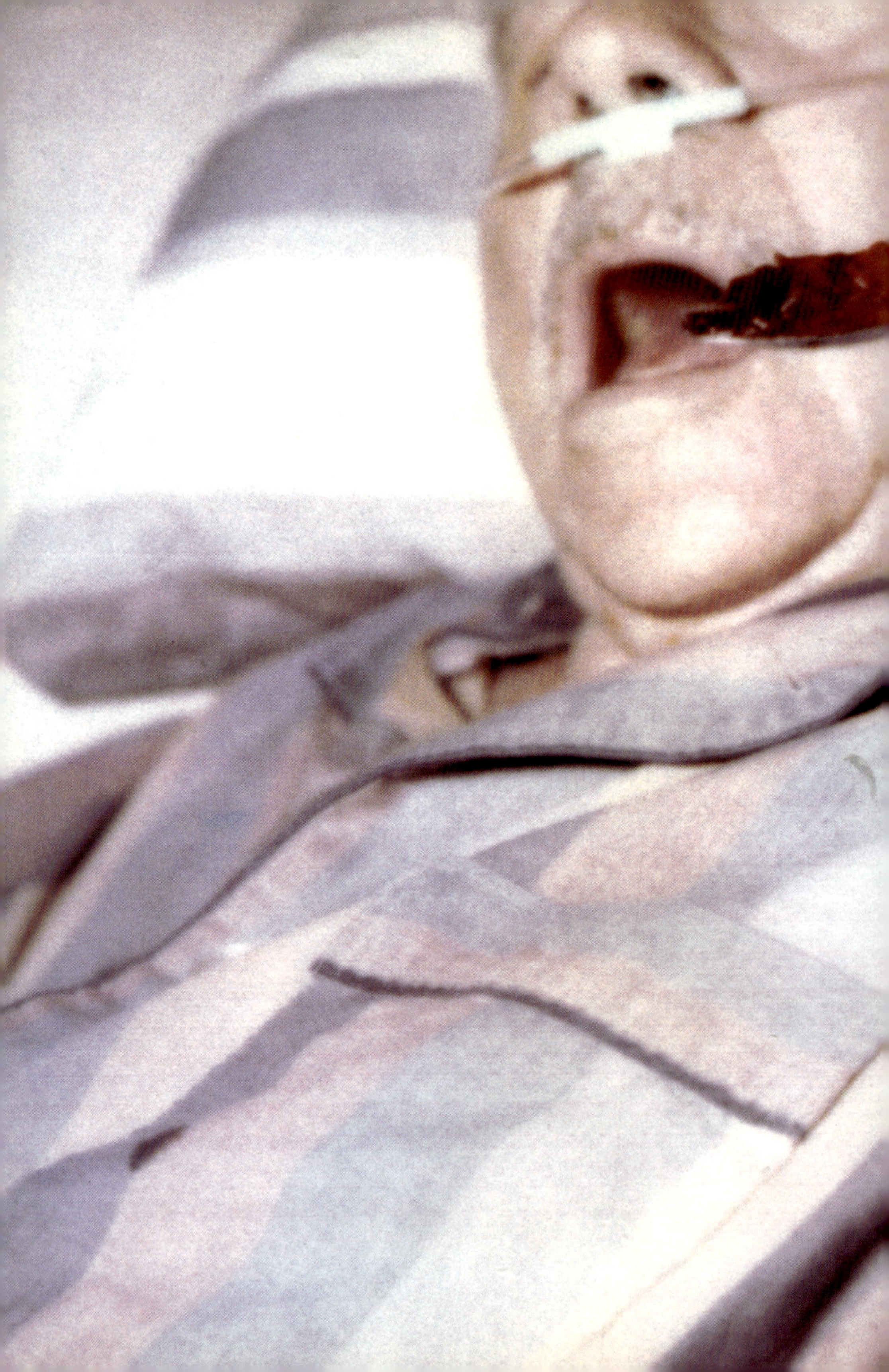

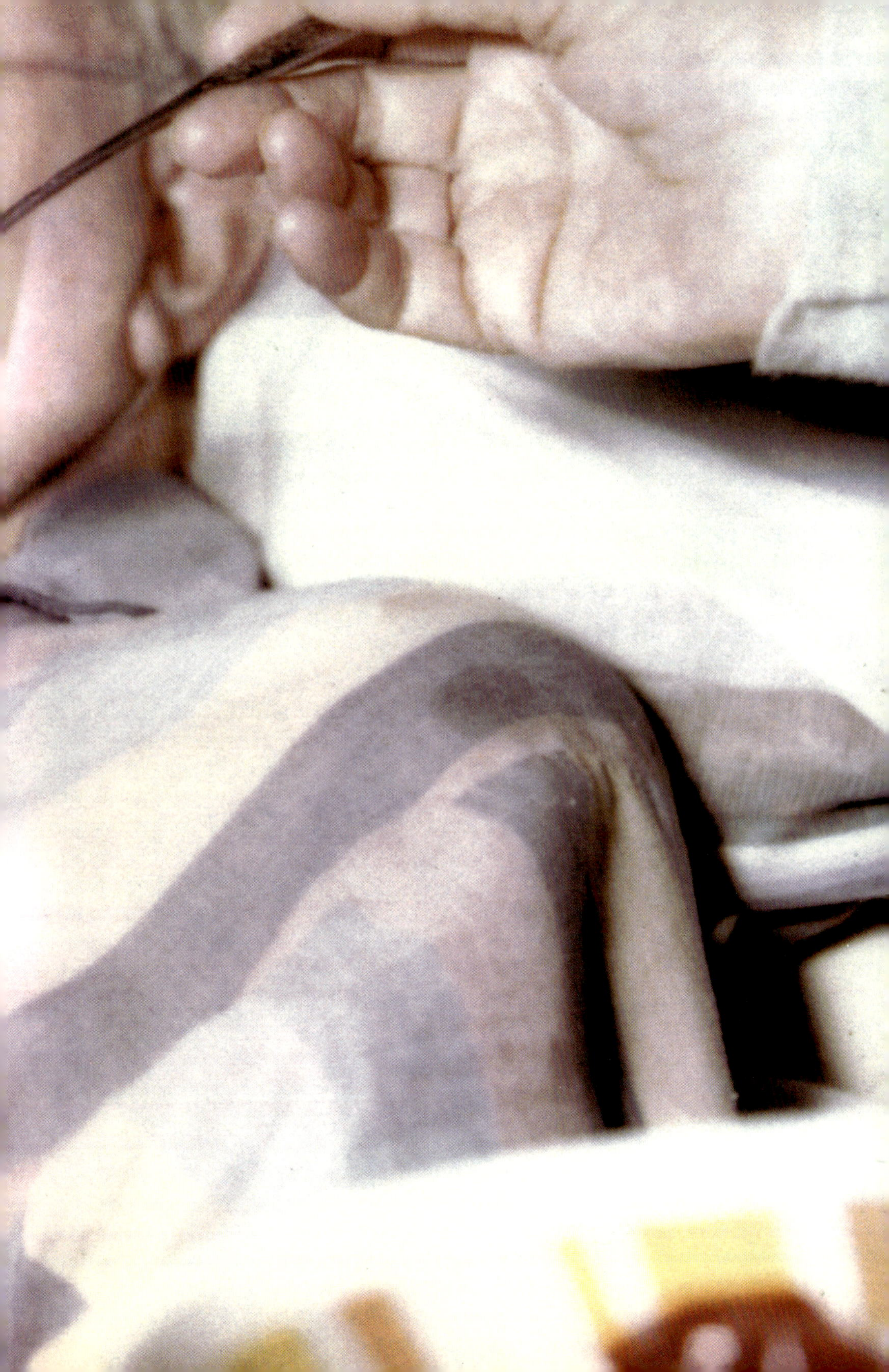

December 24 - Early Morning

I clasp my father, his body limp in my arms, and attempt to adjust his position. Perhaps he can be more comfortable and sleep. "I want my chair," he mumbles. He shuts his eyes. His breath is shallow and short. It's hard to tell if he's sleeping. His mouth is wide open, eyes half-shut. The oxygen machine drones.

It's the final round of *Wheel of Fortune*. The puzzle reads, T-E EN- -ONE. The clock is ticking. From somewhere in his unconscious mind Dad mutters, "The End Zone."

I move Mom's chair into their bedroom, next to my father's hospital bed. She sits and knits while Dad lies there tilted up in front of the large-screen TV. She is persistent in her attempts to comfort him. "Herb, darling, you can beat it," she says. She turns to me, stating, "Ever since your father had to get into this bed, he's let himself go downhill, thinking he's not going to make it." She turns back to him, leans close, and reiterates, "Sweetheart, you know you can do it, you've done it before. Do you want something to eat? I'm going to recharge the battery on your cart just in case you're feeling better. Okay, Goldie? You want to go for a ride?"

"Let me be," he blurts out.

Mom doesn't stop. She tells me about a dream he had last week, in which he hiked all the way to the county courthouse in Clearwater, screaming, "I can walk, I can walk!" When he woke up, he complained to Mom about pains in his legs. This is the first time I can remember that he can feel anything there. We give him Advil for the pain and Xanax to help him relax. We know he won't relax until we get him to his chair. Fran is out sick with the flu. No one from hospice can be here until tomorrow morning. I call the Utopia Home Care Agency. They agree to send Adam at eleven tonight. Mom isn't happy about "some stranger sleeping in my house."

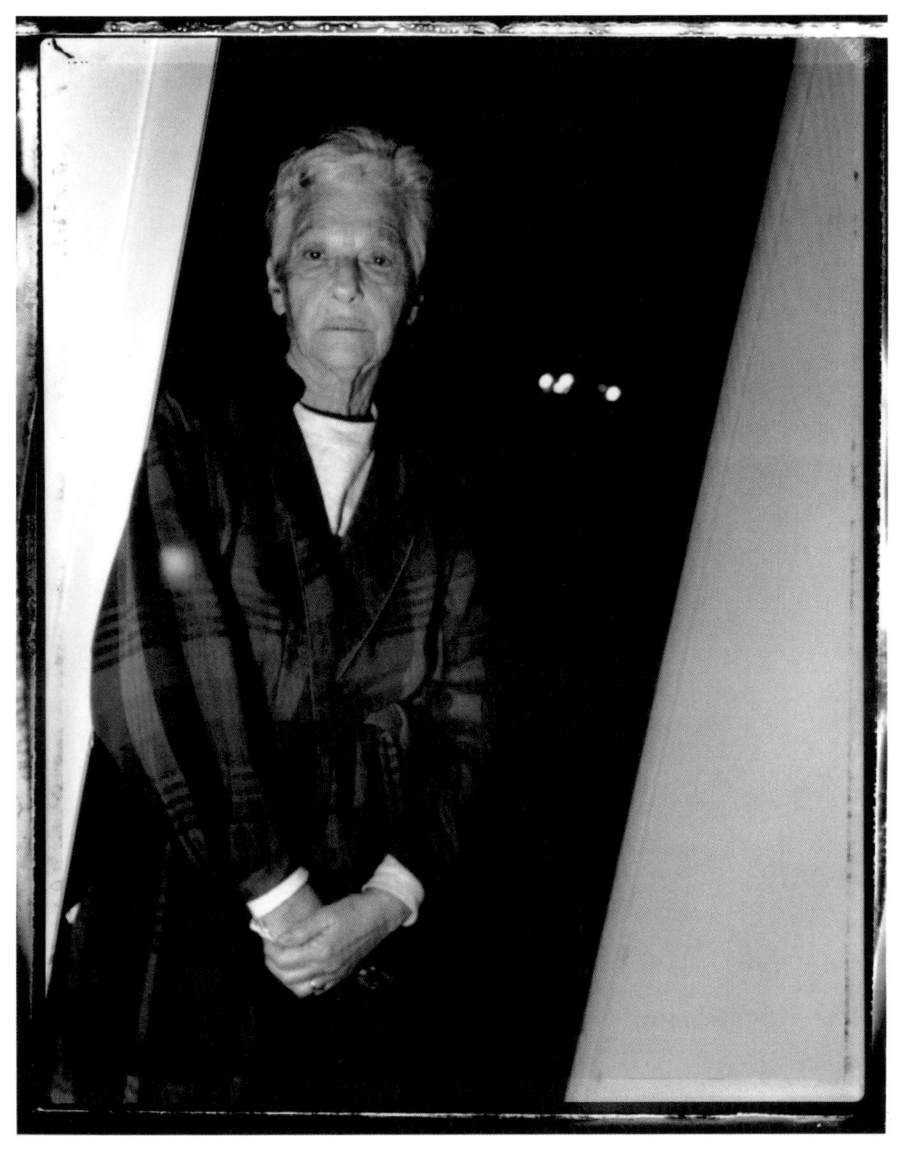

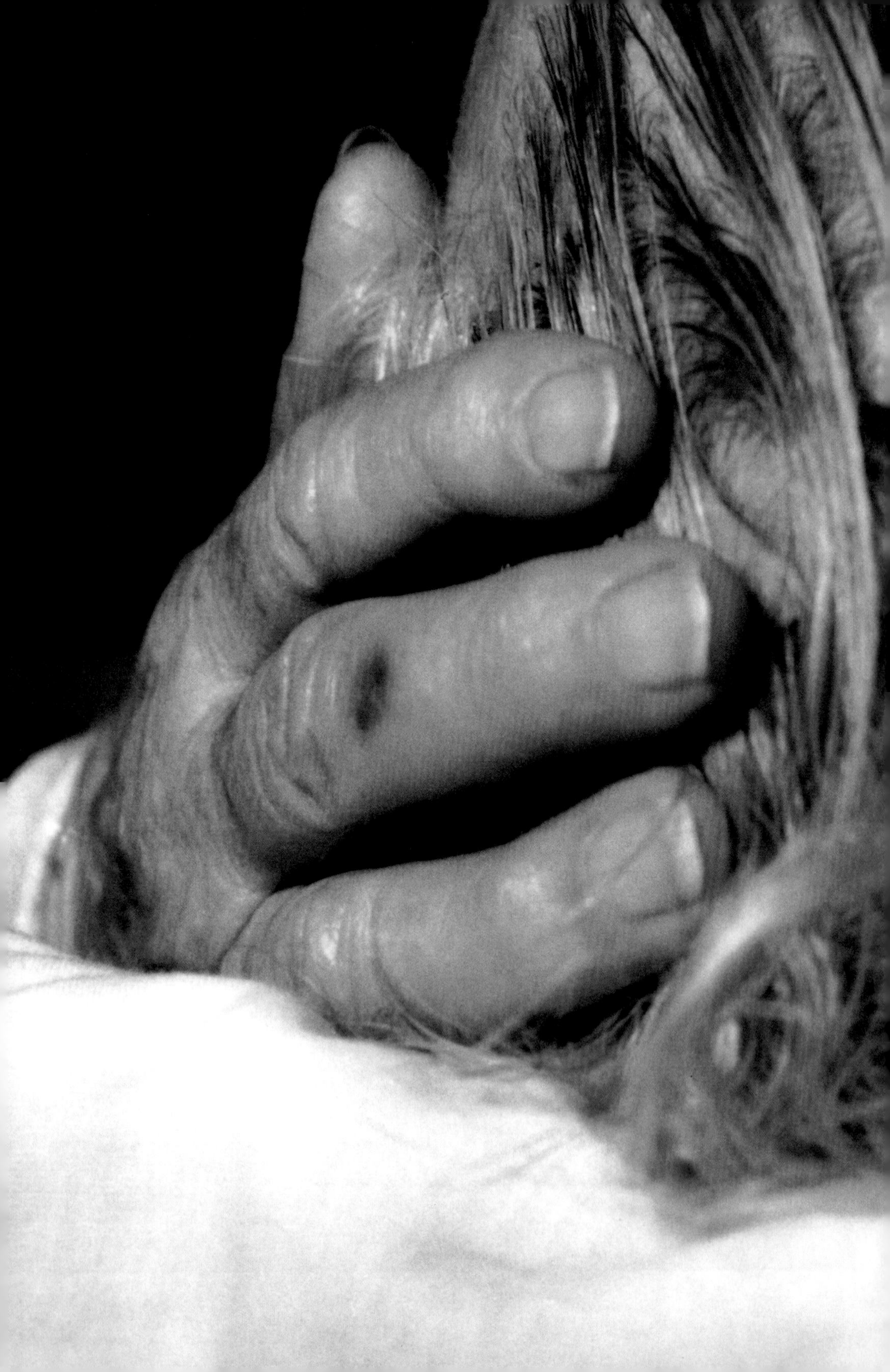

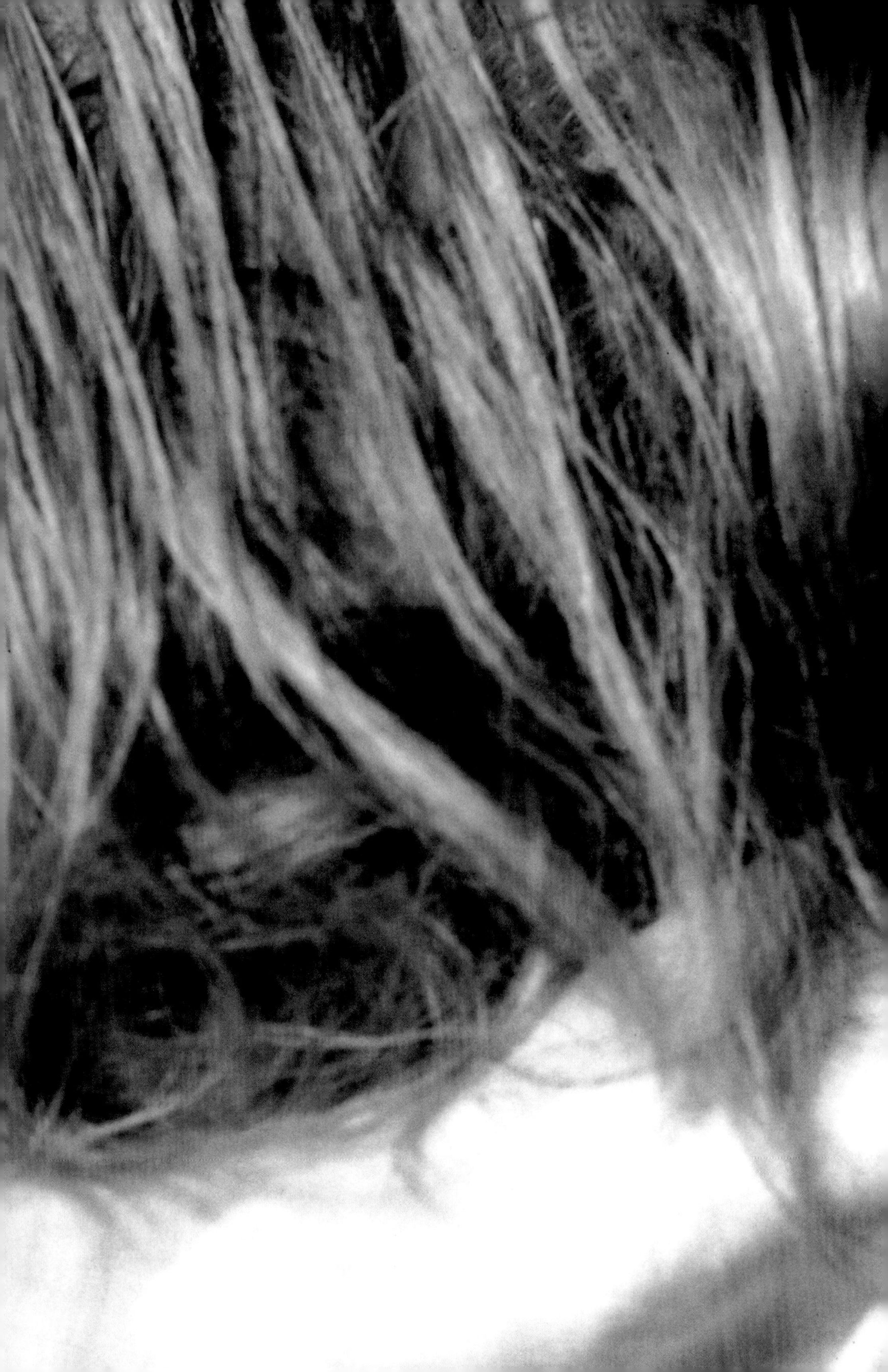

December 24 - Late Afternoon
Eyes shut, Dad's voice rises to a whisper: "Get me to my chair." My mother is hunched over Dad, singing a song from *Fiddler on the Roof* they used to sing to each other: "Goldie, do you love me? Goldie? Do you love me?" His part is to answer, "Do I what?" but he doesn't.

The house is hot from the oxygen. A Polish woman comes to clean and vacuum the house. I step back for a moment to see what she sees here: the two of us scurrying around a sick man hidden away in a room, the door mostly closed. The feeling of death is everywhere.

Nighttime
It's raining. Melody Drive is a field of blurry Christmas lights. Cars filled with sightseeing old people—here to view the lights and get in the holiday spirit—roll by. I forget where I am for a moment.

Adam arrives. He is young, maybe nineteen, with lots of acne. His hair is short except for a tail hanging down his back. He wears a peace-sign earring and a Marlboro Gear T-shirt. Adam is introduced to Dad. My father shakes his head, indicating that he shat in his pants. Adam and I pull the sheet from underneath and carefully roll him to one side. Adam's pack of Marlboro Lights spills across the bed, cigarettes rolling between the sheets and my father's body. The diaper comes off and we find that Dad was mistaken. There is no mess. He expresses a fuzzy recognition that he has no idea what is going on. This is the moment I first see him lose control.

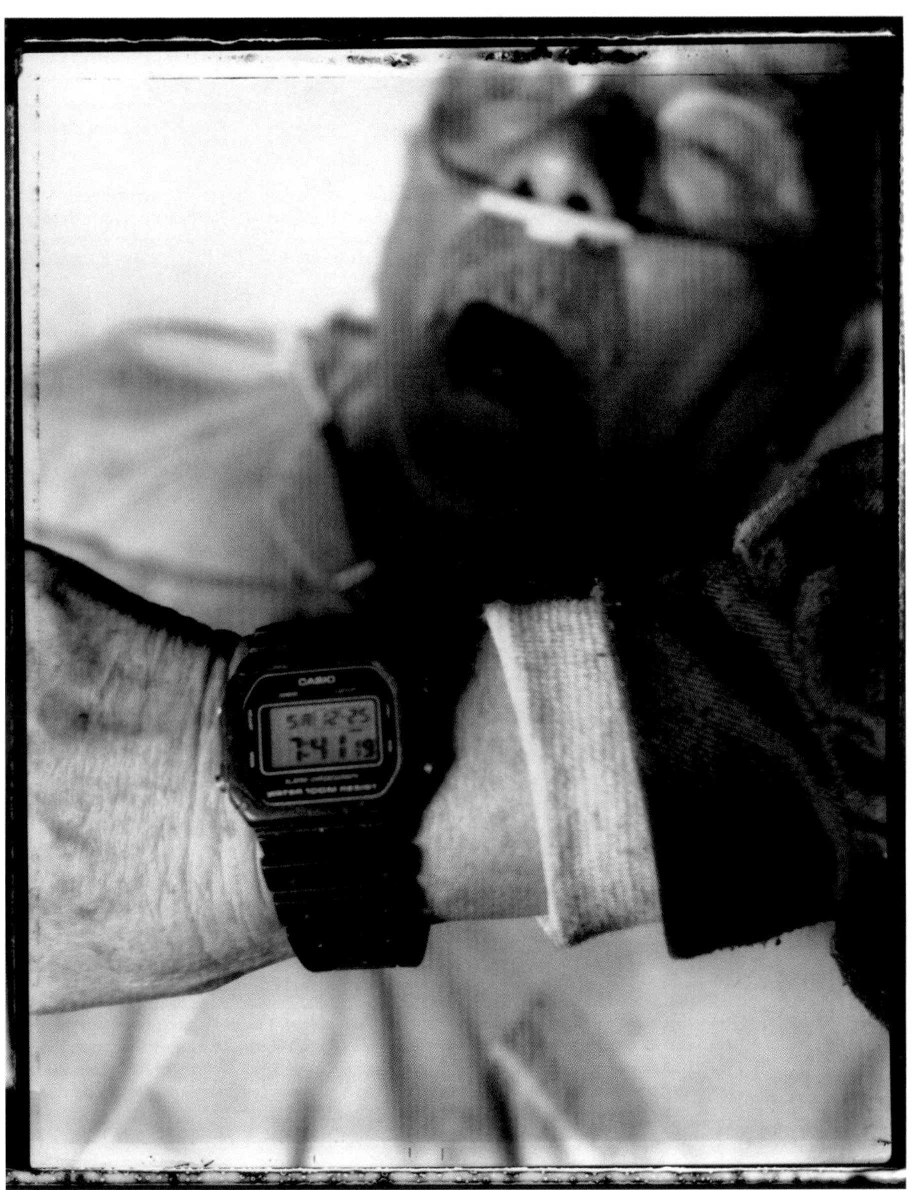
CASIO
SU 12-25
7:41
WATER 100M RESIST

December 25 - 6:30 a.m.
There is an insecure tap, tap, tap on the door. "It's me, Adam. Your mom wants you to come out here, now." Mom is collapsed over Dad, crying and calling out, "I can't understand him. What do you want, Herb? Do you want me to raise the bed higher?"

Mom implores me to do something. "He's not breathing well. Can you help? Jimmy, you must help." I move to Dad and put my ear to his lips. Faintly he says, "I can't breathe." I ask about the oxygen, and Adam says he tested it fifteen minutes ago. My father looks lunatic. I lean closer still and he says, "Say thank you," "To who, Dad?" I ask, going through the list of possibilities and finally arriving at Adam. Dad agrees with his eyes. Even in dying he is ever graceful.

All of a sudden, with as much force as he can muster, Dad yells, "CHAIR!"

I ask Adam about his experience and his confidence wanes. Still, I'm determined to get Dad into his chair, I call hospice and leave a message for the Green Team nurse to call. I direct Mom to comfort Dad.

Mom begs, "Help him breathe, Jim."
I turn up the oxygen machine. Dad's eyes are glazed over. I tell him, "I'm right here, Dad."
"Chair," he whispers. The word is not quite discernible.
"I'm trying, Dad." I want to call Fran.
"No, it's Christmas and I don't want you to disturb anybody," Mom says. "It's not right."
"Mom, I don't know what's right now. I just know that he's dying and I've got to get him to his chair."
"Don't be so negative, Jimmy," she says. "Your father will make it. He always has." Mom kisses Dad while I photograph their last time together. It's an incredible stars-shining-in-your-eyes-as-tears-fall-down-on-us moment.

I see that Mom is about to offer coffee and cookies to Adam. He is nice, but I don't want him here now. "Not now, Mom," I declare. "We need to be alone with Dad." Adam leaves. I realize that all the things that my father couldn't be in his life don't matter now. I think that he's a strong, focused, great man. I must get him to his chair.

Time Speeds Up
Dad is losing consciousness, mumbling coma words. "What's he saying, Jim?" Mom asks.
"I don't know, Mom. 'Chair,' I assume."
Hospice calls back. I describe how he can't breathe, and Rena, the nurse, says, "It sounds like the 'Death Rattle.'" She tells me to rub Dad's hand and help him push forward, and that she'll check back in an hour. I'm pleading to Dad, "Hold on till Fran gets here. Can you hear me?"
No more whispers.
No more breathing.
No more nothing.

7:41 a.m.
He is dead. My mom is begging me to give him more oxygen. I explain it won't help. Hospice calls, someone will be over in thirty minutes. Mom is crying and goes out to get the paper. She comes back in. It's a beautiful, clear, cold morning. The headlines read, FLORIDA GETS A WINTRY SLAP FOR THE HOLIDAY and BETHLEHEM CHRISTMAS IS JOYOUS AND POLITICAL. The house is still warm from the oxygen. Dad is now cold.

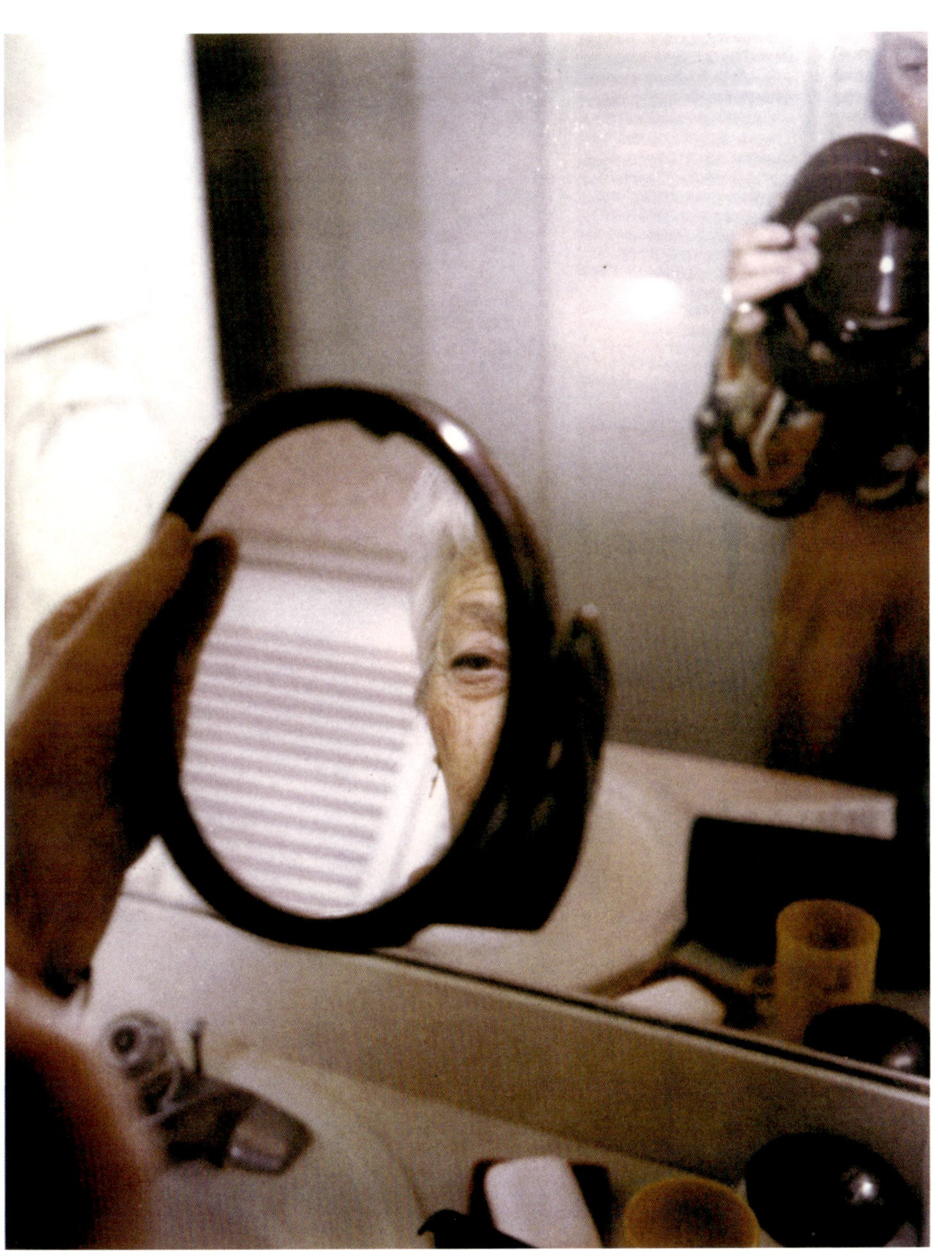

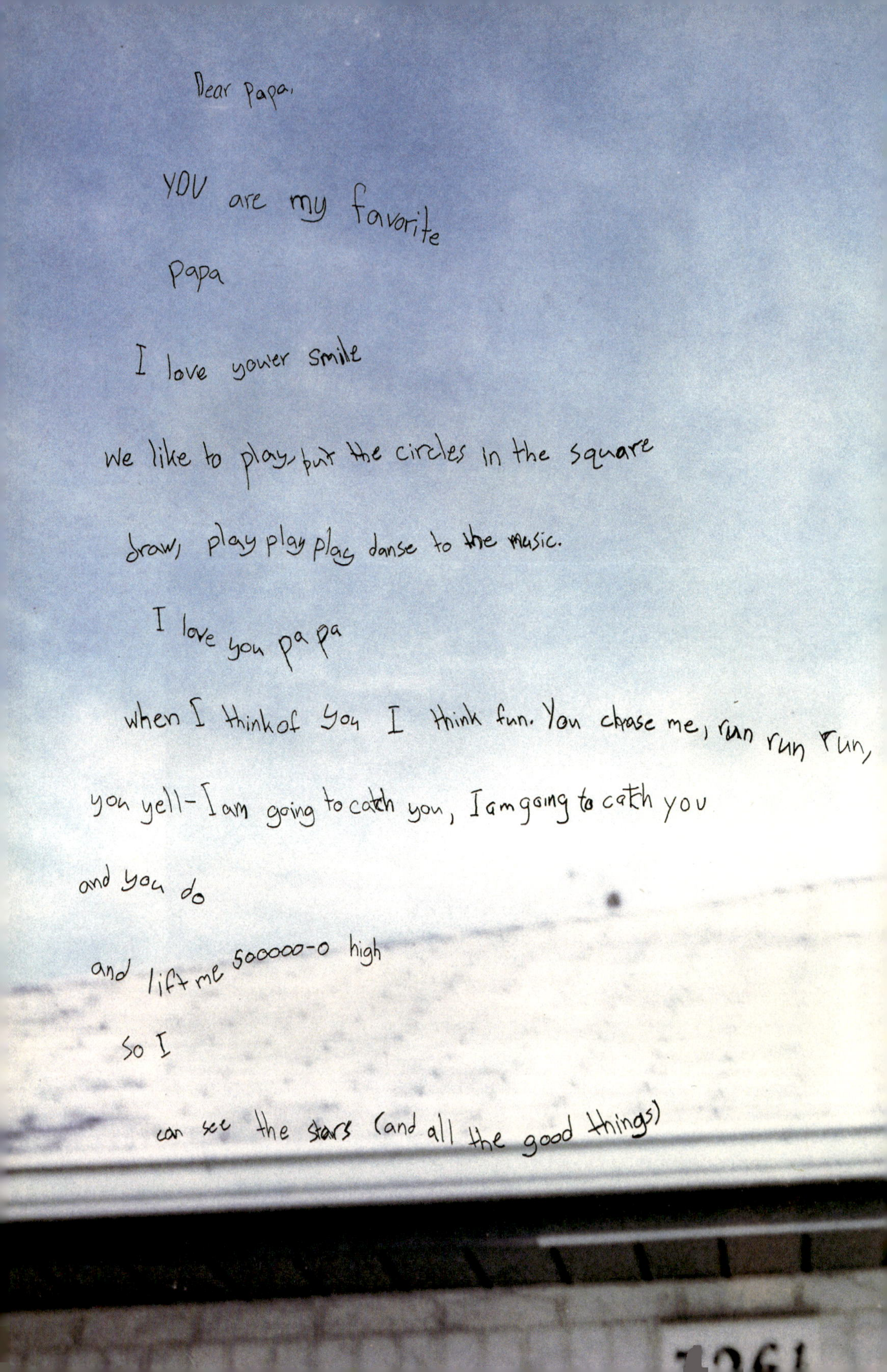

Dear Papa,

YOU are my favorite Papa

I love youer smile

we like to play, put the circles in the square

draw, play play play danse to the music.

I love you papa

when I think of you I think fun. You chase me, run run run, you yell—I am going to catch you, I am going to catch you and you do

and lift me 500000-0 high

So I

can see the stars (and all the good things)

lie down all tired
crickets at night are pretty
see the night,

nighty, night

I dreem I am out in the grass, running down the hills so fast

so fast

and I fall and cry

I wake up in my bed so sad papa

because I get so lonely

I wish that you and Mama sleep with me

But you come to me in my eyes

then I sleep. dont wake up and cry now.

I am happy

You are my only PaPa

I dreem my Mommy and Daddy.

Gone (almost)

She's almost gone.

Dwindling . . . tiny . . .

Finally, at the end of her life,
I see in the thinness of her spiderweb body
signs of where mine came from
once, she was *zaftig,* my mother said.
I'll tell her you said hello,
and then I'll remind her who you are.
Again, I think.
But she's gone, nearly
and I can't forget (remember) yet,
if I ever truly knew her.

She told me last time
that her Jewish name is Blima,
she remembers that it means *flower.*
I am, in more lucid moments,
Judy, her oldest daughter,
(which makes me my mother's older sister)
Lowie, her youngest,
or any of my three male cousins
also known as Judylowiejeffdavejoejenni,
any and all of us at the same time,
but never, quite,
really . . .

Jennifer Gwirtz

Like a long, educated guess,
or wishful thinking
that we are all there, wrapped up in one single body
to surround her with our child-selves,
holding her here.
She sits in the hospital bed,
my mother by her side.

Sam will be home soon, won't he?
did I make dinner?
I don't smell anything cooking.
maybe I never bought the chicken.
Are the girls back from school?

She drifts again, a small raft floating on a big, big ocean.
she is (we are) alone, unmoored.

My mother (we)
reminds her again
of some things, and not others.
Judy is gone,
Sam is gone,
and she is . . .

Peter Cordova

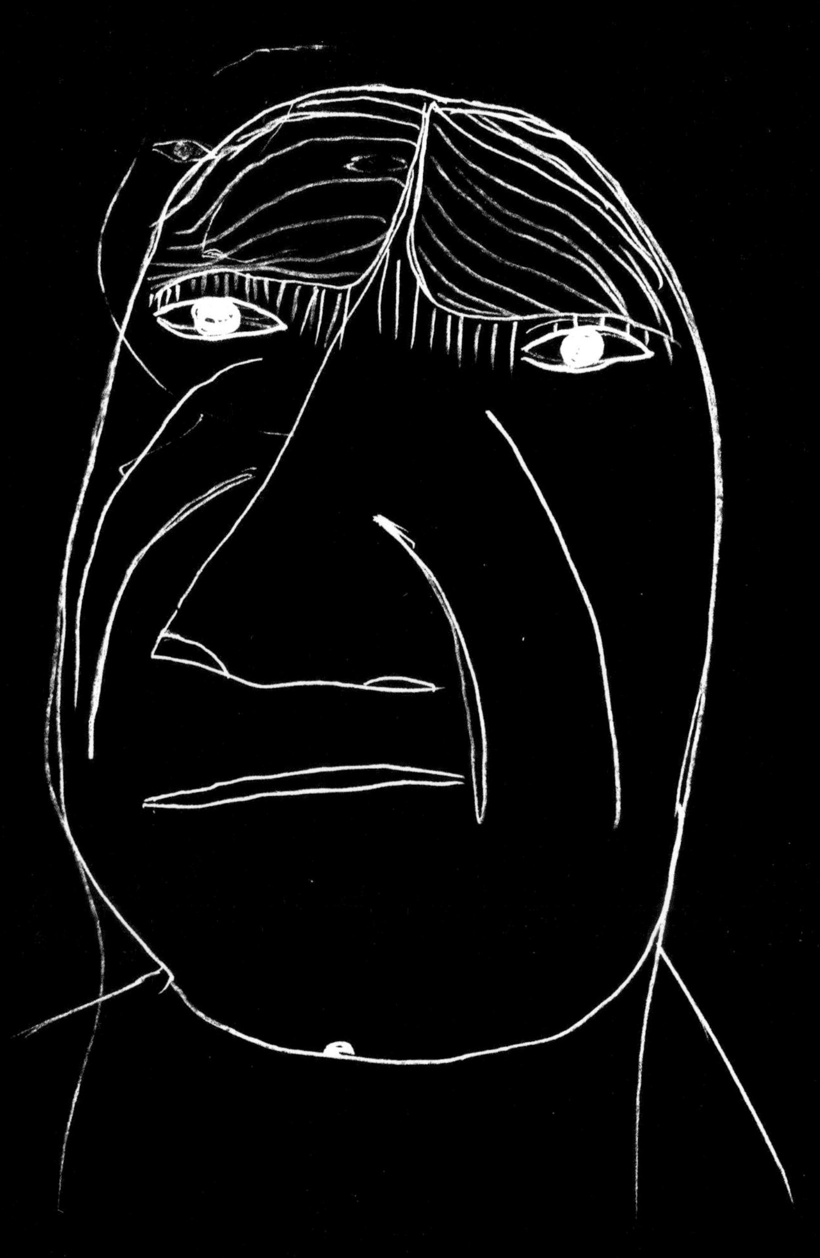

My dad passed away of sickness. Lung cancer. This is a picture of him.

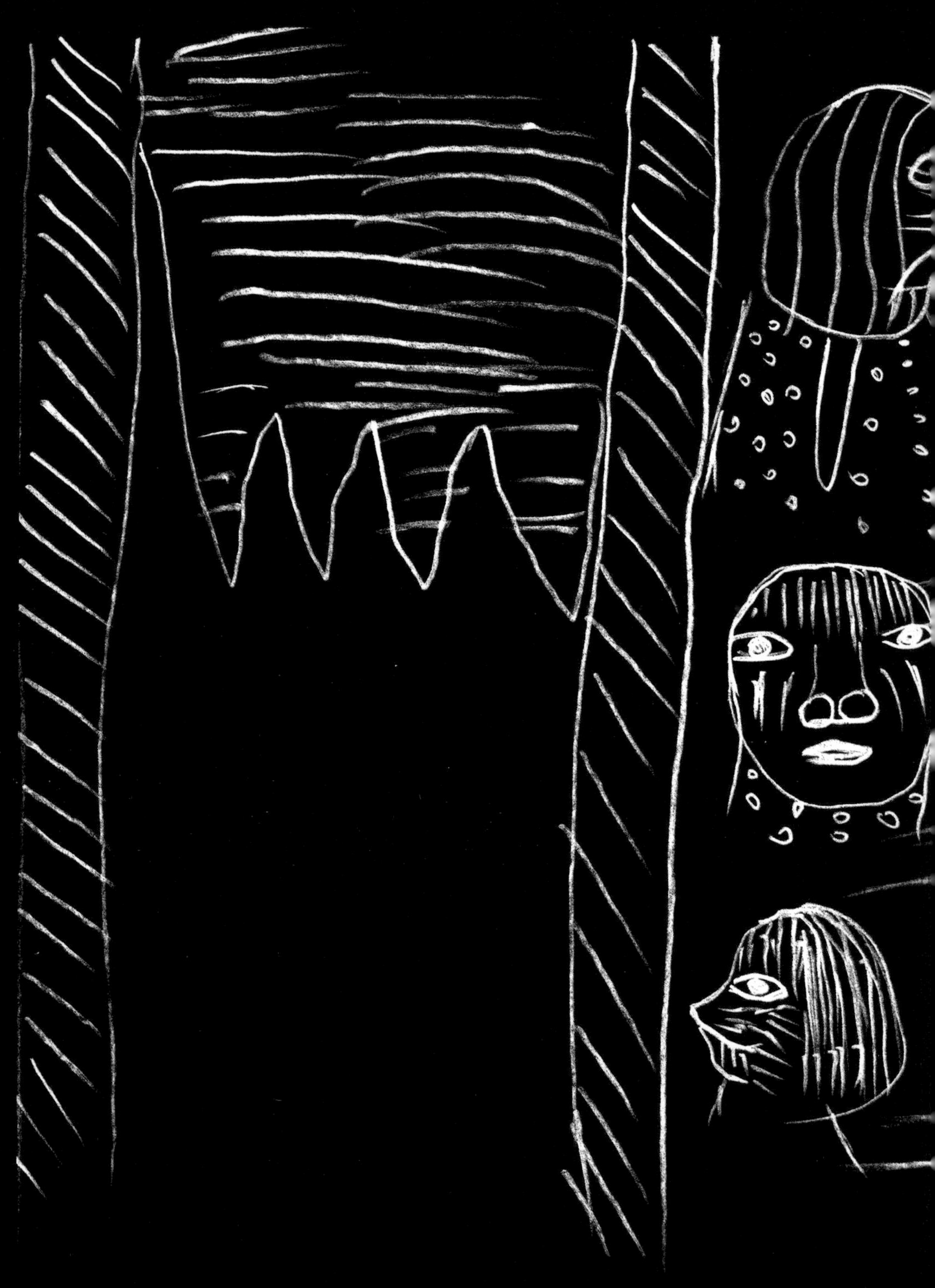

I came home and I saw my family all in one room together and that day I saw my dad on the bed and he was passed away on that day. We accept the day he passed away and my family decided to let it be behind us.

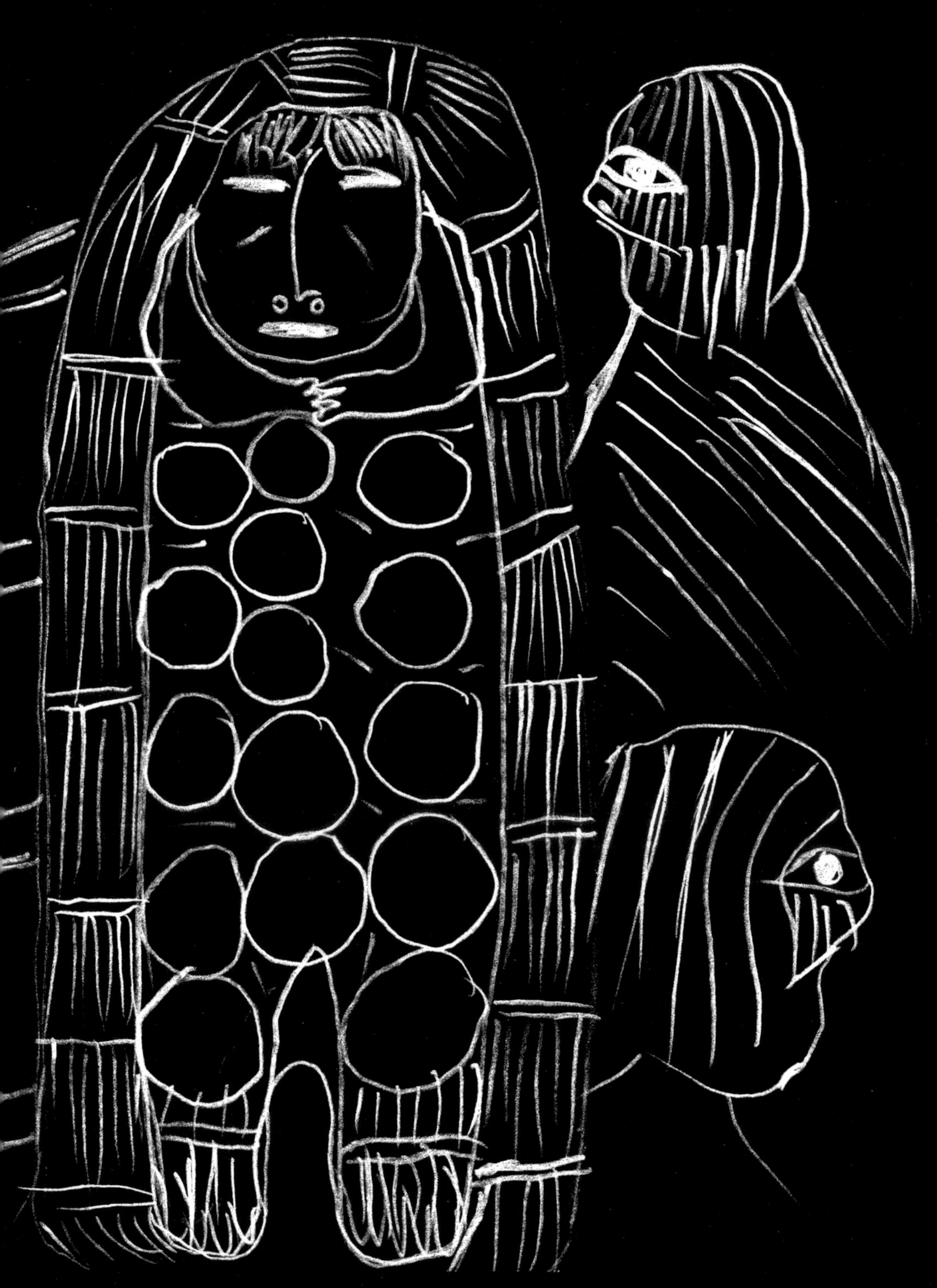

And my dad is happy. This is the way he wanted to be so he can be rest in peace.
I notified my workplace to let them know that I have to have off for one week.

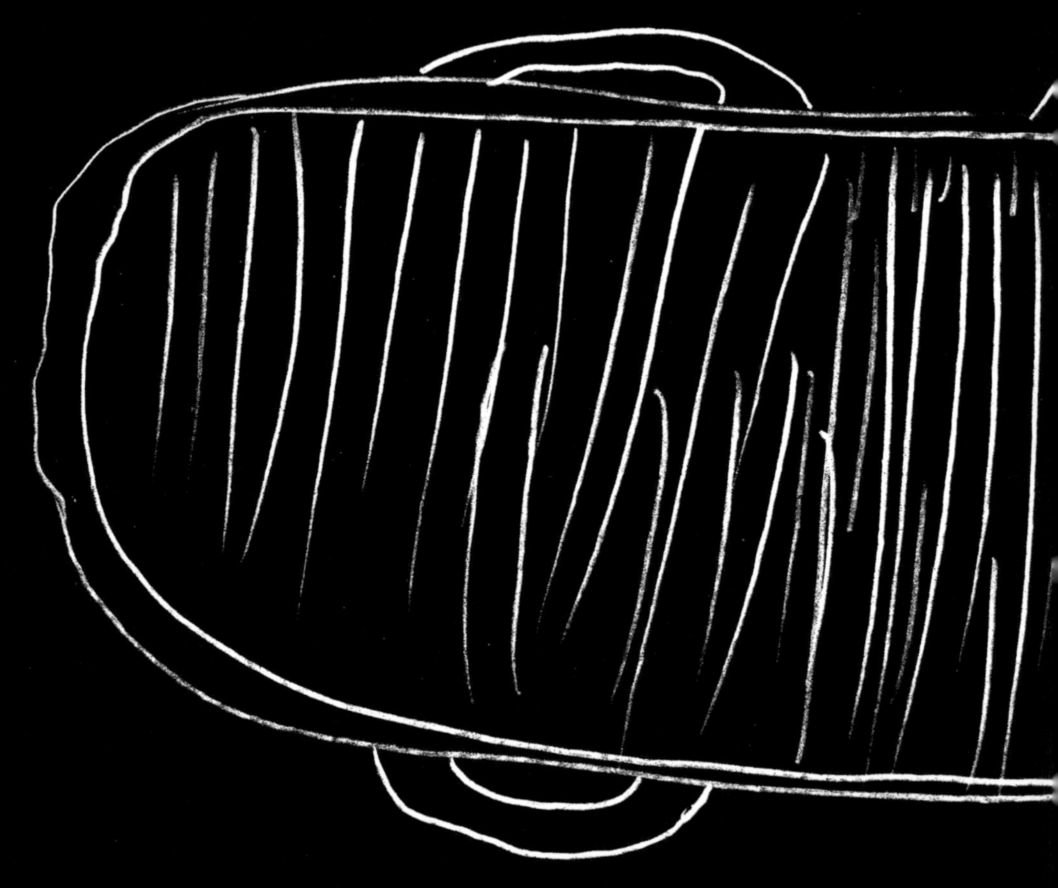

After two days of praying before the burial of my father, I accept all the good days and bad days. I was beside him when he needed someone to look after him.

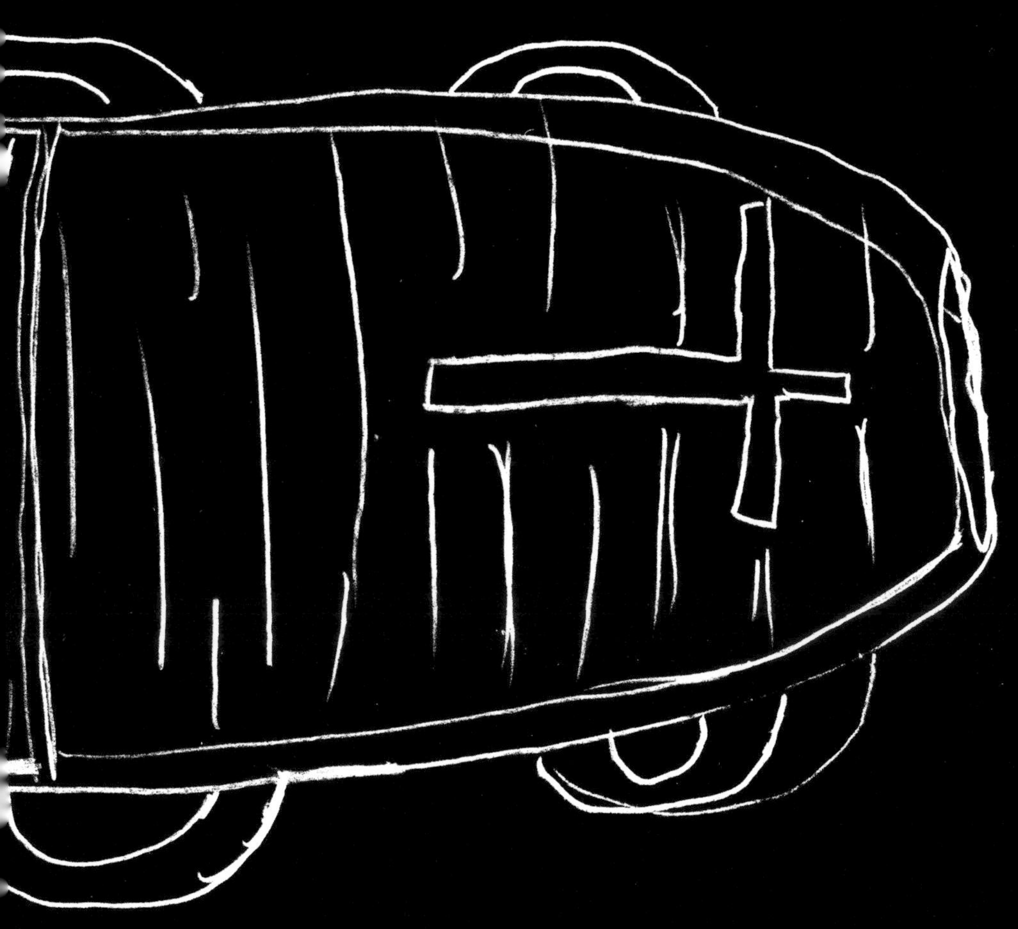

I watched him in the suffering and the sickness before the day he died. I am happy that the suffering is come to an end of his day. Now he's gone but it's time to move on.

Paula Levine

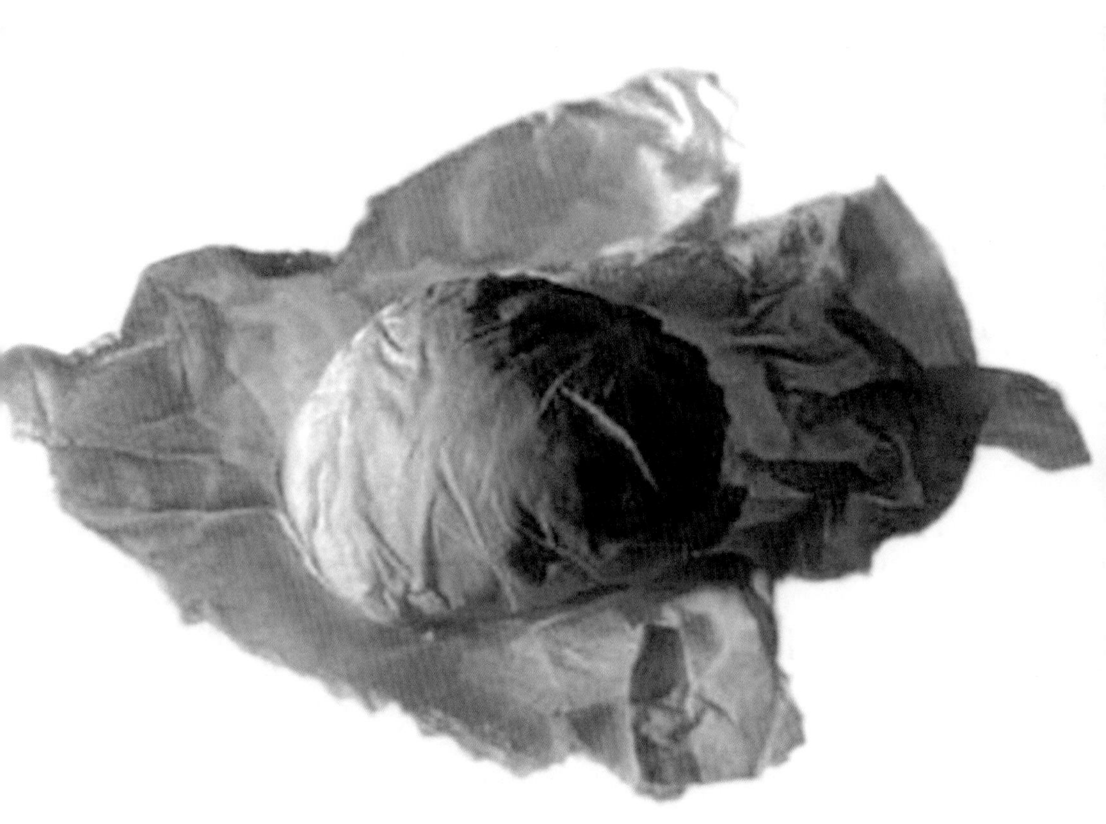

One year of mourning.

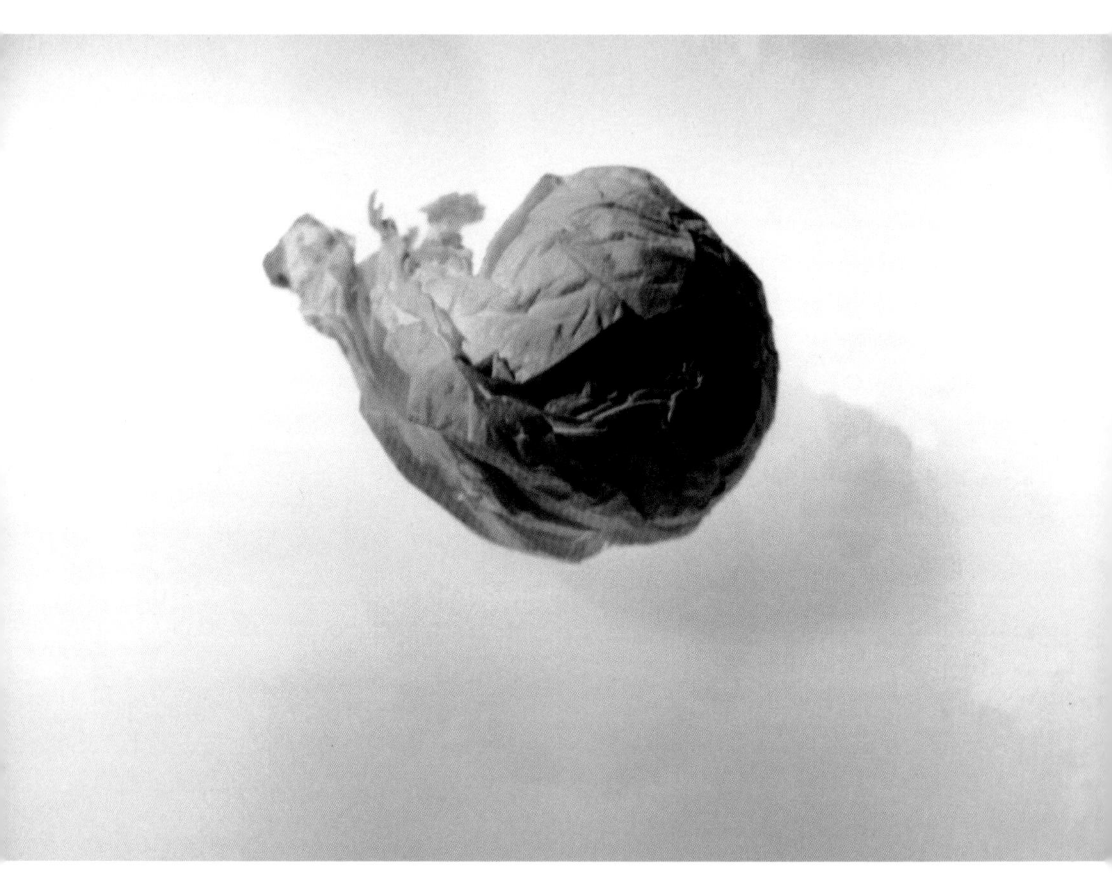

October 1993–October 1994

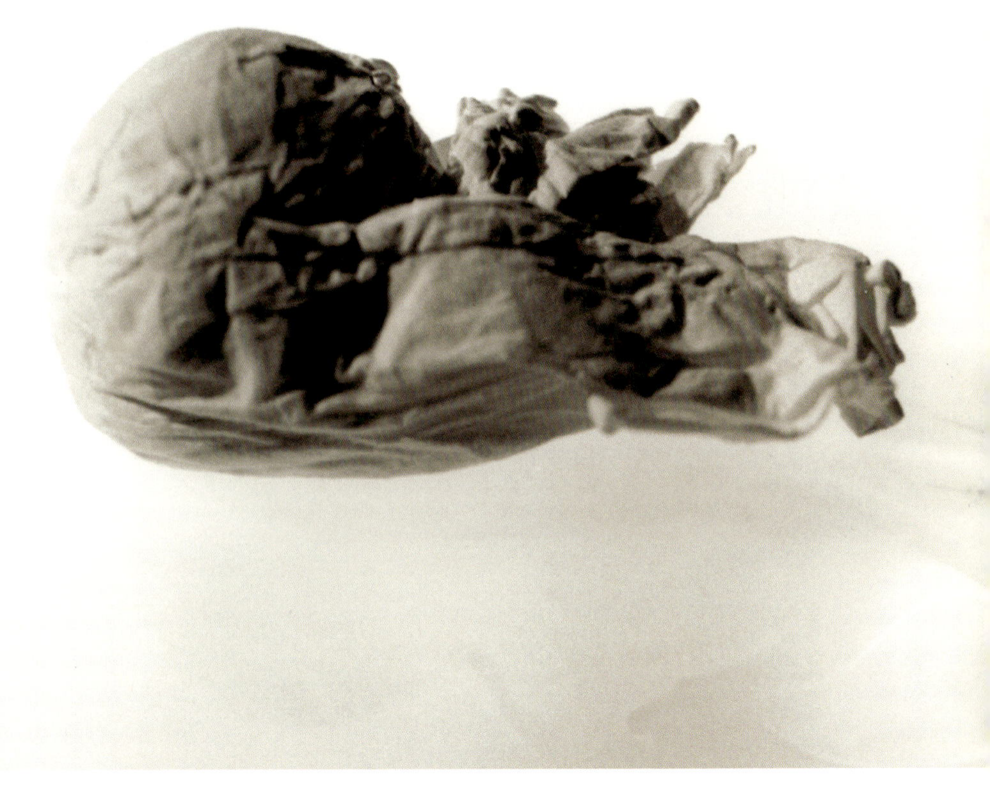

For one year, I collect the tissues I use to grieve.

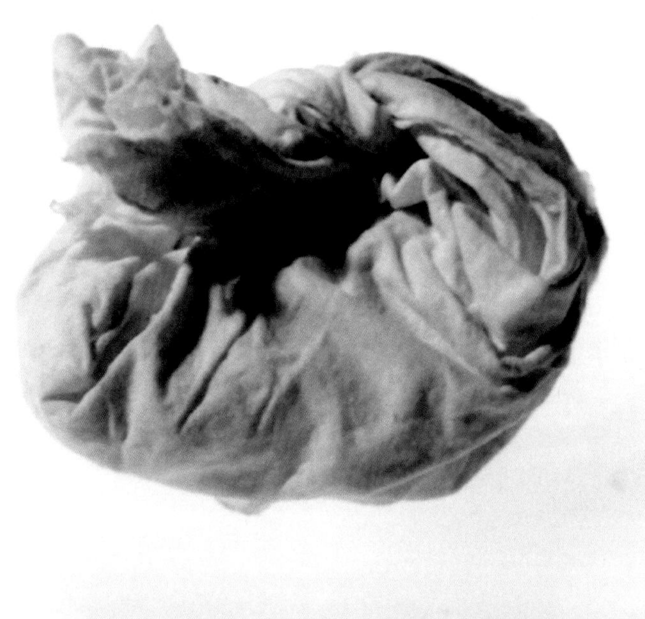

Not to hold on to mourning . . .

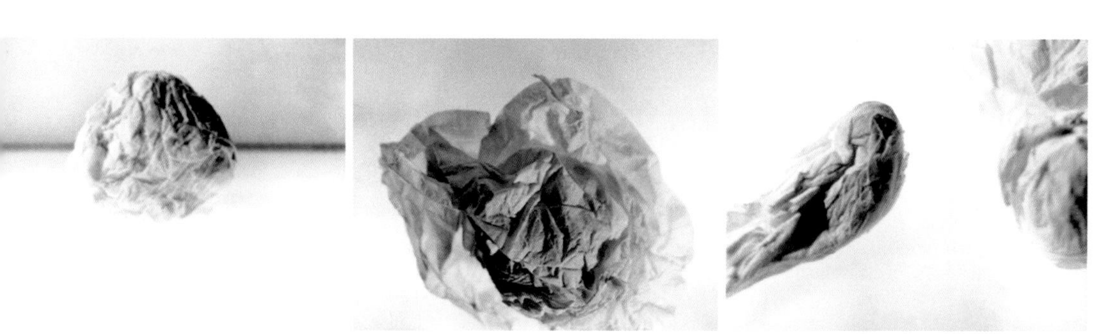

. . . but to mark a path through it.

David Hale

I woke up. I didn't know what day it was: I knew the time, 5:41 in the morning. I know this time well even today, for at this time I get up every day. I took my morning shower, and went down to watch the news for 30 minutes. By the time I had finished watching the news, it was 6:30 and it was time to wake up my younger brother. This morning was different. At 6:33, I heard a loud scream from my mother as she turned on the light in my brother's room. I had no idea what was happening, so I waited for a second froze in the position I was in at the TV, and after about two seconds of the passing of the scream, I shut the TV off. Then I heard my father scream. I knew it was serious. I ran into the recreation room and I screamed, *"Shma Yisrael Addonai Eloheinuu Addonai Ekhad!! Shma Yisrael Addonai Eloheinuu Adonai Ekhad!!"* I didn't know what else to do except pray. I didn't know what was going on until I heard my mom call 911. She was screaming, "Hello, 911, my son, my son is, my son is dead, he died of what we think is a seizure, we checked his pulse he has none, he's all cold!" After that I am assuming the operator asked where we lived and how old my brother was. "He is only nine years old, we live at 4004 Nunn Road, please hurry! Hurry!" My mom came downstairs to talk to me. She said I could go upstairs if I wanted to see him, and I did. I went up the stairs, it was 6:43, I had never seen a corpse before. I went into the room. I saw the body of an innocent nine-year-old boy lying in a mourning father's arms. My brother's eyes were not even closed, you could see the white part of his eye under the eyelid. His mouth was encrusted with dried saliva, his pajama shirt was coming a little above his waistline. I couldn't stand to see it, looking at a loved one's corpse. I ran downstairs, I didn't know what to do. I ran outside, I didn't know what to do. I went back in. My mom had called our friends, the Bells, and she was in the process of calling the Rabbi.

The Bells came and the Rabbi was lost. Then after the Bells came the paramedics came. They asked us questions and I had no idea what to say. I was so frightened, nothing like this had ever happened to me before. At about 7:00, my good friend since age of two came over. He didn't know what to say except, "I'm sorry." My dad came down the stairs to tell us that we were soon to go tell my grandmother because she didn't know yet. We left at 7:30 after I talked with the Rabbi a little bit. We got in my dad's truck and went to the Summerby Senior Center. When we went to tell my grandma my dad told me, "David, make sure that your grandma is sitting down when you tell her." I did so. After I told her, she was crying hard, so I ran into her TV room and found the Orthodox prayer hook and I read from it. *"Yitgadal v'yitgadash sh'mei rabo ba'olmah divra khiruteh. V'almilikh malkhuteh, b'khaiyekhon, uv'yomekhon, uv'khaie d'chol beit yisrael bagla uzman kareev, viemru; amen. Yehei sh'me rabo minvarokh l'olam ulmeh . . ."* After I said *"ulmeh,"* tears were running down my face like rain hits palm trees in a tropical storm. The words were so blurry from my tears that I couldn't read them. Today the words are stained with tears. I cannot imagine that sadness of a grandmother, who sees her many years flash before her, finding out that a grandchild is dead. A child she had lived 74 more years than. I don't know what she was thinking other than misery but if I were in her position I would think, "Why not me?" Though it may seem bizarre that's what she said after I thought that. She said "Oh God, why not pick me instead of an innocent little boy, or he was still not more than a baby." This and the prayer previous to it brought my friend Fredrick to tears.

We stayed at my grandma's for a little while, and then my dad took us all home. I didn't know what to do. They said that they would be taking his body away for an autopsy. Fredrick and I went into the backyard so we didn't have to see it. Although before they did, I went up to his room for the last time to say good-bye to him. I hugged him. I sang into his ears, which were as cold as granite inside a cave, his favorite song for one last time. After I said good-bye we went out back. That is where I told Fredrick when our band practices, the first song we are learning is his favorite one no matter what we had to do, and fortunately today we can play it.

Today is January 22, 2002, one month and twenty-four days since his passing. At the one-year mark of his passing, I will put this under his tombstone, so that he may know how much people cared for him. Now that I am at the end of my essay (for I will not talk about the funeral because I do not wish to discuss what happened there yet), I would like to thank everyone who has helped me get through this hard time. I realize that hardly anyone can understand. I learned about a month after his passing at a yeshiva, that according to Jewish customs, he passed away because his soul was perfect. According to custom you pass away once your soul is perfect. The student I was studying Torah with said he must have been a perfect boy, not to even need a Bar Mitzvah. I smiled at him and said, "You're right my friend, you're right."

Luke ♡
Thank you for all the love you gave me. All the big smiles and special times. You are a wonder-ful teacher and an amazing friend to me. All I can remember is your beautiful eyes that told me everything. I still can't believe it!
Love you so much
Love Summer

Radiant Spirit boy thank you for such love. Be well on your journey knowing you were well b[illegible] ♡ gayle

Luke—
You brought sunshine to my life. ♪

To Luke, The boy with the [illegible] smile. Good luck a[illegible]
To Luke, I barely kn[illegible] were a son that[illegible] we all [illegible]

Luke- you took up such beautiful space here!
Go gentle, sweet boy. -Catherine

on earth.

...journey. ♥Elyta

...You... isn't that a song... o that
loved w/ Mindy o Lucy...
K

Luke though I never
knew you I can feel
how much you are
loved   go on
sweet boy !
Melinda

Luke-
Thanks for the fun
times and Thanks
for the lessons! We will
all miss you -
Until we meet
again -
Love, Ed

-it was good to
meet you any family
as memories of you-
Debbie Taylor John Lindsay

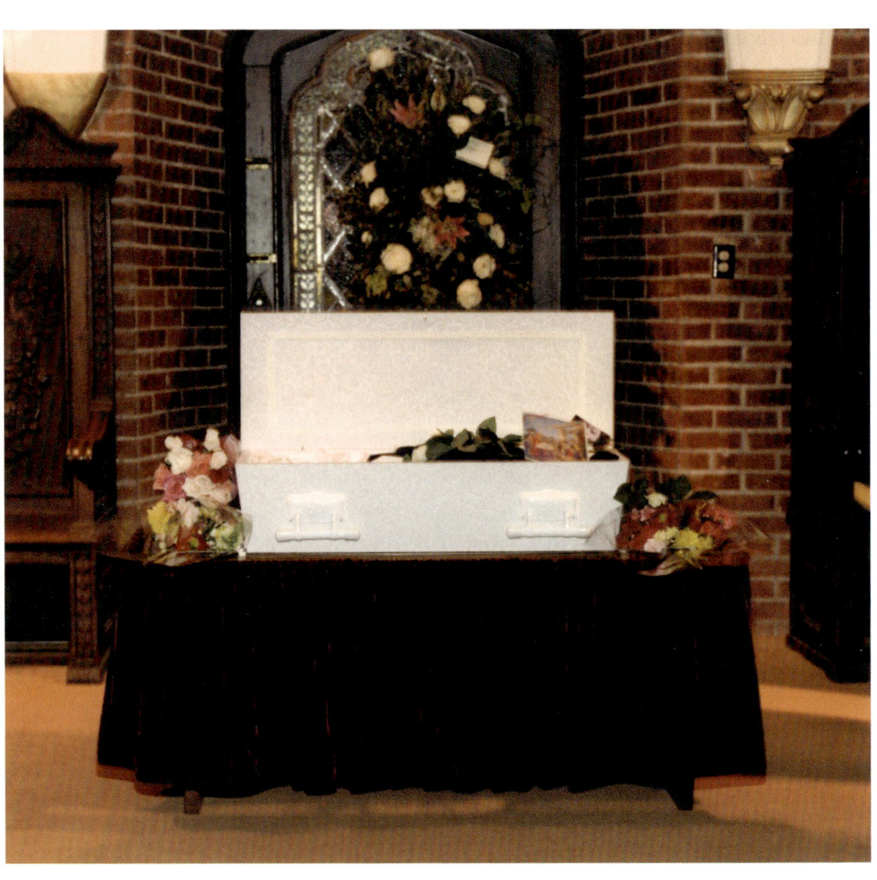

Luke, who was 3 years old mid-October, died quite suddenly on November 5. He has been the foster child of Mindy Zlotnick and Larry Miller since he was 4 days old.

Luke got to experience school with his other friends at the Presidio Early Intervention Program. He had just transferred to his first preschool class in the SFUSD. He had the opportunity to show everyone that he could use his wheelchair HIMSELF as well as the walker.

In the last year Luke had had the opportunity to do a bit of traveling to Seattle for a conference of the national MPS Society and several time to the East coast for two weddings, a Bat Mitzvah and vacation in the ocean and lakes of New England.

Luke is remembered by many friends for many different reasons: his smile, his rendition of The Wheels on the Bus, his ability to scoot all over on his back, his love of chocolate pudding, his pure joy of being here. He was a teacher in life and remains a teacher in death.

Mindy and Larry would like to thanks all the support they have received from friends and family throughout this period. Their presence, food, love, telephone calls and support have helped to make this an easier transition.

Donations can be made to the National MPS Society, 17 Kraemer Street, Hicksville, NY 11801. This is an organization that provides parent to parent support for families with kids with MPS.

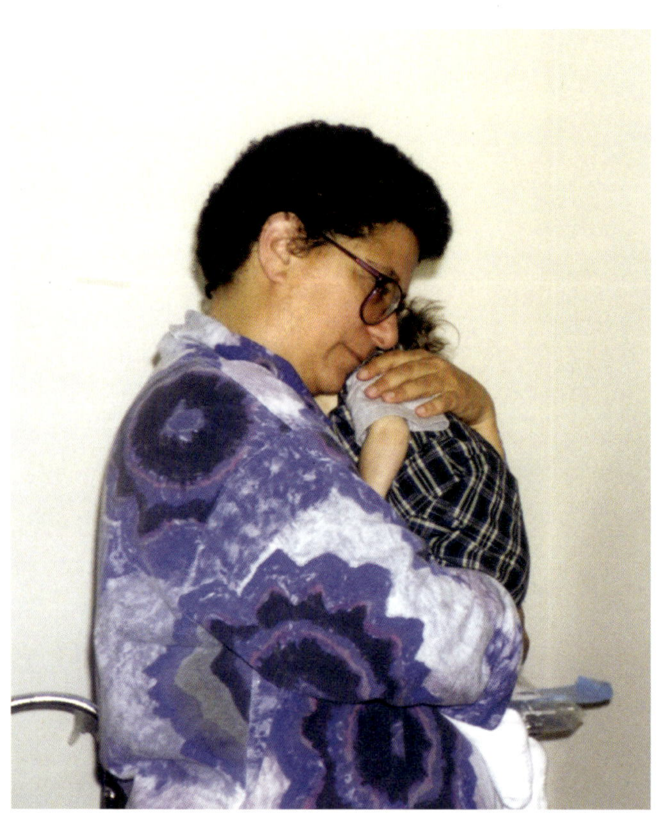

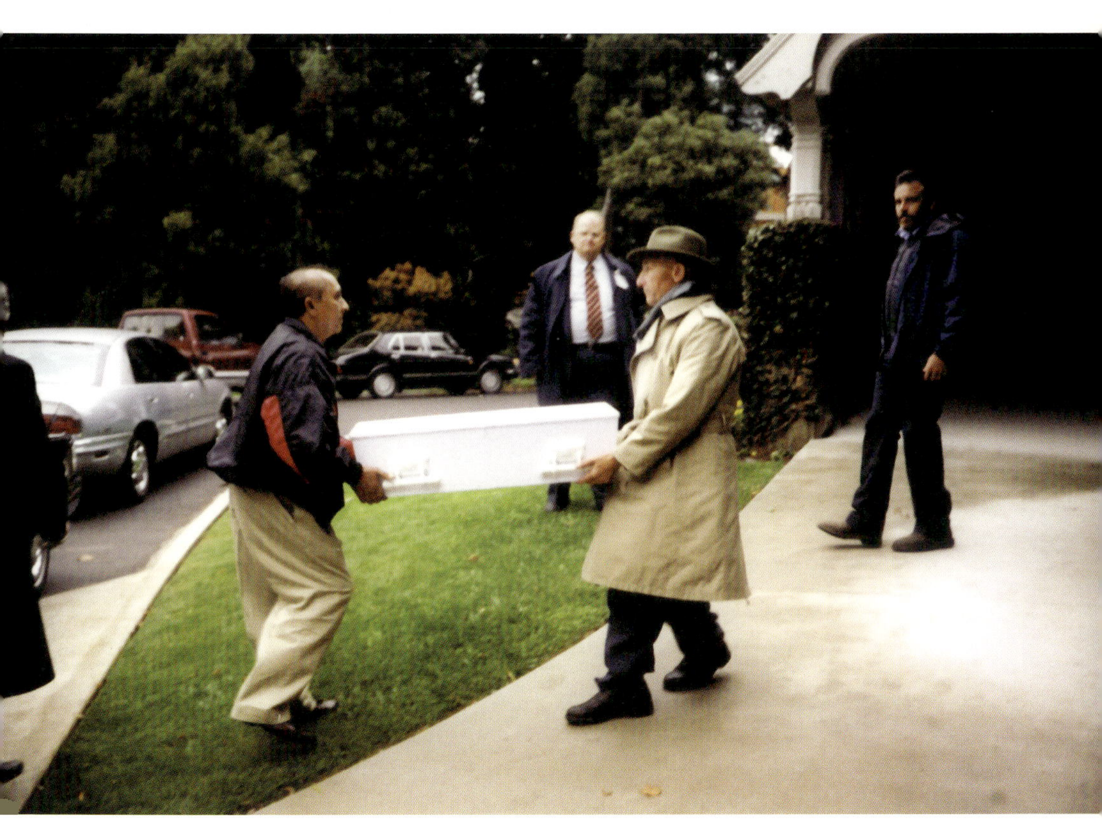

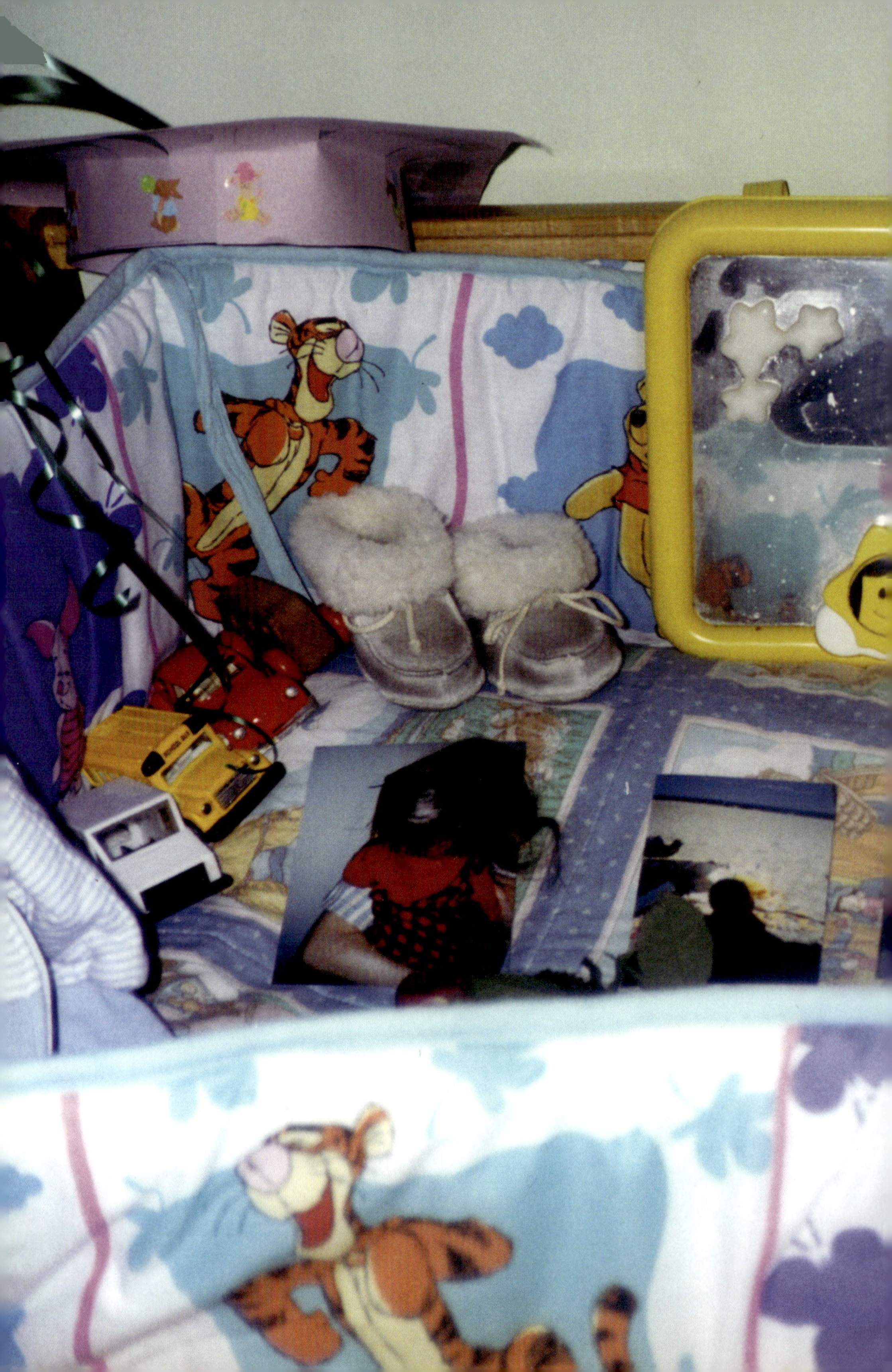

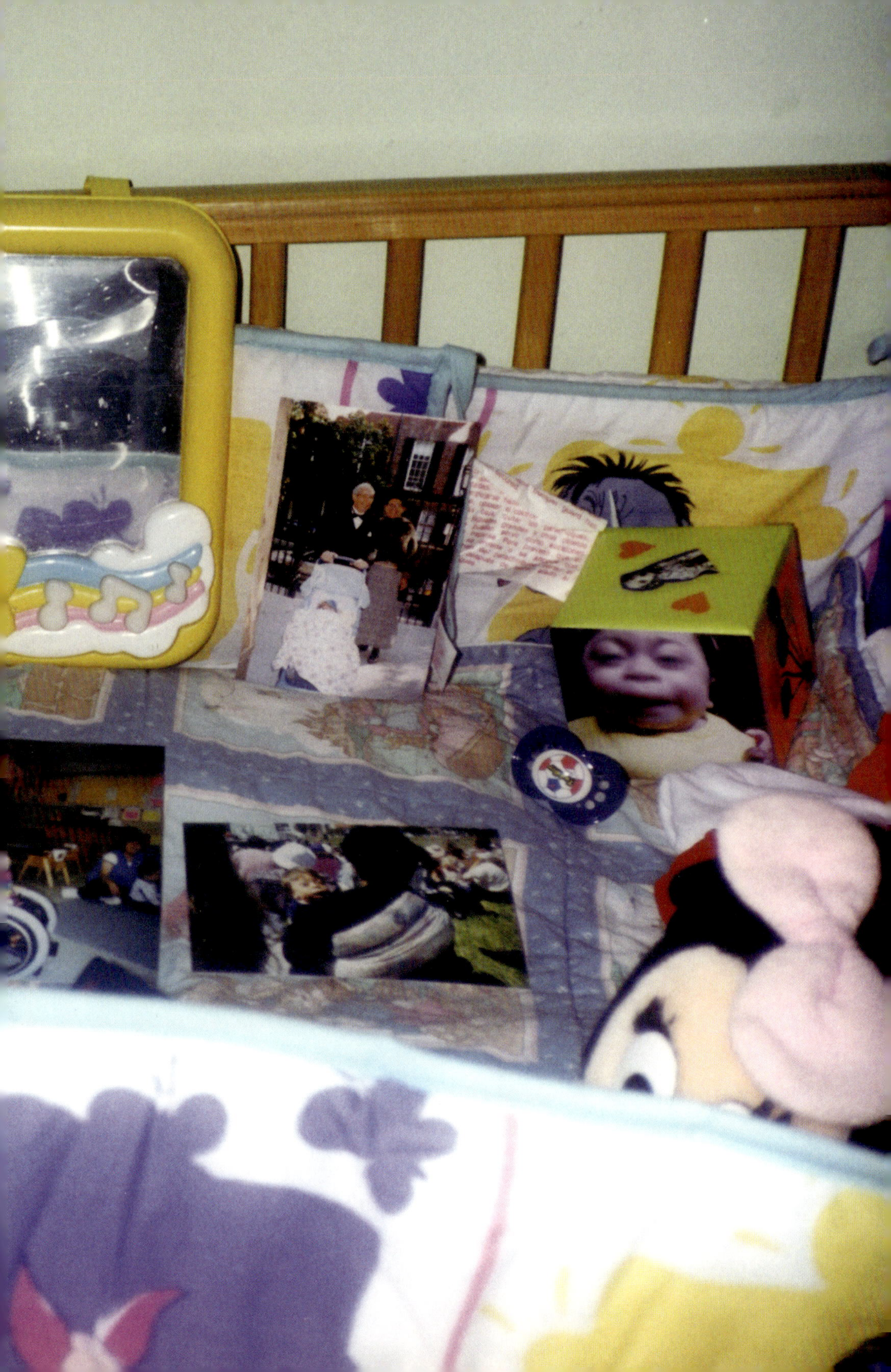

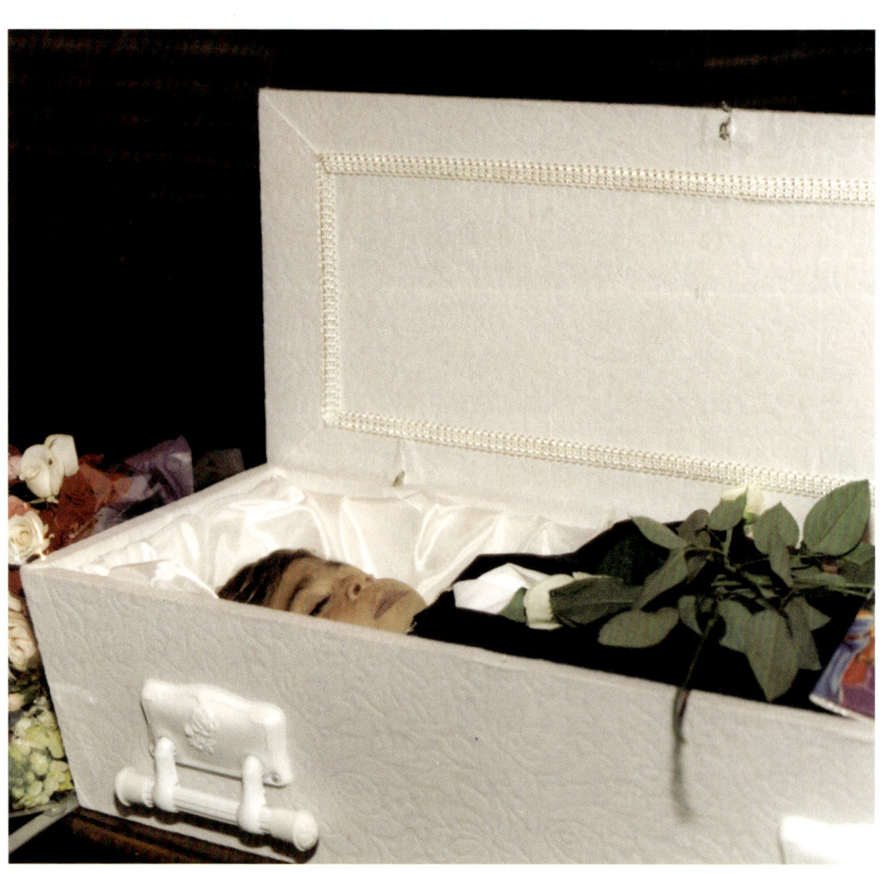

There is a place where
feelings have not yet formed
into words.

A full (and at the same time empty)
space of being.

Some call it love.

A place where babies hang out,
a place between there and here,
where we return
when we die.

Listen to the wind coming through the
trees
watch a leaf
fall

This is the place where
feelings have not yet formed into words.

Now you know Luke.

Larry Miller
12/98

Richard Lichtman

Reflections on a Passage from *Dying in America*

When I wrote the memoir of my parents' dying and death, I had an extremely dif-
ficult time deeding how to select from their lives, each of which spanned more than
85 years. Exactly what was I to include and exclude? There is no logical answer to
this question; lives are made up of millions of experiences and from one reason-
able point of view, each of them is relevant.

The answer is provided to a large extent by what prevails in the memory of the
observer. It is not so much their story that insists upon itself, but the meaning of
their life for you, the child, that establishes the motif that asserts itself. This is only
to say the obvious; it is the impact of their death upon your life that asserts itself.
And this fact follows a familiar pattern, in that what we tend to remember of our
parents is their effect upon us.

But what is the nature of their lives as they lived it independently of their children,
so far as this distinction can be made. The obvious fact that they had their own
lives before our birth is not something we ordinarily focus upon. We come to know
them as parents, as our mothers and fathers, rather than as persons with a history
of their own. And even if we attempt that biography of their lives that an independ-
ent narrator would attempt, someone not their children, we are faced once again
with the fact that what we note in them is what seems important to us. For always
we must select, and the primary principle of selection is what is most crucial to us.

That being said, on this occasion of selecting a passage from a work that already
bears the hand of extreme exclusion, I have chosen to present a passage that pre-
sents something of my father's life, which while not independent of mine, is simul-
taneously his. For in the passage that follows, he evidences a struggle that is his
alone; so much his that I do not believe he could have articulated it if asked. He
is presenting that unspoken penumbra of a life that lives in the shadow of the self
and makes up its implicit and covert being, that nurtures the manifestations that
derive from this source of personal being. Something appeared; something did not
appear. I look back in sorrow at what bound him so tightly to the conventions of his
life and wonder at the life unlived he harbored unspoken. But I also recognize in
joy and gratitude the unspoken voice that struggled so valiantly to speak.

He comes out to visit us for a week. It is very difficult for him to orient himself in
these new surroundings; he often needs help locating the kitchen or bathroom. But
he seems quite happy, and when L comes over to visit, he launches into one of his
Catskill routines made up of the Marx Brothers, Willie Howard, Gallagher and

Sheean, Henny Youngman, and all the vaudeville and burlesque bananas he has caught along the way. I've heard some versions of this shtick so often I can play straight man or comic; one of us begins: "Vus villa?" and the other replies, "I knew his brother Pancho." Followed by, "You ought to be on the stage; and there's one leaving in 20 minutes," and so on and on. . . . The routine just rolls into place. After he has begun, my father can dispense with my services and the routine becomes a monologue which moves on its own. There is nothing here that is not familiar though the pace has become more frenetic. (After all, the first memory I have of anything my father said to me was: "A very funny bird was the pelican/ Its beak holds more than its belly can.") Finally L takes me aside, somewhat exhausted, "Is he always this way?" "It's one of his ways."

We spend one day at the aquarium at Monterey. He is completely enchanted and reminds me that when I was a child, he often took me to the aquarium at the Battery in lower Manhattan. His interest goes back even further, to the times he would play hooky from school so that he could visit the museums of New York, particularly the Museum of Natural History. For he was and would always be basically self-taught, inspired by Mrs. Fraelich's opinion that he had real ability, as she presented him with a copy of *Swiss Family Robinson* when he graduated from the 6th grade. And encouraged again by Mr. Goldin, accepted to Townsend-Harns High School, but leaving school to work for his family, he grew up reading what he could and attending lectures, like the debate between Walter Lippmann and Clarence Darrow at Cooper Union that he spoke of so often and with so much delighted excitement.

Years before my mother became ill, I had developed the practice of sending him books on modern American history, one of his favorite subjects. I had hoped by this device to pull him somewhat out of my mother's orbit of incessant domestic tasks that she continually found to occupy him, to encourage some interest of his own with which to counter her impositions. One of the books I sent was Ronald Steele's biography of Walter Lippmann. It was to play a part in a crucial episode between my father and me that deeply affected my understanding of his life.

The occasion was the Thanksgiving dinner to which I have already alluded, to which B's parents had invited my parents and the two of us. Despite our trepidation it was a very pleasant evening, and it was after dinner my mother gave B the bracelet that had been a gift from her mother. Of all the jewelry she had, it was the most beautiful and the most appropriate. After years of regretting my divorce from S, it was, I believe, her way of finally accepting this second marriage. My father then removed the tie pin he was wearing and offered it to me with a letter he drew from his inside jacket pocket. It was his handwritten copy of a letter, included in the Steele biography, that Lippmann had written to his wife Helen.

The circumstances were these: for both the Lippmanns this was a second marriage. Walter Lippmann and Helen's first husband were close friends who dined frequently at each other's homes. One evening after dinner, when Walter was helping Helen on with her coat, without premeditation he confessed that he had always loved her; shortly afterward, she reciprocated. They divorced their current partners, married each other and lived a loving life together. Walter found it difficult to express his love for her directly, though he often wished he could. On the occasion of their leaving Washington he felt the need to articulate his feelings for her. Steele comments and then quotes the passage my father had copied out:

> There was no way he could say this to her directly. He would have been too embarrassed. But on her seventieth birthday, Feb. 19, 1967, as they were beginning to prepare for their departure from Washington, he left a note on her desk:
>
> My dear Helen,
> I feel I must write you a letter on this day.
> For in it I can say how happy I am that I
> married you and how deeply and everlastingly
> grateful I am. Looking back, I feel as if I had
> never really begun to live until we set out
> together, and that I have known from you not
> only unimagined happiness, but also the secret of
> starting life anew. You have been the
> decisive influence. But for you I would have
> settled down dully thirty years ago in the
> grooves I cut when I was young. But for you I
> would now be settling into a dull old age
> instead of feeling that we are at a new and
> fascinating beginning.
> All my love always, my darling
> Walter

I continue, after all these years, to be deeply moved by the rich complexity of my father's gift of this letter. Was it that my father, too embarrassed to speak to me directly, utilized this letter by Lippmann, who was to embarrassed to speak directly to his wife, to inform me of his acceptance of. . . of what? Of my second marriage, as Lippmann had expressed his deep gratitude for his second marriage? Or, of me, of his love for me, whom he had never told he loved in the over 50 years I had been his son. It seemed an assault to ask him anything further, since the whole point of the letter was to speak indirectly to me. I would have violated the manner of his speech—even, perhaps, the mode of his reflection on his life. In my milieu introspection, self-consciousness, and shared disclosure were the norm. But our parents were different. My friends and I often remarked on the largely objective nature of our parents' conversations, so directed as it was toward the affairs of the world and the comings and goings of relatives and friends, and so little to their own internal springs of action, their subjective lives.

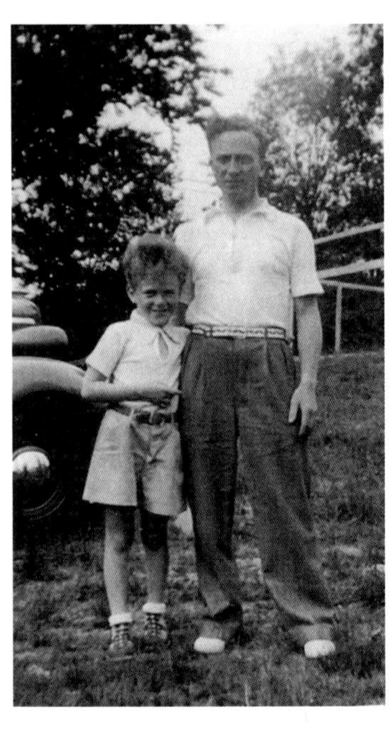

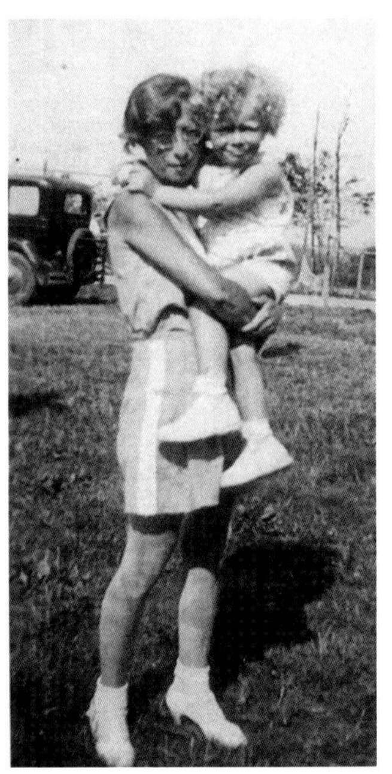

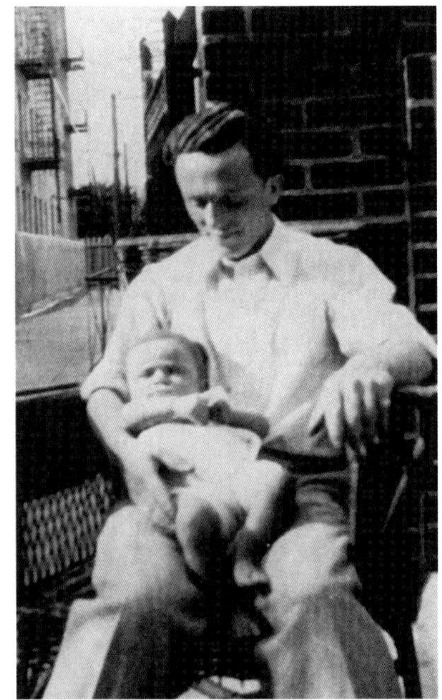

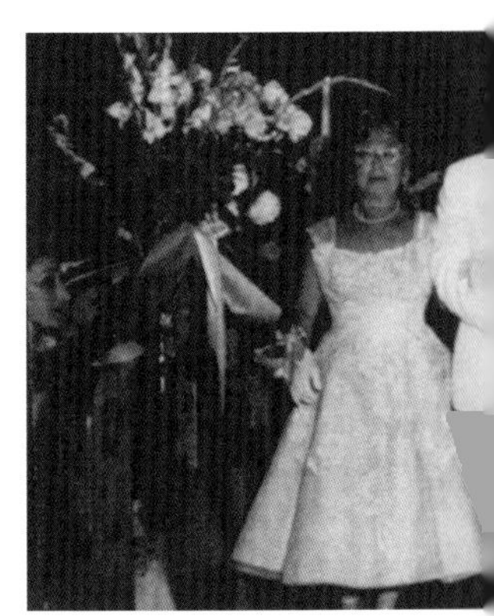

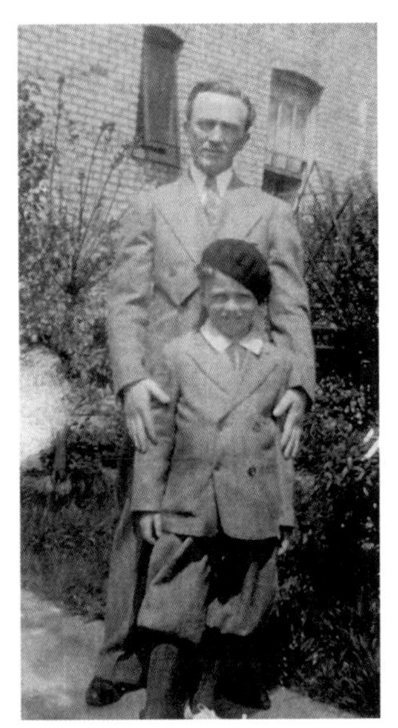

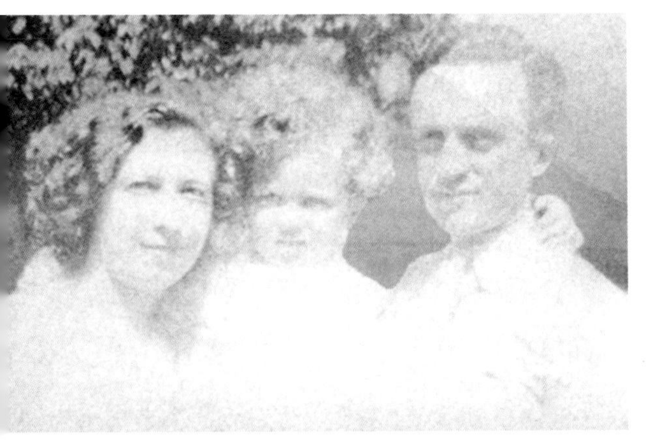

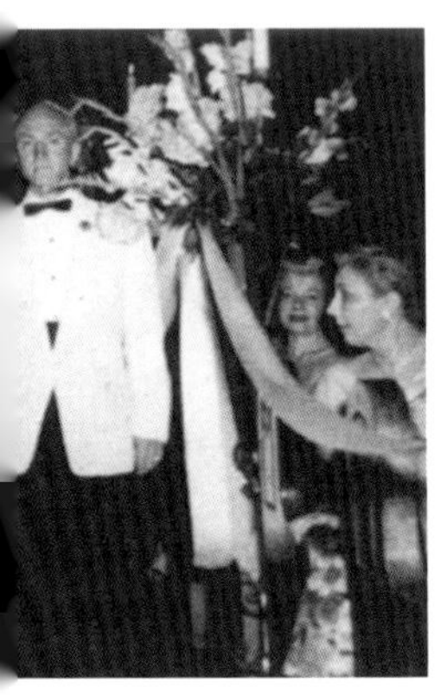

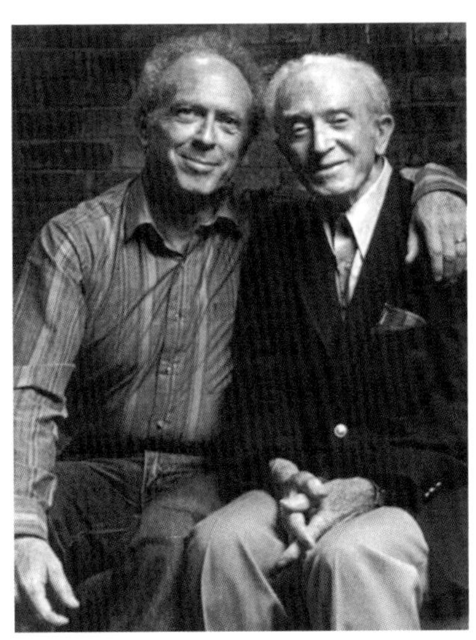

My father was a man who never entertained the thought of being a different person. He had been educated in a culture that cared more for character than personality. He might, of course, have chosen other things in his life, but he would have remained the same nevertheless. My friends and I, on the other hand, seemed always to live under the gaze of relentless questions that would not let us rest wholly at peace in our present lives. There was for us generally some set of alternatives that we needed to consider and some choice made painfully at the expense of other possibilities. I am not speaking here merely of jobs, or marriage partners, or even personas. For us there were moments of critical intersection between our personal agendas and the sociopolitical currents of the time that forced us to recalibrate our moral equilibrium. So the Women's Movement forced us to reconsider the meaning of our gender, and the Sexual Revolution the balance of our desire and constraint.

But my father never seemed to travel this path. He was guided by a somewhat un-self-conscious sense of what needed to be done and he constructed his self-definition in the course of meeting these permanent imperatives. At the time, I thought his life stultified by this lack of explicit, self-conscious choice. But now, after apparent choices of my own have returned me more disorder and pain than I could have anticipated, I am much less sure. It is clear enough what the generation of our parents lacked in "heroic self-determination." But it is also clear to me that they simultaneously avoided being continually assaulted by the ravages of a cruel self-scrutiny, directed by constantly shifting criteria, whose ostensible self-evidence was only exposed after the actions they inspired had long ago produced too much misery to be redeemed.

And yet, what was I to make of my father's consciousness on this occasion? It was not without reflection, but it seemed to need another's articulation to realize itself. My father, who had never spoken to me of his feelings about my second marriage, had transcended his silence through this complex parallel voice which spoke for him. It was as though he stood at the limit of his own immediate capacity for self-reflection, and was able by the stroke of this other articulation, to transcend himself, to leap a chasm he had not previously dared.

Later, when B and I drove my parents home, we stood with them for a few moments in the entranceway to the lobby of the apartment house in which they lived in Brooklyn. It was cold and the sky was very clear. Excited, emboldened by the success of the evening, my mother asked me if there was anything else I wanted. It was a time, a question, a moment wholly separated from the usual course of our lives. She was happier and more open than I ever remembered. I believed she also loved B, perhaps the daughter she had never had, who treated her with great warmth and kindness. I said I would like her to tell me that she loved me, something I had never heard from her in the entire course of my life, something she had never even approached saying to me. And yet on this clear night she immediately told me that she loved me. Much to my own astonishment, I was not astounded. I held my pleasure for a moment, told her that I loved her, and turned to my father. And with the tone of our vaudeville banter but insistently, I asked him too to tell me that he loved me. I was violating my own previous reflection; but I was ecstatic this evening, quietly delirious. I felt strongly loving toward B, and I had heard something I never expected to hear from my mother—her love for me. I was emboldened to close this magic circle around me. "You're okay in my book, kid," he replied. He was back in his own element. I would not let go of him: "Oh no, that won't do it. It's not that hard—I'll tell you: I love you, Dad." I could see that he was moved but not enough to give up his shtick—that light, fast, clever, responsive, ethereal world where you floated above reality, each gesture returned in kind in a perpetual hall of echoes. "You're okay in my book." I refused this offer but he only offered it again. And again, I refused and persisted. Finally, his voice giddy with embarrassed laughter, against the urgent background of my mother's exasperated "Oh Nat, tell him so we can go up already," he uttered the words I so wanted to hear from him. The evening was concluded, special hours out of the whole life we had with each other, a strange and wonderful eruption of light out of the very gray feeling I had assumed would be the color of my life with them forever.

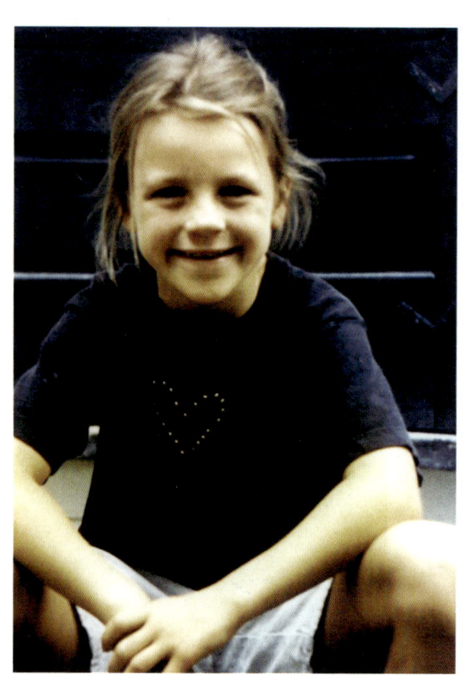

Elizabeth Knox

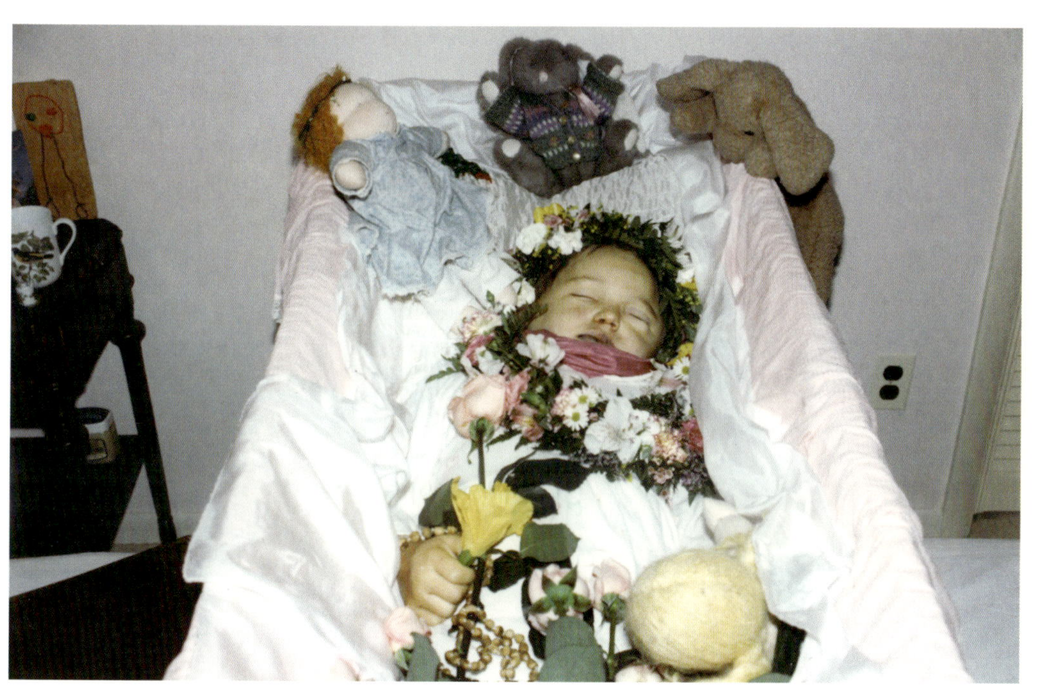

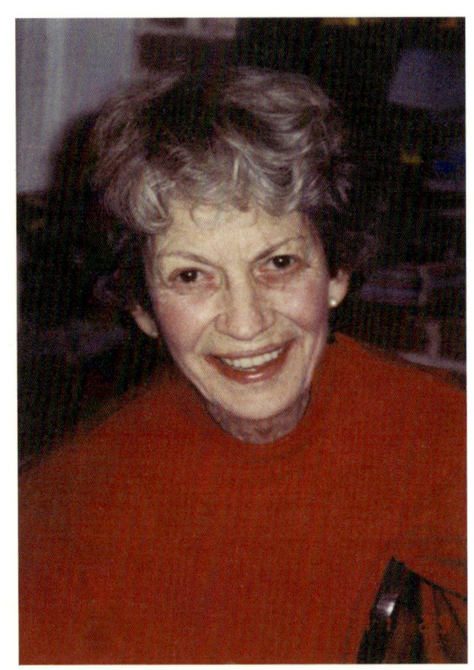

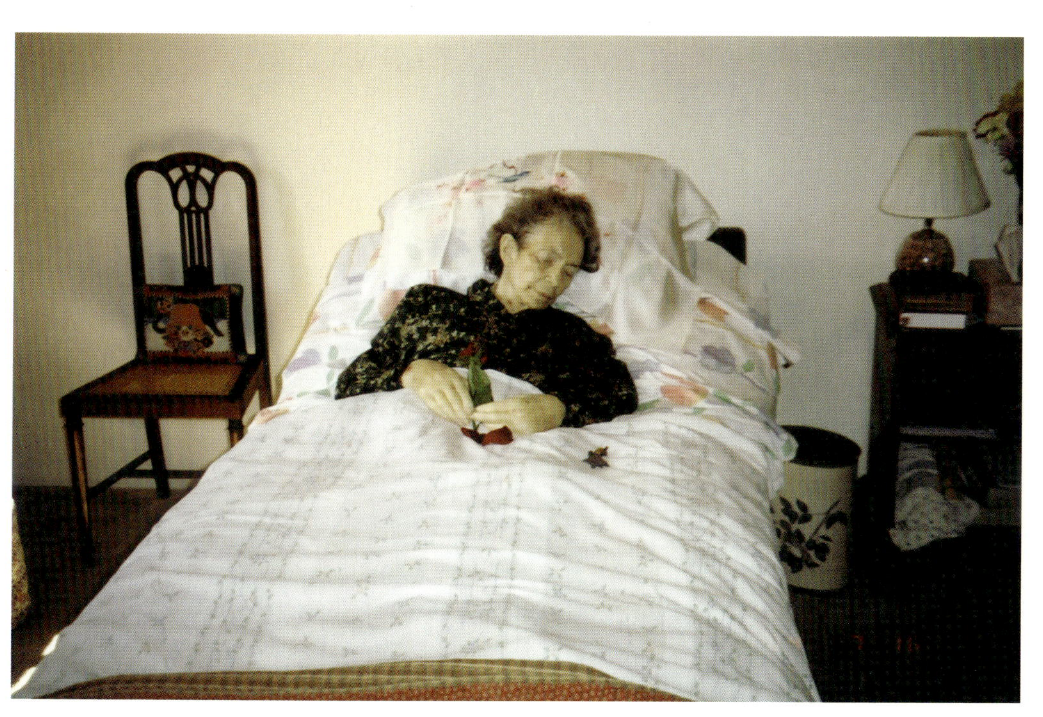

Pilar Olabarria

For Vicenta Ibarretxe Aritzmendi
Spring of 1944

The river ran high that springtime
swollen to a fast flowing body of water
She had thirteen children
a dozen cows
a hundred chickens
land to work
She loved to wash her hands in the river
Over and over

As a young bride
she came from the high mountains
where the river is born
She had thirteen children
a dozen cows
a hundred chickens
land to work

She loved the way the river caressed her hands
as no one else could
Hands that worked the soil
fed the chickens
milked the cows
caressed the children

And as the water ran through her fingers
she heard the loudness of the fast flowing waters
she heard the birds in flight
she admired the birch trees, tall and slender
reaching high
she loved the strength of the boulders
keeping the river in place

It was that spring
when the river had accumulated
every drop of water that had fallen on the land

that the river took her body away
floating on its thunderous carriage

She could not hear the birds' wild call:
Remember the children
the cows
the chickens
the land

She could see the birch trees reaching tall
unable to offer her a branch
She felt the boulders ejecting her
throwing her back into the stormy waters
Over and over

Her thunderous journey suddenly stopping
when she entered a deep dark body of water
And a beautiful, calm moment engulfed her
She felt the fish touching her face
She heard the frogs chanting a requiem
as her body was gently pulled toward the waterfall

The birds caught up with her
Remember the children, they cried
Too late, at the waterfall she had entered darkness
where silence is thunder
blackness is visible
and breathable

The night soft and silent embraced the land
the children, the cows, the chickens
waited without hope
For they knew of her love for the river

Todd Herman

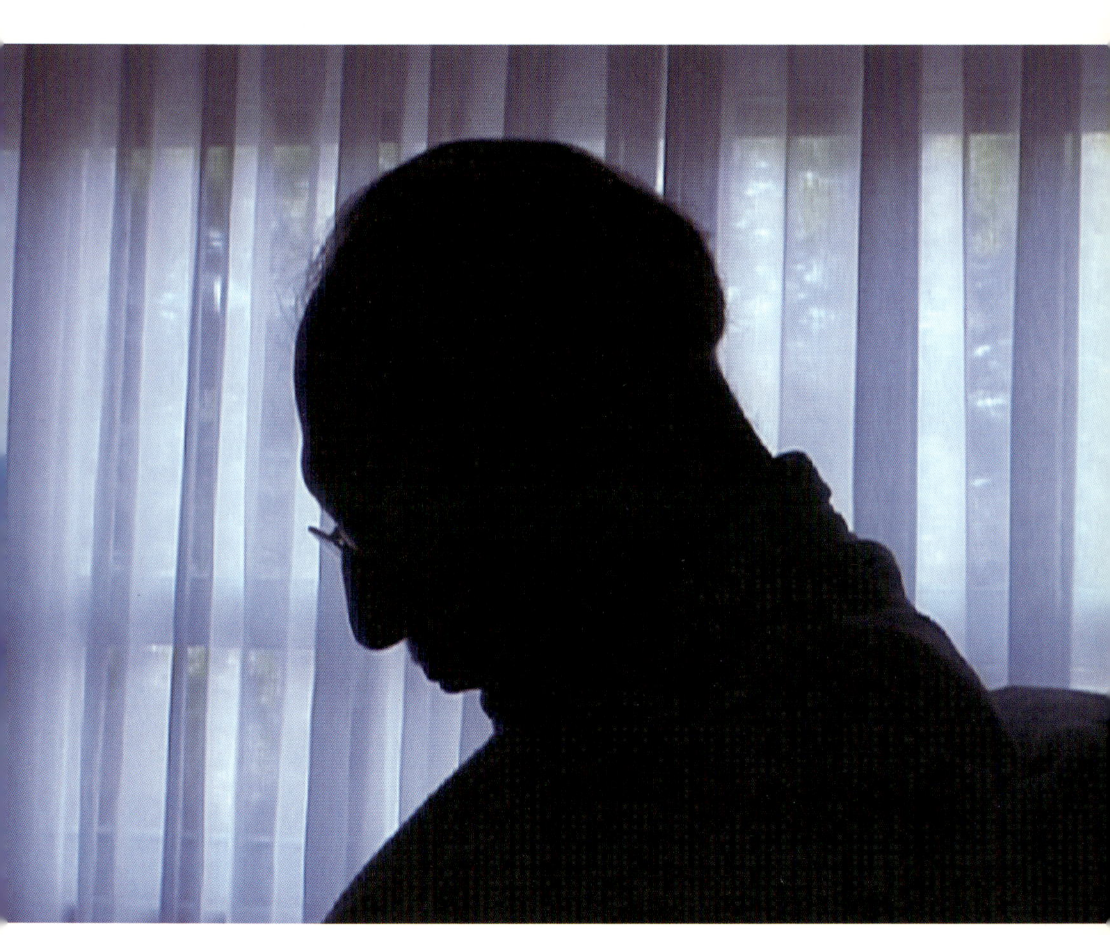

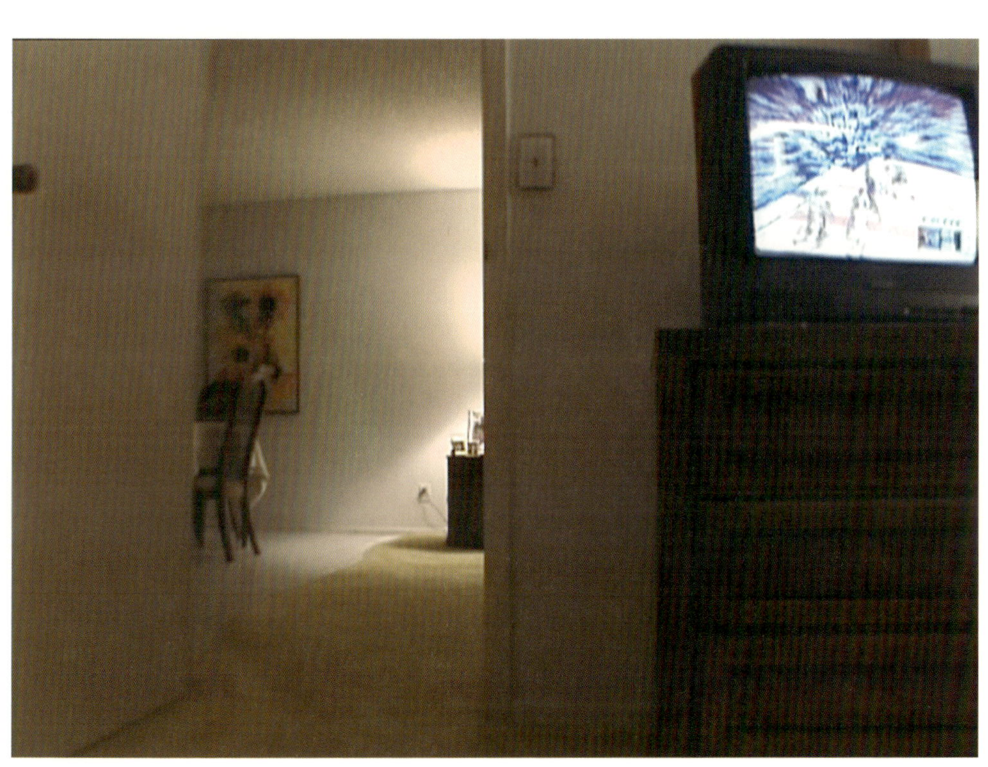

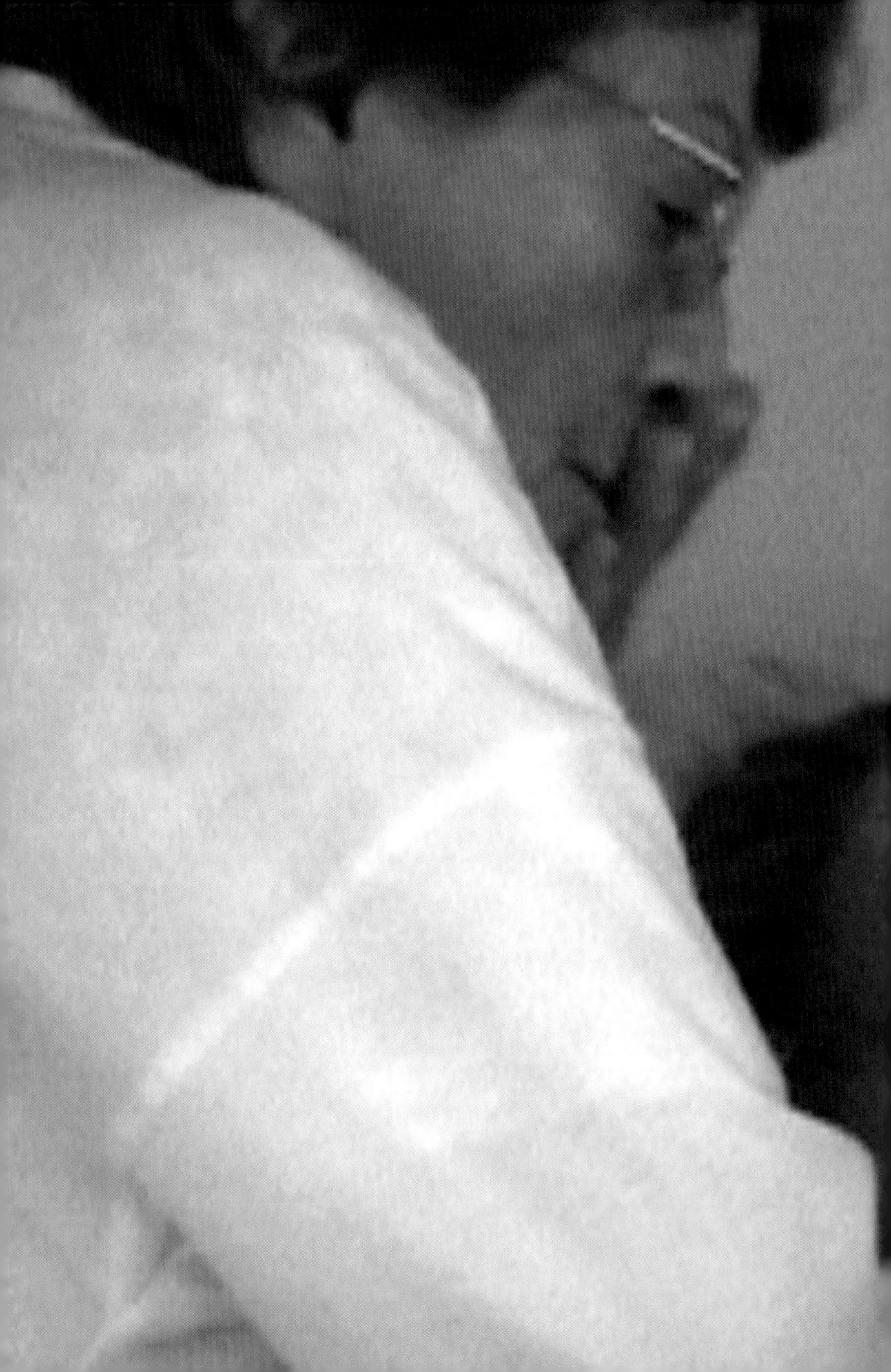

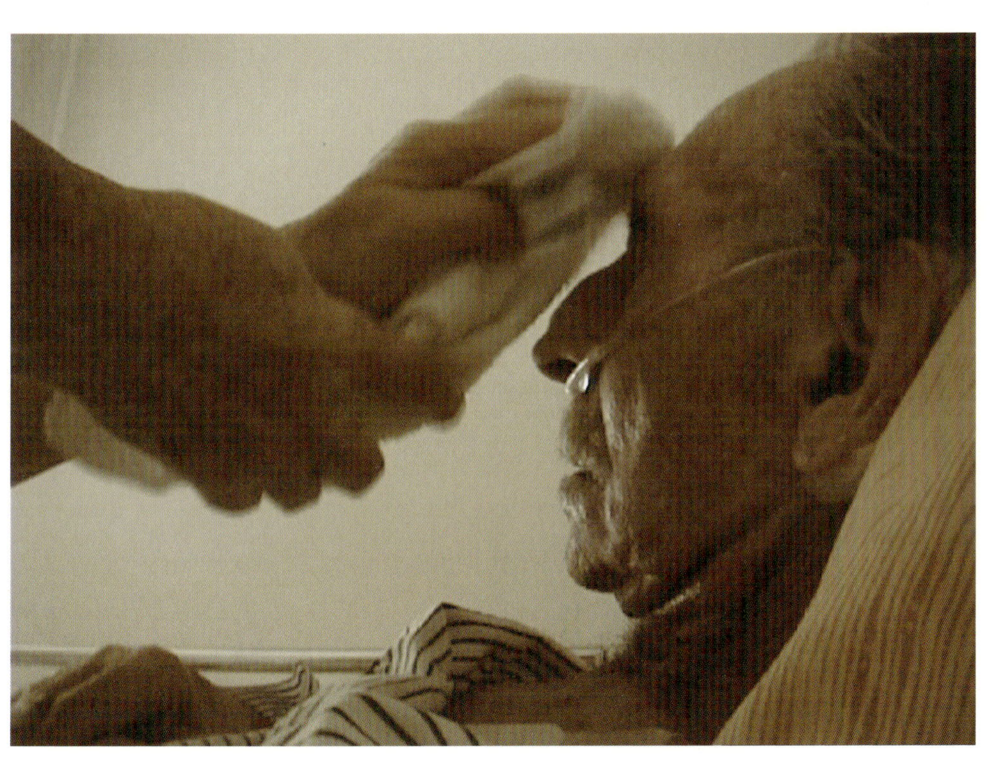

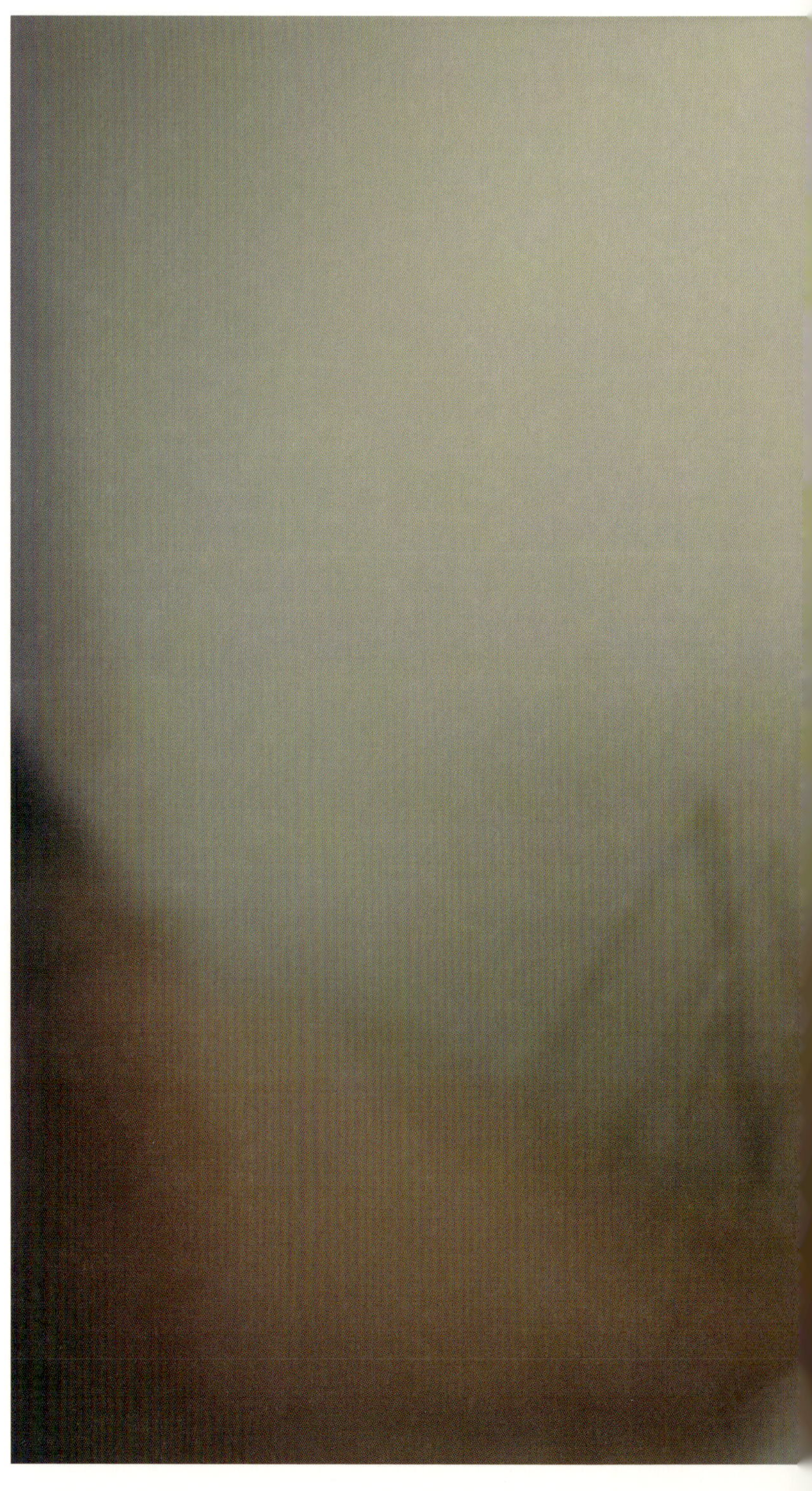

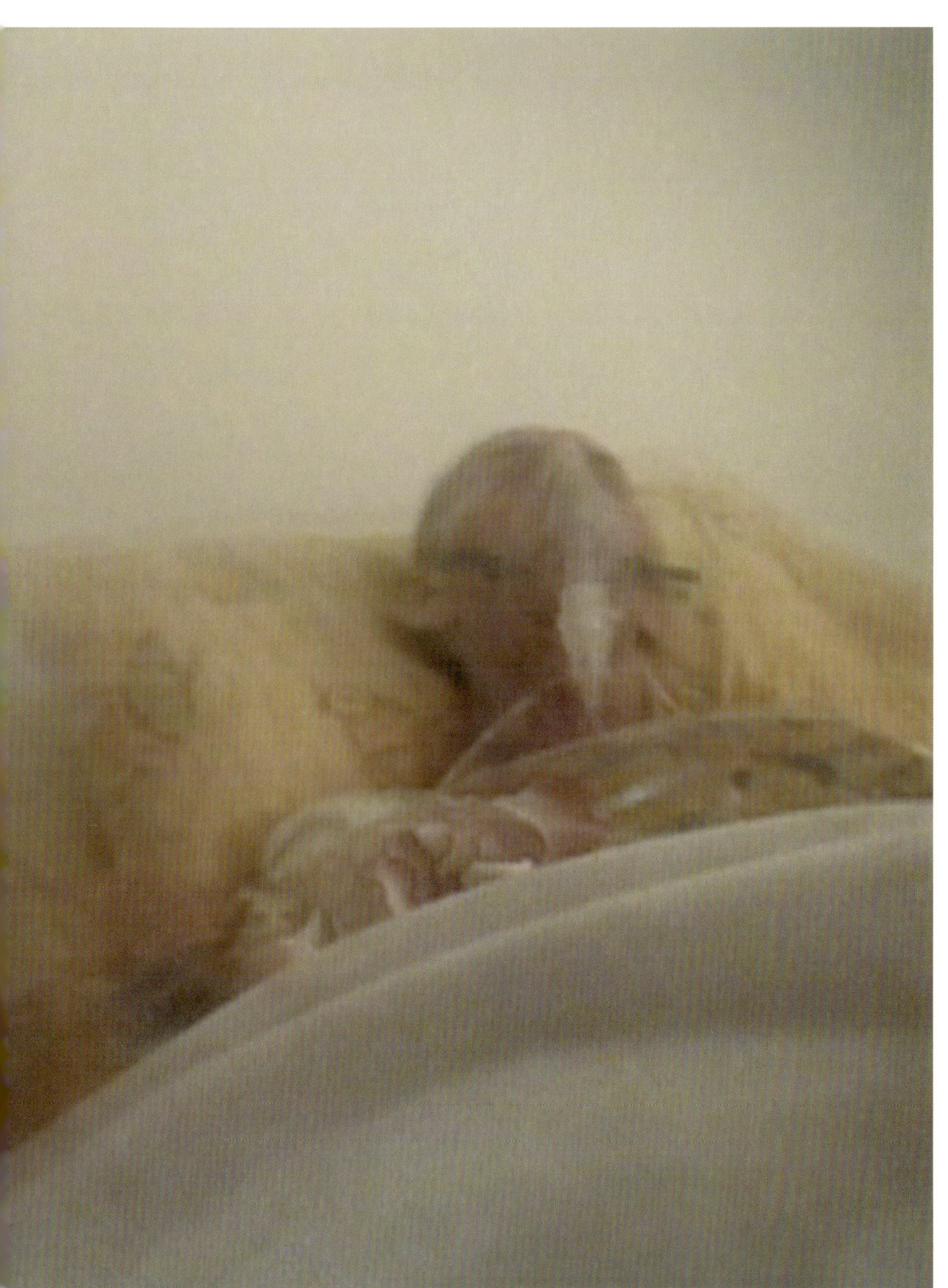

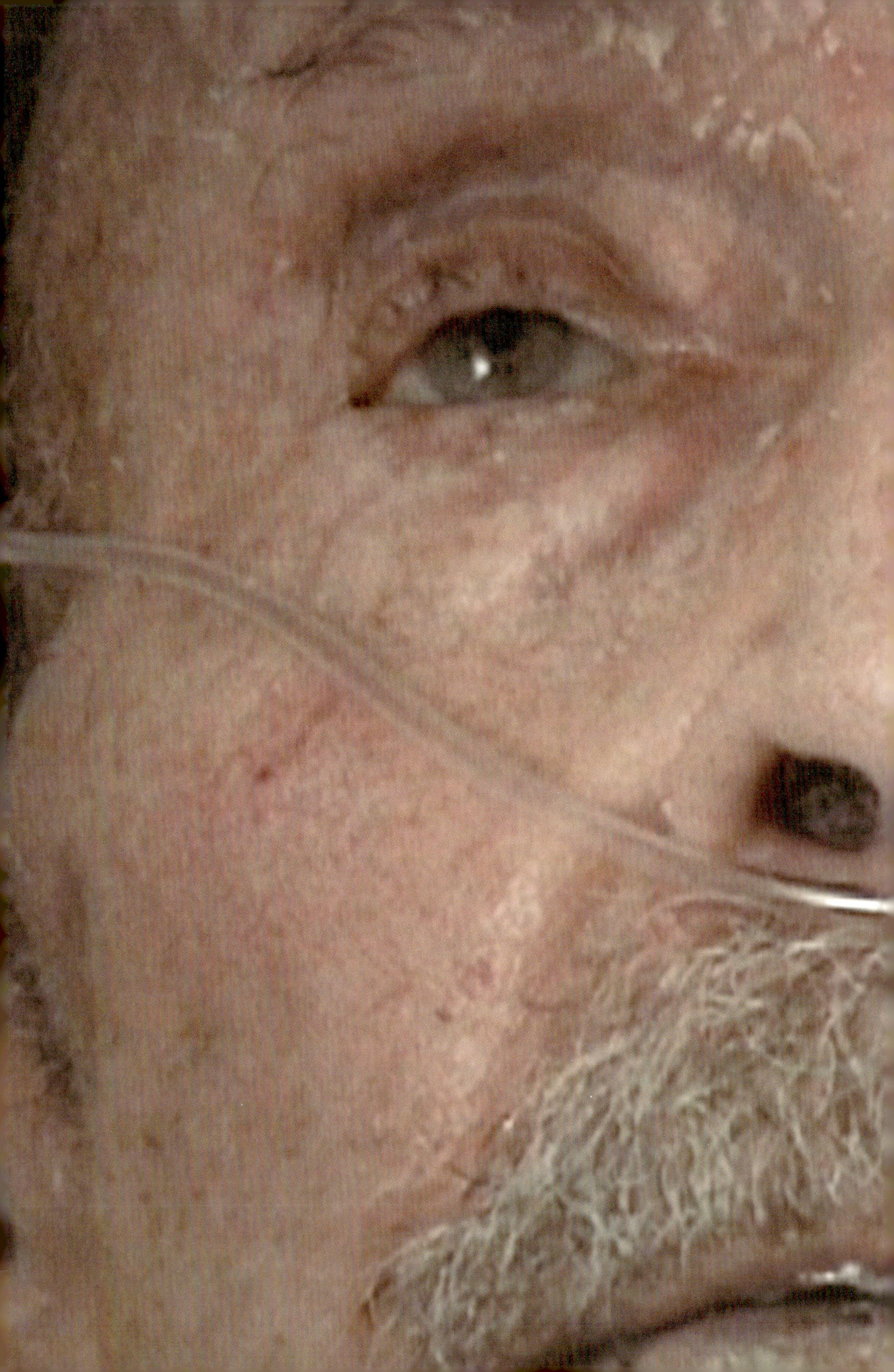

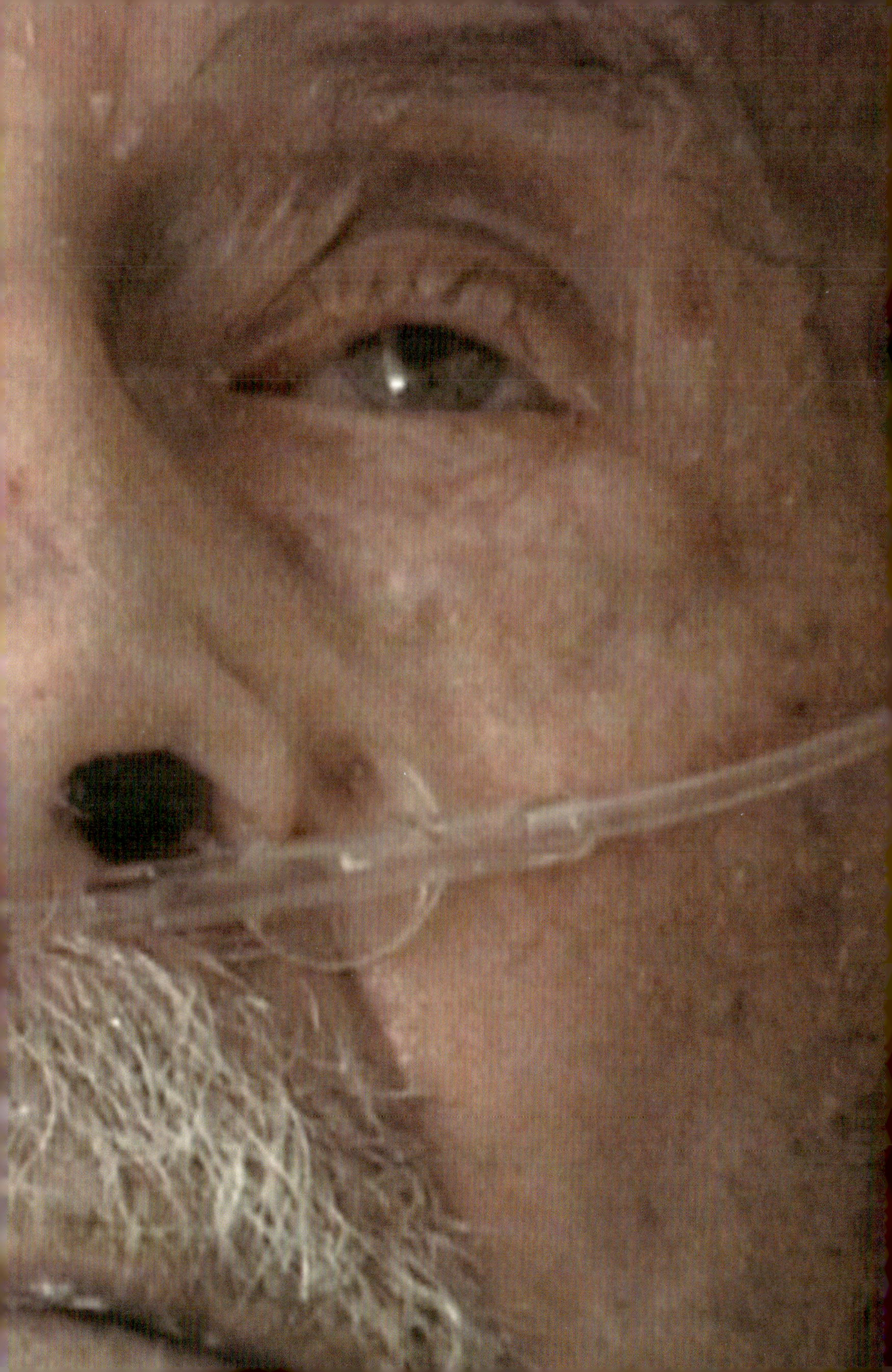

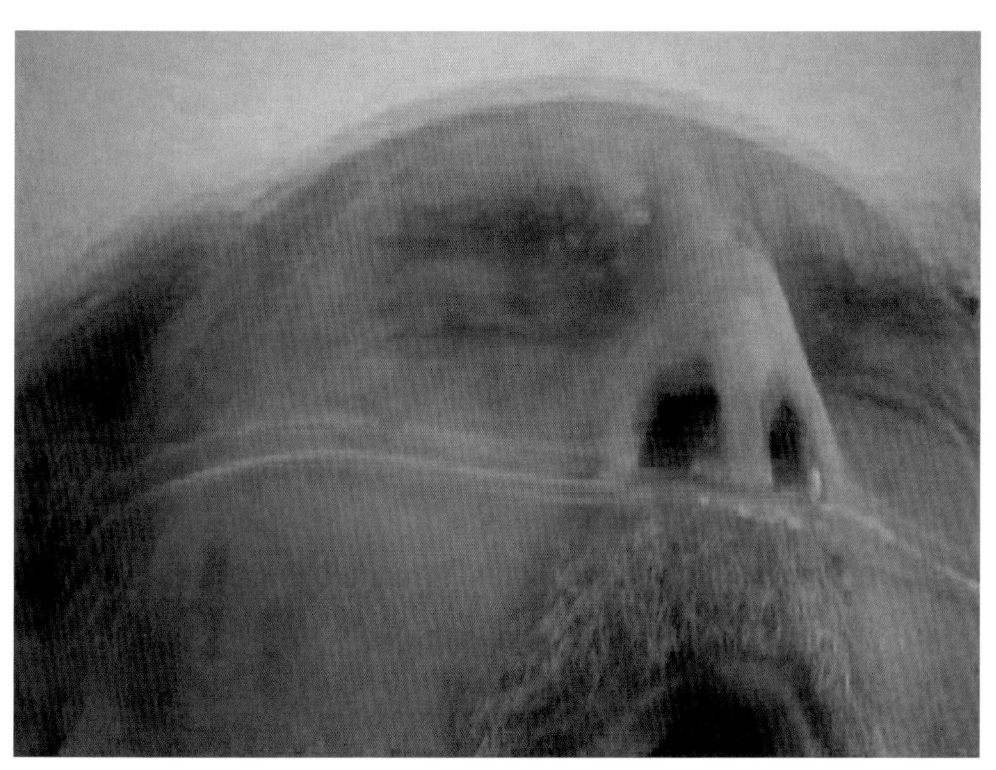

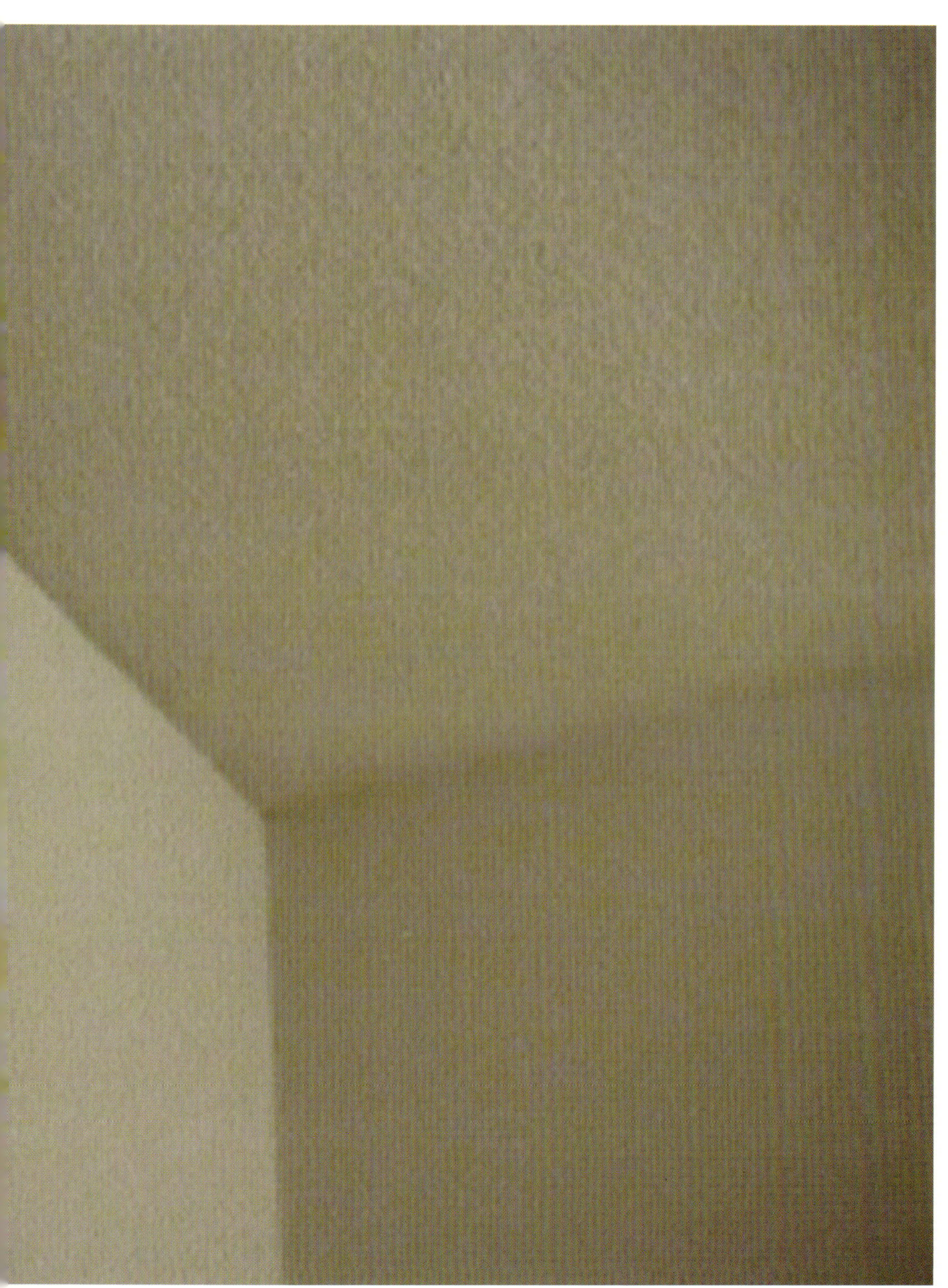

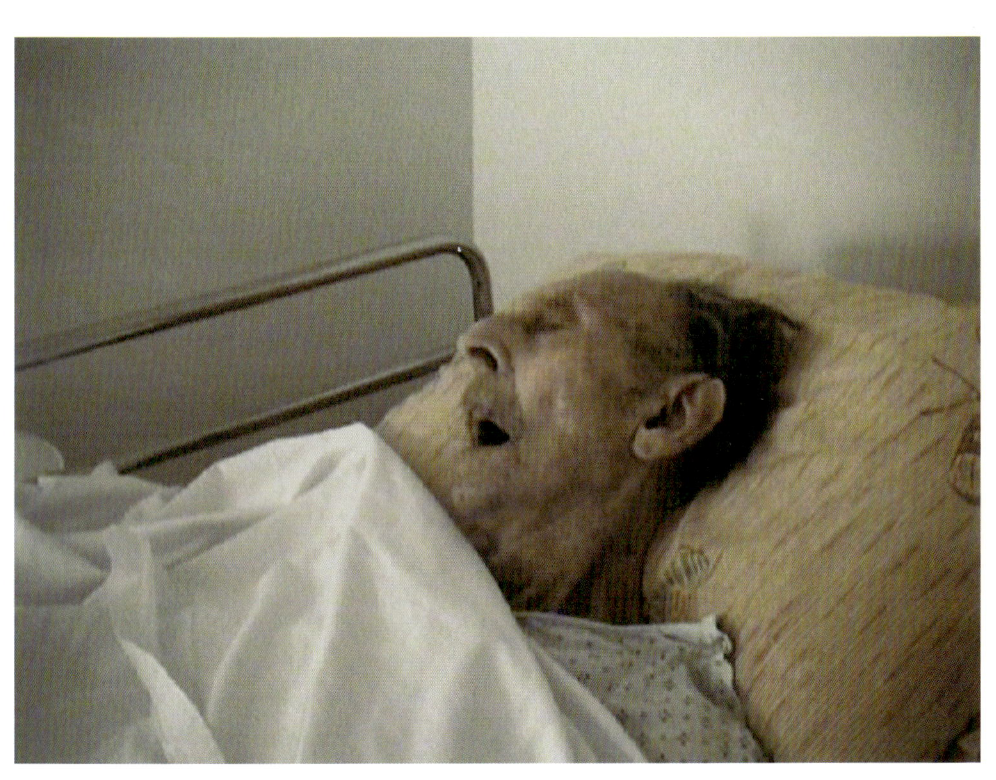

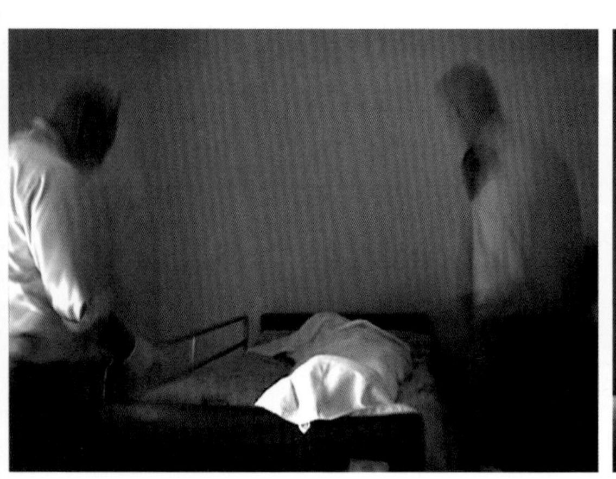 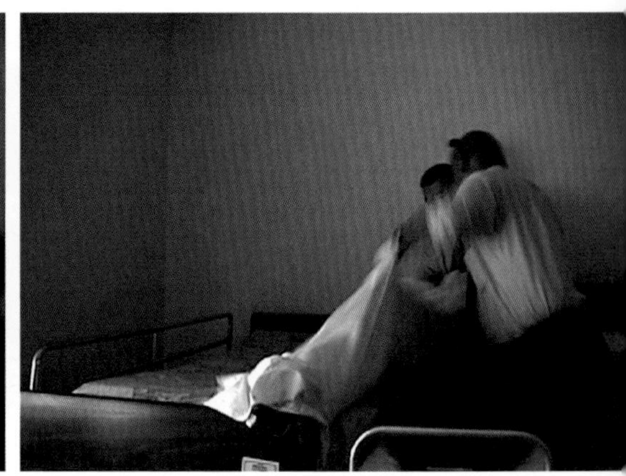

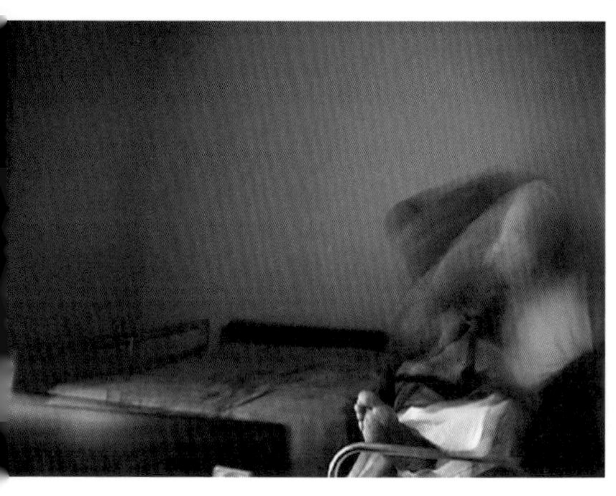 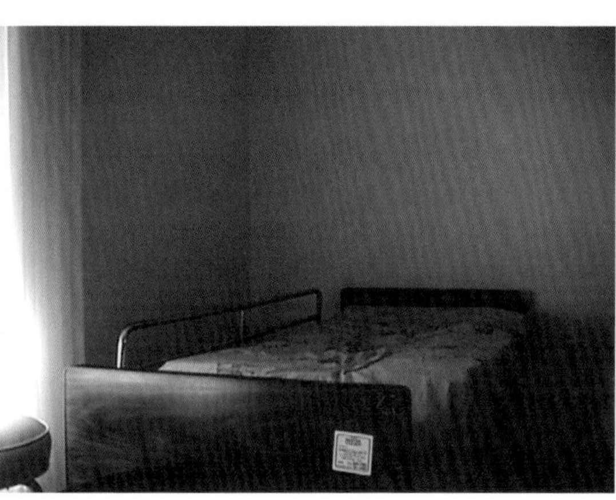

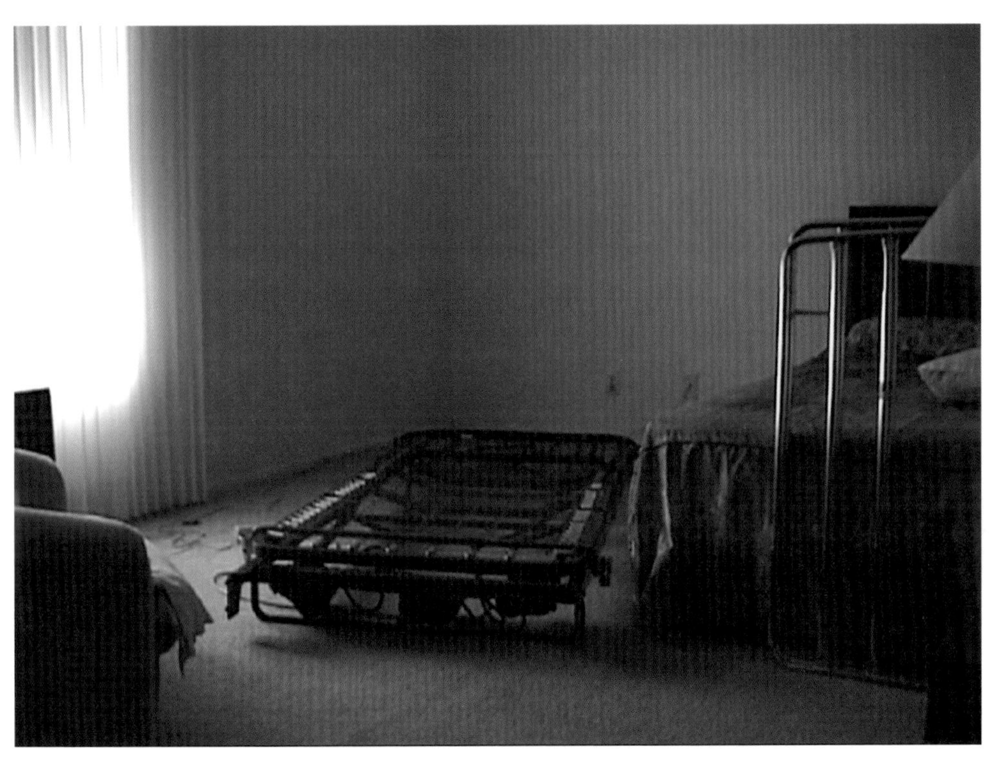

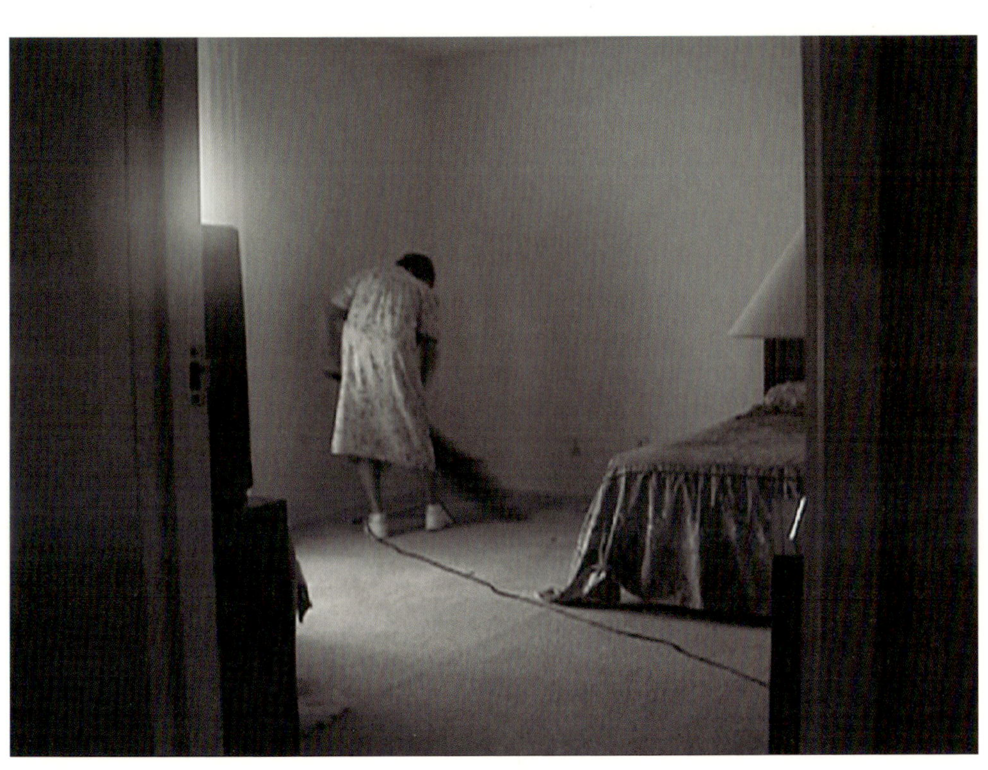

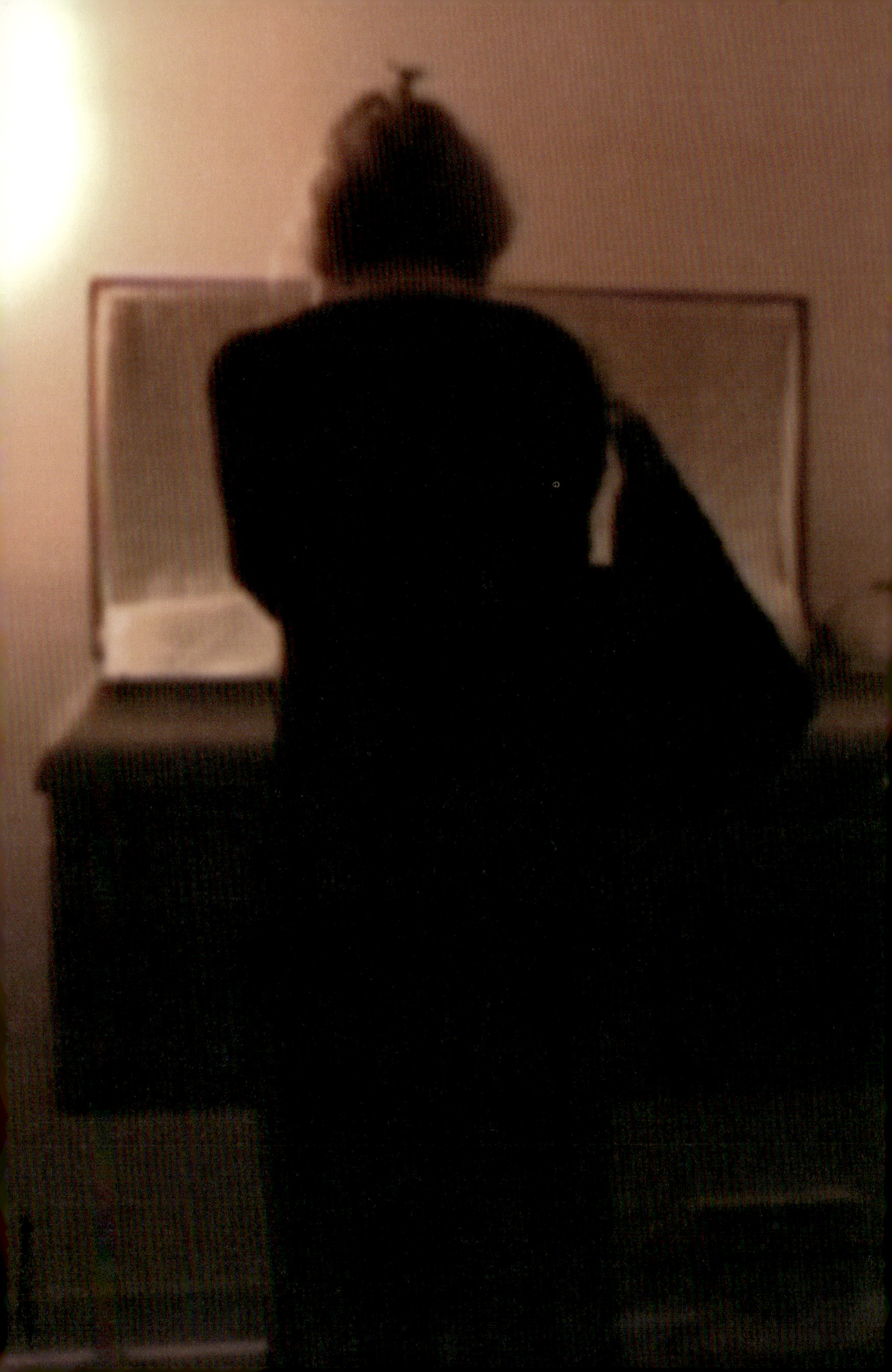

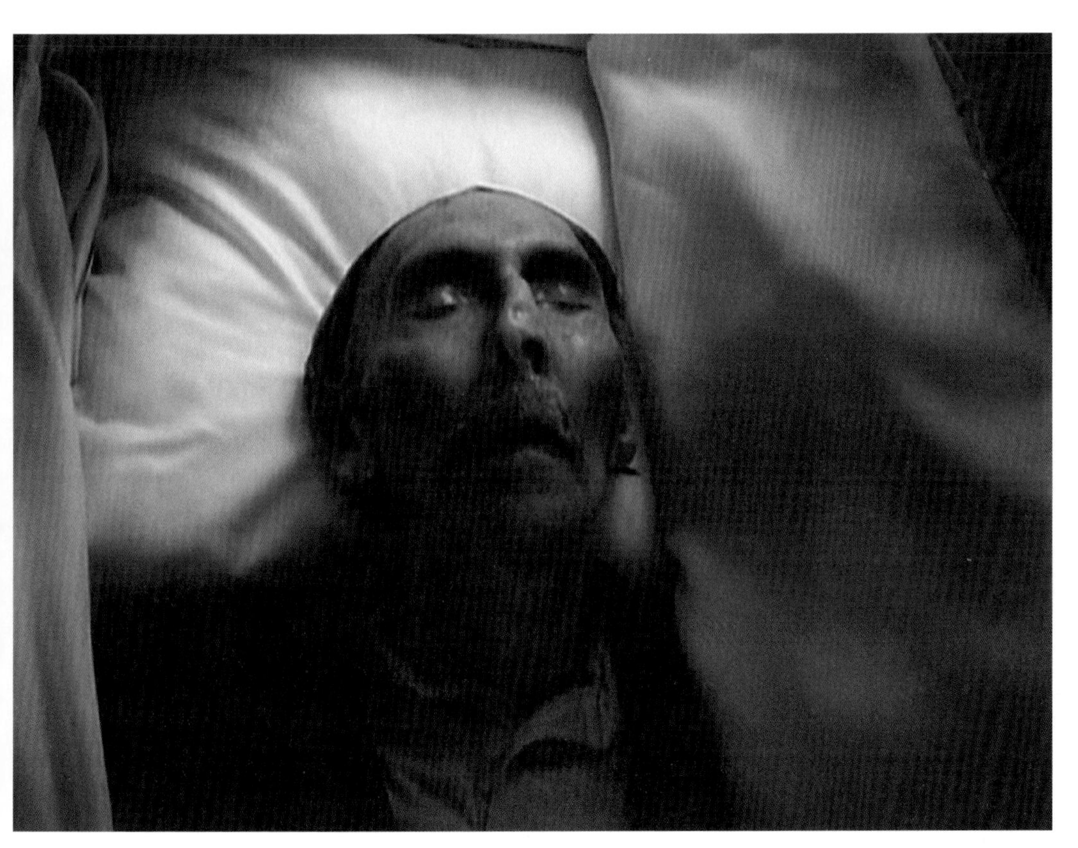

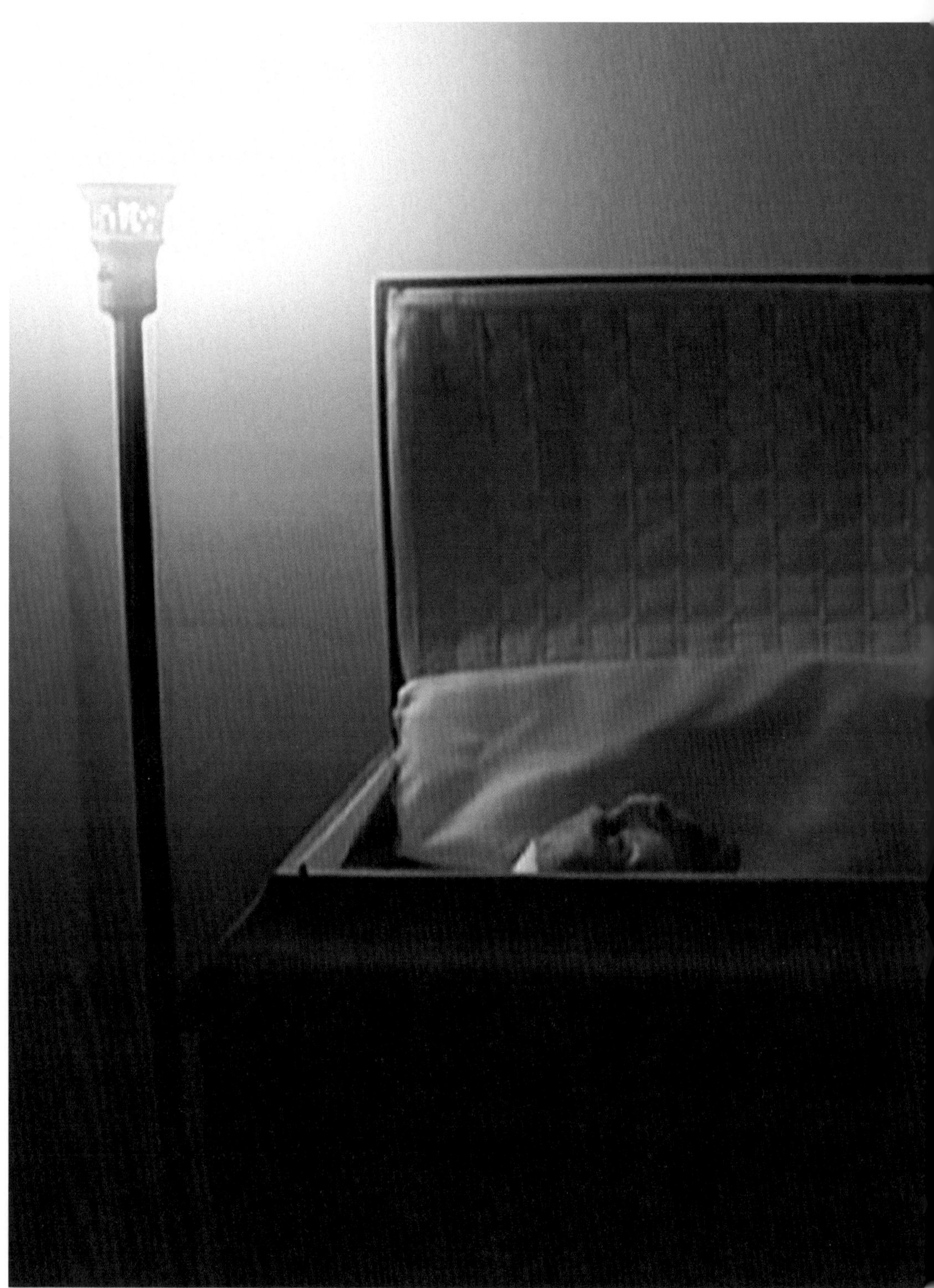

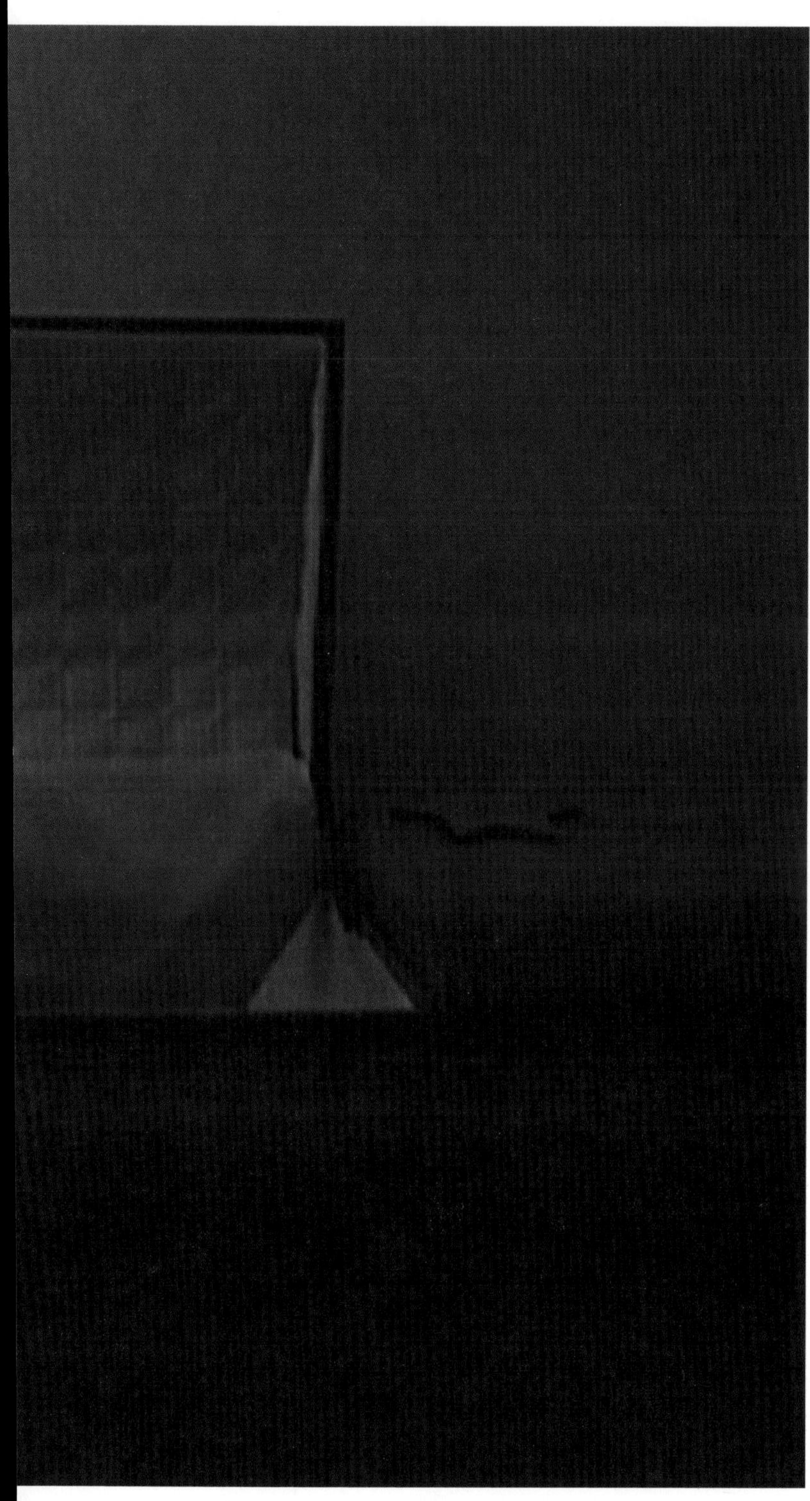

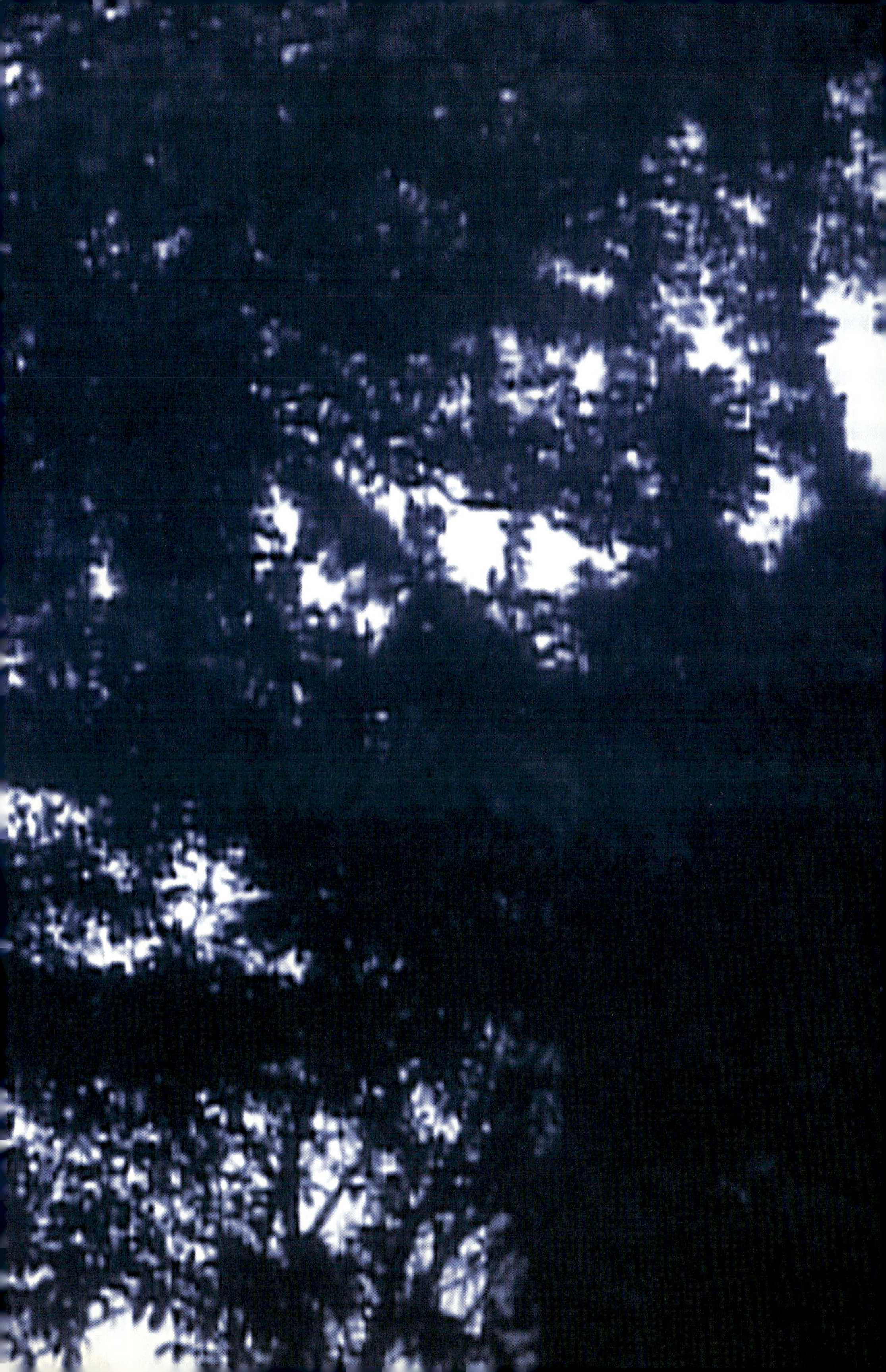

Melanie MacKinnon

The Funeral

I've never watched a dead body
unexplainable . . .
Her spirit has left her.
Her hands carefully holding
her abdomen and each other
cold, stiff, blushed, dead.
It's as if she will sit up
at any moment and acknowledge me
but no . . .
her smile uncomfortable and wrong.
I wish I could change it.
She would be upset with
the way her hair is done.
Her beauty salon perm has
not look like this since
before I was born.
I sit shocked, unmovable,
unknowable.
A stranger among me
I stare in confusion.
The wedge of sunset shrinks
as we
move forward in direction
move westward in motion
move away in flight.
I feel her
She who began me.

Irreplaceable

Everything has its place
Bird curiosities
Bright Pink Lipstick
Cigarettes in the kitchen
Noontime naps
Dessert after dinner
Canned food kingdoms
Dark hallways
"No running in the house"
Fake teeth
Caged bird chatter
Peach Pit melodies
Intercom dinner calls
Suburban mail runs
Wool socks
Whoopee bump thrills
Hidden liquor
Plastic change purse
Blackberry pie
Hair combs
Last breath.
And you left
Everything in its place

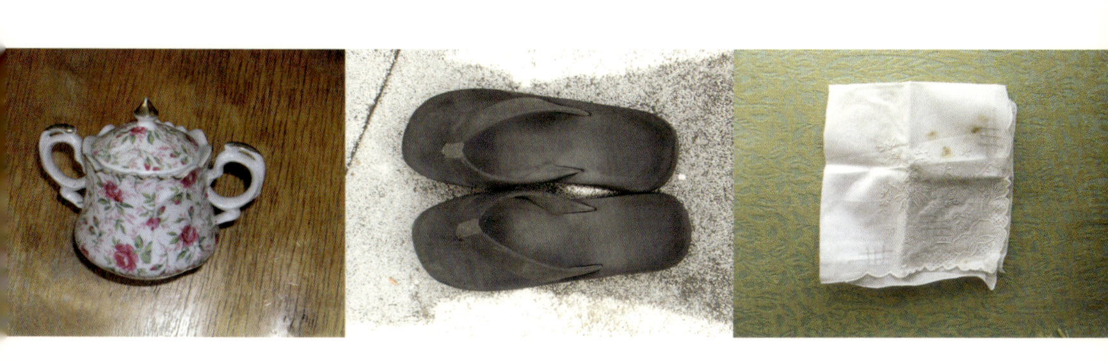

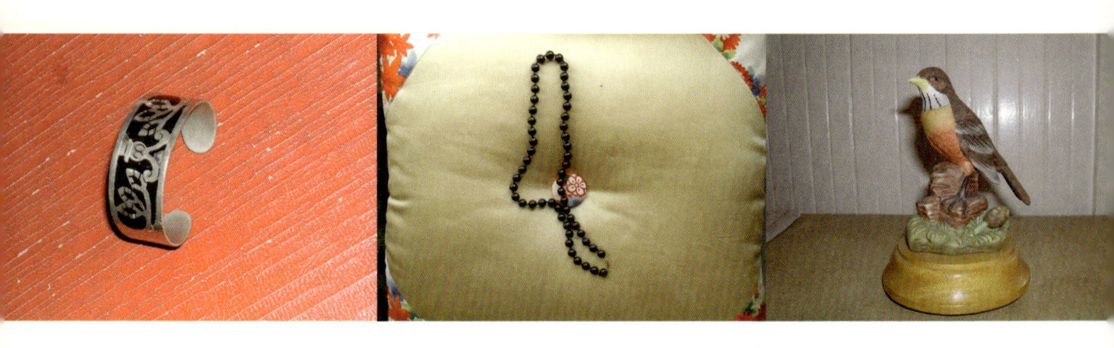

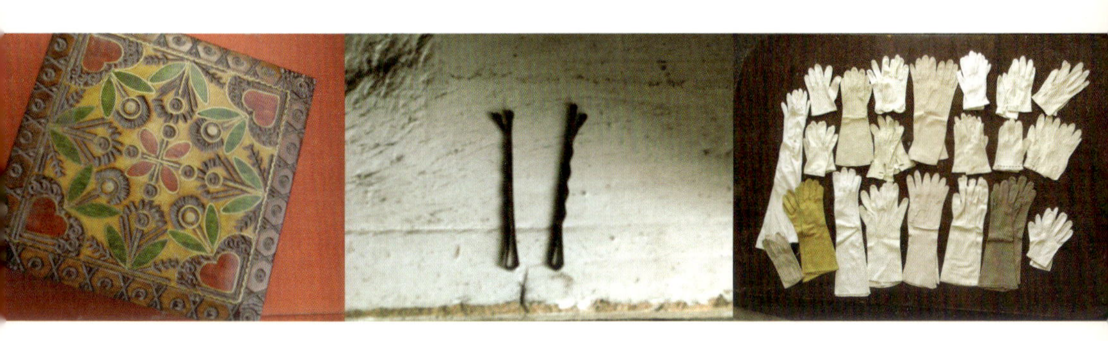

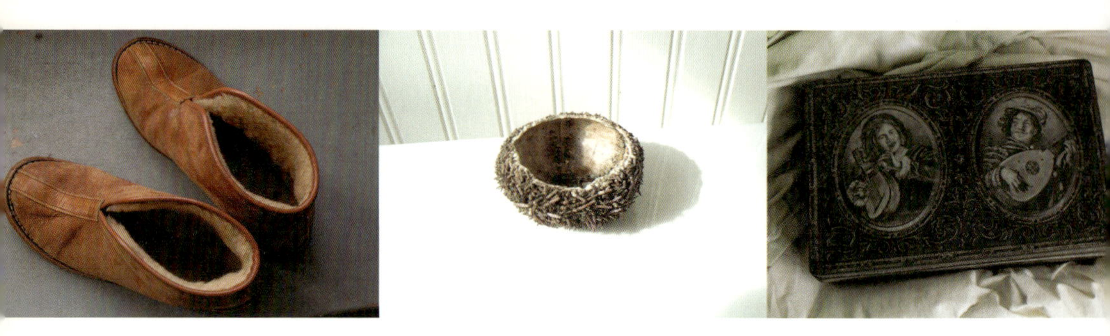

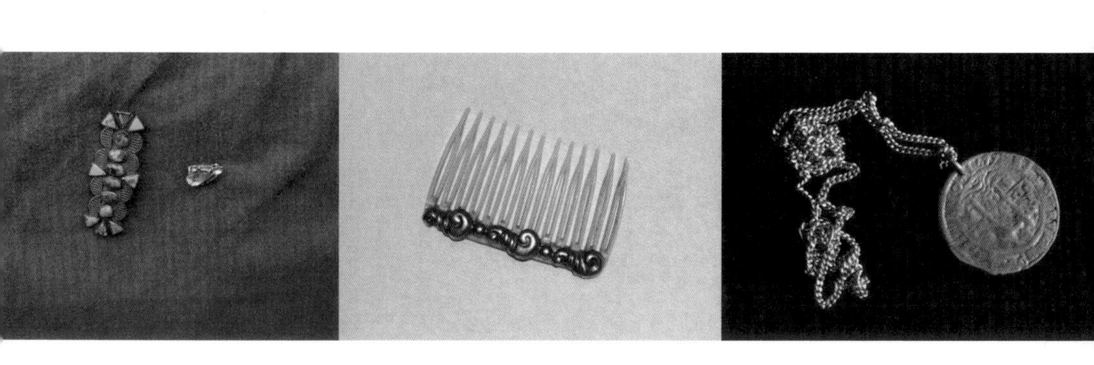

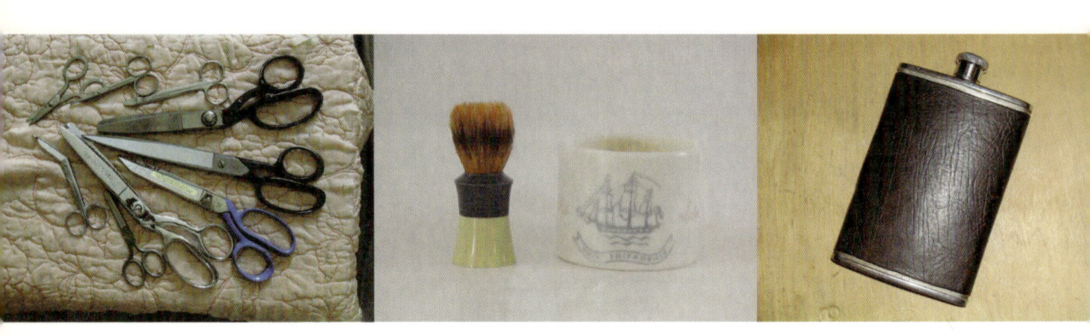

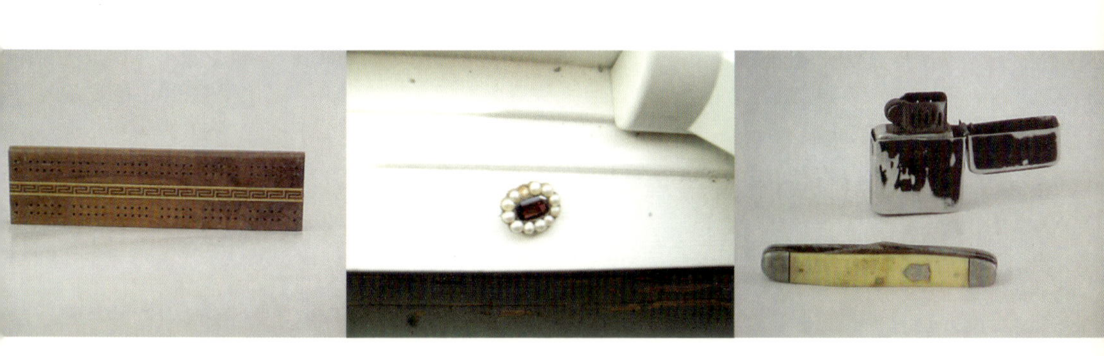

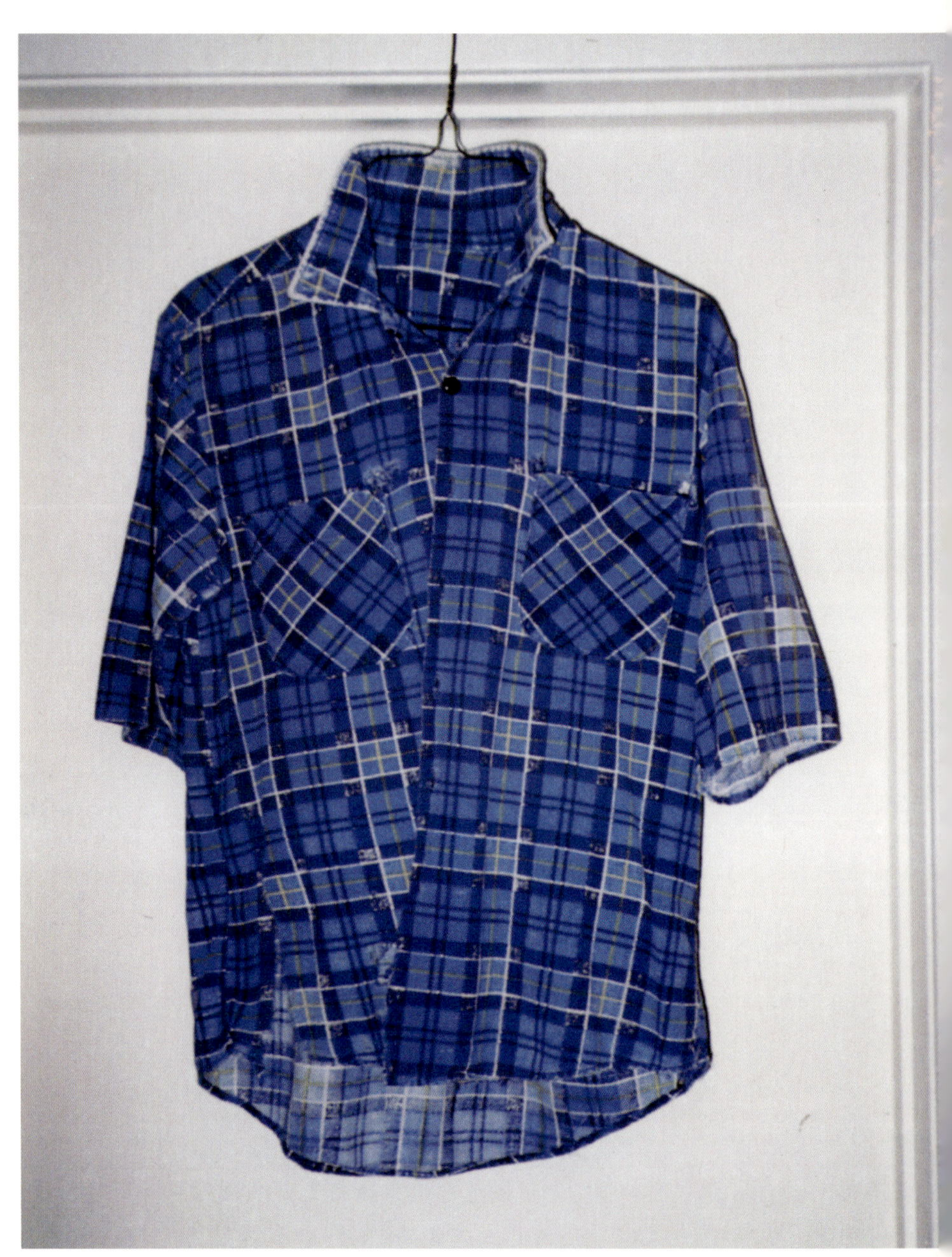

Doug Stoddard

Bill's Favorite Shirt

Bill had many clothes that he liked a lot, but this shirt was his all-time favorite. He looked really cute in it, and it's easy to remember him whenever I look at it and touch the well-worn cloth.

Miria Toveg

I wake up this morning and for the first time in my thirty-two years my heart feels relieved. I look out of my window and see a raven. Some say the raven represents magic and change. I look down and see my two-month-old daughter sleeping, I know there is a connection but I am not quite sure yet what it is. Later today my sister calls to tell me of your passing. I feel relieved. I shed no tears. I feel that the world is a safer and better place without you here. I feel that a balance is somehow being restored. I feel it in my body and in my heart. I can breathe.

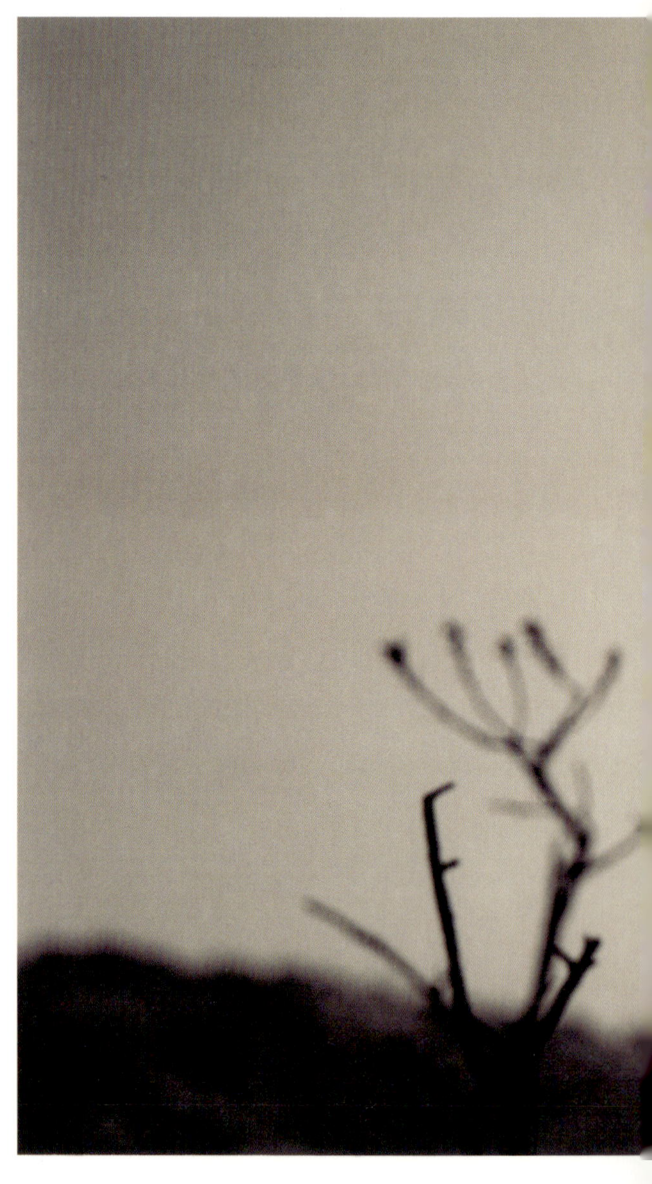

Stefanie J. Atkinson

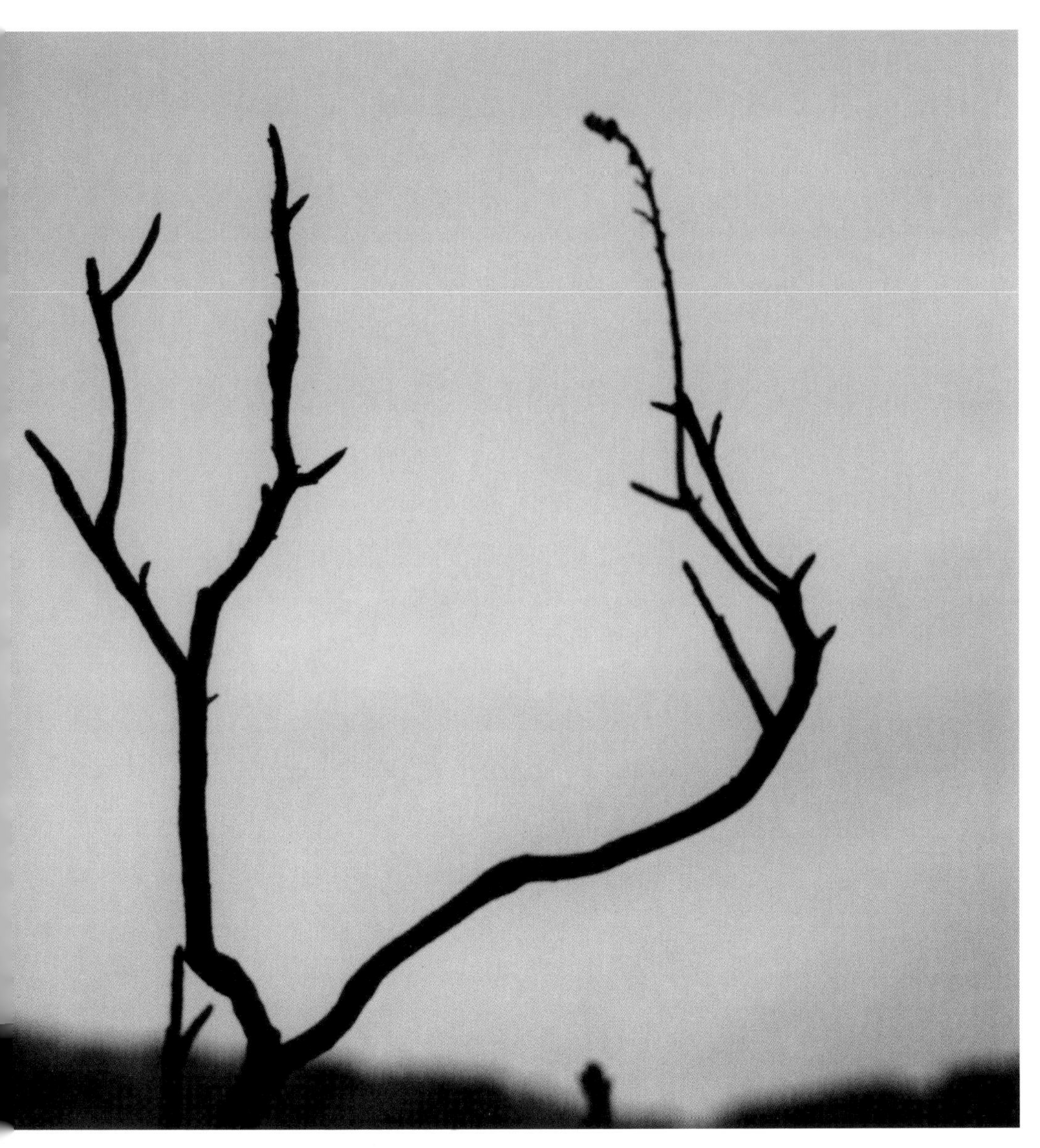

Patricia Coslor

DEAR DON —

SO YOU'RE DEAD. GREG TOLD ME TODAY. ONE OF THE FIRST IMAGES THAT CAME TO MY MIND WAS WHEN LACEY DIED. NOW YOU, TOO HAVE ARRIVED TO THAT "UNDISCOVERED COUNTRY FROM WHOSE BOURNE NO TRAVELER RETURNS"

MY GRIEF IS TOTAL, OVERWHELMING AND CONSUMING. SO IS MY GUILT. AND MY HATRED FOR GIACOMO. AH, WHAT A MESS I'VE MADE. I ALWAYS THOUGHT I'D HAVE A CHANCE TO SEE YOU AND EXPLAIN…

THE LAST TIME I SAW YOU. I ASKED YOU TO FORGIVE ME. IN YOUR NOW OMNIPRESENT KNOWLEDGE I HOPE YOU DO. FORGIVE ME, DON.

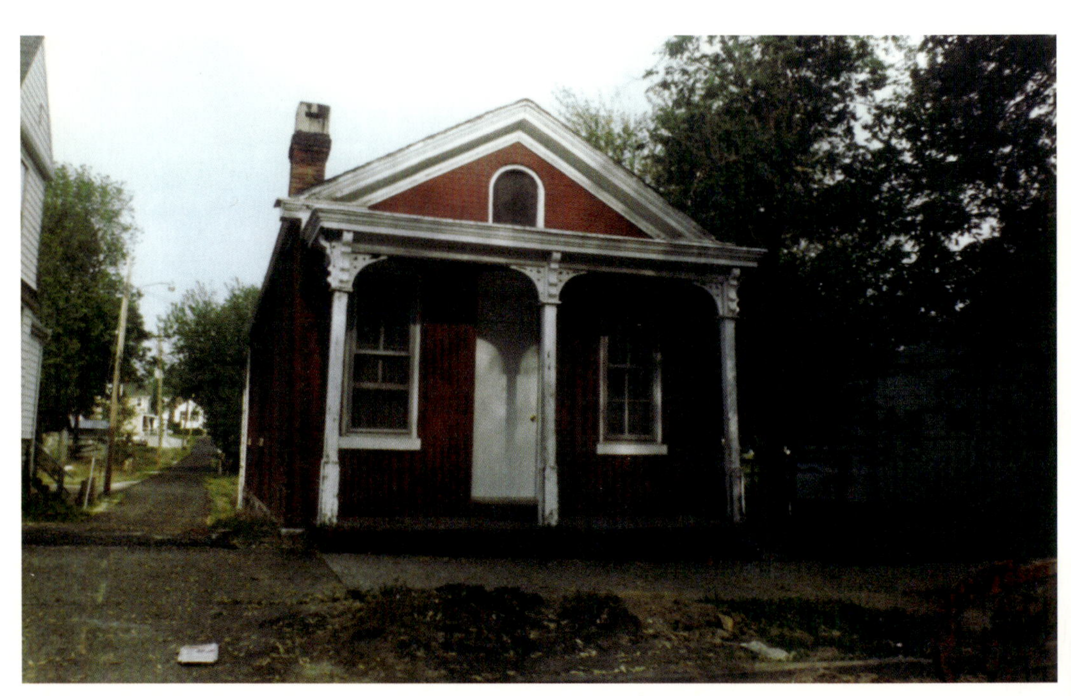

Audrey Frank

Telling Stories

Just another night of telling ghost stories with my brother before bedtime. My turn
. . . except that instead of describing the next adventure of "Bloody Bones," I blurted
out, "Dad is dead." How I knew this at that particular moment neither I nor my
brother questioned. Without missing a beat, my brother started listing out the dif-
ferent items of my dad's possessions that he wanted: his gun, his coin collection,
and his shaving kit. He offered to share the coin collection with me. All I could
think about was that I was free.

We heard the living room door open and close, low murmurs, and my mother begin
to cry. My uncle appeared in our bedroom doorway looking awkward and sorry-
faced. I quickly filled the silence with, "We know. He's dead." My uncle glanced
my way, started to speak, then decided not to. A moment later he was gone. My
brother and I went back to telling stories . . . about how much better things were
going to be now.

Someone I love has died. My grief, shot through with the rage of abandonment, is buried with the beloved, only to resurface again and again in the faces of all the men I have loved, all the times I have been disappointed, and all the ways in which I have been abandoned or abandoned myself in the name of love. To love is to fear losing love. To have been loved is to know that it is worth the risk.

Lori Sampson

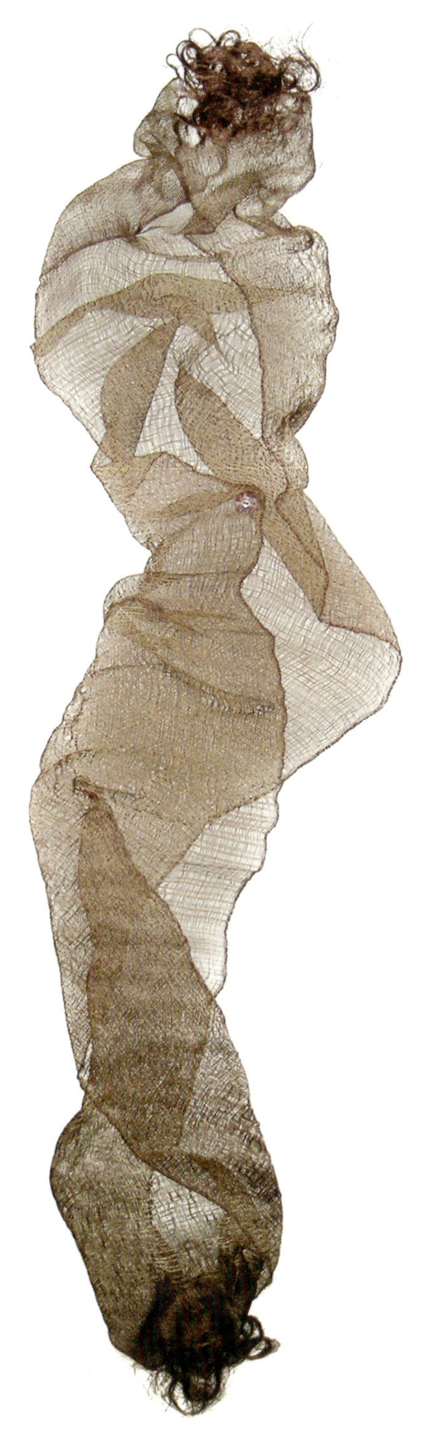

Noemi Sohn

Time Keeper

no named days and months
or faces of clocks

sun, moon, stars
rhythm of waves

blooming buds
morning dew

late sunsets
fiery red days

bites of apples
abundant orchards

deep slumber
long frosted nights

time keeper
the vast heavens.

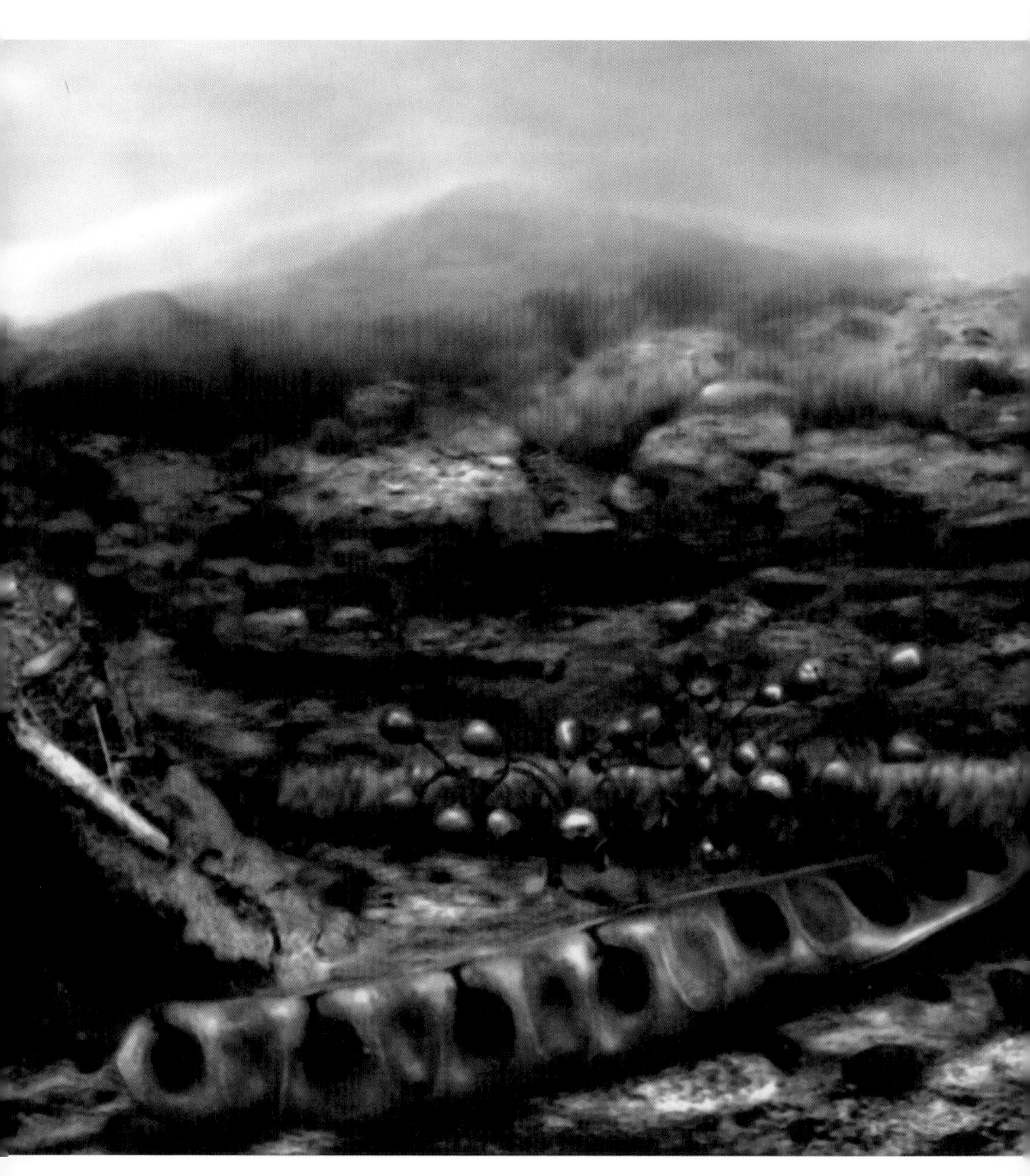

Katherine Wiemelt

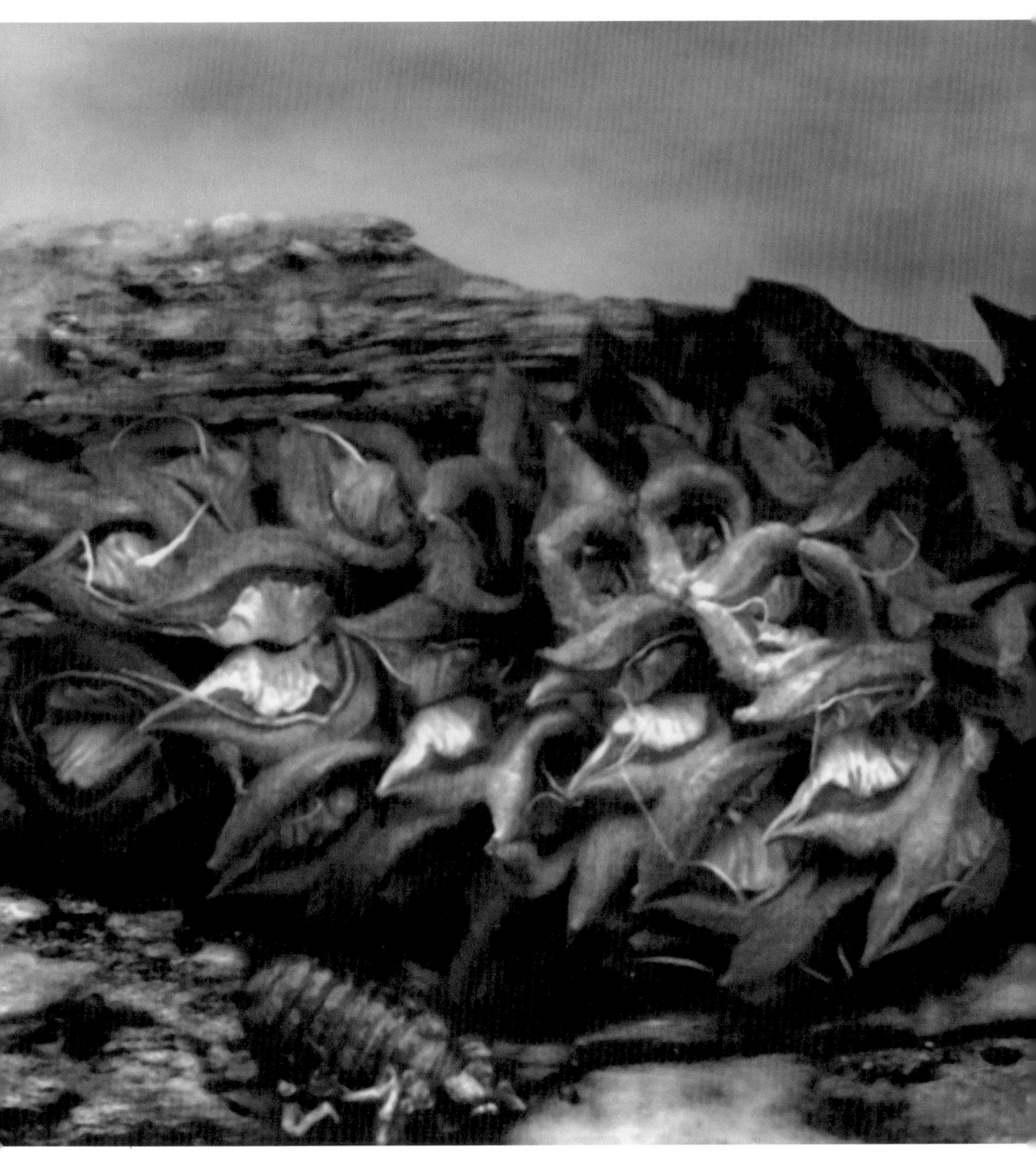

Banira Giri

Widowed Night:
An Expression

Incalculable sighs of sorrow
sprout on night's branches
A thousand groans of
emptiness
cling to each plane of the dark

A single flower from the magnolia tree
has wilted silently
on the bed

This night
a widowed night
a night harrowed by herself
a night dimming within herself
a night weeping to herself
a night lost unto herself
a night sold by herself
a night which has left in her wake
all alone in this grotesque world a widow
abandoning her
disarraying her heart

Incalculable sighs of sorrow
sprout on night's branches
A thousand groans of
emptiness
cling to each plane of the dark

A single flower from the magnolia tree
has wilted silently
on the bed

Defenseless night
A widowed night
Washed in moonlight
yesterday's night
was heavenly, glowing in gold
The breaths of Shah Jahan and Queen Mumantz

swirled about, filling the room
and heating up in each caress

All inspirations, all truths
every beauty decked like a bride
encircled by powerful, muscular arms
Tonight's widowed night
has buried Cleopatra's youth
beneath soil and granite

A night like a graveyard this night—
an expression unto herself
an inhalation unto herself
a lunacy unto herself
a malady unto herself
a nakedness unto herself
an injury unto herself
a funeral procession trailing her own corpse

It could be that the morning will place
dawn's vermilion on her hair's parting
The light of the morning might place
a veil over her nakedness
The rays of the sun may arrive
to circle her unadorned wrists

—becoming bangles of new couplings

But at sunrise
exchanging herself
for tuberculosis germs
in each direction of the morning horizon
this widowed night
has already retched pools of blood
has already retched pools of blood

Wolf Gomez

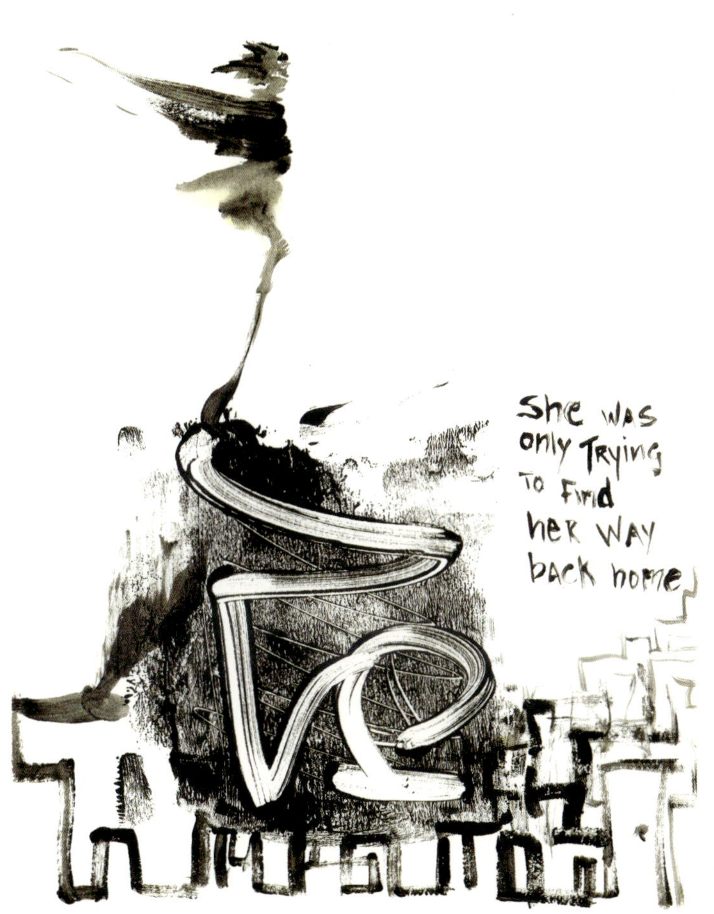

she was
only Trying
To Find
her WAY
back home

Winifred L. Montgomery

Finity

Crows are playing in the wind;
Thick black beetle-shiny wing-fingers
Cupping gusts gritty from the bleak, deserted beach.

Joyful, beaks agape, they
Hover motionless in vicious updrafts, or hop daintily in silly sideways leapfrogs
Over one another's backs.

With glittering black knowing eyes, they silently watch me from
One side of their heads and then another,
Waiting.

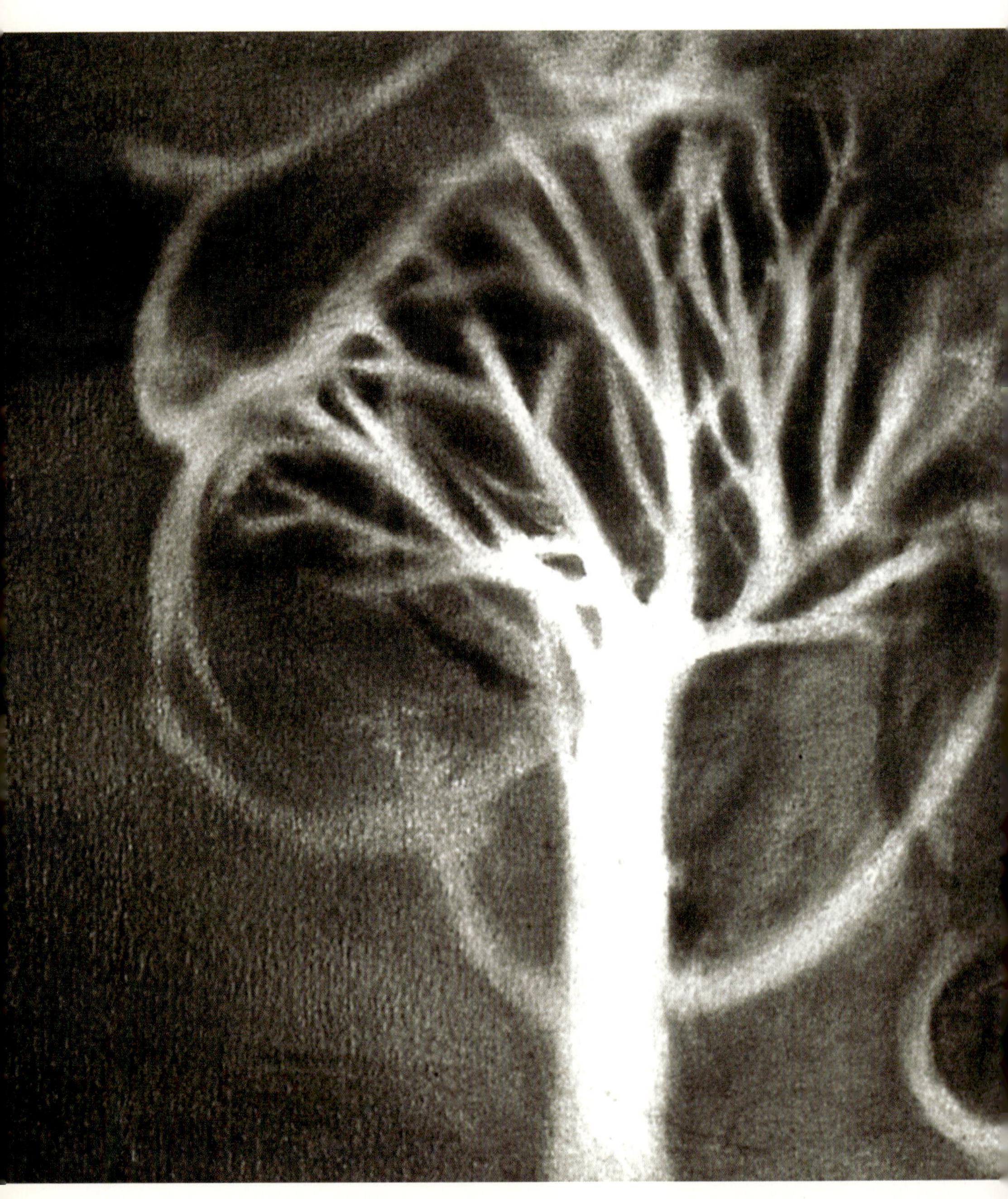

Enrique Andrade

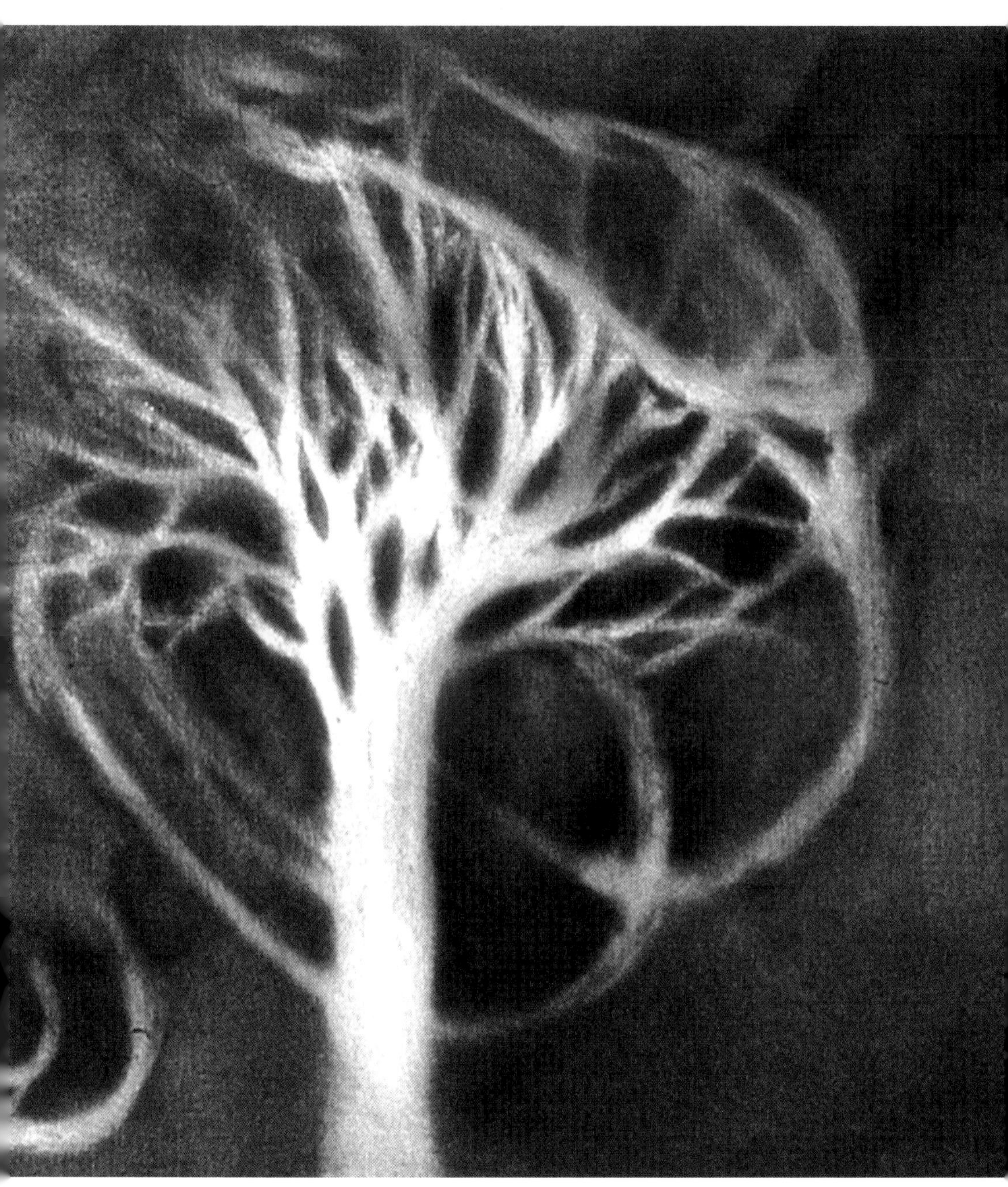

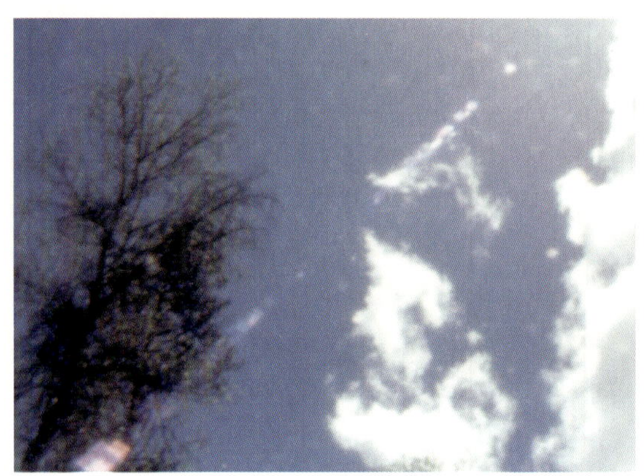

E. Francis Kohler

My Grandmother

It was around late autumn in 1982. My grandmother had been diagnosed with mouth and throat cancer. My sister, our father, and I went to visit her in the hospital where she was undergoing experimental treatment. When we arrived outside her room, we saw a bold graphic on her door. It was a black and yellow sign with three triangles. Y'know, the kind you'd see on a building advertising its bomb shelter status. There was accompanying text with a statement that pregnant women should not enter the room, and visitors should stand back at least ten feet from the patient in addition to limiting their visit to ten minutes or less. We pushed the door open and saw Grandma propped up in bed with a cluster of glass vials hanging from under her jaw. Filled with radiated iodine, these vials had needles in one end that allowed them to be stuck into her skin. We tried to act unalarmed, but whenever she spoke the vials would clack together, making it impossible to ignore. After a bit of uncomfortable chitchat we left. In the elevator going down, I glanced over at my dad. He was biting his lower lip and tears were welling up in his eyes. Almost breathless he said, "It really kills me to see her like that." My dad is one of those guys (from that generation) who on only the rarest of occasions demonstrate any capacity for emotional demeanor of this type. Seeing him like that made it difficult for me not to begin bawling uncontrollably.

My dad came over to visit in late December of that same year. I was living with my sister in downtown Sacramento. He gave us an update on how our Grandma was doing. One of the surgeons had suggested removing my grandmother's jaw. He admitted that this procedure was no guarantee that the spread of cancer would cease and, he managed to add, she may not even survive the surgery. All of us, including our grandmother, decided immediately that this was not an option. What our grandmother did want though was to die at home, in a familiar setting with people she knew around her. My dad enrolled her in a hospice nurse program, which provided skilled nursing care when needed. But what was essential was that someone would live with her and perform all the day-to-day tasks such as grocery shopping, laundry, cooking, and so on. Since I was the only immediate family member currently unemployed, I was the "logical" choice to fill the role. This made me a little anxious. Granted I was 20 (technically an adult), but I was a very young 20-year-old. Naive, self-involved, insecure. I think my dad sensed my apprehension. He stressed that if I felt the responsibility was too much for me to handle, at any point, some other plan would be made. I timidly agreed to the proposition. My sister was certainly happy to see me relocated. I had been living in her smallish one-bedroom apartment for six months now. We got along just swell, but I think I was cramping her style somewhat when she'd have to explain to her dates who that lump was on the inflatable pad on the living room floor.

Within a week I moved in with my grandmother. Despite my best attempts to imagine a gloomy and suffocating situation, it was far from that. We had our own bedrooms and she was terrifically self-sufficient. She was also very sweet and accommodating on every level. Within a month though, she began to quickly deteriorate. Up to this point she would turn off the TV in the evening and make her way back to her room with little or no assistance. Increasingly she was content to sleep in the living room chair. During this time family and friends were exceptionally attentive and came over often. Out of respect for my grandmother, only women would assist her with toileting. I would follow them though and observe in I case I was needed, and to prepare myself for the day when I may need to help her in this manner. It was not a difficult job to lift my grandmother. She was always petite (slim and under five feet tall), but the results of cancer had reduced her to a mere 60 pounds. The first time I witnessed people helping her in the bathroom I was startled by her wasted figure. I was reminded of scenes in *Night and Fog*, a film I saw in high school whose documentation of concentration camps appalled me.

My grandmother's diet at present consisted of a cup of cocoa that I'd make for her in the morning. In the afternoon I would return the empty cup to the kitchen. Then she began drinking less and less each day, until I was pouring a full cup of cocoa down the sink each evening. Despite her seeming disinterest in consuming the drink, she would request a cup every morning, never drinking a drop. She was eating very little too. I'm sure her lack of appetite was due, at least partially, to the painful lesions that lined her mouth and throat. The only thing she ingested on a regular basis was the morphine-laced syrup I gave her every day.

I had a girlfriend at the time, but she was really uncomfortable coming over to my grandmother's apartment. My grandmother would frequently press me to go out in the evening and have fun "like young people do." She insisted she was fine and didn't need me for anything. Later that evening, I ended up at my girlfriend's house. It was getting late and I said I really needed to head home. My girlfriend easily manipulated me into staying overnight at her place, but I told her I absolutely had to get up especially early and get home to my grandmother.

The next morning I raced home wobbling on my bicycle. As I opened the front door it encountered an obstacle. I poked my head in and I saw something that I'll never be able to forgive myself for. My grandmother was on the ground wrapped in blankets. I frantically asked her if she was OK. She appeared to be completely unrattled by it all. She said she was just getting up to use the bathroom and stumbled. There wasn't a hint of blame in her voice. This was no consolation. I felt like shit. By acting this terribly selfish way I had ignored my responsibility to her. It was about ten years later when I was telling a good friend about this incident and the guilt I still had regarding it. She tried to console me by insisting that the good I had done by making it possible for my grandmother to die at home (as was her wish) far outweighed that one evening of poor judgment. I felt somewhat better, but I'll always carry some shame because of my lapse.

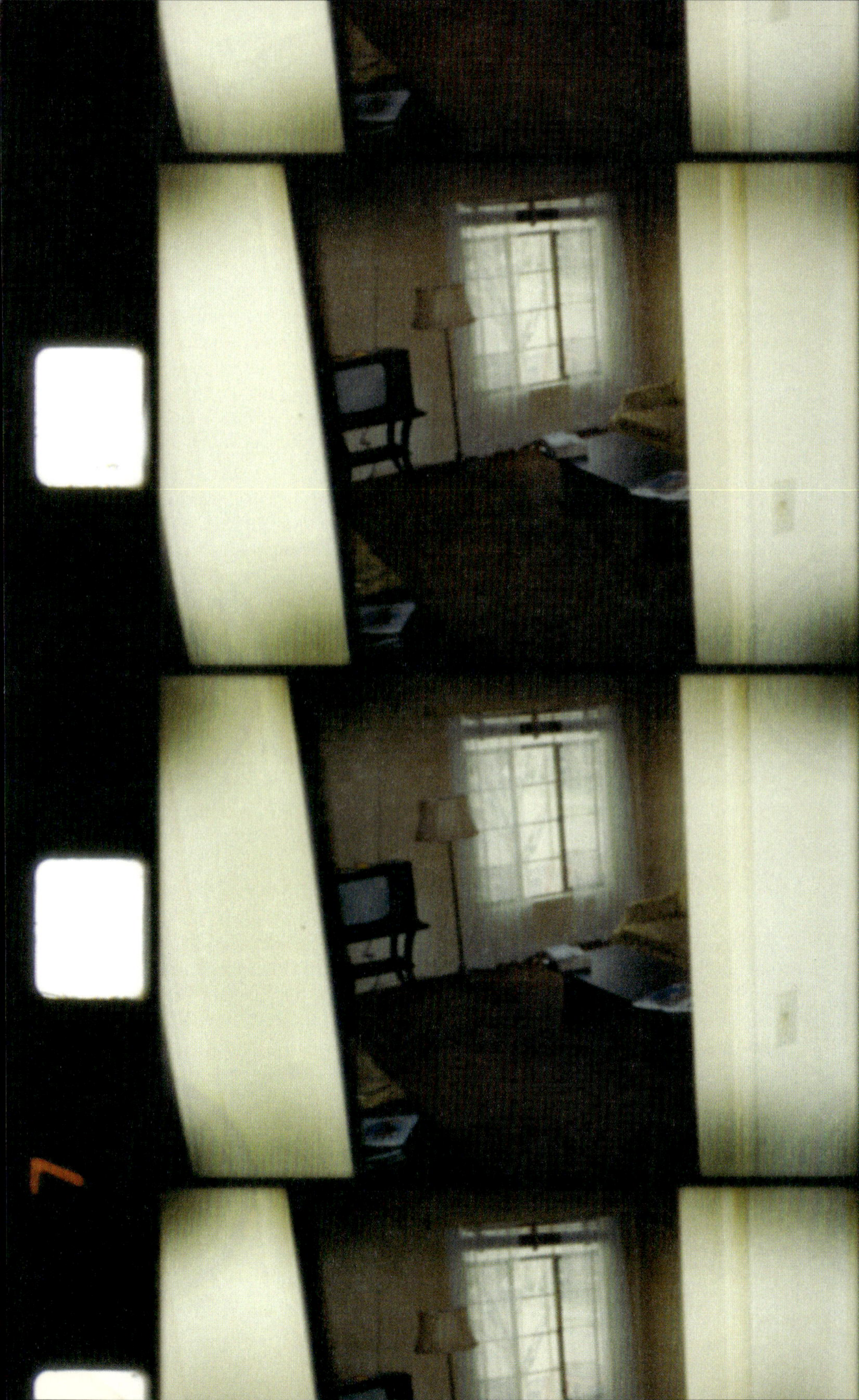

My grandmother's condition proceeded to decline. She was talking less and less. My sister, who had been so involved during the early stages of our grandmother's cancer, was conspicuously absent in the past several weeks. It's possible that the present inevitability of our grandmother's death was something my sister wasn't prepared to accept yet.

The weather had been miserable for weeks, and one wet evening my dad and my sister came to visit. As I mentioned before, my sister hadn't been around for some time, so the sight of grandmother's gray and sunken form was fairly shocking to her. She sat in the farthest corner of the living room and said nothing while my dad and I engaged in the typical interchange. My grandmother, who hadn't spoken a word for at least a week, wasn't participating in the talk. Shortly my father rose, said he was heading home, kissed his mom, and left. My sister remained silent and still for the next few moments and then began to sob. Abruptly she jumped up and rushed out, unable even to say goodbye to either of us. After the door banged shut, I knelt down by my grandmother's side and held her hand. I was overwhelmed by all of this and reluctantly wept. Now even though she appeared pretty well oblivious to all that surrounded her, for some reason I felt bad that I was crying so uncontrollably in her presence. With a weak and cracking voice I looked at her and uttered, "I'm sorry. I'm so sorry." She turned her face to me and squeezing my hand she said, "It's OK. It's OK."

The next morning I was awakened by a sound I didn't recognize. I went into to the living room and found my grandmother moaning. I asked her what was wrong and if she needed anything. I asked her if she was in pain and if there was anything I could do for her. She didn't respond at all and continued to moan. I gave her a dose of morphine and called the hospice nurse. She consulted with a doctor and said I should give my grandmother another dose of morphine and she would be there as soon as possible. When she arrived my grandmother was quiet and still. The nurse commented that my grandmother appeared to be calm and left, saying she would return later. I sat on the couch across from my grandmother and gazed at her. For the first time in at least a month, it was a bright and clear morning. The room was radiant with the light of the rising sun. Despite being a lapsed Catholic well on the way to becoming an agnostic, I looked around the room and thought to myself: if there's a God, take my grandmother today. I slowly made my way back to my bedroom and drowsily watched some loud and idiotic cartoons until I fell back into a doze.

The doorbell roused me from my sleep and I hopped out of bed a little too quickly. As I approached the front door, I felt the blood not quite making its way up to my head and I started to pass out. Instinctively dropping to my knees, I recovered and stood back up and opened the door. My dad's girlfriend Bonnie was here to check on things. As I opened the screen door, Bonnie asked how my Grandma was. I started to relate what had happened earlier that morning, when we both looked over to my grandmother. Something was different. She looked like she was sleeping, but her mouth was slightly open. Bonnie helped me change her, and while lifting my Grandma, Bonnie started to cry. She apologized and I told her she didn't need to apologize to me, I wasn't my dad. Bonnie made some phone calls and various friends and family started to gather at the apartment. The hospice nurse arrived and took my grandmother's vital signs. Her pulse was very weak. This was it. She would be dead soon.

I was handling this all pretty well until a priest of some type showed up. He was wearing one of those brown, Friar Tuck kind of robes. He stood over my grandmother and said something that I'm sure was related to religious blessings of the dead and all that stuff, but what I thought I heard him say was: "Oh my God." This simple mishearing though was enough to destroy my (up to this point) flawless composure. I dashed off to my room to weep and wail. Several folks came in at various points to offer consoling words or a hug. None of them were my father. I was starting to feel better and decided to join the group back in the living room. Unfortunately my timing stunk, because just as rounded the corner, I witnessed the men from the funeral home zipping my grandmother up in a body bag. In an instant she was no longer a conscious being but a soulless decaying substance that needed disposal. This realization hit hard and once again I began to weep somewhat uncontrollably. For whatever reason, I had now chosen the bathroom as my venue of mourning. Everyone came into the bathroom at some point to comfort me. That is everyone except my dad. When he did finally appear he stood at the entrance of the bathroom and blurted, "C'mon son. It's not the end of the world." True, but his astounding lack of sensitivity filled me with a rage that's hard to define. I jumped up and pushed past him screaming, "Like YOU'D fucking know!!" Back to the bedroom. More crying. Eventually everyone trickled out. The apartment was staggeringly empty and quiet.

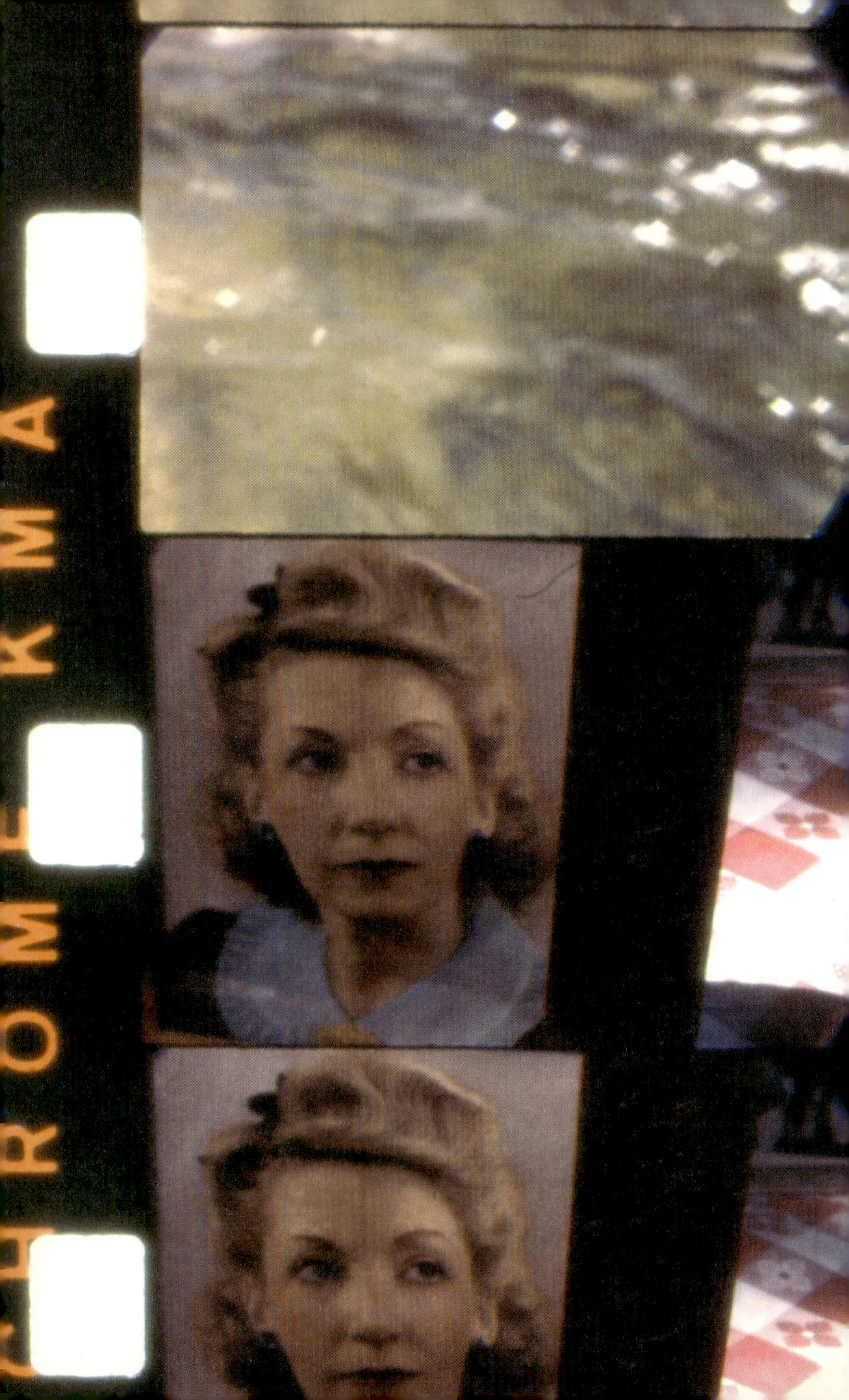

Years later my grandmother's surviving family members finally got together and took turns sprinkling her ashes into a river that runs through the hills of Northern California.

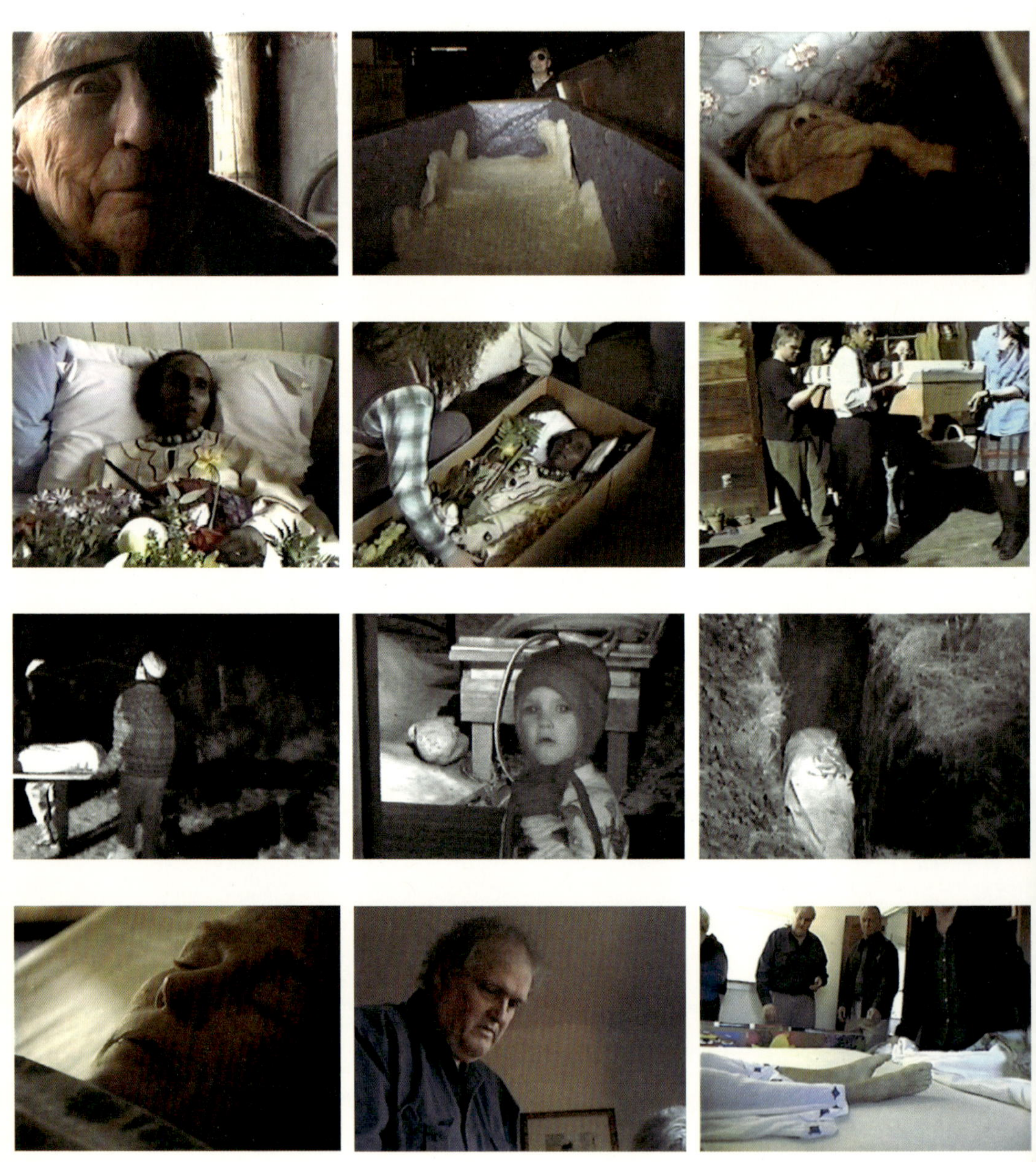

Elizabeth Westrate

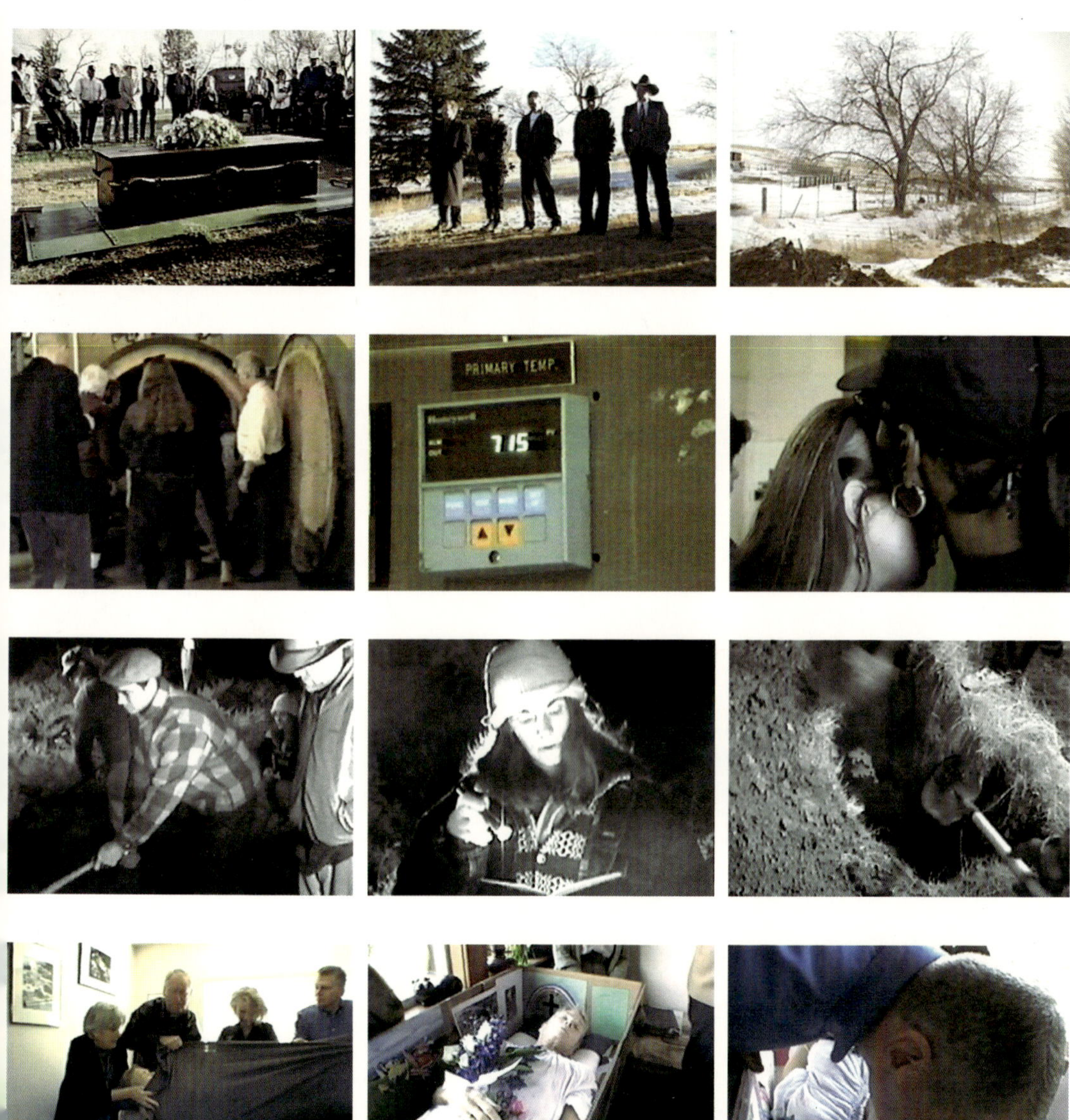

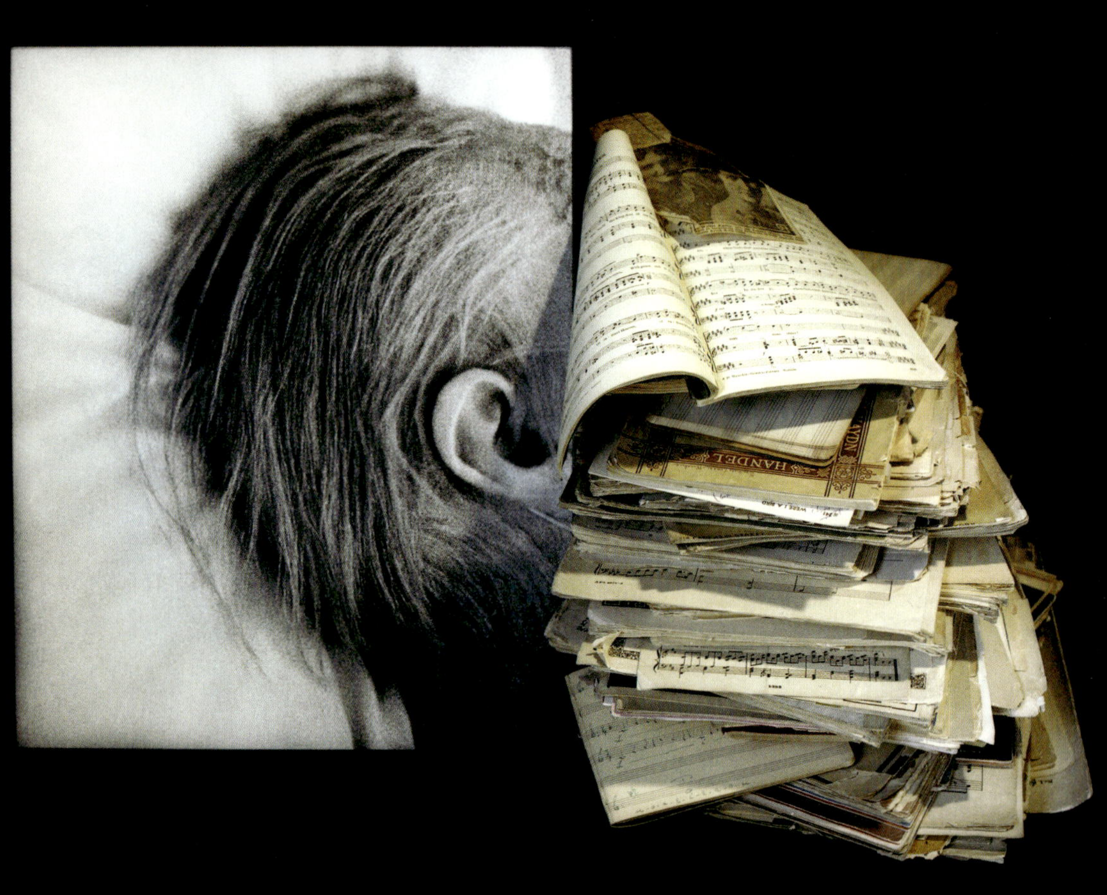

Susan Schwartzenberg

Isabelle

Just before her 91st birthday, my great-aunt Isabelle lay dying in a hospital in Chicago. I went to see her once again, but I also had to go through her things and close her apartment. Each day I spent an hour at the hospital. As I sat next to her bed, I watched the morphine drip, listened to her breathe, and stared out the window vaguely wondering about her life. For most of it, she had worked setting up filing systems for corporate clients, but she had an earlier career as a concert singer. Isabelle and her sister, Roberta, maintained a touring schedule singing opera duets until 1930, when Roberta jumped to her death from an office building.

My mother, Roberta's daughter, had always angrily averted any conversation about her mother, or about her childhood as the daughter and niece of two important singers. So I imagined a great mystery, a mystery sustained by my great-aunt, who talked a great deal, but not often about things I wanted to know. When an interesting subject arose, it was always described in strange euphemistic ways, so I was never quite sure what I had learned. I rested my hopes on a conversation we had a few years before, when she told me she had a suitcase of clippings about her sister's death. "And when I die," she said to me, "I want you to have the suitcase."

Each day when I left the hospital, I went to Isabelle's apartment, and slowly and methodically went through everything. Isabelle lived on the 17th floor of a large condominium complex. I must have gone to the garbage chute one hundred times, throwing away bags full of black lacy underwear, hats, gloves, broken appliances and dishes, strange jewelry, Christmas decorations, knick-knacks, and at least twenty-five years of cancelled checks. In a footlocker in the basement of her high-rise, I even found two military trunks containing documents and photographs—the life history, really, of her late husband. I found a suitcase, but it only contained photographs, a few music reviews, my grandmother's funeral announcement, and most interestingly, several envelopes of old music scores.

The day before Isabelle died it was Halloween, and all the nurses were dressed up as witches and ghosts. The blinds were drawn in her room, so this darkened space was a refuge from the bewildering hospital hallways. As I watched her, I thought how beautiful and peaceful her head looked, pushing itself against the pillow. I took one photograph and she stirred a bit after the shutter clunked. I stroked her head and apologized, and took a few more. I sat beside her, wondering if I'd found the suitcase, wondering if it was a relief to her to finally be dying, and wondering if she had told me more than I was capable of hearing. After awhile, I stood up, looked at her, kissed her, and went back to the apartment.

Suda Changkasiri

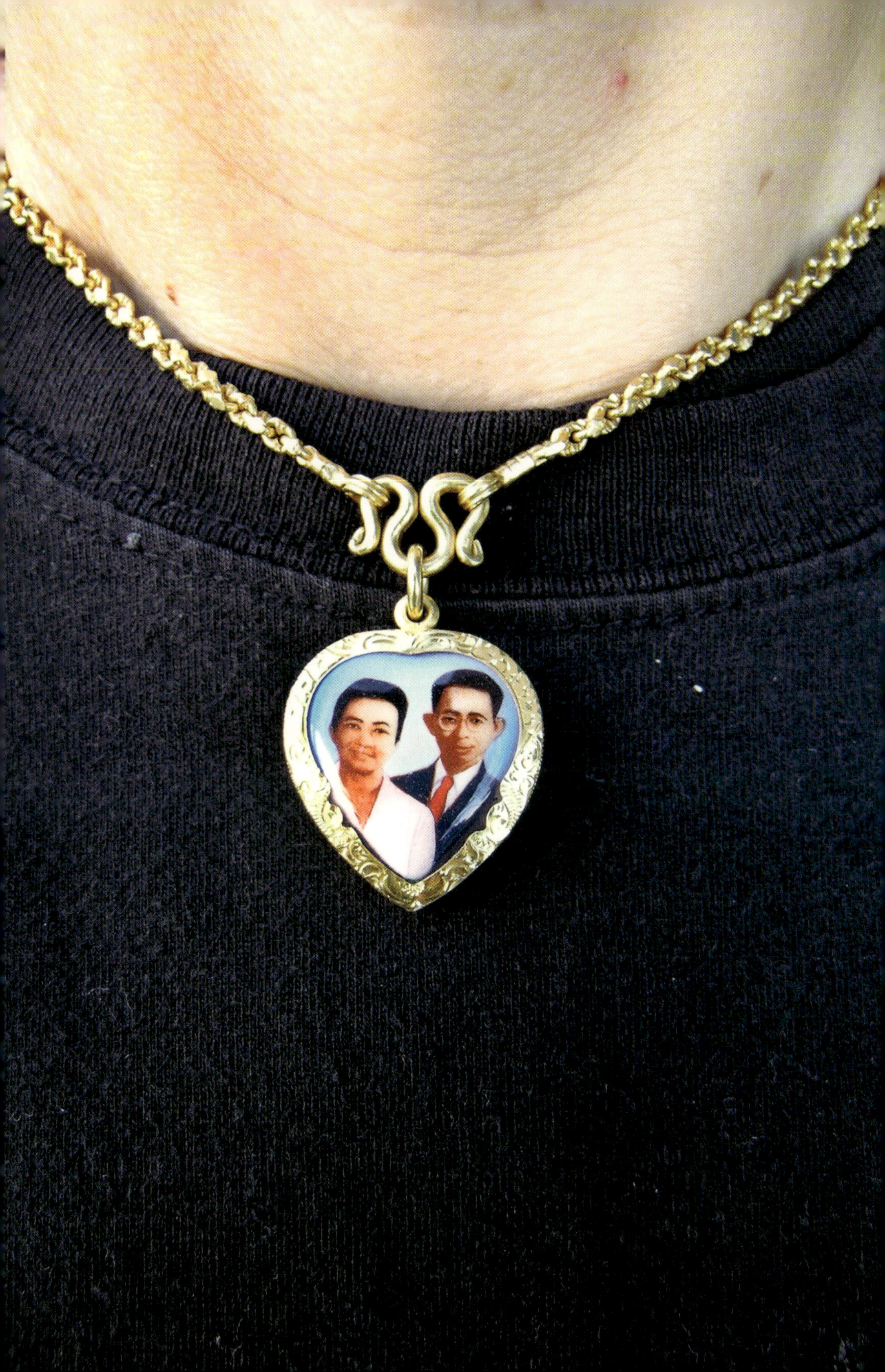

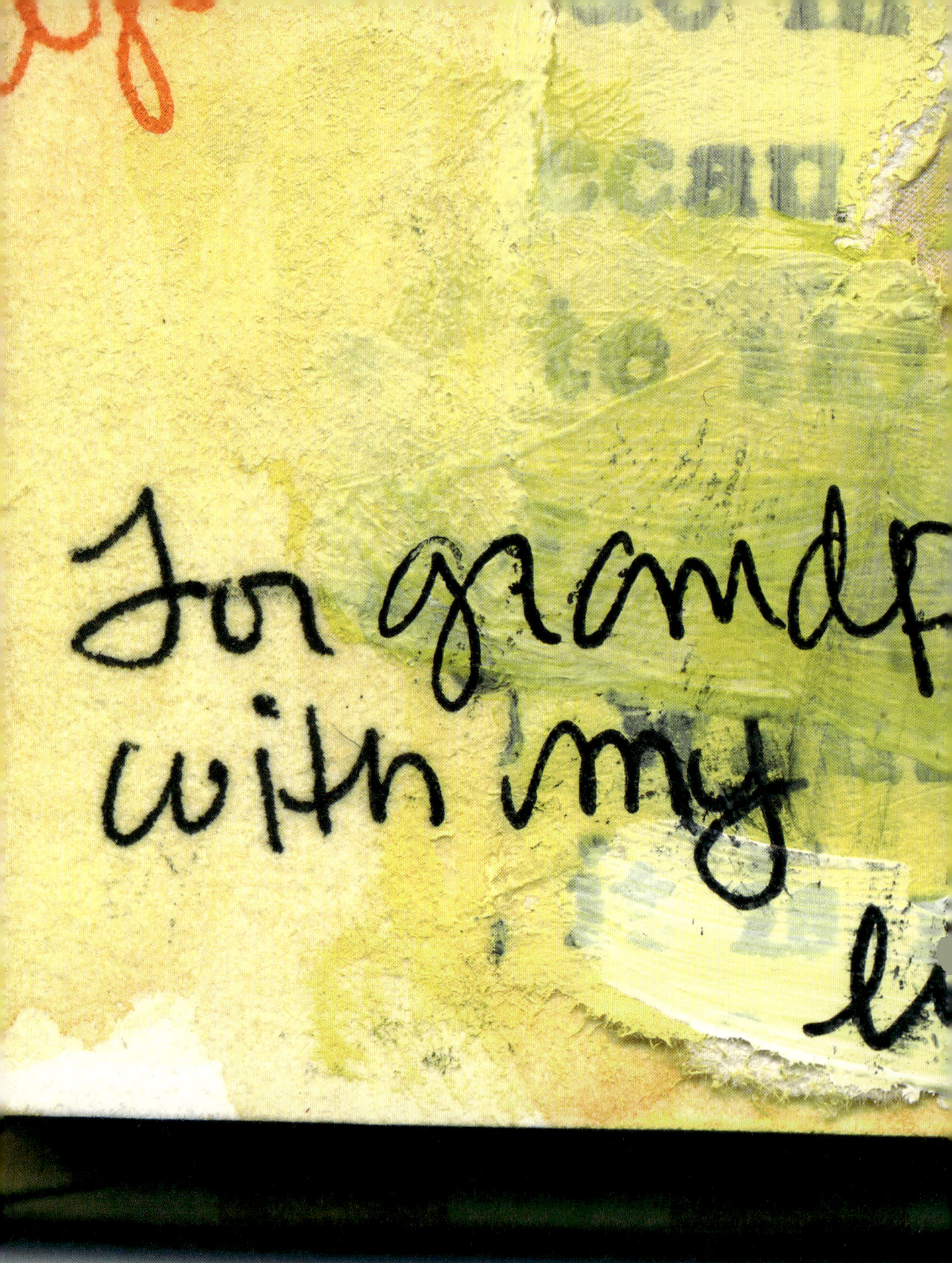

Jessica Herman-Goodson

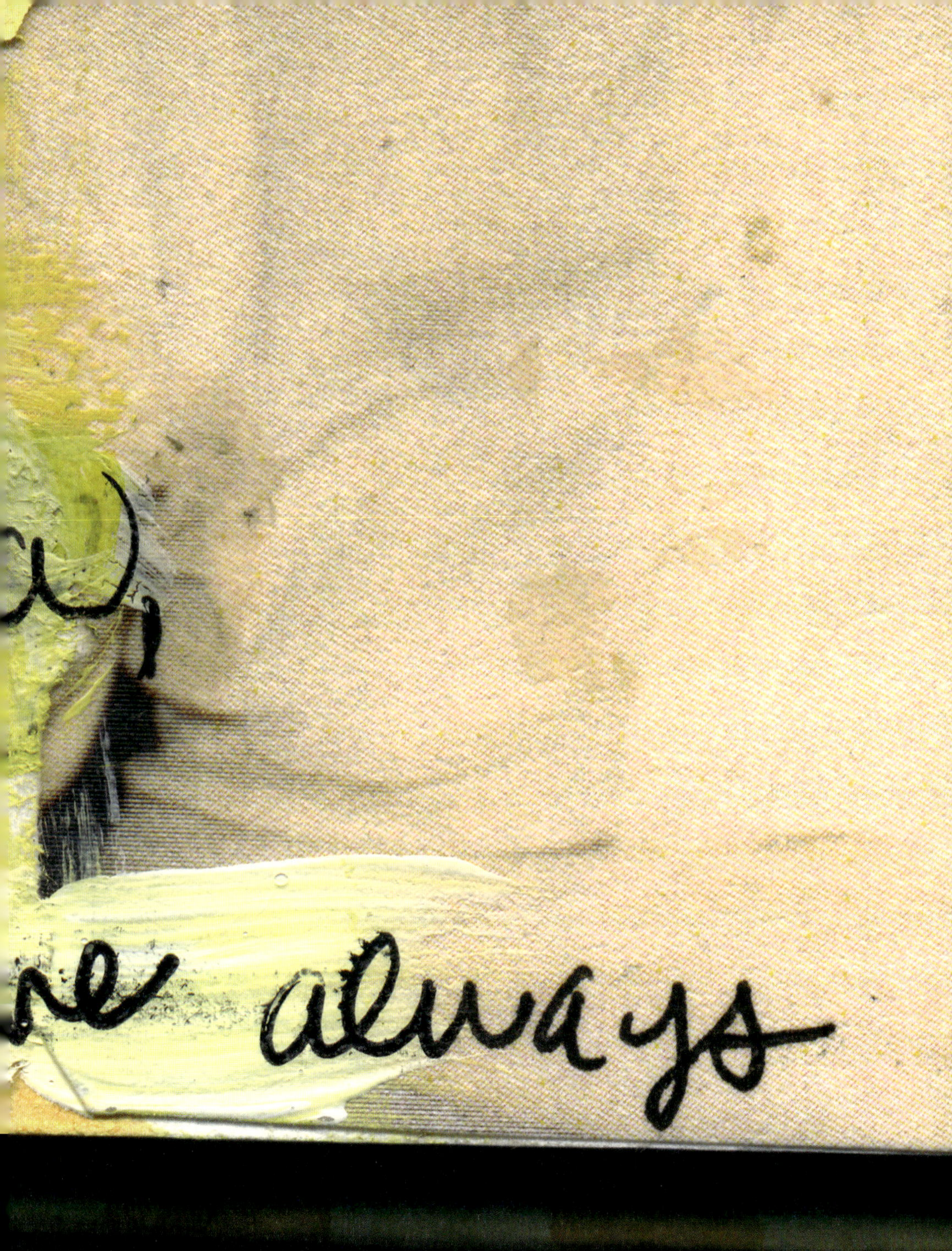

always

My Mother

In June 1990 I got the telephone call, my mother was in a coma after struggling with what her doctors were guessing to be some kind of brain aneurysm. I flew to New York where for two weeks my family and I sat by her bedside. I prayed in my own unique mixture of Jewish upbringing and California New Age Paganism. I also spoke to her quite often because I had heard somewhere that people in comas can still hear you. I remember one doctor saying I was wasting my time, that she was brain dead and could not hear me. The fury that hit me at that moment nearly had me reacting violently toward this doctor, and it also drained all the hope I had for the slight chance that my mother would recover. A few days later, the doctors convinced our family to take my mother off life support and shortly after, she took her last assisted breath.

During the ride home from the hospital, a dove followed the car along the Long Island Expressway and somehow I knew it was my mother's spirit animal. She had always liked birds. She kept a canary named Bijou for a long time, the only pet she really cared for. When she had first gone in to the hospital, my sister said a little bird fell out of a nest and landed at her feet on the sidewalk on First Avenue by the entrance of New York Hospital.

I still think of her when I see doves.

Marco Berger

My Father

My father developed complications after having a triple bypass operation. So he came to California to be near my brother and me. He was famous for smoking cheap cigars and drinking martinis. In fact, he would bring his own flask with previously made martinis to restaurants and ask for a glass of ice. He would even bring his own olives. In a restaurant one night, he told me he could not find the flask since coming to California. He had to actually order a martini from the waiter and I could see it was not a good time for him.

When his health slowly deteriorated, my brother had him admitted to St. Mary's Hospital. I would reluctantly visit him there, not wanting to face the fact that he was dying. One day, he asked me to cut his toenails, as he was too weak to do it himself. I tried, but I just could not get myself to do it. I told him that was what the nurses were for and left in a hurry to enjoy a beautiful day at the beach. To this day I regret that moment, when he really needed me to take care of him and I could not. After a few days in intensive care, he fell into a coma and the doctors suggested we remove him from the life-support machines. It was like a déjà vu. He died later that night holding my wife's hand.

After his death, I went to New York to clear out the apartment where he had lived for thirty years. Going through the house was very painful. I remember opening the drawer of a cabinet in the dining room and finding his famous flask. It was well worn, silver colored, the fake leather peeling away. Without thinking, I turned around quickly and began to say, "Hey Dad, I found your flask."

Nakkali Rupta

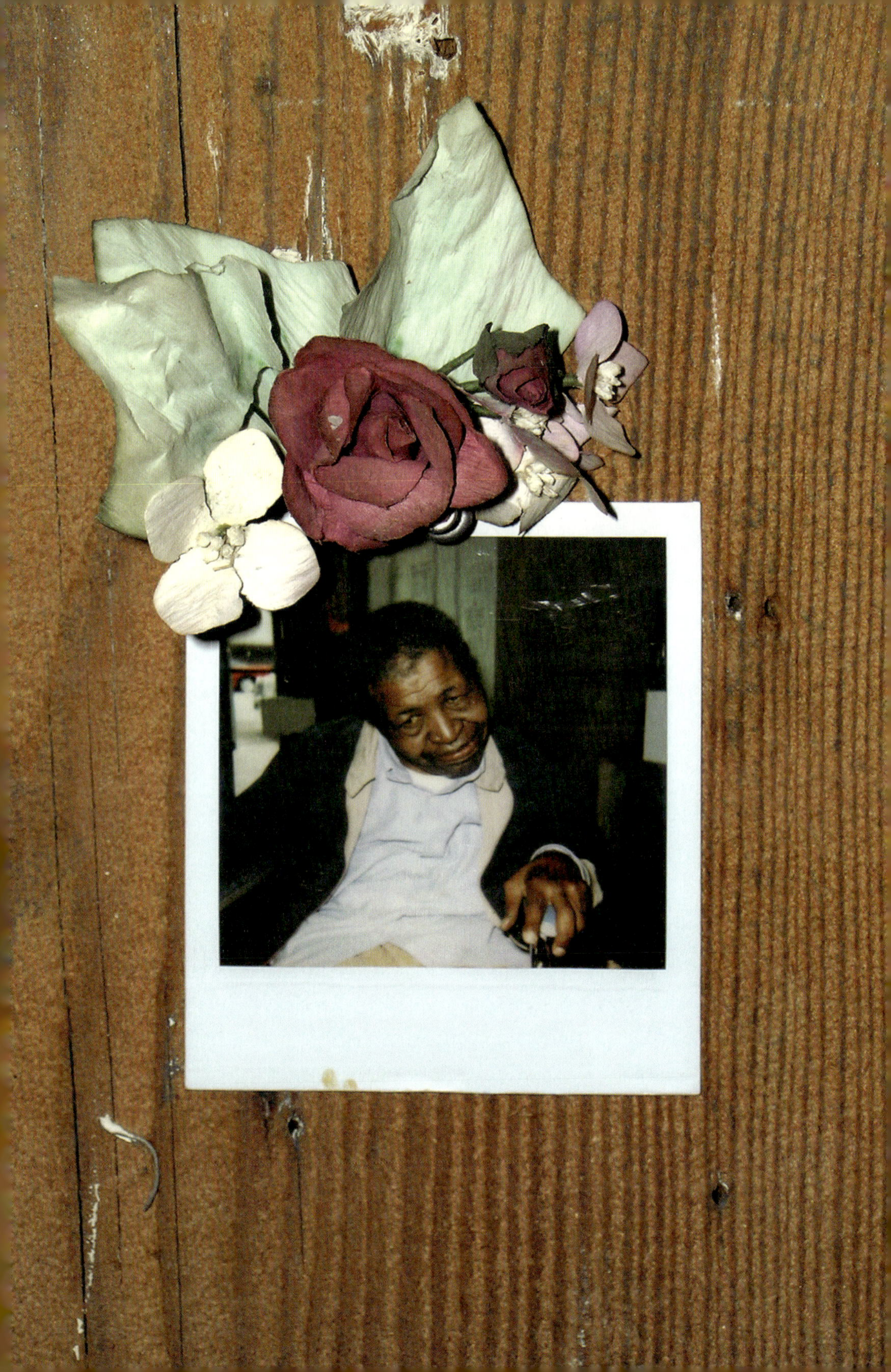

To Seth   Zoë's

I Love you DaD I Miss you So So
Much I cant speer in Words how much I Love
you I am doing my home Worlk. and I am reading vere. We ll.!
I do not no wiy you cod not tell me it rile herts
not to make you fel bad but it gust dos.
ples be ok. nowe remeder ne. miy mom and
Sester and how much ne Love you!

Zoë Ryan

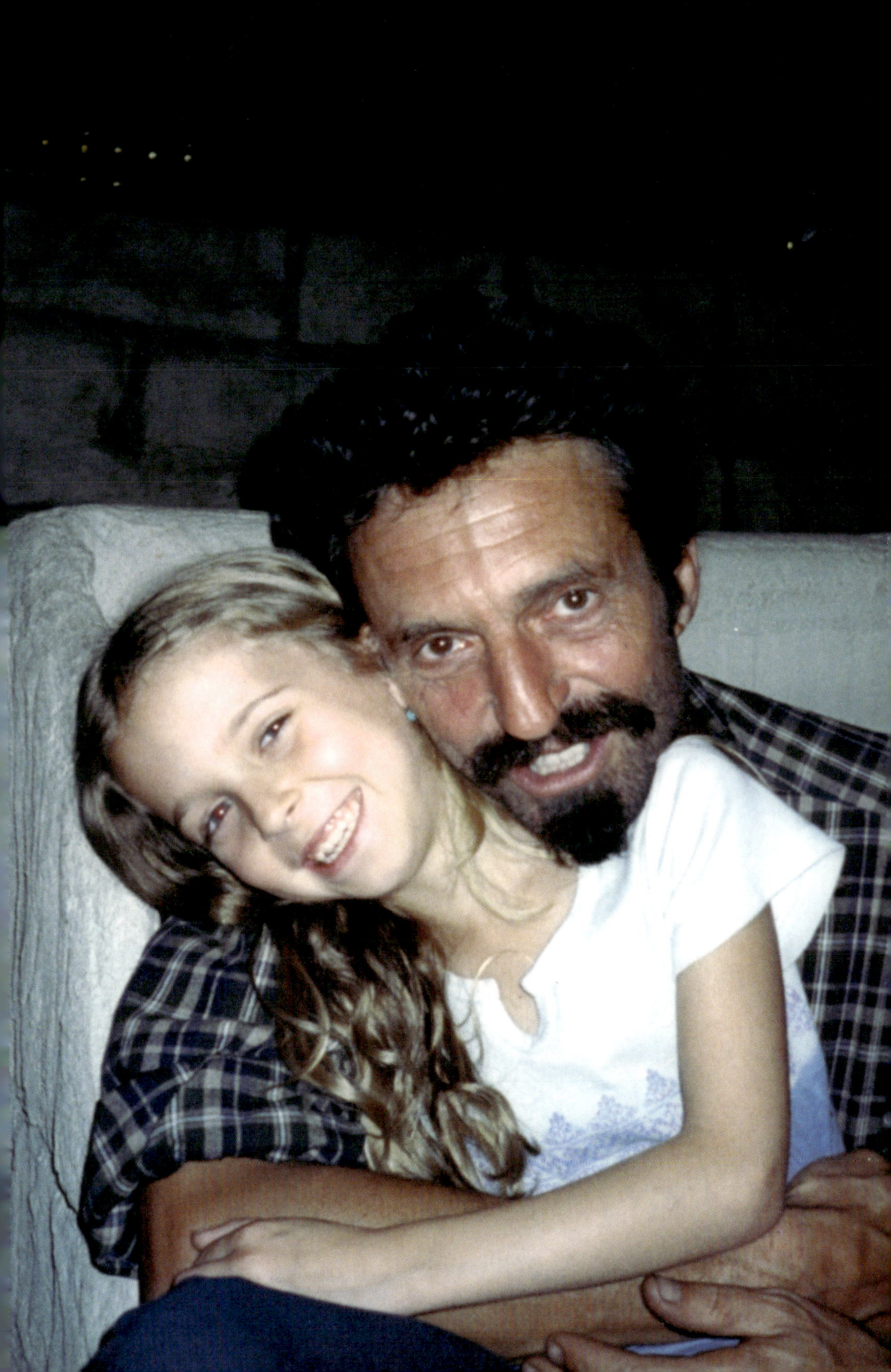

Douglas Morris

Dry Grasses and Burning Hearts

Guy's dusty blue pickup truck drove through the dry California countryside, both of us signing. He explained to me about his former lover who lay dying somewhere beyond. We drove on, winding our way through the live oak trees. The only sounds heard were the hum of the air conditioner and the wind rushing through the cab of the truck. Guy heard nothing. I heard my heart racing with the knowledge of what I would see, and hoped Guy "heard" it too.

With one last dip in the road I could see the grasses of the estuary gold in the noon sun and the dark waters of the bay beyond. Up one more small grade and the truck pulled a sharp left and came to a halt in front of a small brown cottage shrouded in bamboo and palms. I could feel the dust from the road in my mouth. Guy moved quickly from the truck, only looking at me to tell me to follow.

A wooden archway marked our way down a short path to a side porch. A cat, an orange tabby, sat quietly on the railing looking "wanting." The porch was crowded with discarded shoes; he asked me to remove mine. We walked in. It was the kitchen, small and dark, the table and counters covered with food ready to eat, pots and pans filling the sink waiting to be washed. It felt good to enter by the kitchen as we had always done in upstate New York. That was the door reserved for those we loved, friends and family.

Beyond the kitchen was a door hung with white lace pulled to one side. It looked to be the living room although I saw no evidence of furniture, only the corner of a mattress on the floor, a painting, and a vase of wildflowers set carefully at the foot of the bed. Guy stepped through, looked down and started to sign. I stood in the cool of the kitchen amongst the carrot peelings and dirty coffee cups. Finally Guy's large blue eyes turned to me and said, "Come in."

I had seen this same setting once before at our home on Peak's Island, Maine. A room set for one's last days. The flowers from the garden, that only a short distance away were too difficult to visit anymore, and favorite objects set close enough to the bed to remember.

I had seen death lay in waiting some years earlier. I had seen the resignation and sadness to leave this world. I had seen the lifelessness of a body once a whole person now lay stiffly moving and quietly signing to me. Once again I was at "home."

I remember All Saints' Day morning. My lover lay dead in our home. After a full morning of visitors our neighbors were respectfully all gone. I sat in the back meadow some distance from the cottage, only able to see the nose of the gray hearse that had come over on the ferry earlier to carry his body away. I could not bear to watch them "steal" him away, so I sat smoking and waiting. The October air reminded me that winter was not far behind. Colored leaves covered the large boulder I sat on. I heard a rustle behind me and left my vigil to see a large buck standing only feet away. His brown eyes met my blue. The calmness in his eyes was the same I had felt before, such as on a snowy morning before the plows would come to move the snow away or the moment before an afternoon rain. Or when I would look into my lover's eyes before we would go to sleep.

The sound of a car engine broke our steady gaze. I turned to see the hearse pulling away from the cottage. I looked back to see the buck. He stood also watching as the long gray vehicle pulled down the dirt road. The buck shifted his stance, paused and looked at me as if to say good-bye, and bounded off into the autumn foliage. That would be the last time I would feel the closeness of my lover.

Back in California: The figure in the bed motioned me to step closer. I knelt down, reached out and grasped his hand and introduced myself. He said his name was Max. Red hair crowned his head. His fair skin stretched taut against his face. I felt that same feeling, that same awful rush of adrenaline when our eyes met and realized that death was here once more. I wanted to shake him and fluff him like an old feather pillow until he had regained his shape. I wanted to pound the floor so that he might rise and yell in anger at me for disturbing his dying. I wanted to hold him tightly in my arms. I wanted to squeeze this plague from his body. I wanted to curse the "God" that did this.

Instead we exchanged pleasantries as if we had just met on the corner of Eighteenth and Castro and I promised him that I would attend his birthday party that coming week. I smiled and walked slowly from the room, although my heart was racing before me, out the door and out into the heat of the afternoon.

I walked out far enough from the lush growth around the house in order to catch sight of the water. Something to steady me. Something to clear my head. The water glistened dark and cool. The summer grasses burned brown and gold from the sun. (Funny, in the city you don't notice the noise until you stand in front of nature's creations.) The quiet was only broken as Guy walked up from behind me. I turned and he buried his head in my shoulder and cried. I could hear his soft Deaf voice muffled against my body. There is sweetness to a Deaf voice that can only be compared to a trumpet when muted or the flutter of a birds wings beating the ground before taking to the air. This would be one of the few times I would see Guy openly cry.

We walked down and away from the suffering inside the house into the dry grasses of the estuary below. The cattails and midsummer flowers moved ever so slightly in the stiff breeze. Gold and bronze the marshes spread out before us and as always the bay beyond darkly sparkled.

A thin dirt road divided this peaceful scene and led to a small hill beyond. Guy walked slowly and began to talk about all of the men he had loved and all of them dead. I could see the fear of losing his lover in his eyes and in the motion of his hands. We talked of the past and a future that seemed as dark as the waters around us.

Grabbing my hand, Guy led me into the brittle grasses. We walked only a short distance and he knelt down pulling me under a small live oak. I followed his lead. We stretched out on the grass and watched the thin summer clouds with no promise of rain move slowly over head. I turned to him and seeing his eyes filled with the tears of the grief of so many years of pain and loss. I rolled on top of him. Guy did not hear the grass crush beneath us, nor the birds, nor the breeze rattling the leaves of the live oak, only the beat of my heart.

Guy quietly signed to me, "Max and I came here once before and made love." I began to tell him, "You see how life goes on? You see we are here together? One more time you are here in the same place? With me?"

As I tried explain about the fullness of life and the richness in it and how I felt that all of this was part of a greater plan and to see that the death of one more handsome young man had meaning, I almost believed it myself. I knew I was trying to make it right in our minds so that we could go on one more time.

At that moment a deer jumped from seemingly nowhere and stood above us. We lay in stunned silence. The deer's soft brown eyes looked down and met ours. It did not look surprised or even scared, more like a greeting, shifting its weight and making one large leap, it disappeared into the grasses.

Guy, his eyes still sparkling with tears and the blue of the sky above, stamped his fist into his hand, a sign meaning "approval" and kissed me.

I knew I had once more fallen in love.

Alise Murphy

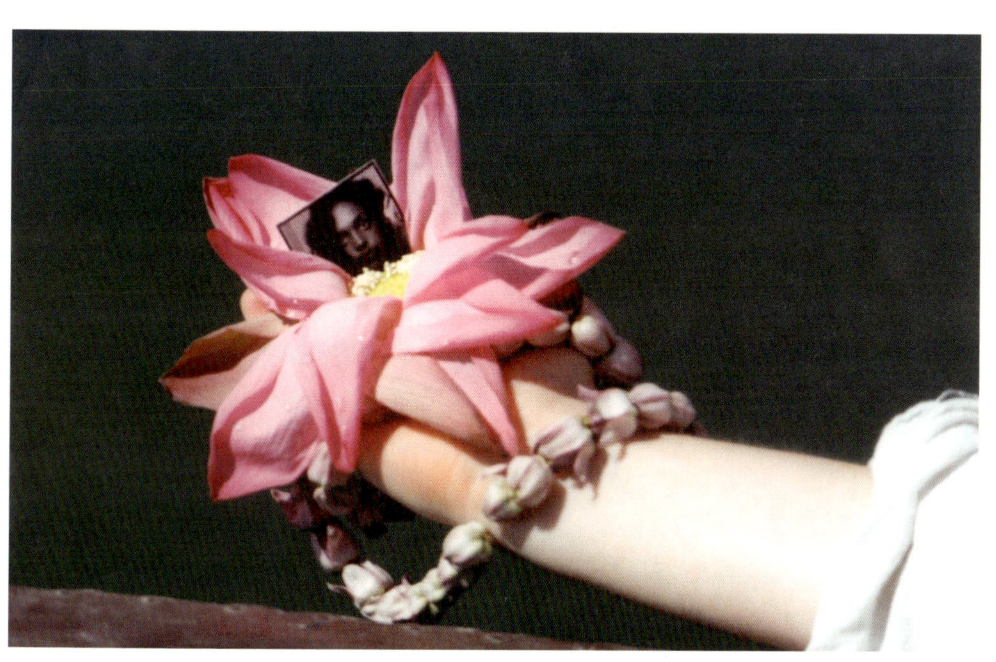

Hey all,

I wanted to let everyone know that Noodle (the cat that didn't like short women)
was put to sleep today after a developing a serious case of fatty liver syndrome.
Here's one of her last pics . . .

David

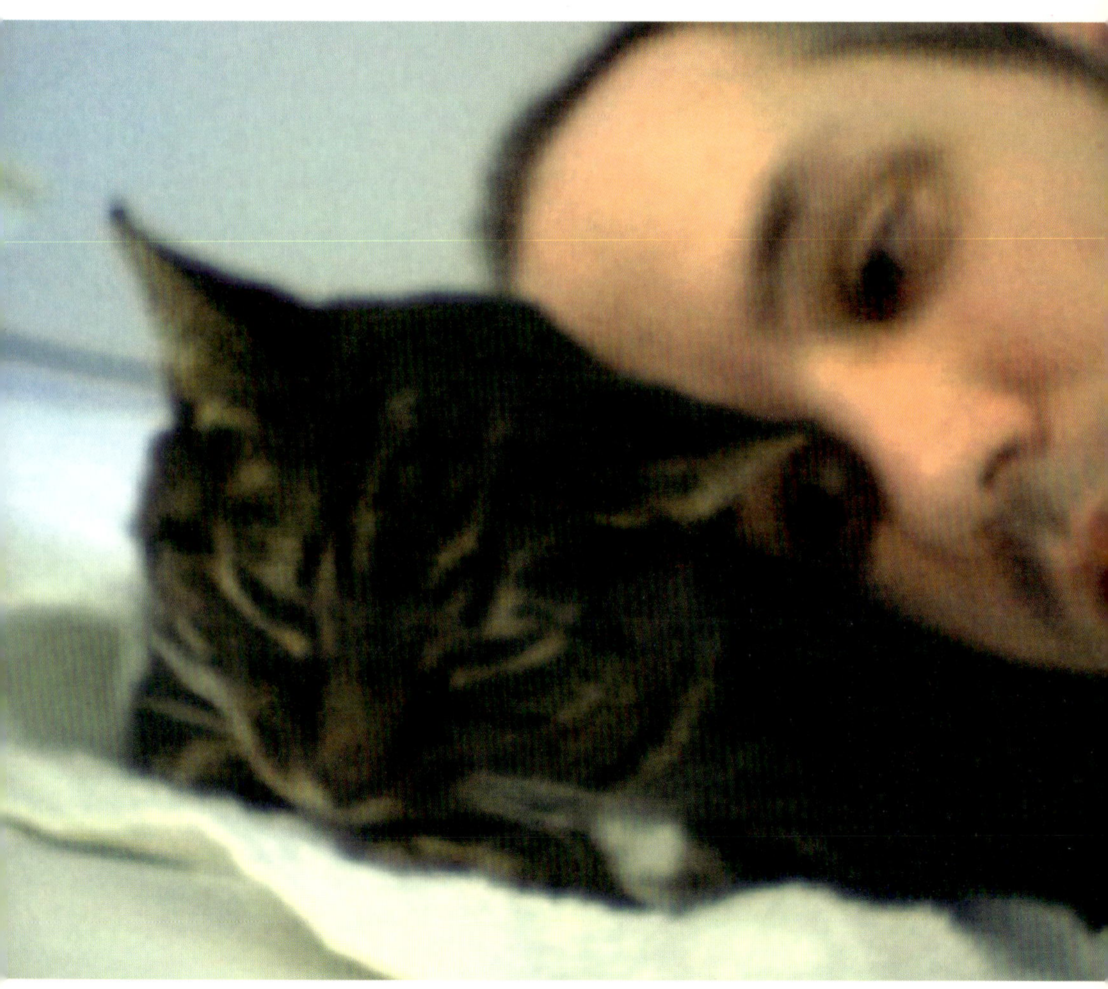

Kelley Kerslake

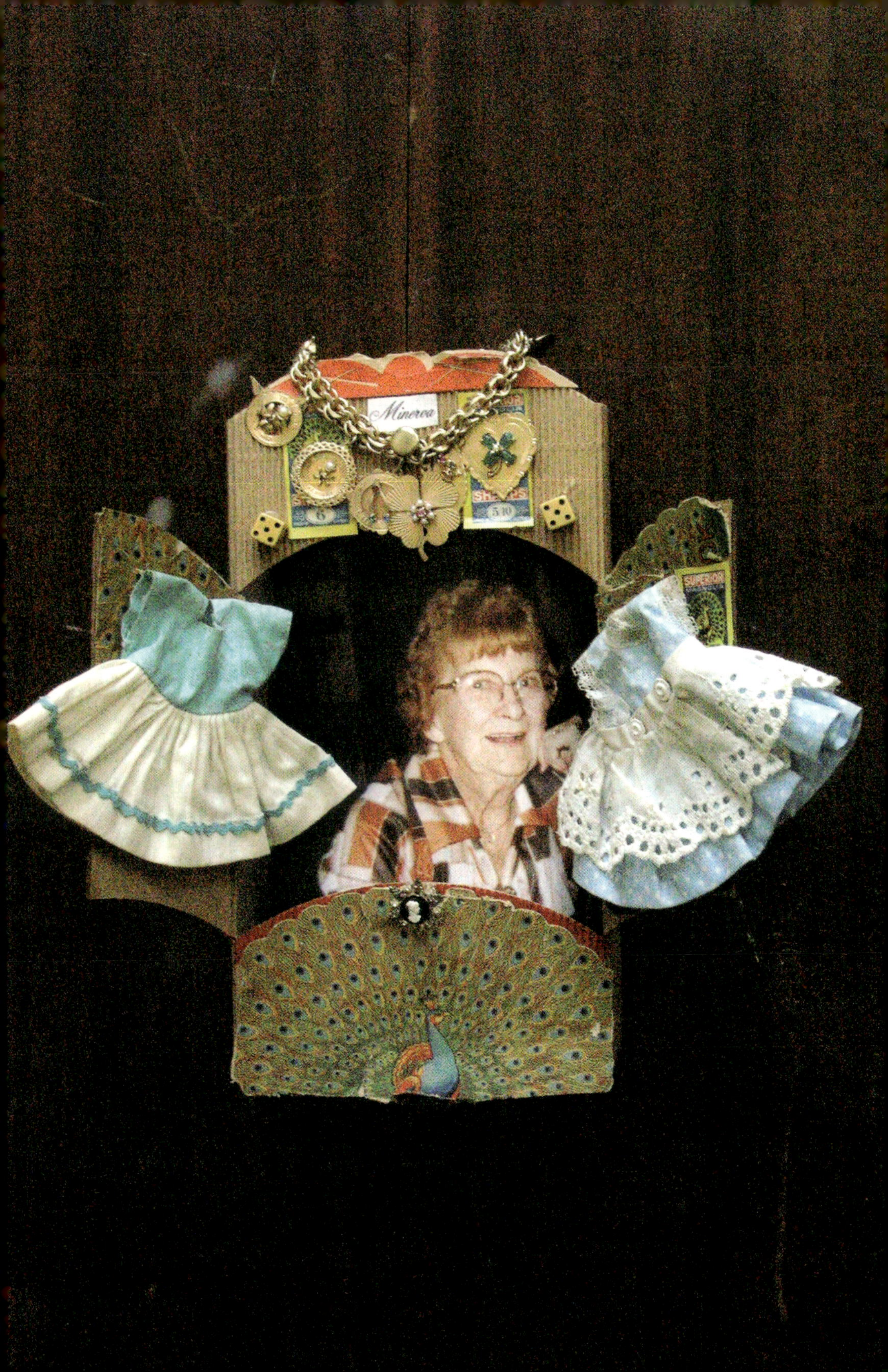

Minerva

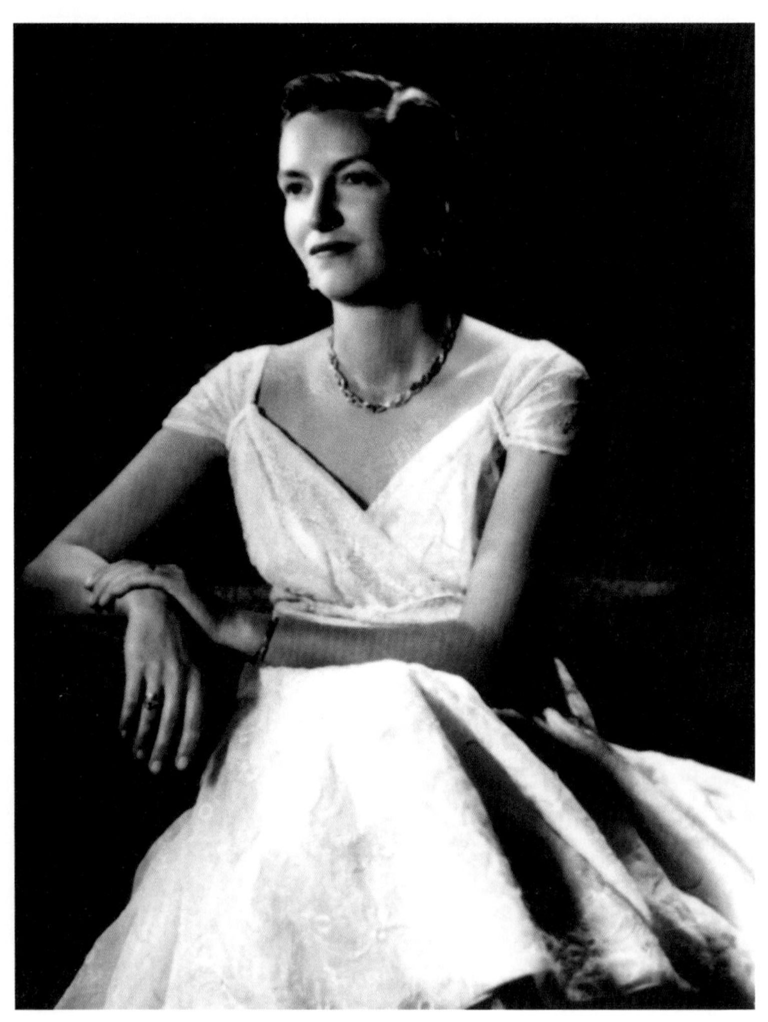

Melissa Stuart

My Mom's Passing

Death . . . I think of death as a transition, that one's energy never dies. Maybe that is why I usually say passing or transition. I tiptoe around the word *death* with most people, not wanting to upset them.

My mom died January 1996, at age 74. She was active up to the last five years of her life. Her body rapidly deteriorated. She was diagnosed with a rare form of Parkinson's, which left her totally incapacitated. She did seem to have her mind, but otherwise was a captive in her body, which grew rigid, crippling her. She experienced a lot of pain. She endured her physical suffering with such dignity, while treated like a baby. She lost her speech and used a talking computer to communicate. She lived at home with help around the clock

I did not have a physically close relationship with Mom, maybe because I did not have an emotional connection with her. Mom never talked about her feelings. I thought she was a perfect enigma. She was mentally acute and a creature of routine. I thought emotional connection was how to be close. Therefore, I felt disconnected with my mom most of our life together and in her dying process.

I wanted to be needed by her, have her ask something of me during her time of illness. She never did. I wanted to know how to feel, and what to do around her. I look back now and see how our dysfunctional relationship kept me from experiencing her just as she was. I felt small for wanting some attention, for wanting some of her things, for wanting . . .

My mom went from a very independent, active woman to her last five years of crippled, painful dependency. Her harsh condition gave her the experience of feeling dependent and emotional, the other side of her independent and lively personality. Through Mom's illness, she would laugh till she cried. She would cry like she never had before. Do we receive certain experiences on this earth plane in order to move through karma, life lessons, to learn how to love?

I feel close to Mom now that she is passed on. I feel like she sees and accepts me, when in actuality, it is more like me seeing, and accepting me.

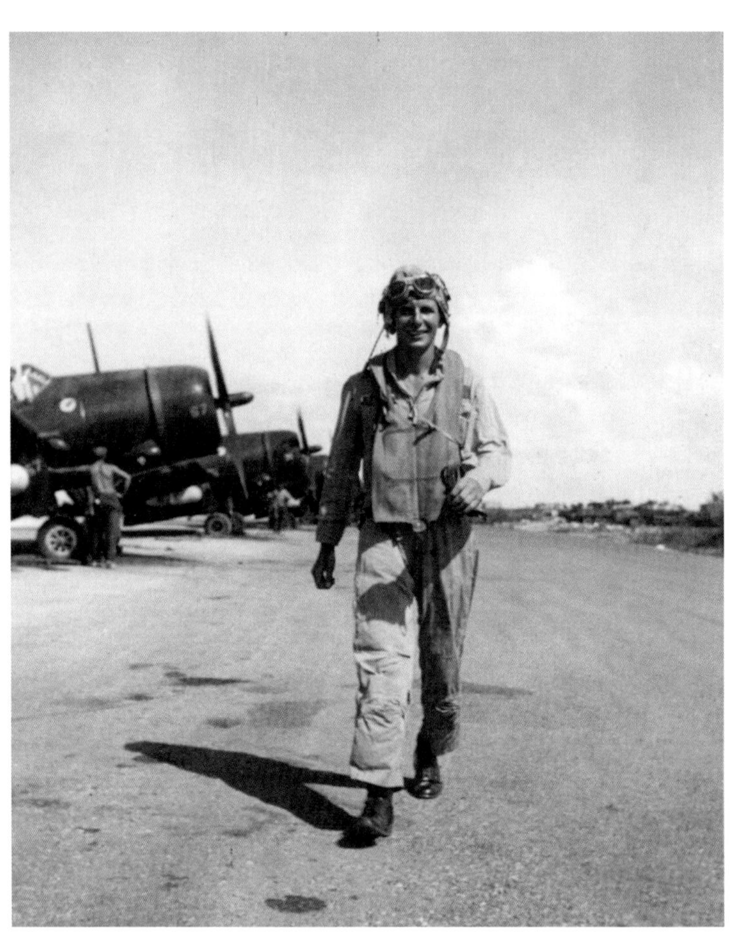

John Baumann

Flight Suit

Mom mailed me some of Dad's clothes this past Christmas: his fuzzy bathrobe, a favorite T-shirt, and the flight suit he wore as a Navy pilot circa WWII. None of us had known about the flight suit. Mom had discovered it in the attic a few weeks earlier in a wardrobe she hadn't sorted through since 1972, the year we moved in.

The T-shirt, from the Glenn Curtis Aviation Museum in Hammondsport ("Wilber and Orville *Who?*"), is the faded veteran of a thousand rinse cycles, palest yellow and stained with the memory of some dark liquid (Skoal tobacco? Almaden Mountain Burgundy?). The robe is brown velour, soft and clean but still harboring a familiar scent of cologne. Dad might have been wearing these when he died, sitting in his chair with a glass of wine watching *Charlie Rose*. I only suspect, and Mom hasn't said.

They're mine now. The T-shirt is already permeated with my runner's sweat, and the robe is gradually memorizing the shape of my slender frame.

The 1946 flight suit, however, will always belong to Dad. "C. F. BAUMANN, ENS USNR" is printed in gilt letters over the breast pocket, beneath a pair of tiny golden wings. The fabric is a shiny, olive-colored synthetic material, US military issue, impervious to time. Wars and soldiers do not last so long. The metallic ink tracing his name is worn mostly away, the only sign of advanced age.

January 31, 2004, would have been Dad's 78th birthday, the first one we commemorated without him. It seemed like the right day to finally try on his flight suit. A month earlier, on Christmas Day, I had held it up to my body, smoothing the empty sleeves over my arms.

A set of zippers peeled open, letting me step inside, then closed tight up to my neck. The fit was snug and flattering. Suddenly, I felt macho. I could picture myself landing on the deck of an aircraft carrier, waving to cheering crowds. My wife, Jennifer, got out the digital camera, and I held a football (substitute flight helmet) tucked under one arm, to complete that *Top Gun* look.

We e-mailed the photos to Mom and my sister Melinda, who were surprised at how perfectly the suit fit. Dad had been thin, like me, until he quit smoking. We got used to seeing a heavier man in the last two decades. Now we must get used to not seeing him at all.

The night after Dad's birthday I had a dream. I was a passenger in a small commuter aircraft, swooping and careening over Pearl Harbor. There were flash-glimpses of small islands and looming shipyard cranes. Then the plane banked hard, and the window was filled with a close-up view of waves rushing by.

Jennifer was strapped into the seat next to me. She reached over and took my hand.

"It feels scary, but the pilot knows what he's doing," I said, pleased to be treated to such a roller-coaster flight.

I woke up and wrote down the dream in my journal. Later it struck me who was probably flying the plane.

I am the pilot, he seemed to say, *and you are just along for the ride.*

Leroy Moore Jr.

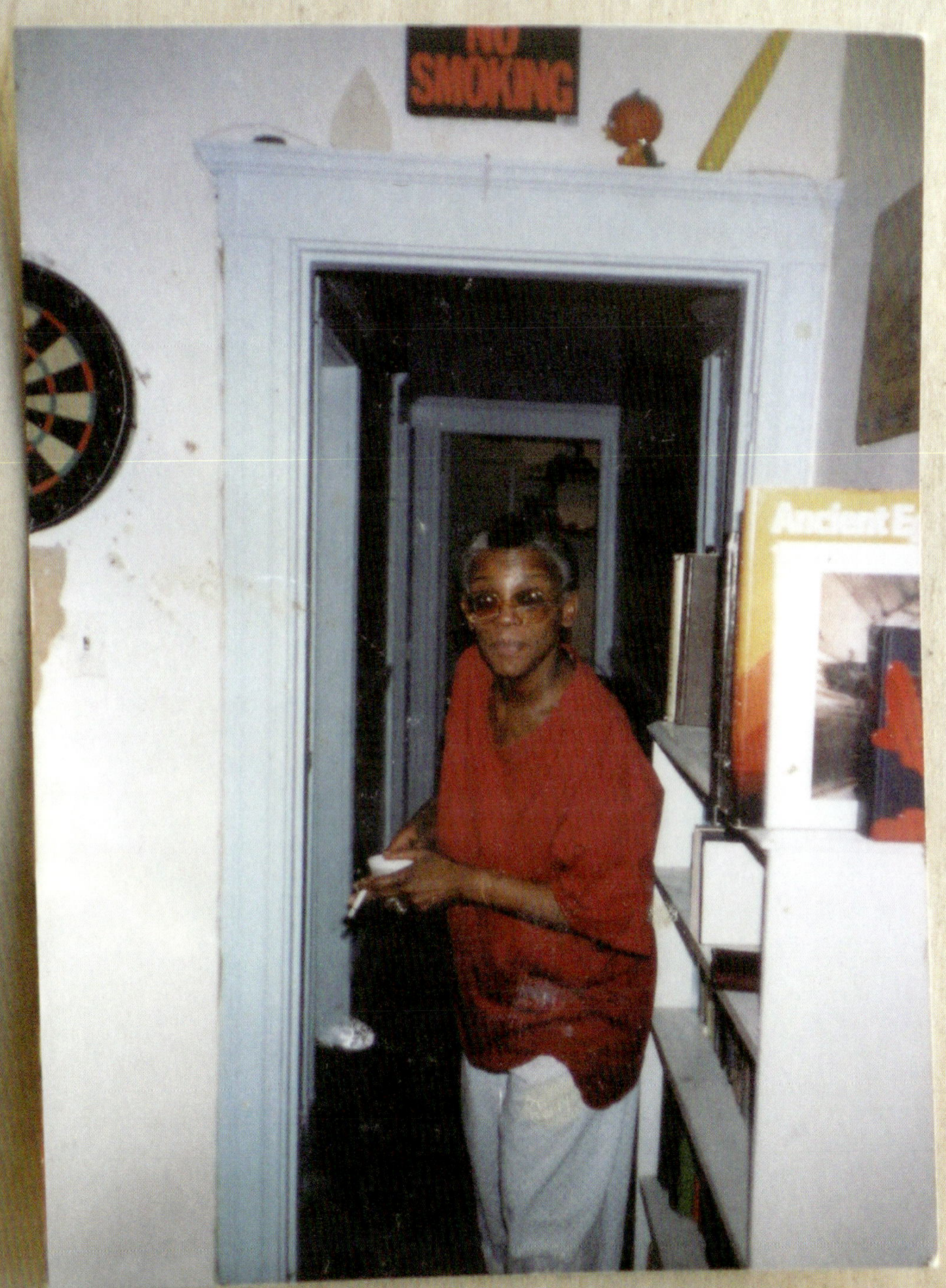

Another Day

It's 6:00 a.m. and she knows her day has to begin.

On the edge of her bed, she wonders how long can she continue with this. Her son pretends to be asleep as she goes through her morning routine. Every morning he wants to hug his mother and tell her everything will be OK, but he knows everything is not OK. He watches his mother go through her painful routine. He shares her pain and is scared of his mother's body because of his own disability. Out of one eye, he watches his mother every morning and feels helpless. He wonders did she feel the same way when he was in the hospital racked with pain?

As she crawls out of bed, she looks down to her breast and slowly shakes her head. Her breasts are crisp and dark black from the radiation. "How many cells and muscles have they cooked in the past year?" Her mind screams. Her breasts aren't hers anymore. They are a different color compared to the rest of her smooth, dark brown skin.

In the shower, she looks down at her body and doesn't recognize it. Dark circles are all over her chest and left arm, she notices. As a tear falls into the bath water, she tells herself to be strong. How can she go on?

Showering, dressing, breakfast and a container of sixteen different pills is her morning routine. The pill container is like a box of crayons filled with every color you might need: blue, red, tan, yellow, etc. The door closes behind her.

He looks out the window to see his mother walking to the bus stop. It is 7:00 a.m. He thinks about her day and night, and prays that she'll make it home safely. Many times he has to wait at the bus stop to make sure she makes it to the apartment.

8:00 a.m.
Sitting in the doctor's office. "Lela!" the nurse announced in a soft voice. Lela knows what she has to do. Naked on a cold table, she hears the sound of the machine, mmmmmmmm. She pops up like nothing has happened and proceeds to get dressed. Before walking out of the doctor's office, he hands her a prescription. Her mind is yelling, "How many pills you want me to take!"

11:00 a.m.
Stumbles out of the hospital. "Wake up, come on wake up!" she tells herself. She is on the bus again.

12:00 p.m.
Punches her time card. "Six o'clock, come on, stay awake until then!" she thinks.

3:00 p.m.
Break time. After lunch, she pulls out her crayon-like pill container. In the last month or so, she has spent more money on medicine than on rent, food, and transportation put together.

6:30 p.m.
Waiting for the bus to go home. The pain of chemotherapy is taking over her left side, but her medicine is slowly kicking in, making her sleepy once again.

7:00 p.m.
On the bus. She starts to doze off. "Whitney Street!" the bus driver announces. She stands up slowly, grabs her bags, and walks down off the bus.

7:15 p.m.
At home. Her son studies his mother and notices she still has her teeth and hair. He takes off her shoes while she is on her bed. He gives her a kiss and a hug. She kisses and hugs him back, and replies in a tired voice, "I'm OK."

12:00 a.m.
He hears his mother crying and he starts to cry.

6:00 a.m.
The next morning.
His mother is sitting on the edge of her bed with her head in her hands. He wants to stop the clock! He wants to take his mother's place today. He wants to hug his mother and tell her everything will be OK, but he knows everything is not OK. His eyes are watery and she begins her morning routine.

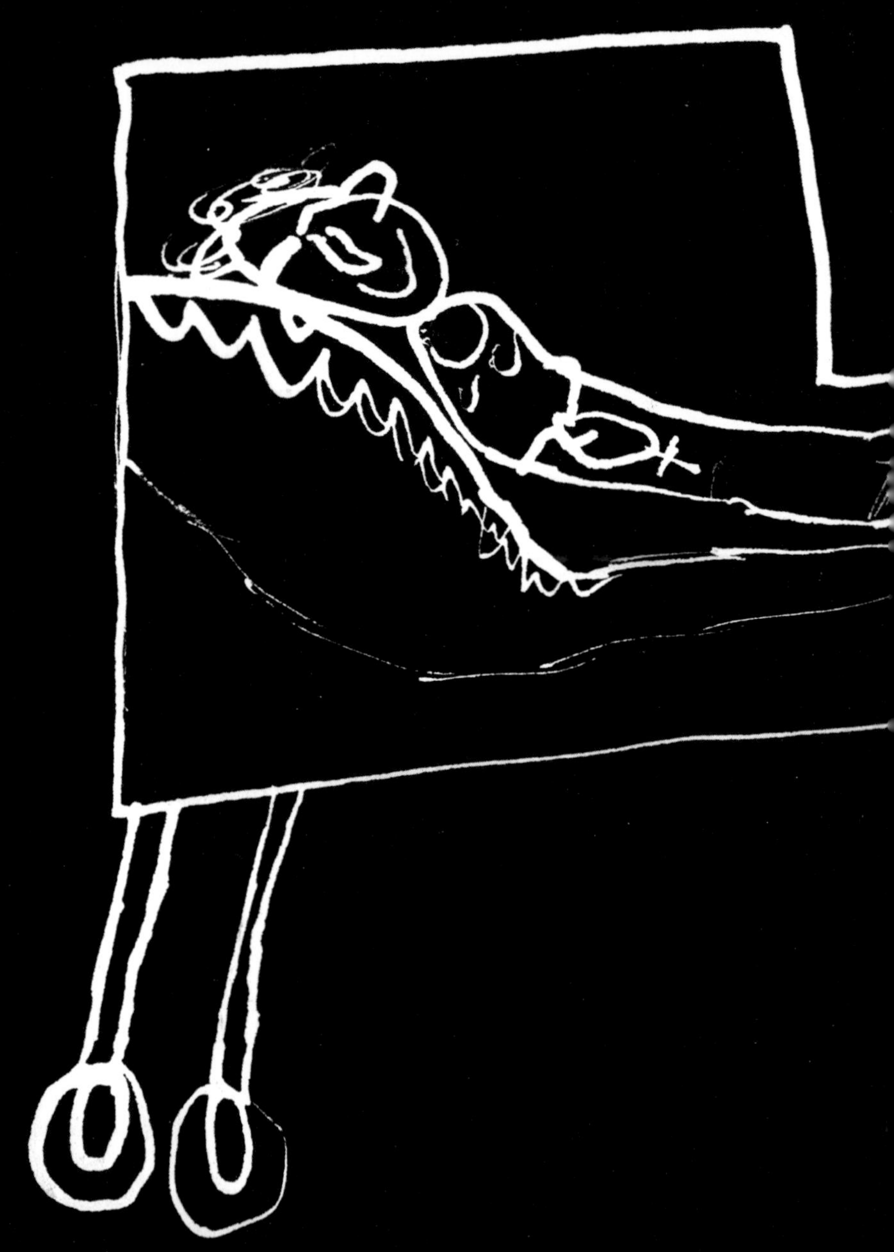

Sara O'Sullivan

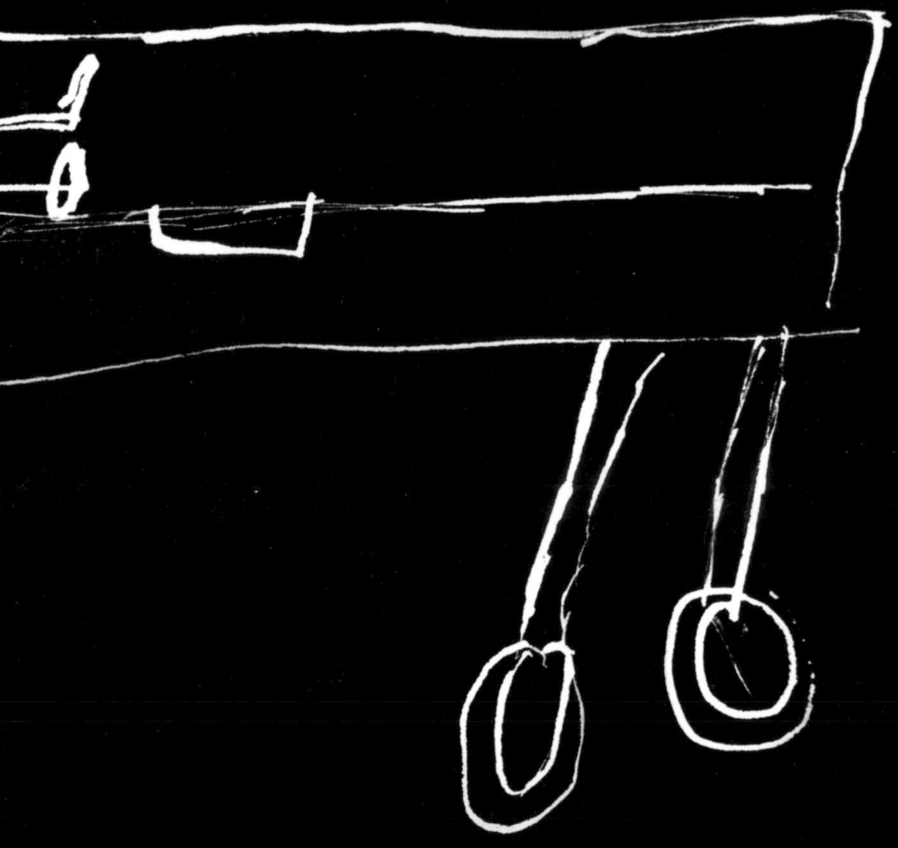

This is a picture of Margarete. I went to her funeral on Friday. Margarete's daughter Anne got upset. So did I. I took it hard. I helped carry Margarete's coffin.

Cheryl Strayed

The Love of My Life

The first time I cheated on my husband, my mother had been dead for exactly one week. I was in a cafe in Minneapolis watching a man. He watched me back. He was slightly pudgy, with jet black hair and skin so white it looked as if he'd powdered it. He stood and walked to my table and sat down without asking. He wanted to know if I had a cat. I folded my hands on the table, steadying myself; I was shaking, nervous at what I would do. I was raw, fragile, vicious with grief. I would do anything.

"Yes," I said.

"I thought so," he said slowly. He didn't take his eyes off me. I rolled the rings around on my fingers. I was wearing two wedding bands, my own and my mother's. I'd taken hers off her hand after she died. It was nothing fancy: sterling silver, thick and braided.

"You look like the kind of girl who has a cat."

"How's that?" I asked.

He didn't answer. He just kept looking at me steadily, as if he knew everything about me, as if he owned me. I felt distinctly that he might be a murderer.

"Are you mature?" he asked intently.

I didn't know what he meant. I still don't. I told him that I was.

"Well then prove it and walk down the street with me."

We left the cafe, his hand on my arm. I had monstrous bruises on my knees from how I'd fallen on them after I walked into my mother's hospital room and first saw her dead. He liked these. He said he'd been admiring them from across the room. They were what had drawn him to me. Also, he liked my boots. He thought I looked intriguing. He thought I looked mature. I was twenty-two. He was older, possibly thirty. I didn't ask his name; he didn't ask mine. I walked with him to a parking lot behind a building. He stopped and pressed me against a brick wall and kissed me, but then he wasn't kissing me. He was biting me. He bit my lips so hard I screamed.

"You lying cunt," he whispered into my ear. "You're not mature." He flung me away from him and left.

I stood, unmoving, stunned. The inside of my mouth began to bleed softly. Tears filled my eyes. I want my mother, I thought. My mother is dead. I thought this every hour of every day for a very long time: I want my mother. My mother is dead.

It was only a kiss, and barely that, but it was, anyway, a crossing. When I was a child I witnessed a leaf unfurl in a single motion. One second it was a fist, the next an open hand. I never forgot it, seeing so much happen so fast. And this was like that—the end of one thing, the beginning of another: my life as a slut.

When my mother was diagnosed with cancer, my husband, Mark, and I took an unspoken sexual hiatus. When she died seven weeks later, I couldn't bear for Mark to touch me. His hands on my body made me weep. He went down on me in the gentlest of ways. He didn't expect anything in return. He didn't make me feel that I had to come. I would soak in a hot bath, and he would lean into it to touch me. He wanted to make me feel good, better. He loved me, and he had loved my mother. Mark and I were an insanely young, insanely happy, insanely in-love married couple. He wanted to help. No, no, no, I said, but then sometimes I relented. I closed my eyes and tried to relax. I breathed deep and attempted to fake it. I rolled over on my stomach so I wouldn't have to look at him. He fucked me and I sobbed uncontrollably.

"Keep going," I said to him. "Just finish." But he wouldn't. He couldn't. He loved me. Which was mysteriously, unfortunately, precisely the problem.

I wanted my mother.

We aren't supposed to want our mothers that way, with the pining intensity of sexual love, but I did, and if I couldn't have her, I couldn't have anything. Most of all I couldn't have pleasure, not even for a moment. I was bereft, in agony, destroyed over her death. To experience sexual joy, it seemed, would have been to negate that reality. And more, it would have been to betray my mother, to be disloyal to the person she had been to me. I'd seen my father break her nose, her finger, the tiny bones around the socket of her left eye. My stepfather had loved her and been a good husband to her for ten years, but shortly after she died, he'd fallen in love with someone else. His new girlfriend and her two daughters moved into my mother's house, took her photos off the walls, erased her. I needed my stepfather to be the kind of man who would suffer for my mother, unable to go on, who would carry a torch. And if he wouldn't do it, I would.

We are not allowed this. We are allowed to be deeply into basketball, or Buddhism, or *Star Trek,* or jazz, but we are not allowed to be deeply sad. Grief is a thing that we are encouraged to "let go of," to "move on from," and we are told specifically how this should be done. Countless well-intentioned friends, distant family members, hospital workers, and strangers I met at parties recited the famous five stages of grief to me: denial, anger, bargaining, depression, and acceptance. I was alarmed by how many people knew them, how deeply this single definition of the grieving process had permeated our cultural consciousness. Not only was I supposed to feel these five things, I was meant to feel them in that order and for a fairly prescribed amount of time.

I did not deny. I did not get angry. I didn't bargain, become depressed, or accept. I fucked. I sucked. Not my husband, but people I hardly knew, and in that I found a glimmer of relief. The people I messed around with did not have names; they had titles: the Prematurely Graying Wilderness Guide, the Technically Still a Virgin Mexican Teenager, the Formerly Gay Organic Farmer, the Quietly Perverse Poet, the Failing but Still Trying Massage Therapist, the Terribly Large Texas Bull Rider, the Recently Unemployed Graduate of Juilliard, the Actually Pretty Famous Drummer Guy. Most of these people were men; some were women. With them, I was not in mourning; I wasn't even me. I was happy and sexy and impetuous and fun. I was wild and enigmatic and terrifically good in bed. I didn't care about them or have orgasms. We didn't have heart-to-heart talks. I asked them questions about their lives, and they told me everything and asked few questions in return; they knew nothing about me. Because of this, most of them believed they were falling instantly, madly in love with me.

I did what I did with these people, and then I returned home to Mark, weak-kneed and wet, bleary-eyed and elated. I'm alive, I thought in that giddy, post-sex daze. My mother's death has taught me to live each day as if it were my last, I said to myself, latching onto the nearest cliché, and the one least true. I didn't stop to think: What if it had been my last day? Did I wish to be sucking the cock of an Actually Pretty Famous Drummer Guy? I didn't think to ask that because I didn't want to think. When I did think, I thought, I cannot continue to live without my mother.

I lied—sometimes to the people I messed around with (some of them, if they'd known I was married, would not have wanted to mess around with me), but mostly to Mark. I was not proud of myself. I was in love with him and wanted to be faithful to him and wanted to want to have sex with him, but something in me wouldn't let me do it. We got into the habit of fucking in the middle of the night, both of us waking from a sound sleep to the reality of our bodies wet and hard and in the act. The sex lasted about thirty seconds, and we would almost always both come. It was intensely hot and strange and surreal and darkly funny and ultimately depressing. We never knew who started it. Neither of us recalled waking, reaching for each other. It was a shard of passion, and we held on to it. For a while it got us through.

We like to say how things are, perhaps because we hope that's how they might actually be. We attempt to name, identify, and define the most mysterious of matters: sex, love, marriage, monogamy, infidelity, death, loss, grief. We want these things to have an order, an internal logic, and we also want them to be connected to one another. We want it to be true that if we cheat on our spouse, it means we no longer want to be married to him or her. We want it to be true that if someone we love dies, we simply have to pass through a series of phases, like an emotional obstacle course from which we will emerge happy and content, unharmed and unchanged.

After my mother died, everyone I knew wanted to tell me either about the worst breakup they'd had or all the people they'd known who'd died. I listened to a long, traumatic story about a girlfriend who suddenly moved to Ohio and to stories of grandfathers and old friends and people who lived down the block who were no longer among us. Rarely was this helpful.

Occasionally I came across people who'd had the experience of losing someone whose death made them think, *I cannot continue to live*. I recognized these people: their postures, where they rested their eyes as they spoke, the expressions they let onto their faces and the ones they kept off. These people consoled me beyond measure. I felt profoundly connected to them, as if we were a tribe.

It's surprising how relatively few of them there were. People don't die anymore, not the way they used to. Children survive childhood; women, the labors of birth; men, their work. We survive influenza and infection, cancer and heart attacks. We keep living on and on: 80, 90, 103. We live younger, too; frightfully premature babies are cloistered and coddled and shepherded through. My mother lived to the age of forty-five and never lost anyone who was truly beloved to her. Of course, she knew many people who had died, but none who made her wake to the thought: *I cannot continue to live.*

And there is a difference. Dying is not your girlfriend moving to Ohio. Grief is not the day after your neighbor's funeral, when you felt extremely blue. It is impolite to say this. We act as if all losses are equal. It is un-American to behave otherwise: we live in a democracy of sorrow. Every emotion felt is validated and judged to be as true as any other.

But what does this do to us: this refusal to quantify love, loss, grief? Jewish tradition states that one is considered a mourner when one of eight people dies: father, mother, sister, brother, husband, wife, son, or daughter. This definition doesn't fulfill the needs of today's diverse and far-flung affections; indeed, it probably never did. It leaves out the step-relations, the long-term lovers, the chosen family of a tight circle of friends; and it includes the blood relations we perhaps never honestly loved. But its intentions are true. And, undeniably, for most of us that list of eight does come awfully close. We love and care for oodles of people, but only a few of them, if they died, would make us believe we could not continue to live. Imagine if there were a boat upon which you could put only four people, and everyone else known and beloved to you would then cease to exist. Who would you put on that boat? It would be painful, but how quickly you would decide: You and you and you and you, get in. The rest of you, good-bye.

For years, I was haunted by the idea of this imaginary boat of life; by the desire to exchange my mother's fate for one of the many living people I knew. I would be sitting across the table from a dear friend. I loved her, him, each one of these people. Some I said I loved like family. But I would look at them and think, Why couldn't it have been you who had died instead? You, good-bye.

I didn't often sleep with Mark, but I slept beside him, or tried to. I dreamed incessantly about my mother. There was a theme. Two or three times a week she made me kill her. She commanded me to do it, and I sobbed and got down on my knees, begging her not to make me, but she would not relent. In each dream, like a good daughter, I ultimately complied. I tied her to a tree in our front yard, poured gasoline over her head, and lit her on fire. I made her run down the dirt road that passed by the house where I'd grown up, and I ran her over with my truck; I dragged her body, caught on a jagged piece of metal underneath, until it came loose, and then I put my truck in reverse and ran her over again. I took a miniature baseball bat and beat her to death with it. I forced her into a hole I'd dug and kicked dirt and stones on top of her and buried her alive. These dreams were not surreal. They took place in the plain light of day. They were the documentary films of my subconscious and felt as real to me as life. My truck was really my truck; our front yard was our actual front yard; the miniature baseball bat sat in our closet among the umbrellas. I didn't wake from these dreams crying; I woke shrieking. Mark grabbed me and held me. He wetted a washcloth with cool water and put it over my face. These dreams went on for months, years, and I couldn't shake them. I also couldn't shake my infidelities. I couldn't shake my grief.

What was there to do with me? What did those around me do? They did what I would have done—what we all do when faced with the prospect of someone else's sorrow: they tried to talk me out of it, neutralize it, tamp it down, make it relative and therefore not so bad. We narrate our own lesser stories of loss in an attempt to demonstrate that the sufferer is not really so alone. We make grossly inexact comparisons and hope that they will do. In short, we insist on ignoring the precise nature of deep loss because there is nothing we can do to change it, and by doing so we strip it of its meaning, its weight, its own fiercely original power.

The first person I knew who died was a casual friend of my mother's, named Barb. Barb was in her early thirties, and I was ten. Her hair was brown and shoulder length, her skin clear and smooth as a bar of soap. She had the kind of tall body that made you acutely aware of the presence of its bones: a long, knobby nose; wide, thin hips; a jaw too pointed to be considered beautiful. Barb got into her car and started the engine. Her car was parked in a garage and all the doors were closed and she had stuffed a Minnesota Vikings cap into a small hole in the garage wall to make it even more airtight. My mother explained this to me in detail: the Vikings hat, the sitting in the car with the garage door closed on purpose. I was more curious than sad. But in the months that followed, I thought of Barb often. I came to care for her. I nurtured an inflated sense of my connection to her.

Recently, another acquaintance of mine died. He was beautiful and young and free-spirited and one hell of a painter. He went hiking one day on the Oregon coast and was never seen again. Over the course of my life, I have known other people who've died. Some of them have died the way we hoped they would—old, content, at their time; others, the way we hoped they wouldn't—by murder or suicide, in accidents, or too young of illnesses. The deaths of those people made me sad, afraid, and angry; they made me question the fairness of the world, the existence of God, and the nature of my own existence. But they did not make me suffer. They did not make me think, *I cannot continue to live.* In fact, in their deaths I felt more deeply connected to them, not because I grieved them, but because I wanted to attach myself to what is interesting. It is interesting to be in a Chinese restaurant and see a poster of the smiling face of an acquaintance, who is one hell of a painter, plastered on the front door. It is interesting to be able to say, I know him, to feel that a part of something important and awful and big. The more connections like this we have, the more interesting we are.

There was nothing interesting to me about my mother's death. I did not want to attach myself to it. It was her life that I clung to—her very, very interesting life. When she died, she was about to graduate from college, and so was I. We had started together. Her college was in Duluth, mine in Minneapolis. After a lifetime of struggle and sacrifice, my mother was coming into her own. She wanted to major in six subjects, but the school wouldn't let her, so she settled on two.

My mother had become pregnant when she was nineteen and immediately married my father, a steelworker in western Pennsylvania when the steel plants were shutting down; a coal miner's son born about the time that the coal was running out. After three children and nine years of violence, my mother left him. My father had recently moved us to a small town near Minneapolis in pursuit of a job prospect. When they divorced, he went back to Pennsylvania, but my mother stayed. She worked as a waitress and in a factory that made small plastic containers that would eventually hold toxic liquids. We lived in apartment complexes full of single mothers whose children sat on the edges of grocery-store parking lots. We received free government cheese and powdered milk, food stamps, and welfare checks.

After a few years, my mother met my stepfather, and when he fell off a roof on the job and hurt his back, they took the twelve-thousand-dollar settlement and spent every penny on forty acres of land in northern Minnesota. There was no house; no one had ever had a house on this land. My stepfather built a one-room tar-paper shack, and we lived in it while he and my mother built us a house from scrap wood and trees they cut down with the help of my brother, my sister, and me. We moved into the new house on Halloween night. We didn't have electricity or running water or a phone or an indoor toilet. Years passed, and my mother was happy—happier than she'd ever been—but still, she hungered for more.

Just before she died, she was thinking about becoming a costume designer or a professor of history. She was profoundly interested in the American pioneers, the consciousness of animals, and the murders of women believed to be witches. She was looking into graduate school, though she feared that she was too old. She couldn't believe, really, that she was even getting a degree. I'd had to convince her to go to college. She'd always read books but thought that she was basically stupid. To prepare, she shadowed me during my senior year of high school, doing all the homework that I was assigned. She photocopied my assignment sheets, wrote the papers I had to write, read the books. I graded her work, using my teacher's marks as a guide. My mother was a shaky student at best.

She went to college and earned straight A's.

She died on a Monday during spring break of our senior year. After her funeral, I immediately went back to school because she had begged me to do so. It was the beginning of a new quarter. In most of my classes, we were asked to introduce ourselves and say what we had done over the break. "My name is Cheryl," I said. "I went to Mexico." I lied not to protect myself, but because it would have been rude not to. To express loss on that level is to cross a boundary, violate personal space, to impose emotion in a nonemotional place.

We did not always treat grief this way. Nearly every culture has a history, and some still have a practice, of mourning rituals, many of which involve changes in the dress or appearance of those in grief. The wearing of black clothing or mourning jewelry, hair cutting, and body scarification or ritual tattooing all made the grief-stricken immediately visible to the people around them. Although it is true that these practices were sometimes ridiculously restrictive and not always in the best interest of the mourner, it is also true that they gave us something of value. They imposed evidence of loss on a community and forced that community to acknowledge it. If, as a culture, we don't bear witness to grief, the burden of loss is placed entirely upon the bereaved, while the rest of us avert our eyes and wait for those in mourning to stop being sad, to let go, to move on, to cheer up. And if they don't—if they have loved too deeply, if they do wake each morning thinking, *I cannot continue to live*—well, then we pathologize their pain; we call their suffering a disease.

We do not help them: we tell them that they need to get help.

Nobody knew about my sexual escapades. I kept waiting for them to cure me, or for something to cure me of them. Two years had passed since my mother's death, and I still couldn't live without her, but I also couldn't live with myself. I decided to tell Mark the truth. The list was long. I practiced what I would say, trying to say it in the least painful way. It was impossible. It was time.

Mark sat in the living room playing his guitar. He was working as an organizer for a nonprofit environmental agency, but his real ambition was to be a musician. He had just formed his first band and was writing a new song, finding it as he went along. I told him that I had something to tell him and that it was not going to be easy. He stopped playing and looked at me, but he kept his hands on the guitar, holding it gently. This man whom I'd loved for years, had loved enough to marry, who had been with me through my mother's death and the aftermath, who'd offered to go down on me in the gentlest of ways, who would do anything, anything for me, listened as I told him about the Technically Still a Virgin Mexican Teenager, the Prematurely Graying Wilderness Guide, the Recently Unemployed Graduate of Juilliard.

He fell straight forward out of his chair onto his knees and then face down onto the floor. His guitar went with him and it made clanging, strumming, hollow sounds as it went. I attempted to rub his back. He screamed for me to get my hands off him.

Later, spent, he calmly told me that he wanted to kill me. He promised he would if I'd given him AIDS.

Women are used to the bad behavior of men. We eroticize and congratulate it and in return we brace ourselves to be dissatisfied, duped, deceived, dumped, and dicked around. I had broken the rules. Even among our group of alternative, left-wing, hippy, punk-rock, artsy politicos, I was viewed by many as the worst kind of woman: the whore, the slut, the adulteress, the liar, the cheat. And to top it all off, I had wronged the best of men. Mark had been faithful to me all along.

He moved out and rented a room in the attic of a house. Slowly we told our friends. The Insanely Young, Insanely Happy, Insanely In-Love Married Couple was coming apart. First, they were in disbelief. Next, they were mad, or several of them—not at us, but at me. One of my dearest friends took the photograph of me she kept in a frame in her bedroom, ripped it in half, and mailed it to me. Another made out with Mark. When I was hurt and jealous about this I was told that perhaps it was exactly what I needed: a taste of my own medicine. I couldn't rightfully disagree, but still my heart was broken. I lay alone in our bed feeling myself almost levitate from the pain.

We couldn't decide whether to get divorced or not. We went to a marriage counselor and tried to work it out. Months later, we stopped the counseling and put the decision on hold. Mark began to date. He dated one of those women who, instead of a purse, carried a teeny-weeny backpack. He dated a biologist who also happened to be a model. He dated a woman I'd met once who'd made an enormous pot of very good chili of which I'd eaten two bowls.

His sex life temporarily cured me of mine. I didn't fuck anyone, and I got crabs from a pair of used jeans I'd bought at a thrift store. I spent several days eradicating the translucent bugs from my person and my apartment. Then the Teeny-Weeny

Backpack Woman started to play tambourine in Mark's budding band. I couldn't take it anymore. I went to visit a friend in Portland and decided to stay. I met a man: a Punk Rocker Soon to Be Hopelessly Held Under the Thumb of Heroin. I found him remotely enchanting. I found heroin more enchanting. Quickly, without intending to, I slipped into a habit. Here, I thought. At last.

By now Mark pretty much hated me, but he showed up in Portland anyway and dragged me back home. He set a futon down for me in the corner of his room and let me stay until I could find a job and an apartment. At night we lay in our separate beds fighting about why we loved and hated each other so much. We made love once. He was cheating on someone for the first time. He was back with the Biologist Who Also Happened to Be a Model, and he was cheating on her with his own wife. Hmmm, we thought. What's this?

But it was not to be. I was sorry. He was sorry. I wasn't getting my period. I was really, really, really sorry. He was really, really, really mad. I was pregnant by the Punk Rocker Soon to Be Hopelessly Held Under the Thumb of Heroin. We were at the end of the line. We loved each other, but love was not enough. We had become the Insanely Young, Insanely Sad, Insanely Messed-Up Married Couple. He wanted me gone. He pulled the blankets from my futon in his room and flung them down the stairs.

I sat for five hours in the office of an extremely overbooked abortion doctor waiting for my abortion. The temperature in the room was somewhere around fifty-six degrees. It was packed with microscopically pregnant women who were starving because we had been ordered not to eat since the night before. The assistants of the Extremely Overbooked Abortion Doctor did not want to clean up any puke.

At last, I was brought into a room. I was told to undress and hold a paper sheet around myself. I was given a plastic breast and instructed to palpate it, searching for a lump of cancer hidden within its depths, while I waited for my abortion. I waited, naked, palpating, finding the cancer over and over again. The Extremely Overbooked Abortion Doctor needed to take an emergency long-distance phone call. An hour went by. Finally, she came in.

I lay back on the table and stared at a poster on the ceiling of a Victorian mansion that was actually composed of miniature photographs of the faces of a hundred famous and important women in history. I was told to lie still and peacefully for a while and then to stand up very quickly and pull my underwear on while an assistant of the Extremely Overbooked Abortion Doctor held me up. I was told not to have sex for a very long time. The procedure cost me four hundred dollars, half of which I was ridiculously hoping to receive from the Punk Rocker Soon to Be Hopelessly Held Under the Thumb of Heroin. I went home to my new apartment. The light on my answering machine said I had three messages. I lay on my couch, ill and weak and bleeding, and listened to them.

There was a message from the Punk Rocker Soon to Be Hopelessly Held Under the Thumb of Heroin, only he didn't say anything. Instead he played a recording of a Radiohead song that went, "You're so fucking special / I wish I was special / but I'm a creep / I'm a weirdo."

There was a message that consisted of a thirty-second dial tone because the person had hung up.

There was a message from Mark wondering how I was.

My mother had been dead for three years. I was twenty-five. I had intended, by this point in my life, to have a title of my own: The Incredibly Talented and Extraordinarily Brilliant and Successful Writer. I had planned to be the kind of woman whose miniature photographed face was placed artfully into a poster of a Victorian mansion that future generations of women would concentrate on while their cervixes were forcefully dilated by the tip of a plastic tube about the size of a drinking straw and the beginnings of babies were sucked out of them. I wasn't anywhere close. I was a pile of shit.

Despite my mother's hopes, I had not graduated from college. I pushed my way numbly through that last quarter, but I did not, in the end, receive my bachelor's degree because I had neglected to do one assignment: write a five-page paper about a short story called "The Nose," by Nicolay Gogol. It's a rollicking tale about a man who wakes up one morning and realizes that his nose is gone. Indeed, his nose has not only left him but has also dressed in the man's clothes, taken his carriage, and gone gadding about town. The man does what anyone would do if he woke up and found that his nose was gone: he goes out to find it. I thought the story was preposterous and incomprehensible. Your nose does not just up and leave you. I was told not to focus on the unreality of it. I was told that the story was actually about vanity, pretentiousness, and opportunism in nineteenth-century Russia. Alternately, I could interpret it as a commentary upon either male sexual impotency or divine Immaculate Conception. I tried dutifully to pick one of these concepts and write about it, but I couldn't do it, and I could not discuss with my professor why this was so. In my myopic, grief-addled state, the story seemed to me to be about something else entirely: a man who woke up one morning and no longer had a nose and then went looking for it. There was no subtext to me. It was simply a story about what it was about, which is to say, the absurd and arbitrary nature of disappearance, our hungry ache to resurrect what we've lost, and the bald truth that the impossible can become possible faster than anyone dreams.

All the time that I'd been thinking, *I cannot continue to live,* I also had the opposite thought, which was by far the more unbearable: that I would continue to live, and that every day for the rest of my life I would have to live without my mother. Sometimes I forgot this, like a trick of the brain, a primitive survival mechanism. Somewhere, floating on the surface of my subconscious, I believed—I still believe—that if I endured without her for one year, or five years, or ten years, or twenty, that she would be given back to me; that her absence was a ruse, a darkly comic literary device, a terrible and surreal dream.

What does it mean to heal? To move on? To let go? Whatever it means, it is usually said and not done, and the people who talk about it the most have almost never had to do it. I cannot say anything about healing, but I can say that something happened as I lay on the couch bleeding and listening to my answering machine play the Radiohead song and then the dial tone and then Mark's voice wondering how I was: I thought about writing the five-page paper about the story of the man who lost his nose. I thought about calling Mark and asking him to marry me again. I thought about becoming the Incredibly Talented and Extraordinarily Brilliant and Successful Writer. I thought about taking a very long walk. I decided to do all of these things immediately, but I did not move from the couch. I didn't set out the next day either to write the paper about the guy who lost his nose. I didn't call Mark and ask him to marry me again. I didn't start to work on becoming the Incredibly Talented and Extraordinarily Brilliant and Successful Writer. Instead I ordered pizza and listened to that one Lucinda Williams CD that I could not ever get enough of, and, after a few days, I went back to my job waiting tables. I let my uterus heal and then slept at least once with each of the five guys who worked in the kitchen. I did, however, hold on to one intention, and I set about fulfilling it: I was going to take a long walk. One thousand six hundred and thirty-eight miles, to be exact. Alone.

Mark and I had filed the papers for our divorce. My stepfather was going to marry the woman he'd started dating immediately after my mother died. I wanted to get out of Minnesota. I needed a new life and, unoriginally, I was going west to find it. I decided to hike the Pacific Crest Trail—a wilderness trail that runs along the backbone of the Sierra Nevada and the Cascade Mountains, from Mexico to Canada. I decided to hike a large portion of it—from the Mojave Desert in California to the Columbia River at the Oregon-Washington border. It would take me four months. I'd grown up in the country, done a good amount of camping, and taken a few weekend backpacking trips, but I had a lot to learn: how, for example, to read a topographical map, ford a river, handle an ice axe, navigate using a compass, and avoid being struck by lightning. Everyone who knew me thought that I was nuts. I proceeded anyway, researching, reading maps, dehydrating food and packing it into plastic bags and then into boxes that would be mailed at roughly two-week intervals to the ranger stations and post offices I'd occasionally pass near.

I packed my possessions and stored them in my stepfather's barn. I took off my wedding ring and put it into a small velvet box and moved my mother's wedding ring from my right hand to my left. I was going to drive to Portland first and then leave my truck with a friend and fly to LA and take a bus to the start of the trail. I drove through the flatlands and Badlands and Black Hills of South Dakota, positive that I'd made a vast mistake.

Deep in the night, I pulled into a small camping area in the Big Horn Mountains of Wyoming and slept in the back of my truck. In the morning I climbed out to the sight of a field of blue flowers that went right up to the Tongue River. I had the place to myself. It was spring and still cold, but I felt compelled anyway to go into the river. I decided I would perform something like a baptism to initiate this new part of my life. I took my clothes off and plunged in. The water was like ice, so cold it hurt. I dove under one time, two times, three times, then dashed out and dried off and dressed. As I walked back to my truck I noticed my hand: my mother's wedding ring was gone.

At first I couldn't believe it. I had believed that if I lost one thing, that I would then be protected from losing another; that my mother's death would inoculate me against further loss. It is an indefensible belief, but it was there, the same way I believed that if I endured long enough, my mother would be returned to me.

A ring is such a small thing, such a very small thing.

I went down on my hands and knees and searched for it. I patted every inch of ground where I had walked. I searched the back of my truck and my pockets, but

I knew. I knew that the ring had come off in the river. Of course it had; what did I expect? I went to the edge of the water and thought about going back in, diving under again and again until I found it, but it was a useless idea, and I was defeated by it before I even began. I sat down on the edge of the water and cried. Tears, tears, so many kinds of tears, so many ways of crying. I had collected them, mastered them; I was a priestess, a virtuoso of crying.

I sat in the mud on the bank of the river for a long time and waited for the river to give the ring back to me. I waited and thought about everything. I thought about Mark and my boat of life. I thought what I would say to him then, now, forever: You, get in. I thought about the Formerly Gay Organic Farmer and the Quietly Perverse Poet and the Terribly Large Texas Bull Rider and the Five Line Cooks I Had on Separate Occasions Over the Course of One Month. I thought about how I was never again going to sleep with anyone who had a title instead of a name. I was sick of it. Sick of fucking, of wanting to fuck the wrong people and not wanting to fuck the right ones. I thought about how if you lose a ring in a river, you are never going to get it back, no matter how badly you want it or how long you wait.

I leaned forward and put my hands into the water and held them flat and open beneath the surface. The soft current made rivulets over my bare fingers. I was no longer married to Mark. I was no longer married to my mother. I was no longer married to my mother. I couldn't believe that this thought had never occurred to me before: that it was her I'd been wed to all along; and I knew that I couldn't be faithful any more.

If this were fiction, what would happen next is that the woman would stand up and get into her truck and drive away. It wouldn't matter that the woman lost her mother's wedding ring, even though it was gone to her forever, because the loss would mean something else entirely: that what was gone now was actually her sorrow and the shackles of grief that had held her down. And in this loss she would see, and the reader would know, that the woman had been in error all along. That, indeed, the love she had for her mother was too much love, really; too much love and also too much sorrow. She would realize this and get on with her life. There would be what happened in the story and also everything it stood for: the river, representing life's constant changing; the tiny blue flowers, beauty; the spring air, rebirth. All of these symbols would collide and mean that the woman was actually lucky to have lost the ring, and not just to have lost it, but to have loved it, to have ached for it, and to have had it taken from her forever. The story would end, and you would know that she was the better for it. That she was wiser, stronger, more interesting, and most of all, finally starting down her path to glory. I would show you the leaf when it unfurls in a single motion: the end of one thing, the beginning of another. And you would know the answers to all the questions without being told. Did she ever write that five-page paper about the guy who lost his nose? Did she ask Mark to marry her again? Did she stop sleeping with people who had titles instead of names? Did she manage to walk 1,638 miles? Did she get to work and become the Incredibly Talented and Extraordinarily Brilliant and Successful Writer? You'd believe the answers to all these questions to be yes. I would have given you what you wanted then: to be a witness to a healing.

But this isn't fiction. Sometimes a story is not about anything except what it is about. Sometimes you wake up and find that you actually have lost your nose. Losing my mother's wedding ring in the Tongue River was not OK. I did not feel better for it. It was not a passage or a release. What happened is that I lost my mother's wedding ring and I understood that I was not going to get it back, that it would be yet another piece of my mother that I would not have for all the days of my life, and I understood that I could not bear this truth, but that I would have to.

Healing is a small and ordinary and very burnt thing. And it's one thing and one thing only: it's doing what you have to do. It's what I did then and there. I stood up and got into my truck and drove away from a part of my mother. The part of her that had been my lover, my wife, my first love, my true love, the love of my life.

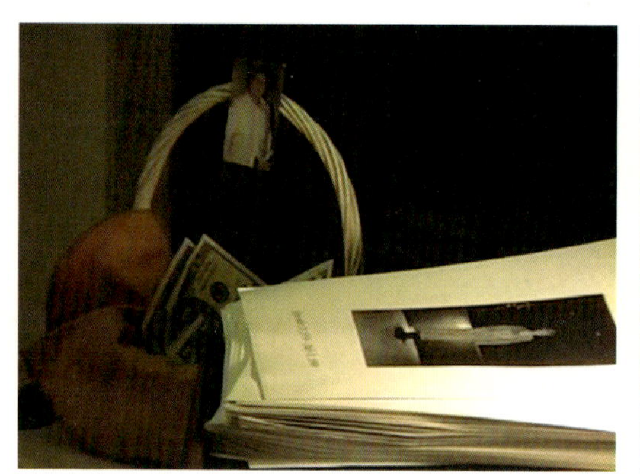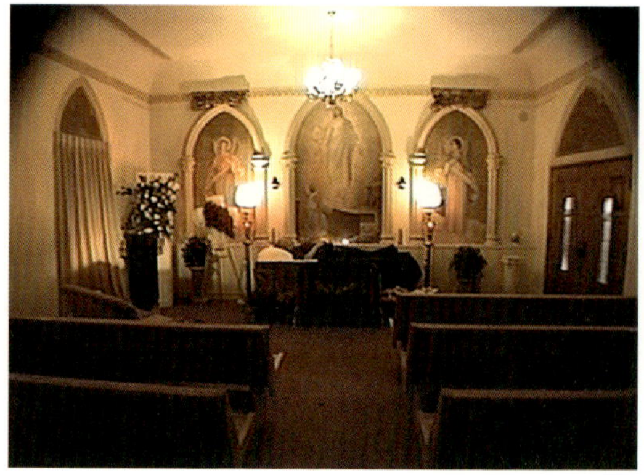

Nakkali Rupta

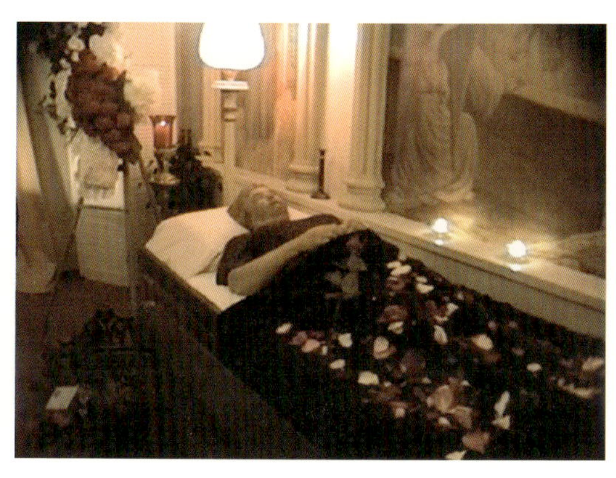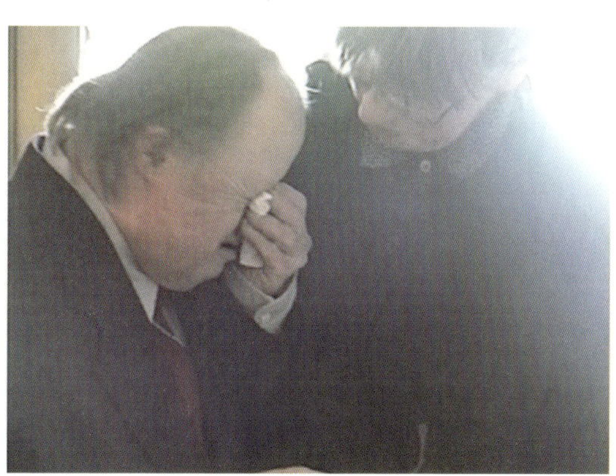

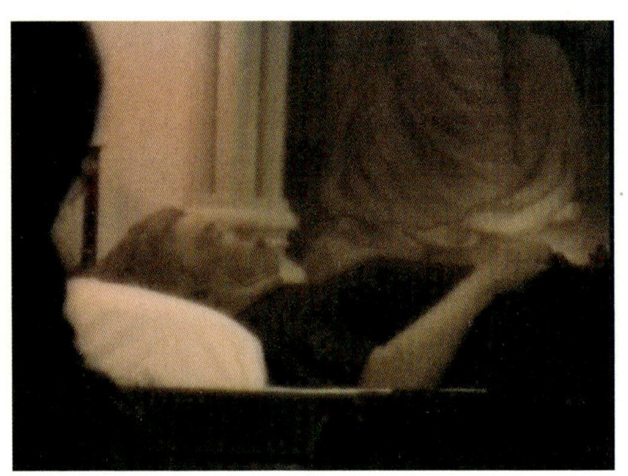 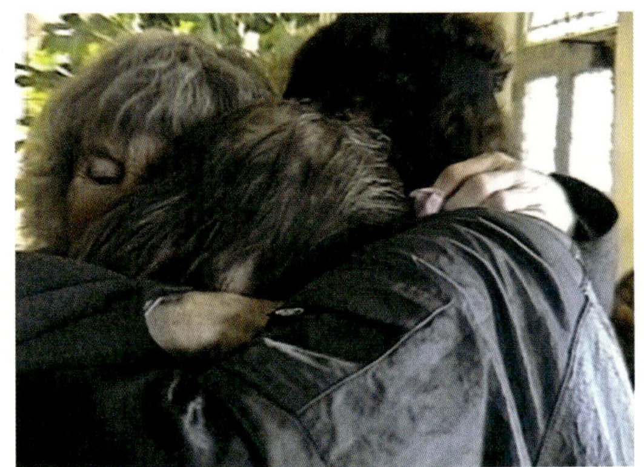

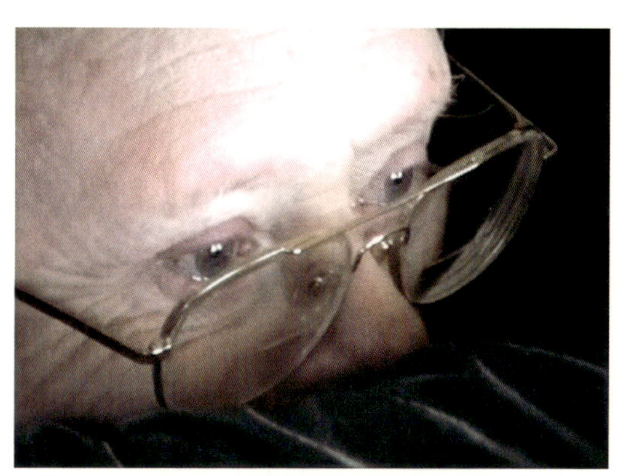

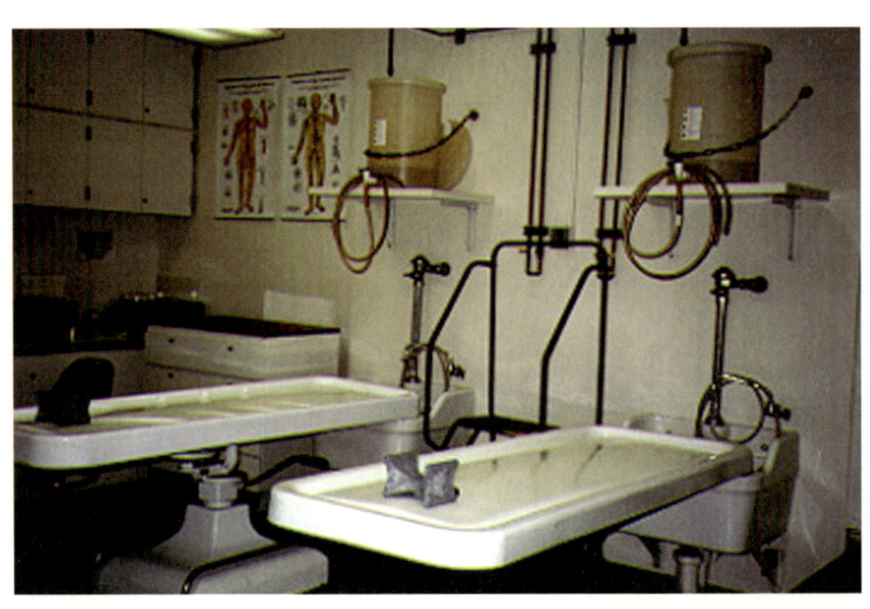

Albert Baris

Q. How long does embalming preserve the remains?

A. We must understand that embalming is only a temporary hindrance to decomposition. Decomposition is a natural and scientific process that begins immediately after death. In order for decomposition to take place you need to have two elements present . . . air and water, which make ideal hosts for aerobic and anaerobic bacteria. Logically, it would make sense that if we can stop these two elements from coming in contact with the remains, then we can stop decomposition from taking place. The only way to retard decomposition 100% is to vacuum seal the remains—logical and scientific, but not practical. Other factors that come into play are:

Mode of death—Traumatic deaths do not embalm as well as a "natural cause" death, due to the breakdown of circulation.

Weight of remains—The more weight, the more water the remains contain.

Type of casket and outer enclosure—A protective casket and vault will seal out more water and air than a non-protective.

Soil and climate conditions—A dry, sandy soil cemetery is better than a wet, clay soil cemetery due to water retention.

Skill and thoroughness of the embalmer—As in any other profession, shortcuts and inferior materials will make for a shoddy job. If the funeral director takes pride in his work, then he will do a more thorough embalming using only the highest quality materials available to him.

No funeral director should warrant to a family, that by embalming or buying certain merchandise, the remains will last forever . . . this is NOT true. It may hinder the decomposition process for a short time . . . but nothing is forever.

In summary, this question is almost impossible to give a definite answer, but I hope the answer gives you further insight as to how and why these factors can determine the length of time a remains will last after death.

Q. What causes the face and hands to swell?

A. Again, there are many factors that determine this. The primary cause is usually water retention due to kidney failure. There are many times that you may go to calling hours and notice this, but unless you were a close family member, at the decedents side at death, you really don't know whether that swelling was apparent before death or not. Another cause may have been due to a blood clot in one of the facial arteries or veins. Embalming makes use of the circulatory system, and if there is a blockage, then the chemicals that are being injected cannot flow smoothly . . . usually a good funeral director can notice this before it gets out of hand, and work other ways around this to prevent swelling. A third factor to consider is interaction of certain medications. Cancer patients are usually given these types of medications, and one of the side effects is what is commonly called "moon face." The face of the patient swells and "rounds out." This effect is hardly ever removed by embalming. A final factor to take into consideration is traumatic death. An accident, a fall, some trauma to the face will cause swelling to occur due to the disruption of the circulatory system.

Q. How do you keep the eyes and mouth closed?
A. Eyes are kept closed in one of two ways. We use a small plastic oval-shaped eye cap. These eye caps are a bit larger than a contact lens, and have tiny grippers on the surface which grasp the insides of the upper and lower eyelids. Another method would be to apply a small line of adhesive on the top of the lower lid, and bring both lids to close naturally.

The mouth is kept closed by taking what is known as a mandible-septum suture. A suture is taken under the lower lip's septum and passing it through the nasal septum, then closing the jaw by tying the two ends of the suture thread together. Another way is to use what is known as a injector needle gun. This gun places one wire into the lower jaw, and another into the upper jaw. The two wires are then twisted closed. I believe these are two most common ways of closing the mouth securely.

Q. Have you ever had a body sit up or spasm while you were embalming?
A. No, and I have never heard of this happening to another funeral director either. I think this stems from stories back in the 18th century, when there may have been times that the person was pronounced dead, but in all reality was not.

Q. Do you use special cosmetics?
A. Yes, we use mortuary cosmetics, although regular commercial cosmetics may also be used. The benefit of a mortuary cosmetic is its ability to hide certain imperfections or marks that may be on the person's skin.

Q. Can I watch you do an embalming?
A. Laws usually prohibit anyone except for staff of the funeral home, doctors, registered nurses or immediate family members from being in the preparation room during the embalming process.

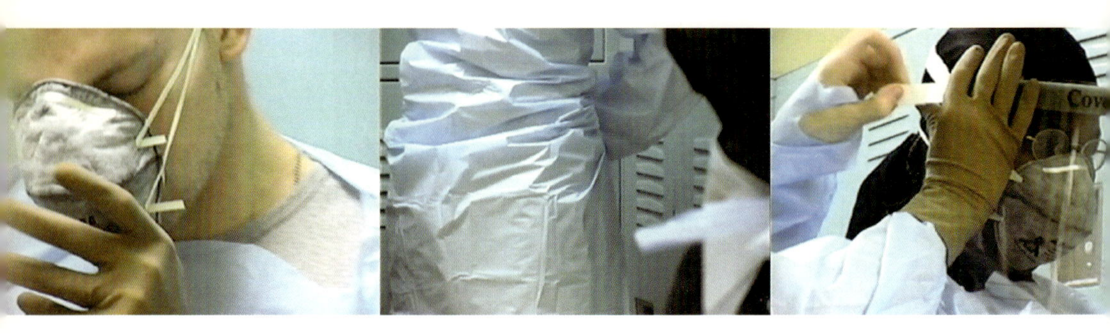

Elizabeth Westrate

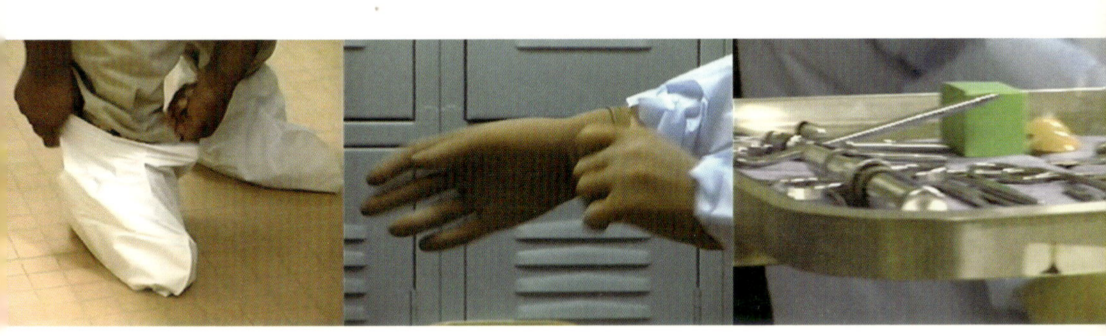

ATTACH TO TOE
DANGER
FIRE
BLANK

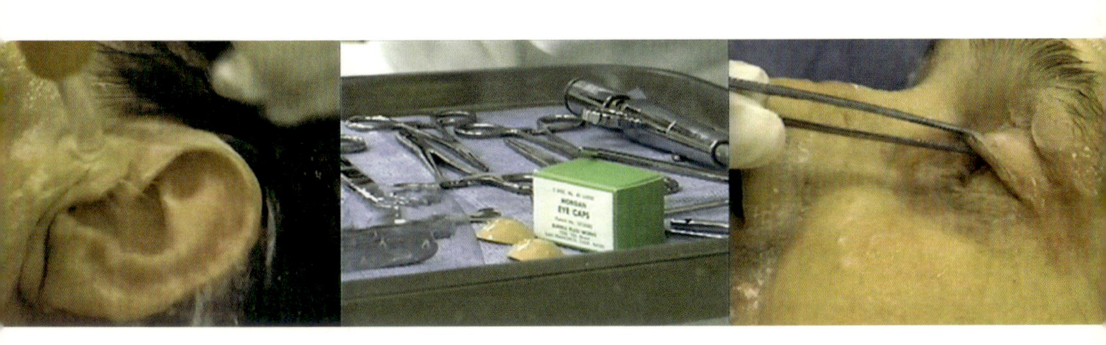

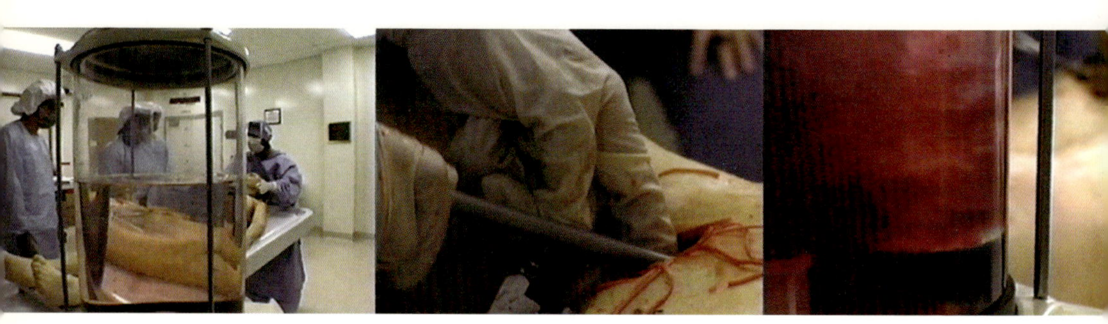

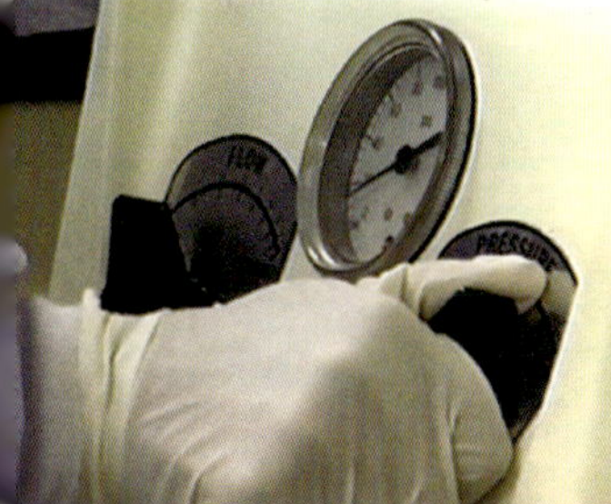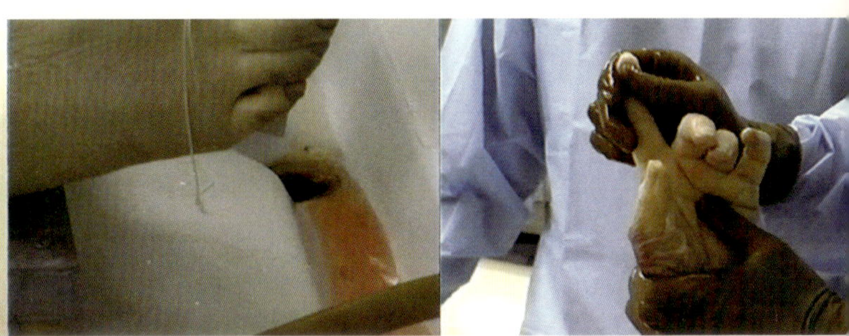

Gordon Shepard

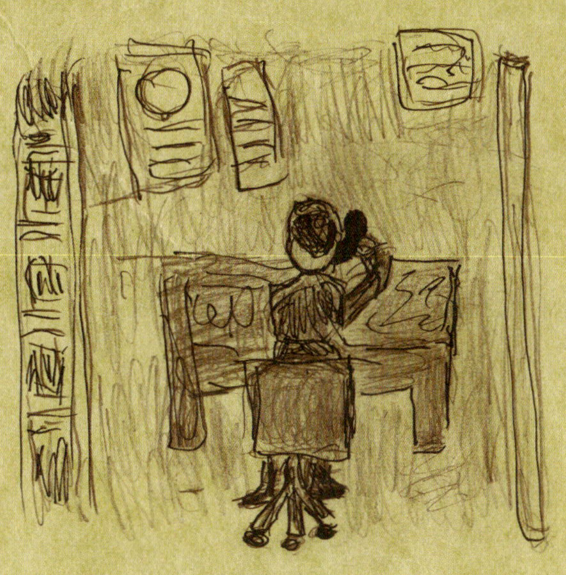

I GOT A CALL FROM
MY BROTHER. HE TOLD
ME THAT OUR MOTHER
HAD PASSED AWAY.

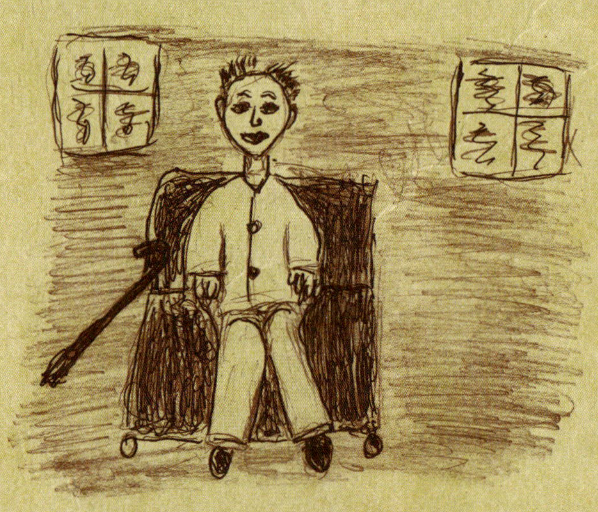

I KNEW THAT
HER HEALTH WAS
DETERIORATING. SHE
WAS BEGINNING TO
LOSE HER HAIR.

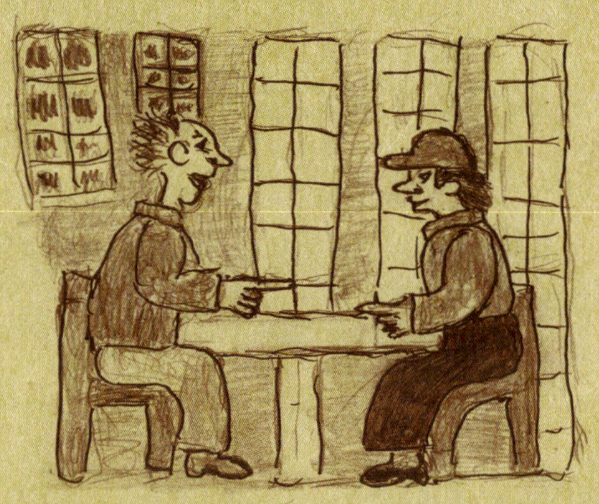

THE LAST TIME I SAW
HER SHE TREATED ME LIKE
I WAS A CHILD.
SHE WAS A LITTLE
ABSENT MINDED.

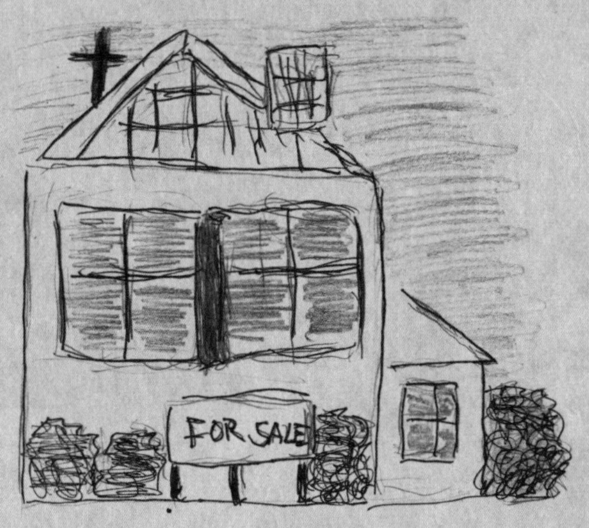

HER HOUSE IS STILL STANDING,
BUT IT HAS BEEN SOLD.

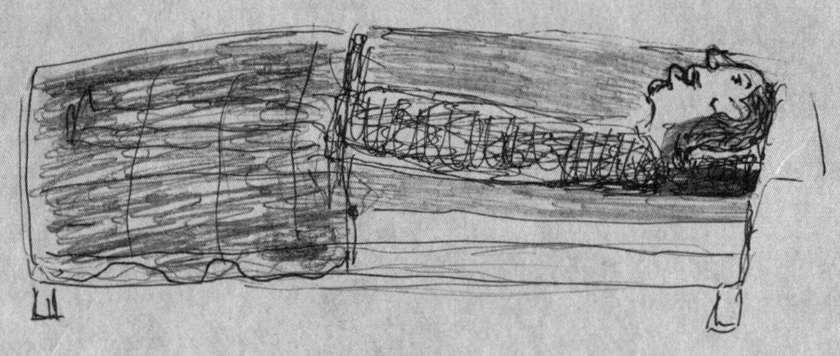

I LOVED HER.

Camille Holvoet

WHEN WILL THIS WICKED WORLD END?
I ONLY WANT ONE LIFE.

I WANT TO REST IN PEACE

Lt. Col. Dave Grossman

The Mud of Guilt and Horror

Beyond fear and exhaustion is a sea of horror that surrounds the soldier and assails his every sense.

Hear the pitiful screams of the wounded and dying. Smell the butcher-house smells of feces, blood, burned flesh, and rotting decay, which combine into the awful stench of death. Feel the shudder of the ground as the very earth groans at the abuse of artillery and explosives, and feel the last shiver of life and the flow of warm blood as friends die in your arms. Taste the salt of blood and tears as you hold a dear friend in mutual grieving, and you do not know or care if it is the salt of your tears or his. And see what hath been wrought.

Strangely, such horrifying memories seem to have a much more profound effect on the combatant—the participant in battle—than the noncombatant, the correspondent, civilian, POW, or other passive observer of the battle zone. The combat soldier appears to feel a deep sense of responsibility and accountability for what he sees around him. It is as though every enemy dead is a human being he has killed, and every friendly dead is a comrade for whom he was responsible. With every effort to reconcile these two responsibilities, more guilt is added to the horror that surrounds the soldier.

A colleague of mine spoke of "a brave and distinguished" old veteran who, after nearly seventy years, "wept softly . . . as he described a popular officer who had been literally disemboweled by a shell fragment." Often you can keep these things out of your mind when you are young and active, but they come back to haunt your nights in your old age. "We thought we had managed all right," he told my colleague, "kept the awful things out of our minds, but now I'm an old man and they come out from where I hid them. Every night."

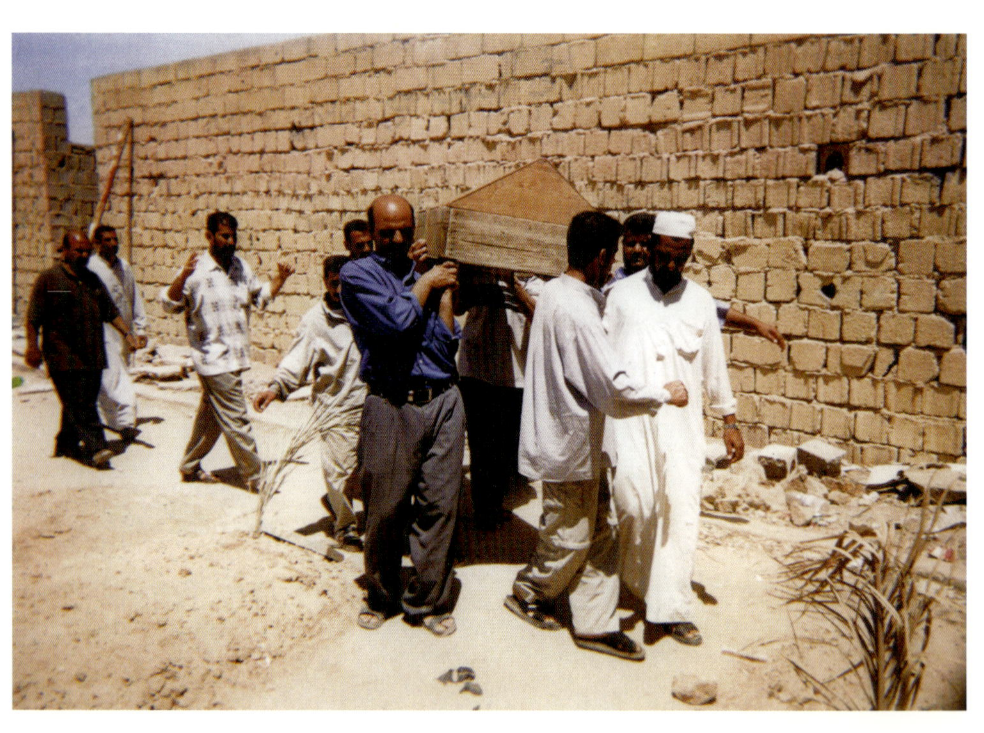

Jassim Mohammad Al Khafajy

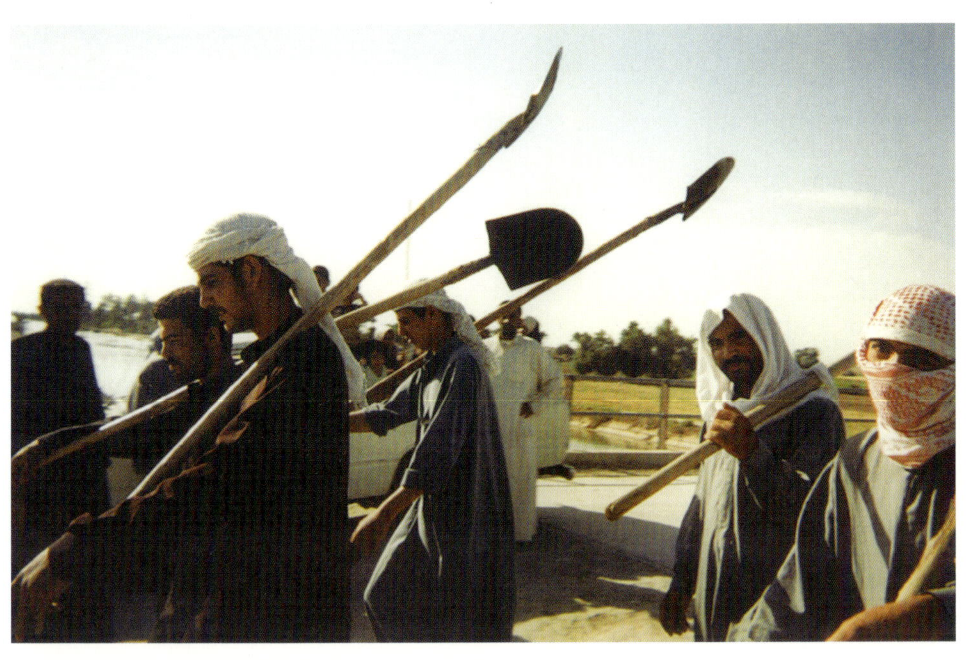

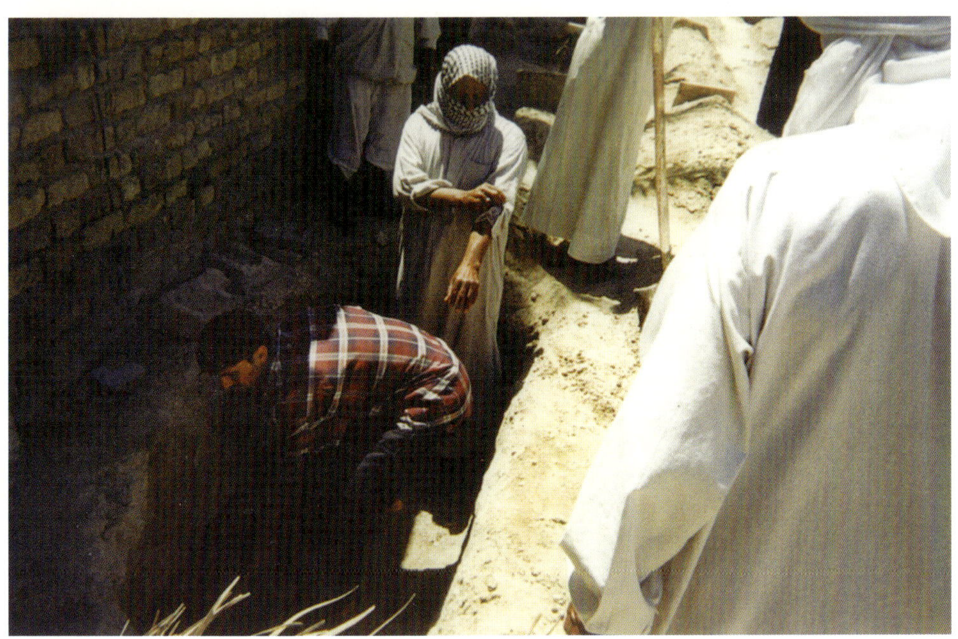

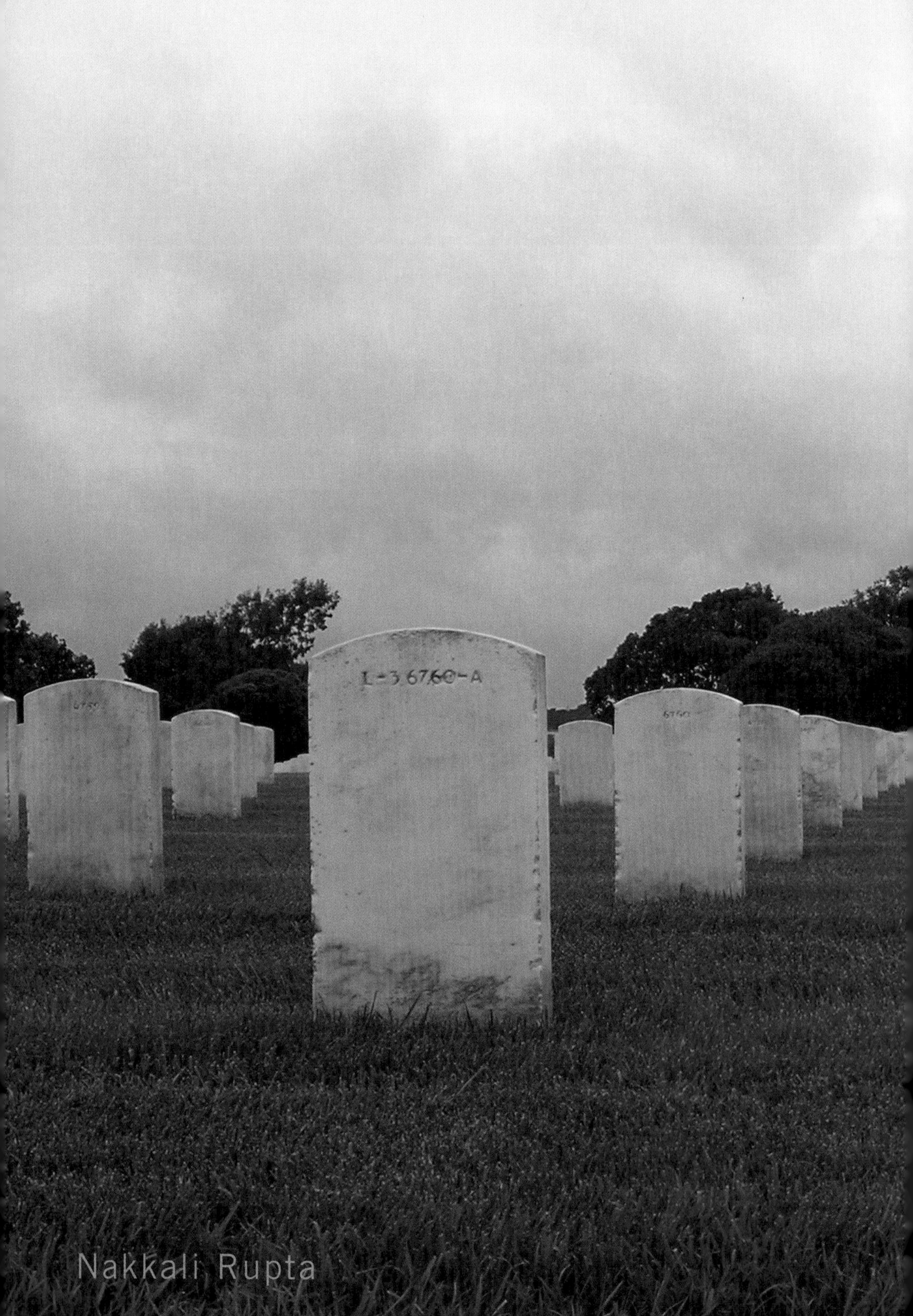
L-3 6760-A
Nakkali Rupta

L-3 6761-A

Brenda Rasmussen

HELEN I
JAN 14 1924
AUG 25 1950
WIFE OF
TEC5 DALLAS L FOOTE
US ARMY

Alena Natalia Charow

My Angels

When I was young,
They would always visit,
bringing me toys and other fun things,
I loved back then.
He would sit me on his lap while he drank his martinis,
They always had a green olive,
and he would eat his tortilla chips with salsa,
He would always give me the olive.
She would always take me for walks,
spoil me with love and all the little things I liked.
When my mother went off to work,
she would always come,
and it was the best thing in my life.
Then one day after my mother left for work,
A new face came,
I cried.
My mother had to stay home.
He didn't come as often either.
But I saw him with her in a big building.
She had lots of tubes attached to her.
I was worried.
But when she kissed me and spoke with that same voice,
I knew it would be okay.
I never saw her again after that.
That same new face soon got familiar,
I often saw my mother crying,
I wondered where her mother was to give her a bottle or a nap.
Soon I got used to the fact,
She would never return,
But he always was there for me.

He became something like her,
however played his role, too.

Many years went by.
Every year we visited a field with many stones,
to remember her.
I took him for granted,
Not knowing someday he would join her.
Then one day I visited him in the same building where she was,
this time I wasn't as assured,
I was older,
and smarter,
and I knew more.
The last time I saw him,
He was wrapped in a blanket in my uncle's house,
I had found a crab pincher on the beach,
I wanted him to hear it.
But all he did was apologize saying he couldn't hear now,
But he would be able to soon.
He stopped visiting,
I knew he had joined her,
I cried,
I could absorb what death was now.
We sold his store,
It's now a bar.
Even though they are both gone,
I remember them perfectly.
They were the most important people in my life,
And still are.
When something goes wrong,
I ask them to fix it,
and sooner or later,
in some way,
Everything goes right.
They are my grandparents.
They are my angels.

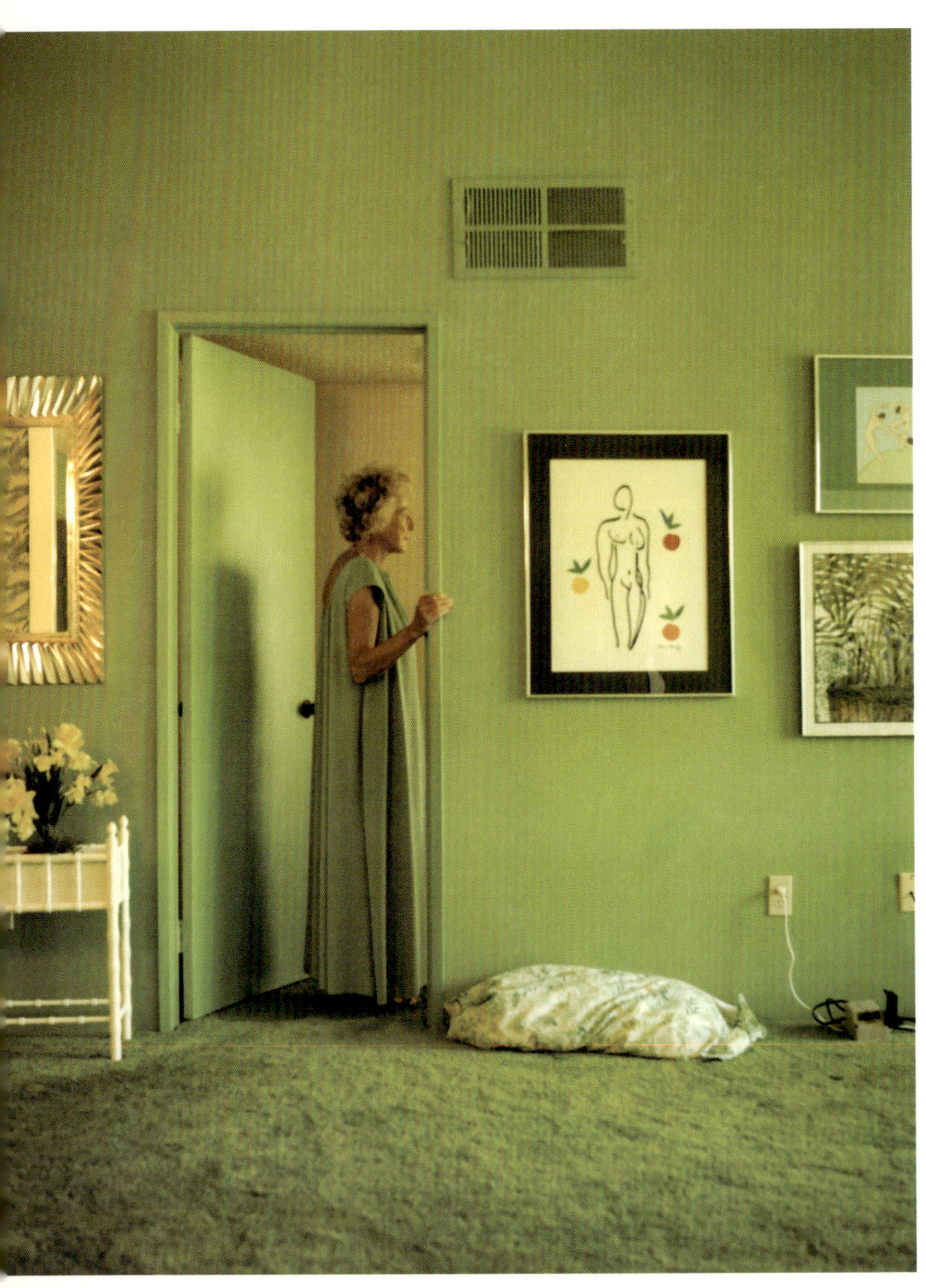

Larry Sultan

Last year, at our annual family reunion at Lake Tahoe, I sneaked into their bedroom while my mother was taking her afternoon nap. I stood by the door for several minutes to be sure that she was asleep and then carefully tiptoed over to the bed. She was lying on her stomach with her head turned toward me. I was so apprehensive of waking her that I breathed in rhythm with her. Standing at the foot of the bed, I realized that I had never seen the underside of her foot. I had my camera, so I photographed it. I could see the slight grass stains from walking barefoot that morning to the lake.

I wanted to photograph it again and again, to use up an entire roll of film. Then it struck me that she was not really asleep, that her breathing, like mine, was controlled. We were co-conspirators. Just as I was secretly photographing, she was secretly awake.

She felt me looking.

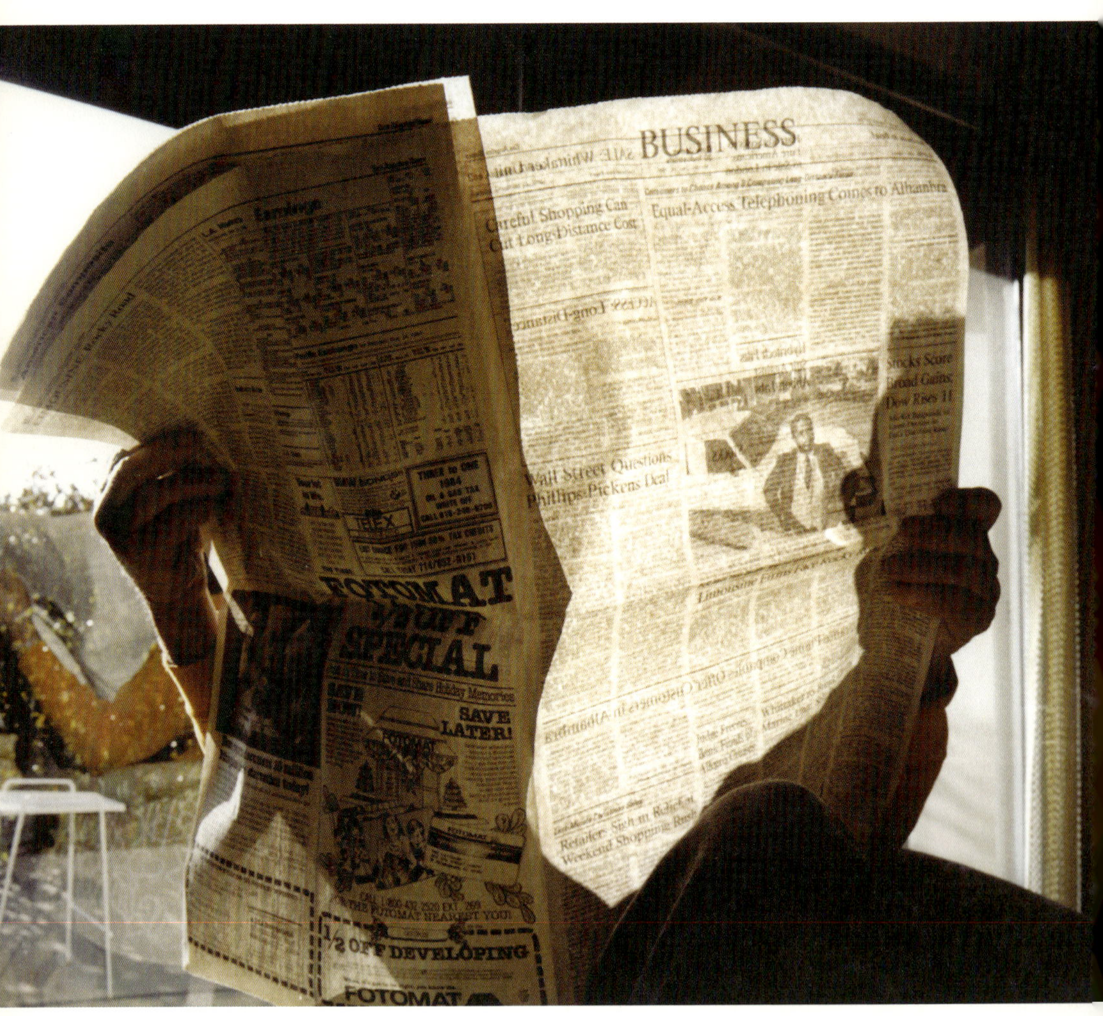
BUSINESS
Careful Shopping Can
Cut Long-Distance Cost
Equal-Access Telephoning Comes to Alhambra
Wall Street Questions
Phillips-Pickens Deal
Stocks Score
Broad Gains;
Dow Rises 11
FOTOMAT
WIPP
SPECIAL
SAVE
LATER!
1/2 OFF DEVELOPING
FOTOMAT

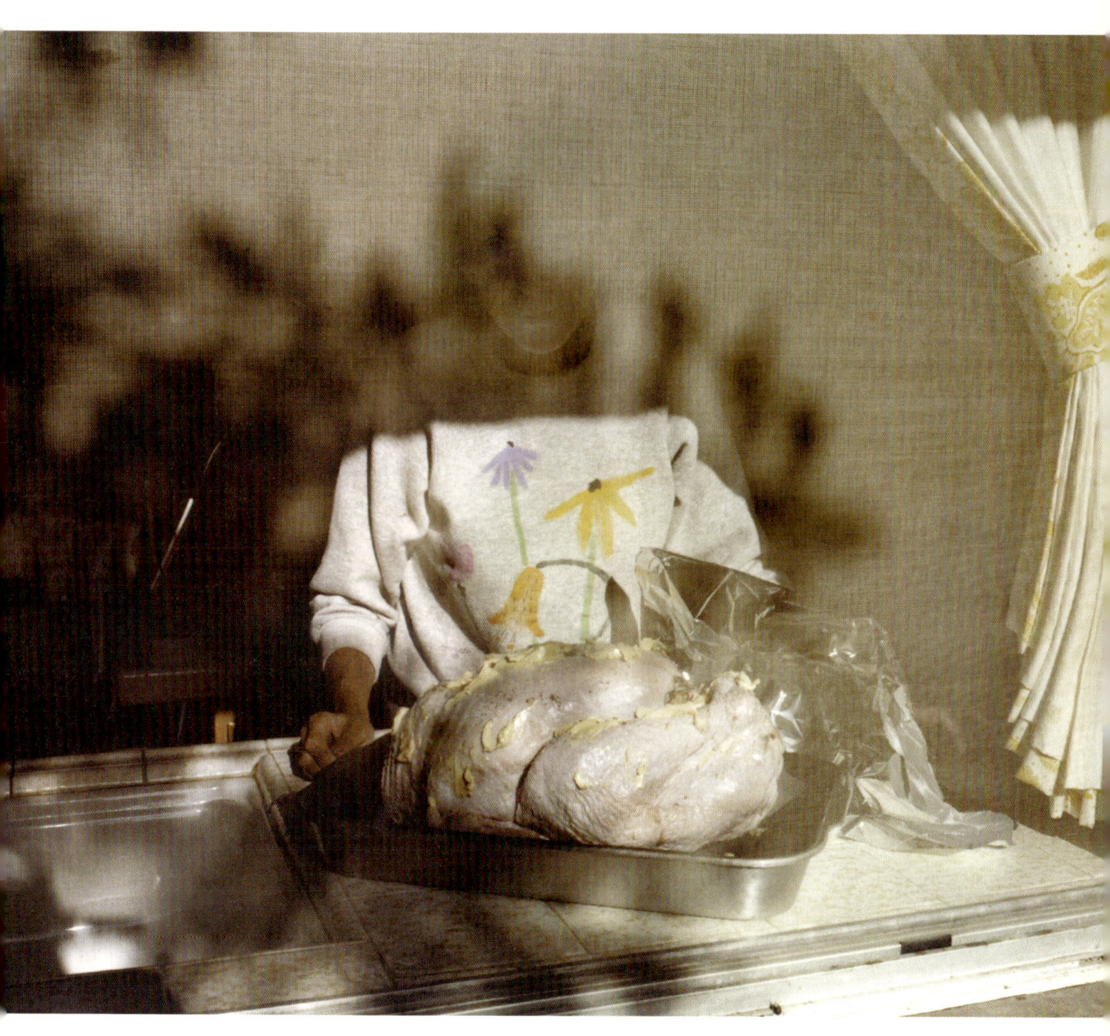

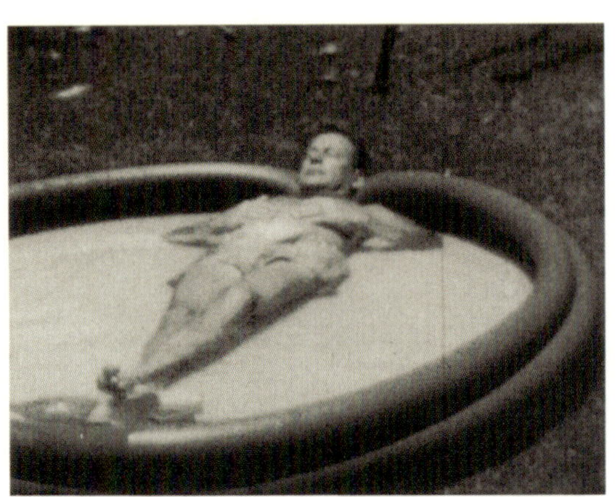
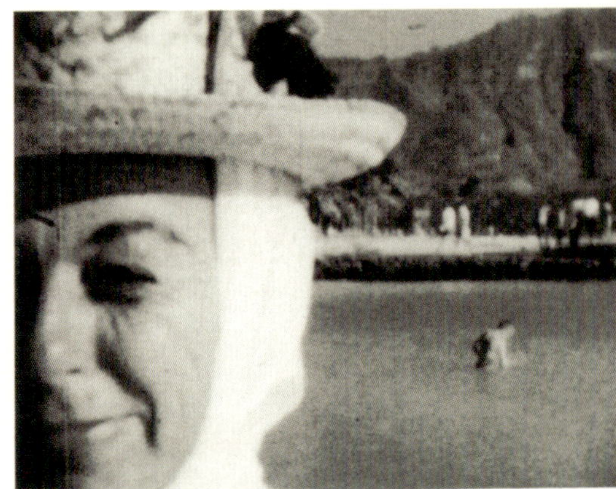
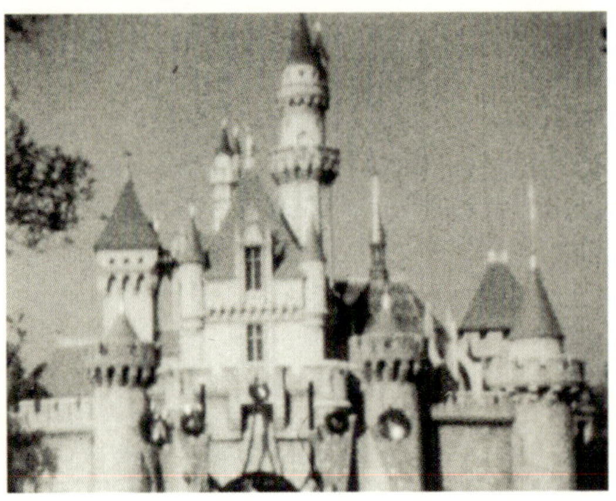
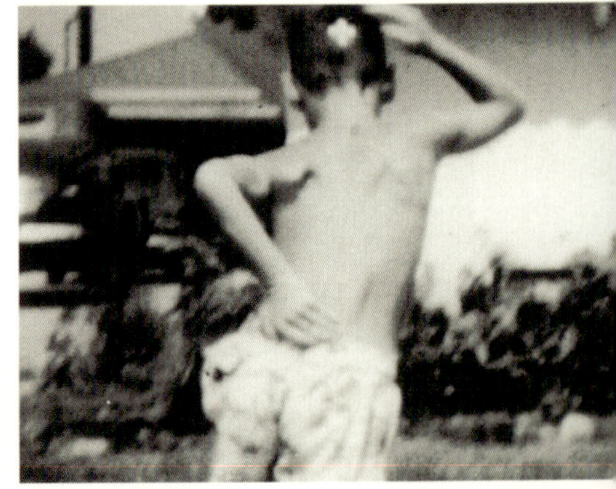

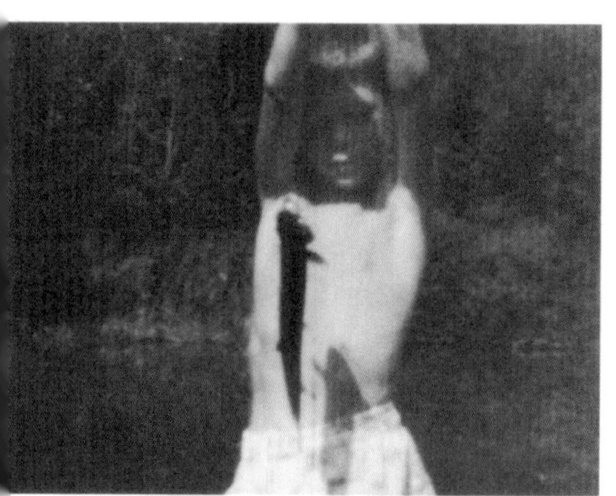
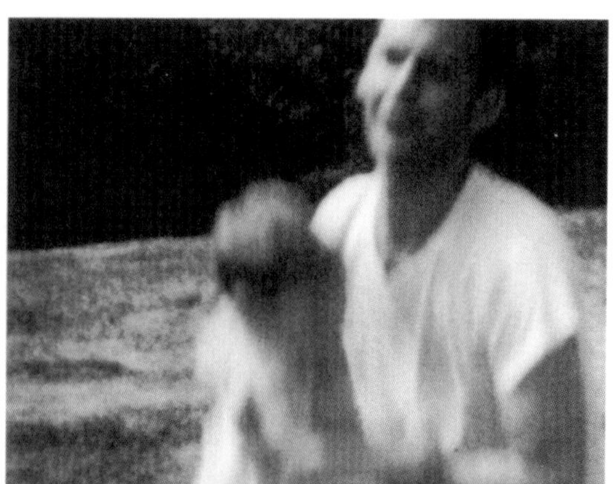
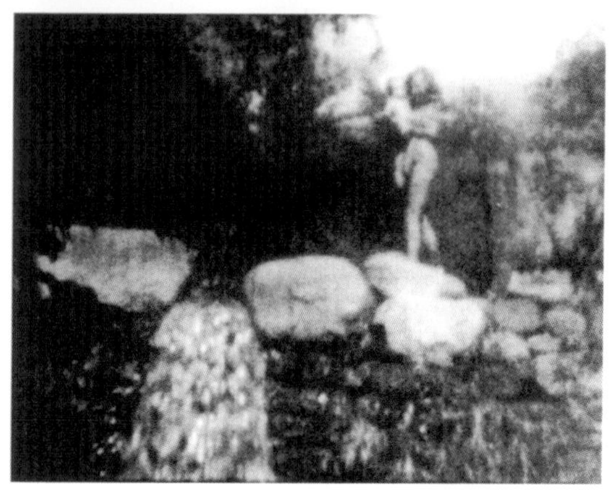

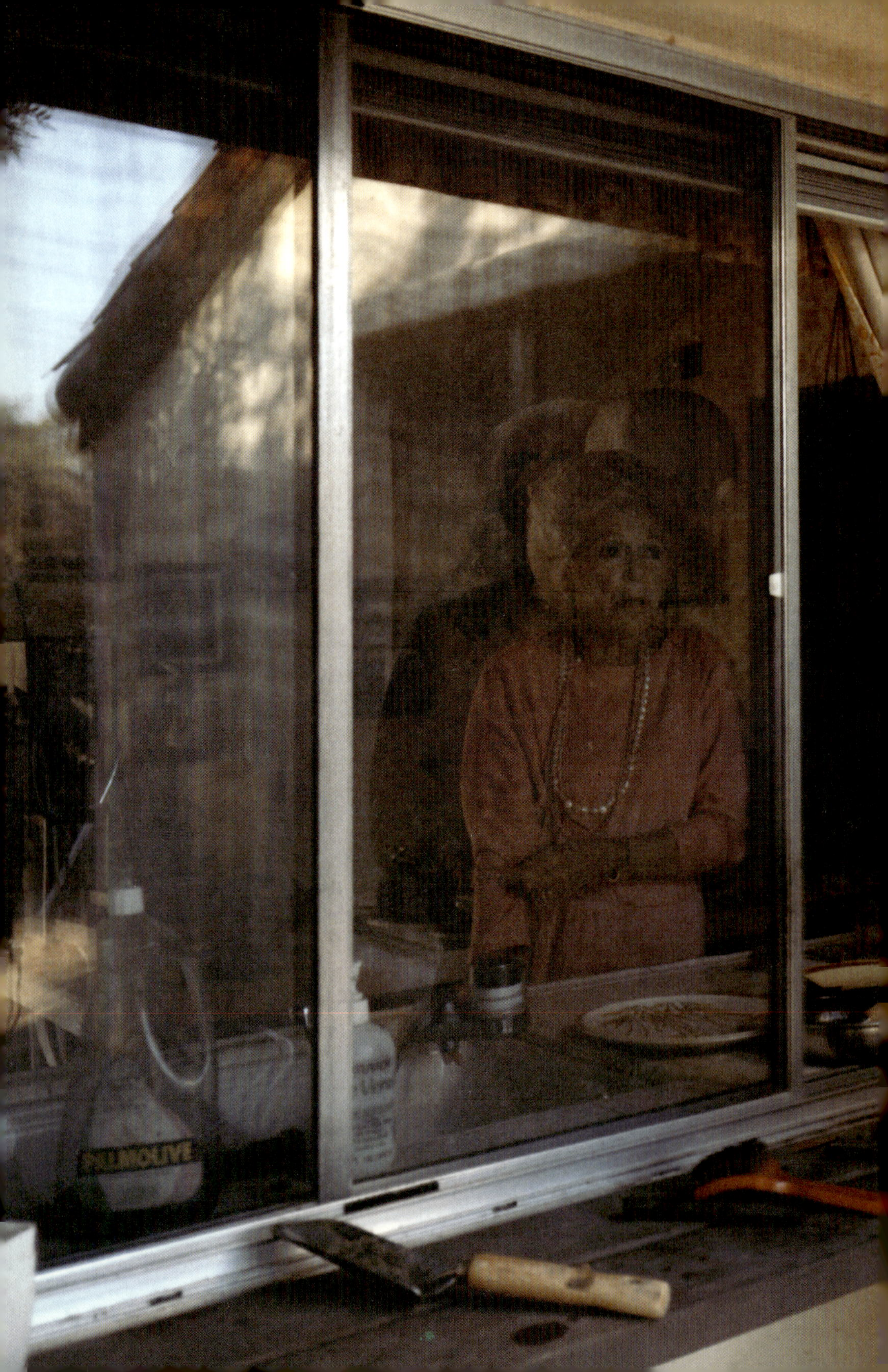
PALMOLIVE

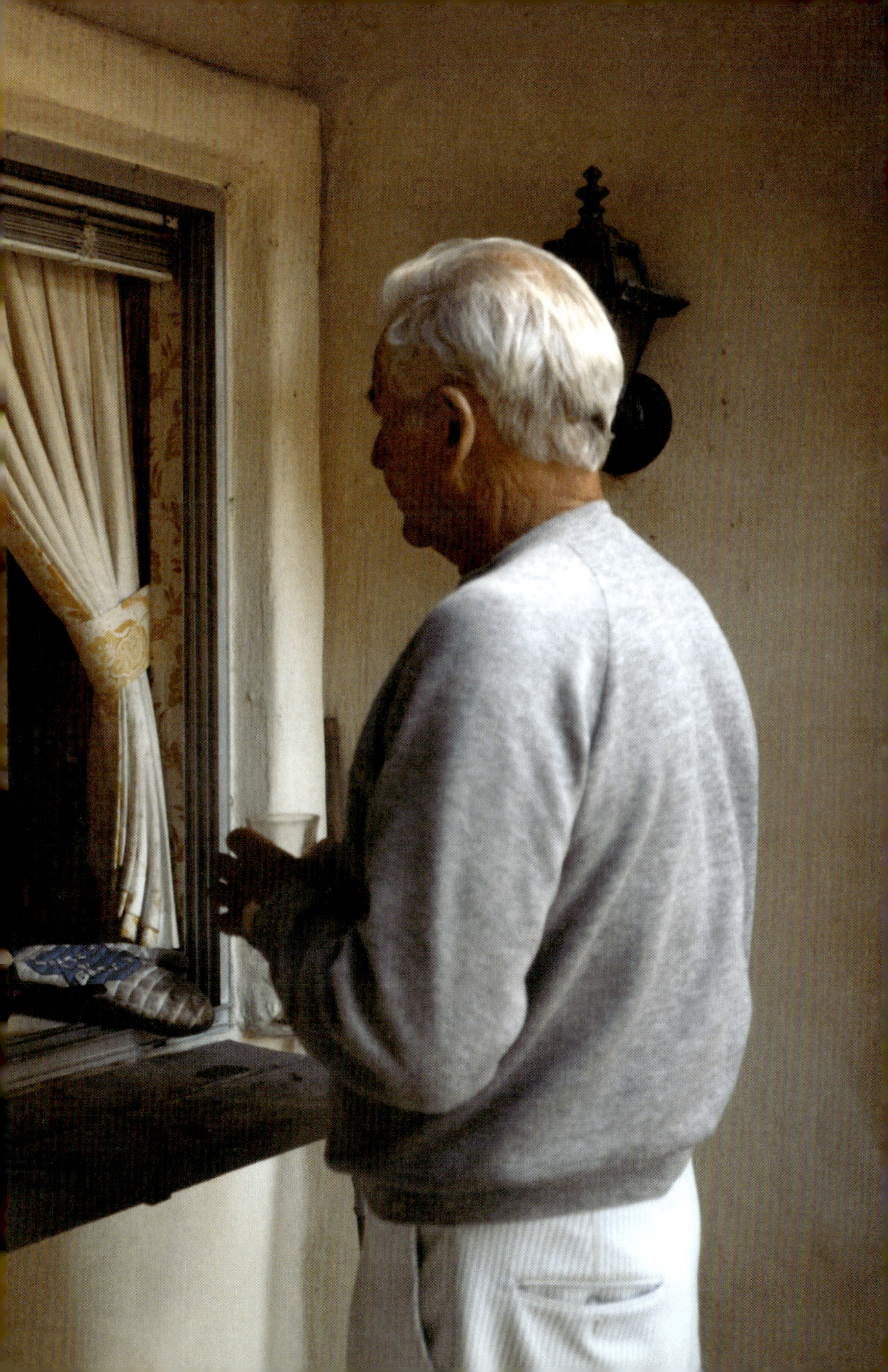

Amy Auerbach

This Envelope Contains the

PERMIT FOR DISPOSITION OF HUMAN REMAINS

Department of Health, State of California

for the cremated remains of

GEORGE R. BROCKELT

Final Disposition: RESIDENCE: 1101 G. STREET

PETALUMA, CA 94952

Section 7054 of the California Health and Safety code states as follows: "... *every person who deposits or disposes of any human remains in any place, except in a cemetery, is guilty of a misdemeanor.*" However, the code does make exception for cremated remains scattered at sea if done pursuant to Section 7117. Further, Section 7054.6 states that "*Cremated remains may be removed in a durable container from the place of cremation and kept in the dwelling owned or occupied by the person having the right to control disposition of the remains ...*" This person may dispose of the remains but first must obtain a permit for disposition from the local Registrar; and, within ten days after disposition must file with the Registrar a copy of the permit with description of the place of disposition. This person who elects to dispose of remains must comply with Sections 7054.6 and 10376.5 of the Health and Safety Code.

Russell & Gooch Funeral Chapel

License #FD-633

270 Miller Avenue, Mill Valley, California 94941

Do Not Destroy

LAW REQUIRES THAT THIS PERMIT ACCOMPANY THE
CREMATED REMAINS TO THE FINAL RESTING PLACE

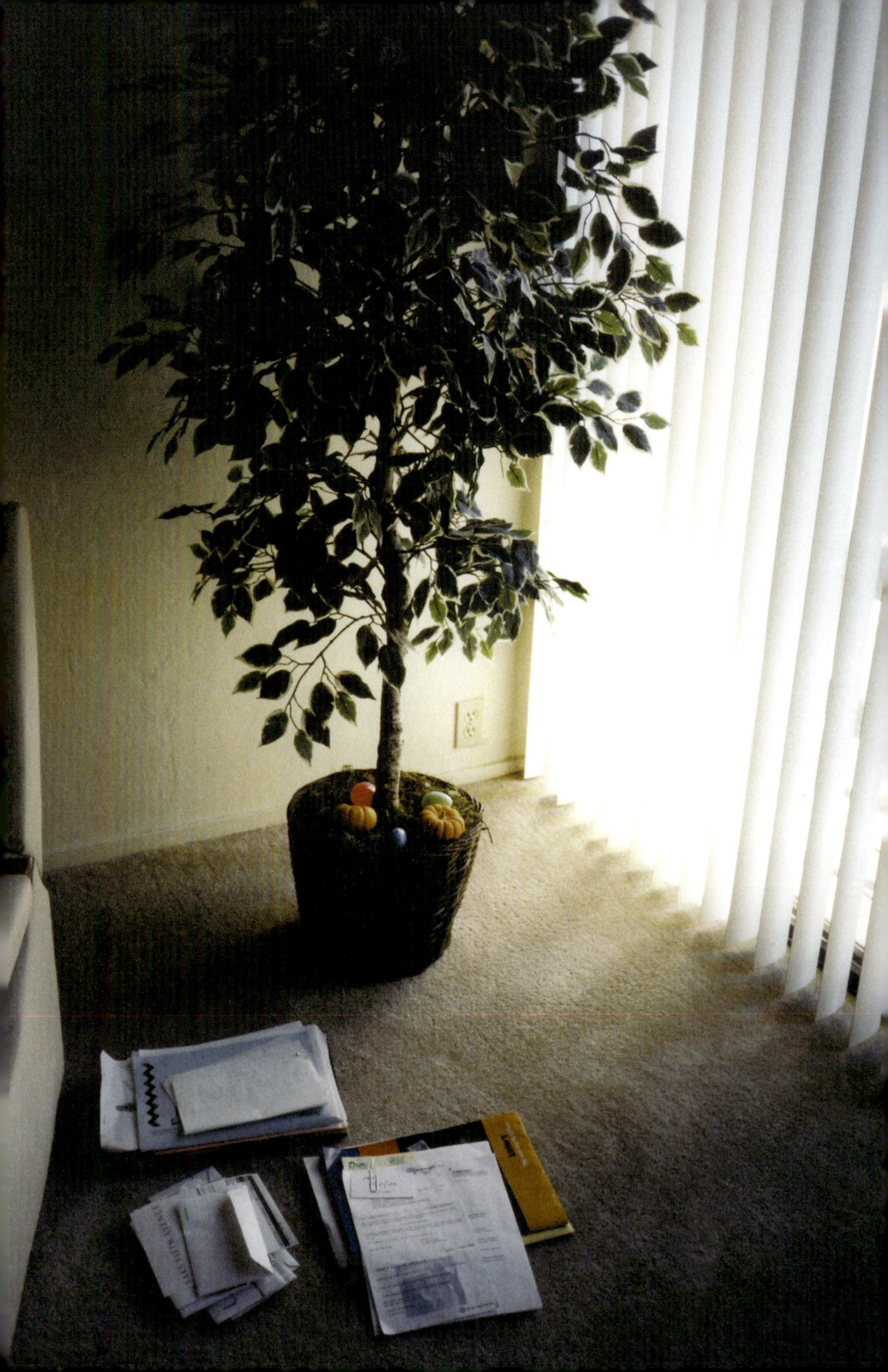

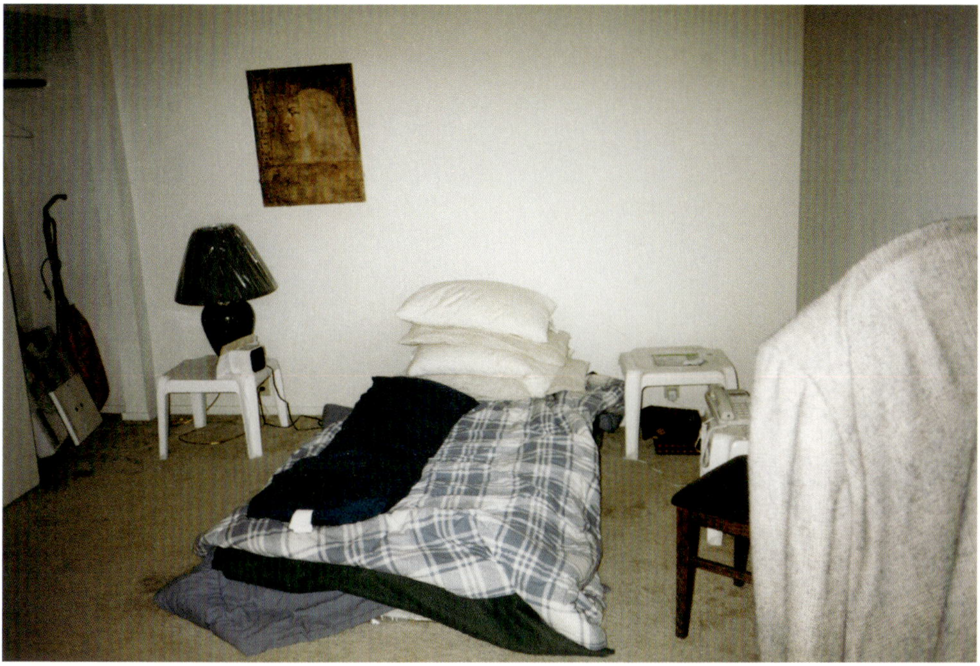

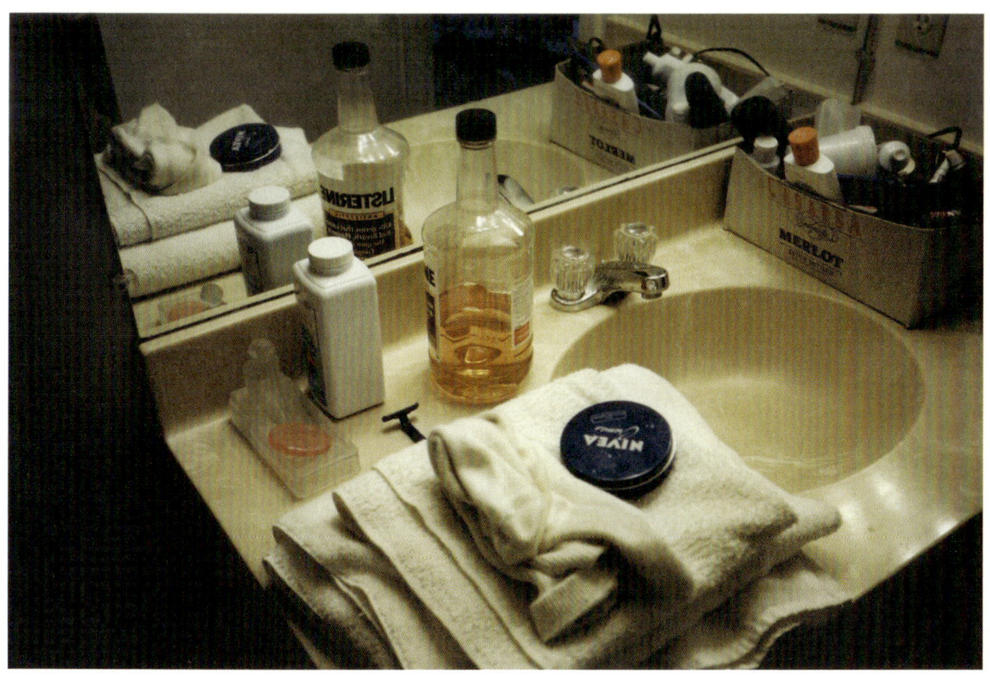

LISTERINE
MERLOT
MERLOT
NIVEA

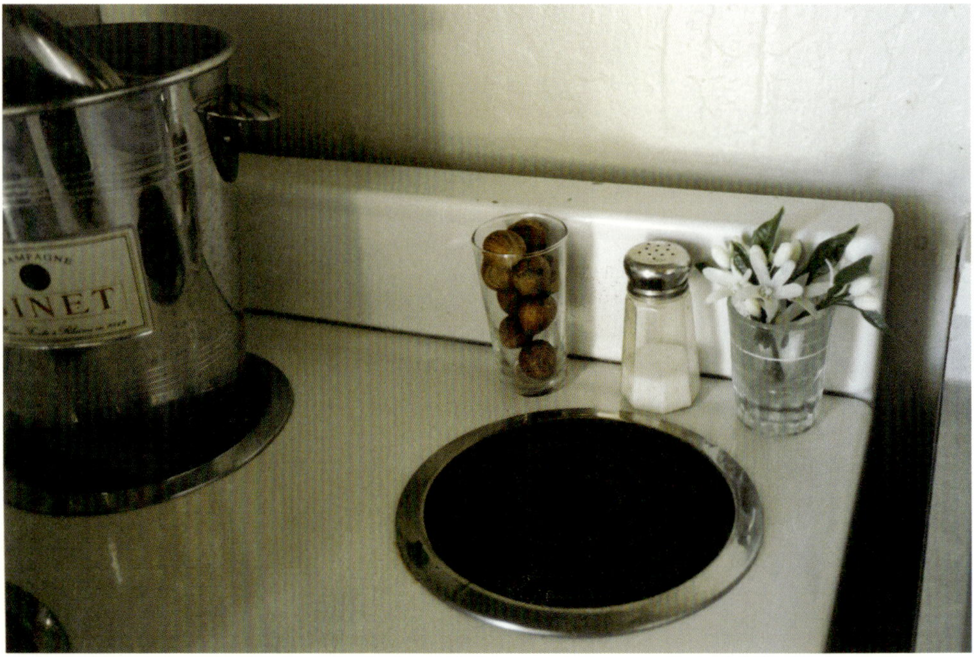

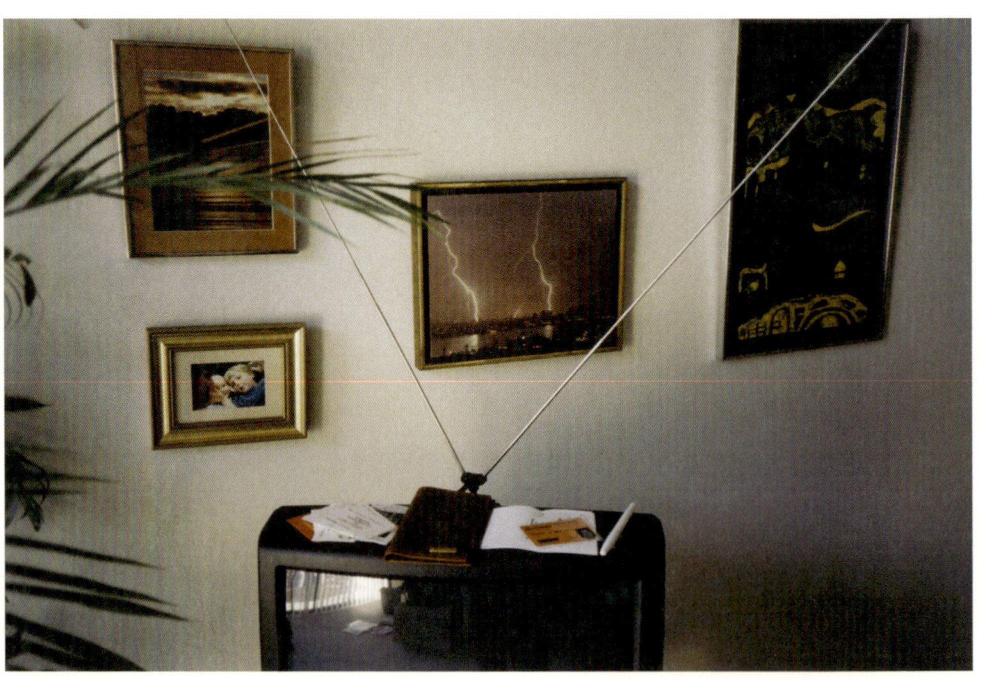

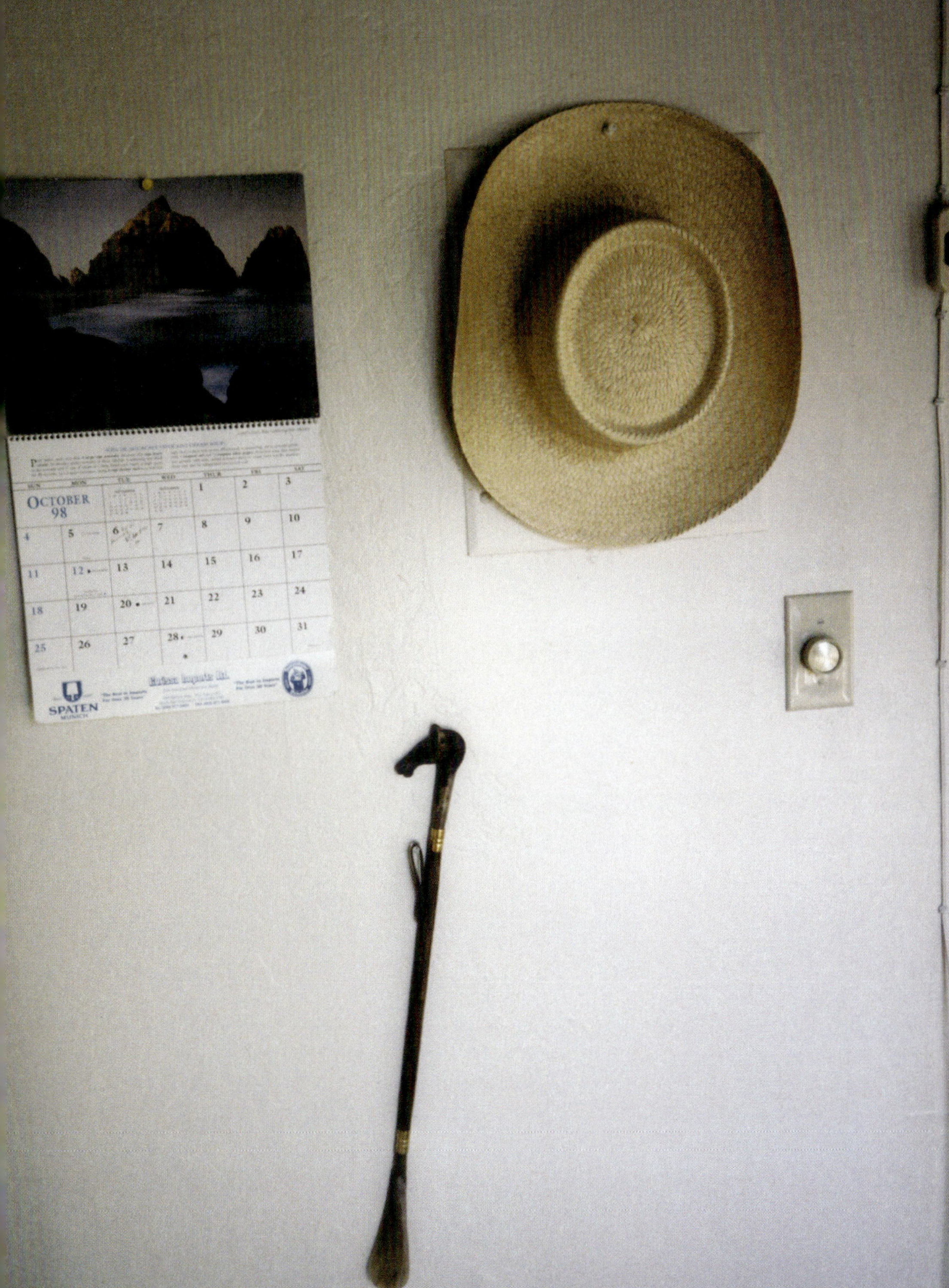

OCTOBER
98
SPATEN
MÜNCHEN

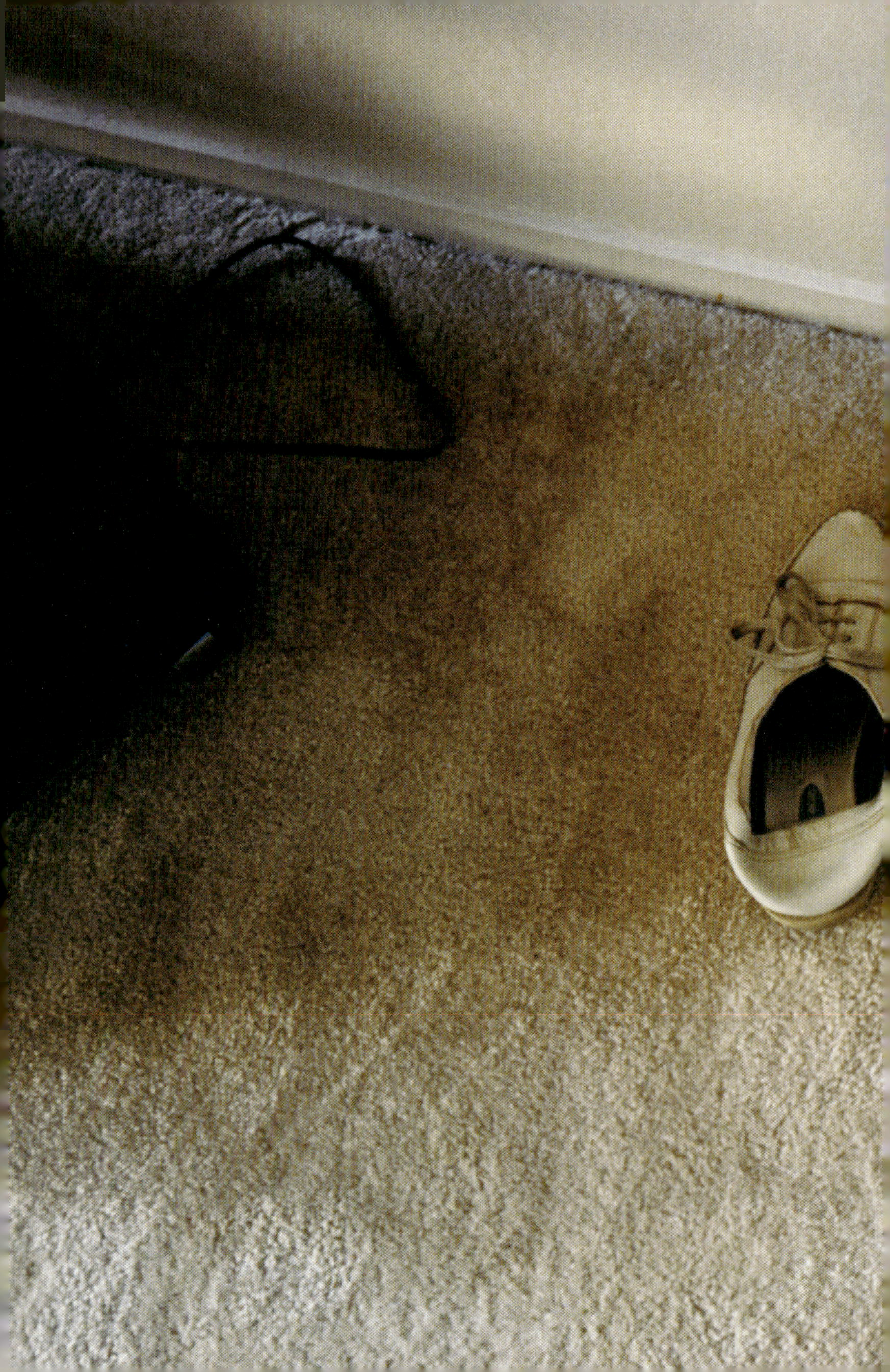

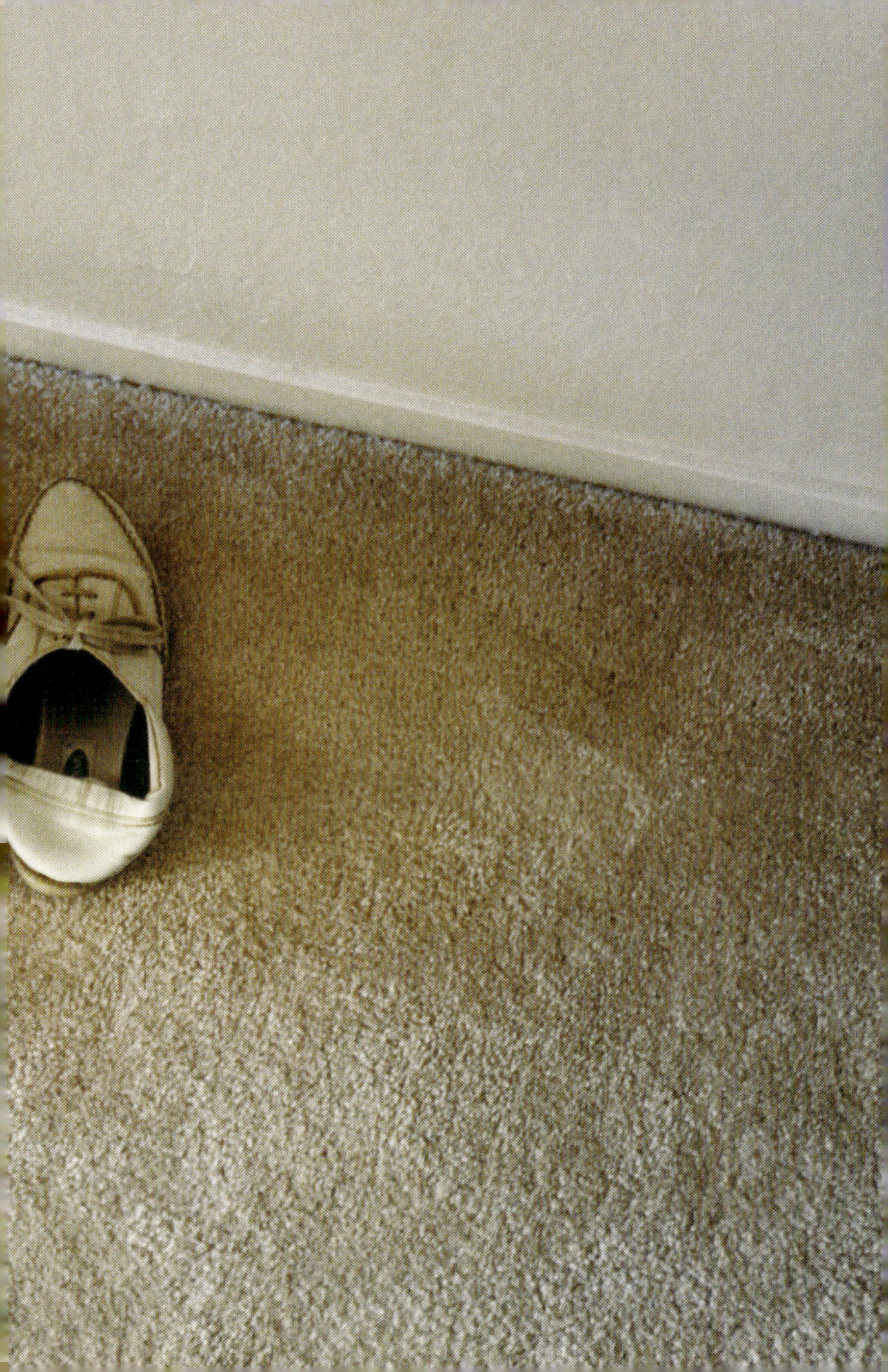

Willy Whitefeather

I'm going to tell you a little story about my experience with life and my Cherokee heritage. From what I've learned from my elders, death is passing on to what the Cherokee people call the "real world." The world we're in is only an illusion and the "real world" is one we pass on to.

Years ago while I was eating, I started to choke on a piece of tomato skin that went into my windpipe. The friend of mine who I was with started working on me, trying to revive me. But I just stopped breathing altogether. While I was out, I saw this light like a beautiful pulsating heartbeat. And I went towards that light. It was as if I went right through it and onto the other side of it. It was so beautiful. There was a person standing there on a little pier and he was all in white. His face was like looking at the brightest light ever, like looking into the sun. And he held up his hand to me and said, "You have to go back, it's not your time."

Then, I was in this beautiful river winding around a bend. And I knew that there were going to be many surprises on the other side of the bend. This light being, I call it a "light being," he's standing on a little wooden pier watching. And there were willow trees and the sunbeams were shining through the willow trees. And the water on this section of the river was as smooth as glass. And a big bird flew across from the other bank and flew in front of me. It was so low to the water that the end of one of its wing tips was just touching the water. And then the other wing tip touched the water. I noticed that the wave circles made by each wing slowly began to join together on the surface of the water.

Well, my friend just kept working on me and working on me, and I finally spit that tomato skin right out of my windpipe and I came back into my body. I'll never forget what I saw over there. So now I don't have any fear about dying. I think that if we're afraid of death then we don't live life. It's like that song that goes, "Some say love it is a river, that bends the tender reed. And the fool afraid of dying never learns how to live." It goes like that.

So, we learn our lessons and then we go on. No big deal. But you don't have to believe any of this because this is just what I know, it's my own thing. But it makes you strong when you know.

Betty Benard

WHEN I GETS REALLY UPSET
AND CANT SLEEP, MY MOTHER'S
SPIRIT COMES AND SITS
AT THE SIDE OF MY BED
AND TALKS TO ME. THEN
I FEELS ALRIGHT.

Michele Kunard

A Lot Of times youR soul
kind of like drifts — drifts away a little bit.
Kind of like a magic little Thing
that happens in life to people.
It come Right Out and Just fades away.

Amanda Coslor

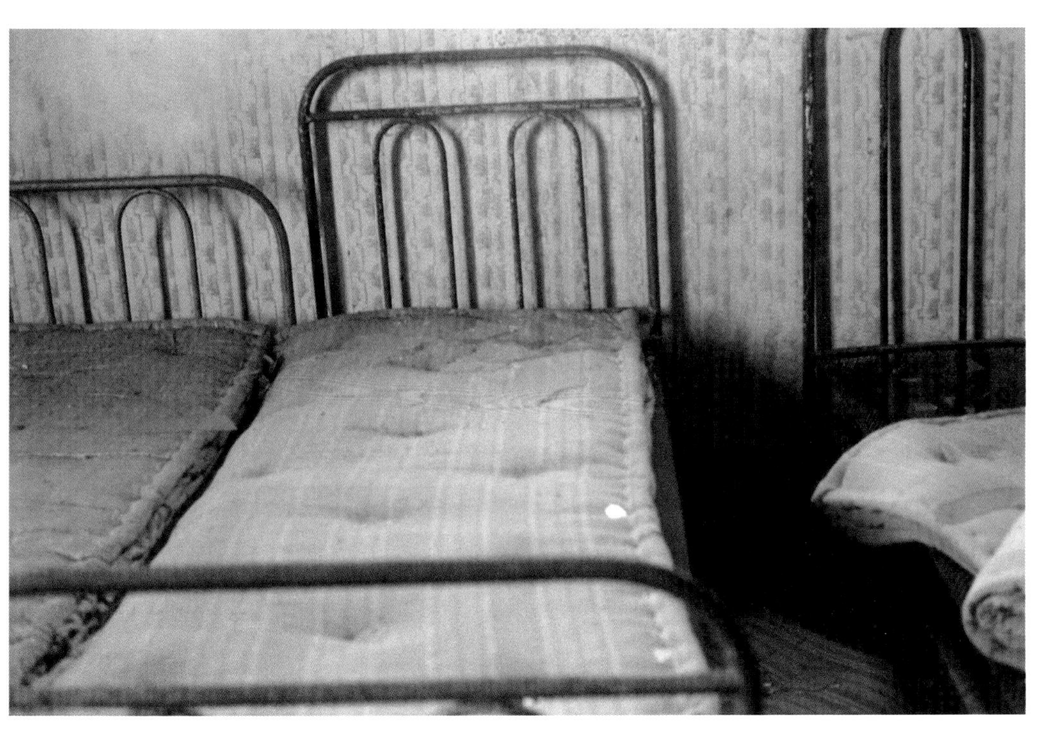

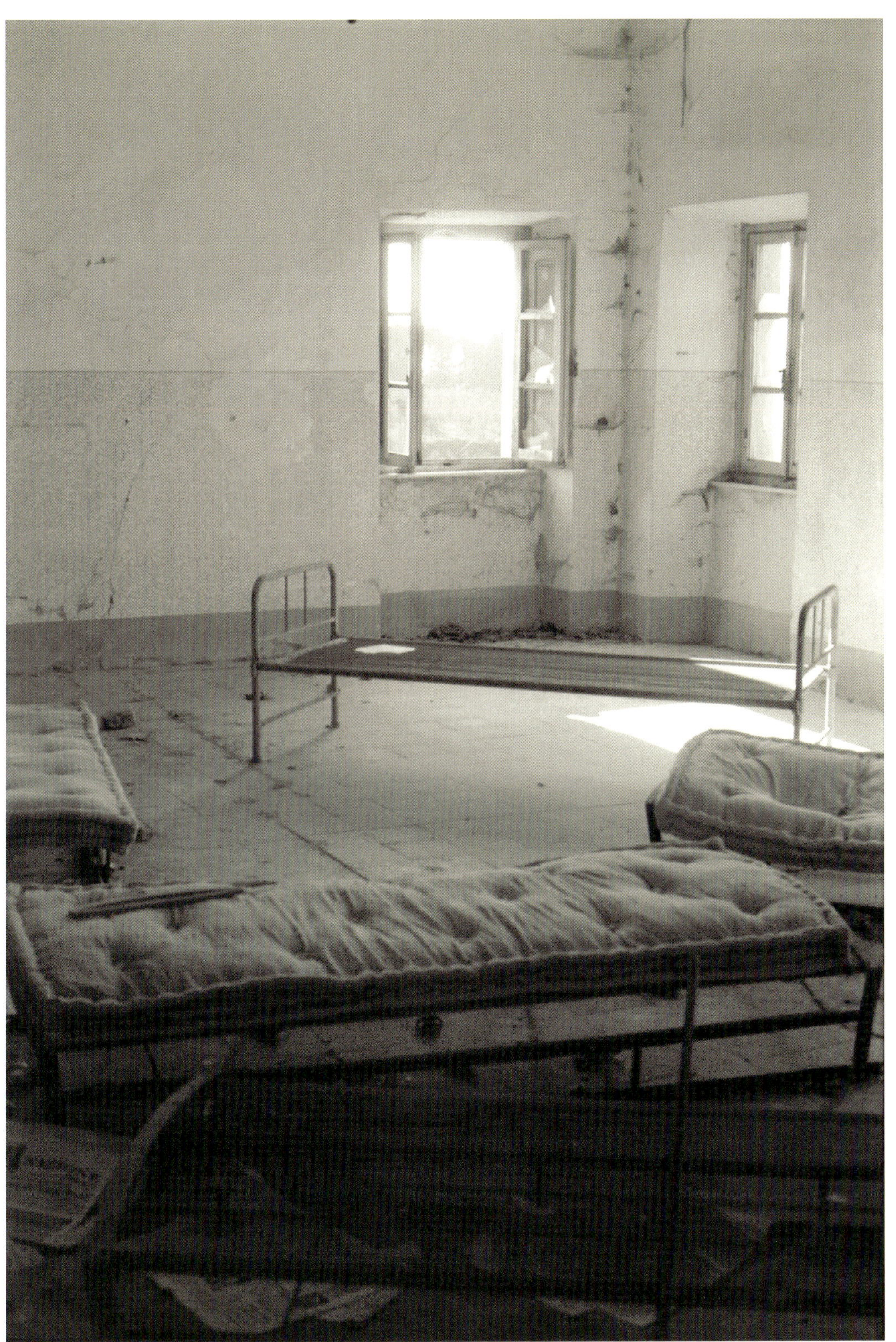

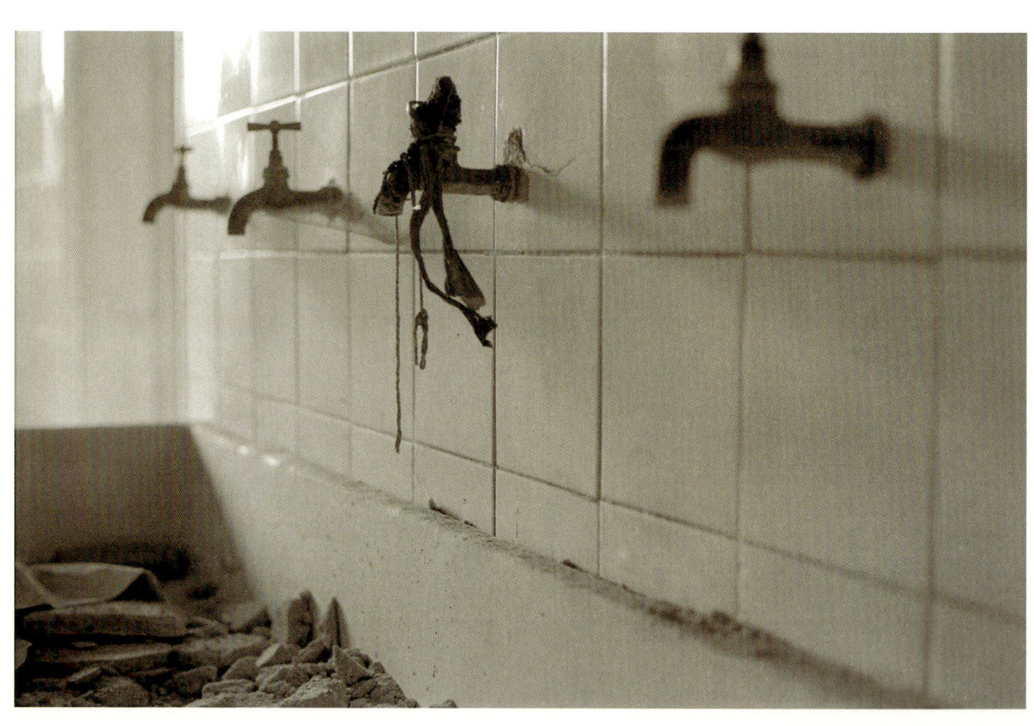

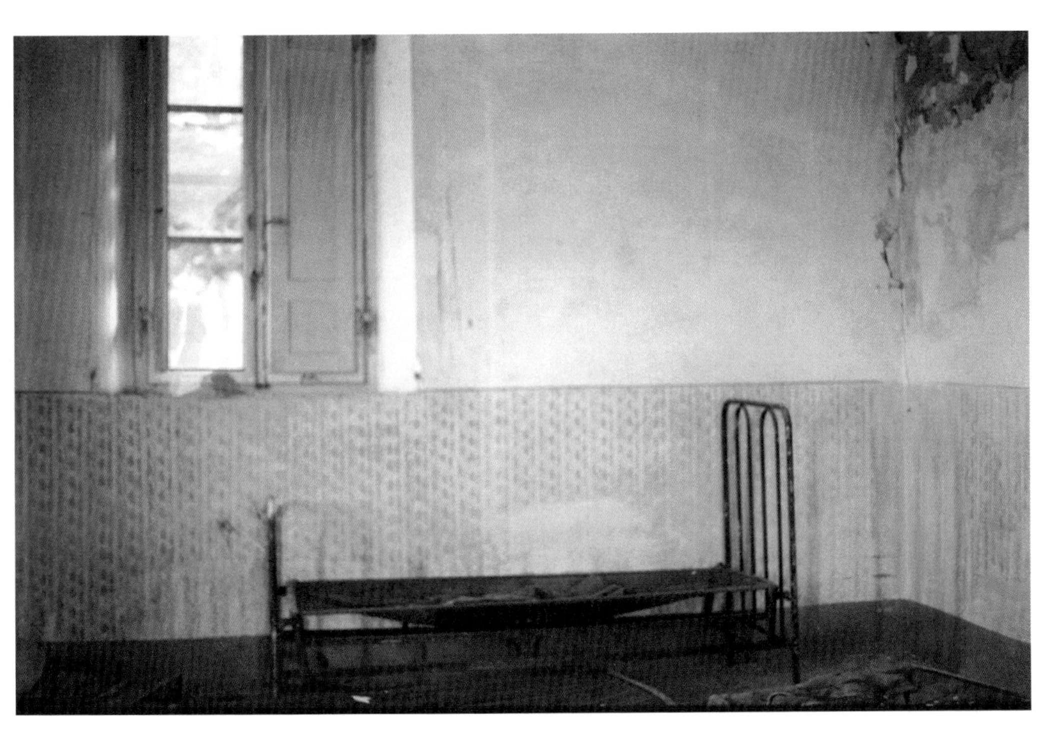

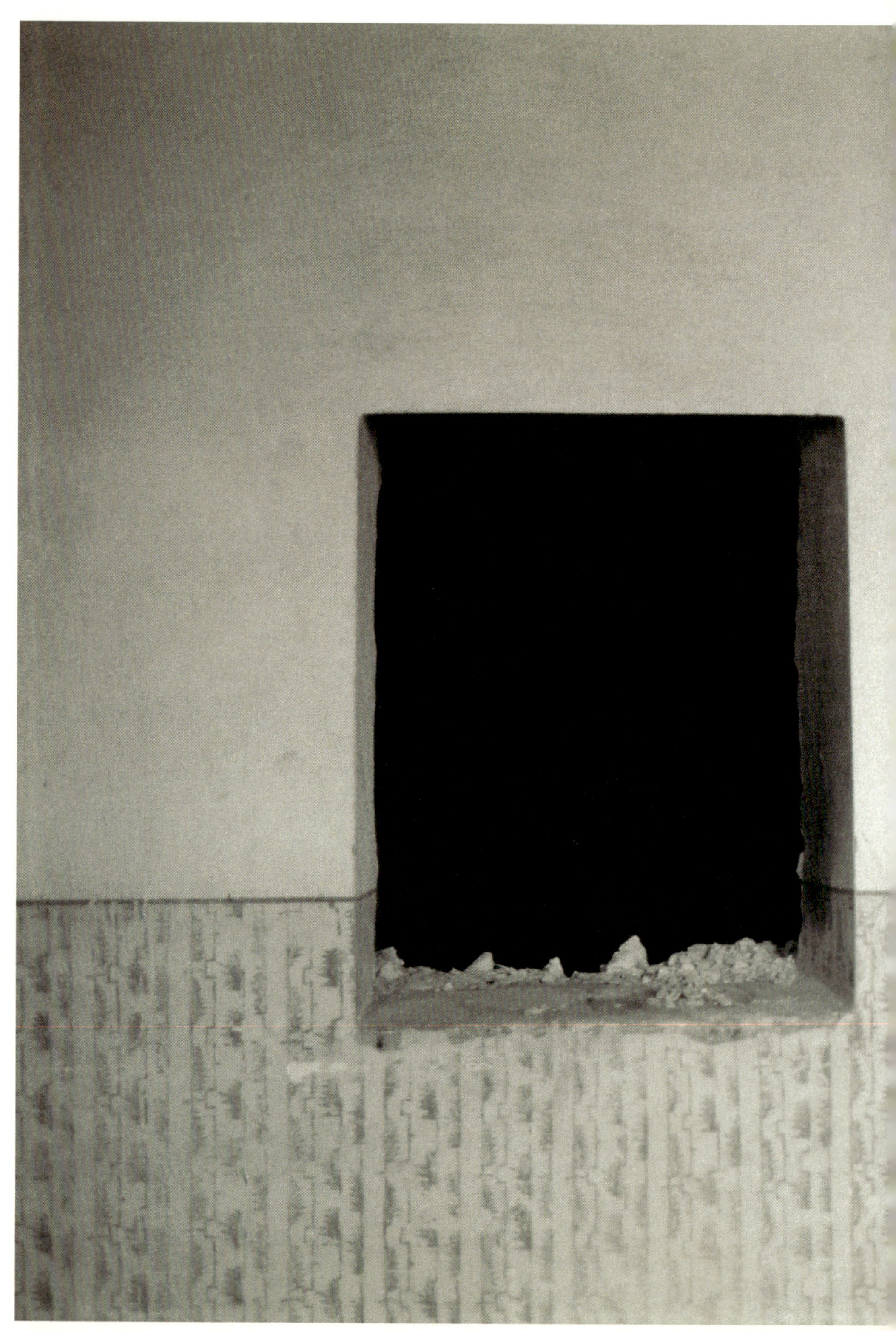

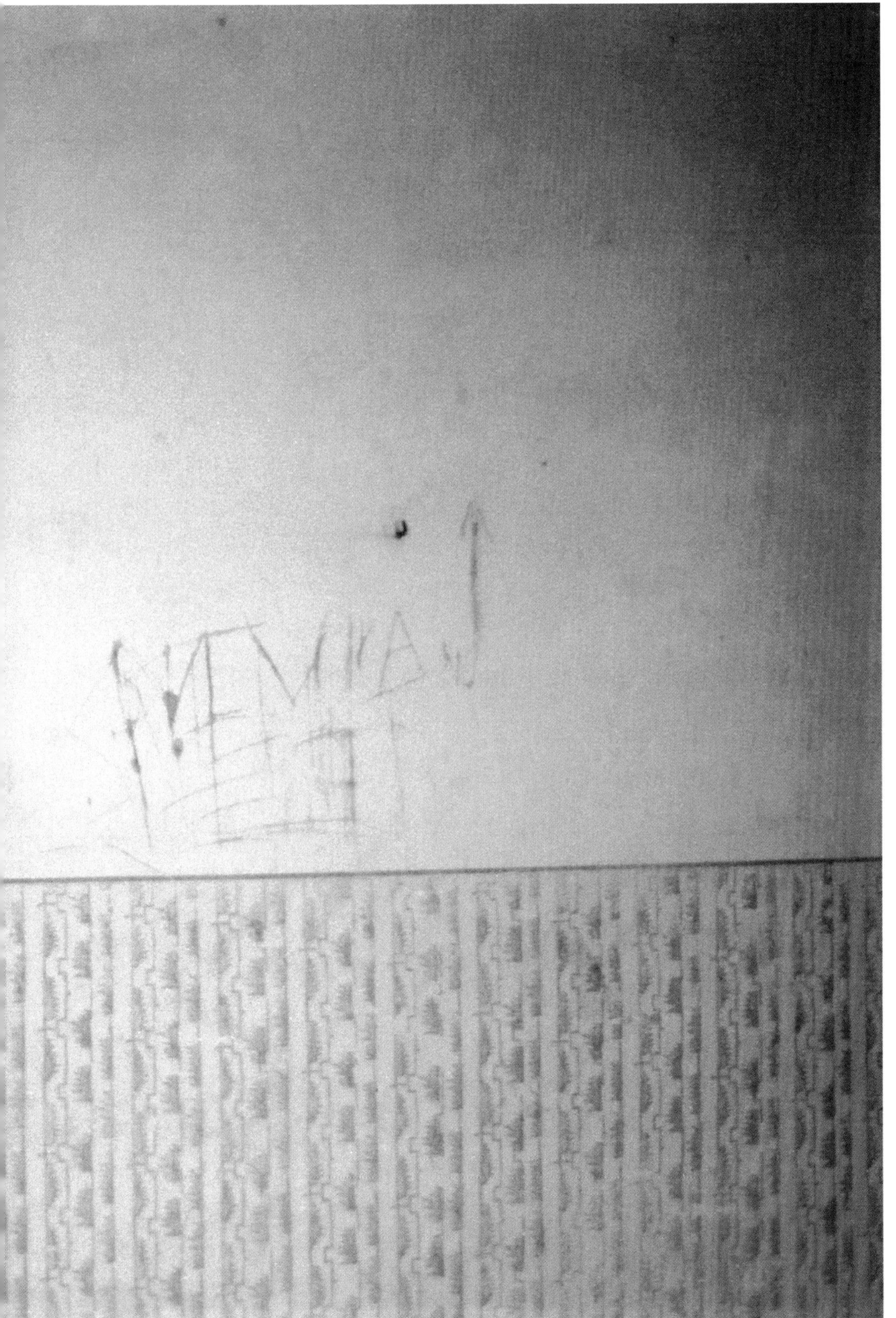

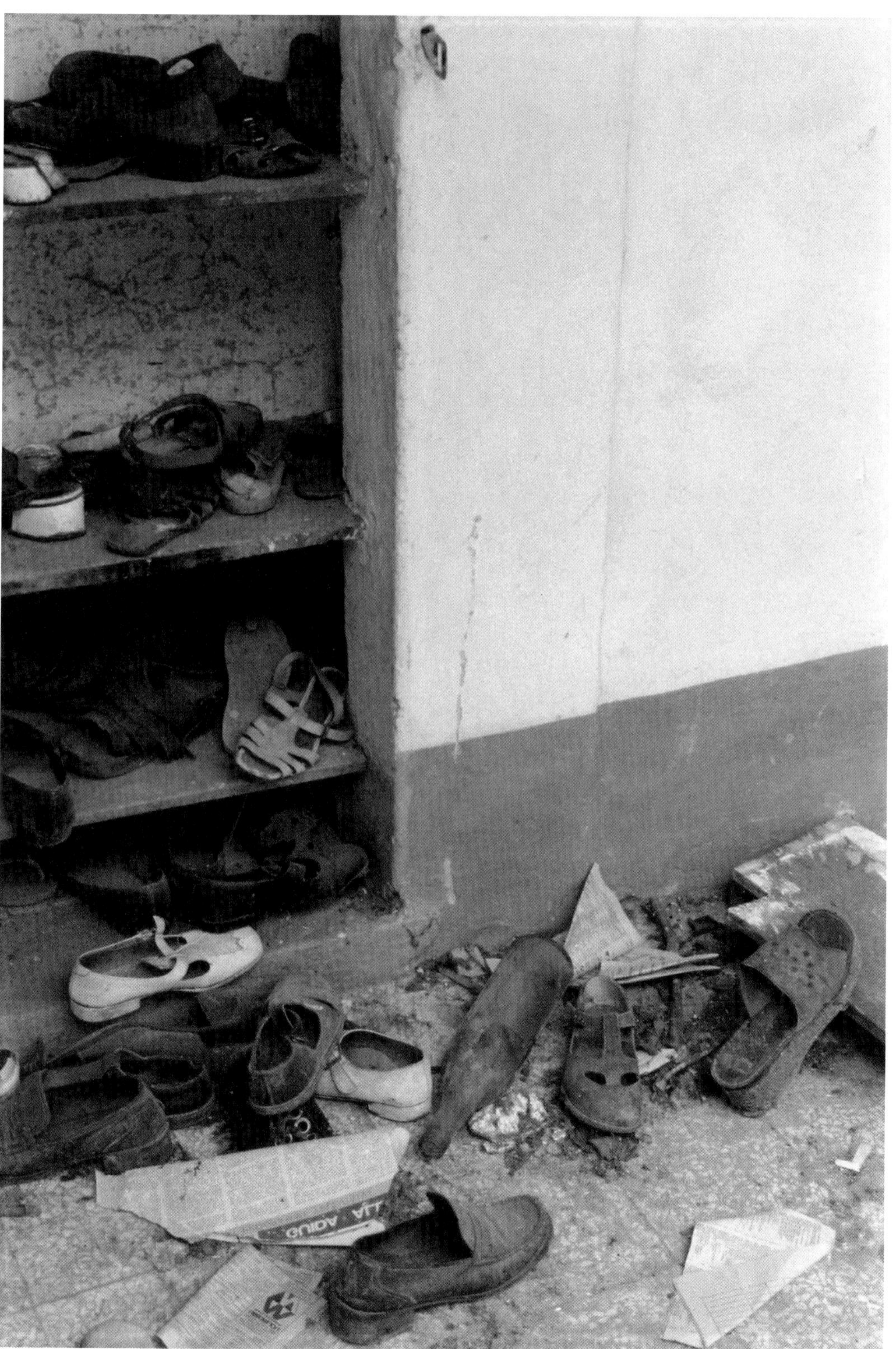

you go slow. toes barely pr
gently. realizing how great t
keen awareness of being
clear to be true. the ceme
i'm shocked to find my life.
existing and living. i see ea
lead me to her grave. i'm sor
loud silenence loud silenc
feet can't hold me up
be what a crashing ph
and 'come to' shaking' like a
clinching fistfulls of gra
sound i hear is harrowing.
me.

Beth Griffin

driving to the grave
sing the accelerator ever s
e sense of touch in one toe. th
h motion. vision too pierci
ry coming into focus. In awe
at is th...if...we
blade of grass as my shoes
that my steps crushed the g
uilds up inside me 'til m
this
ilty drenched earthquake
o keep from drowning. th
an't be human. it might b

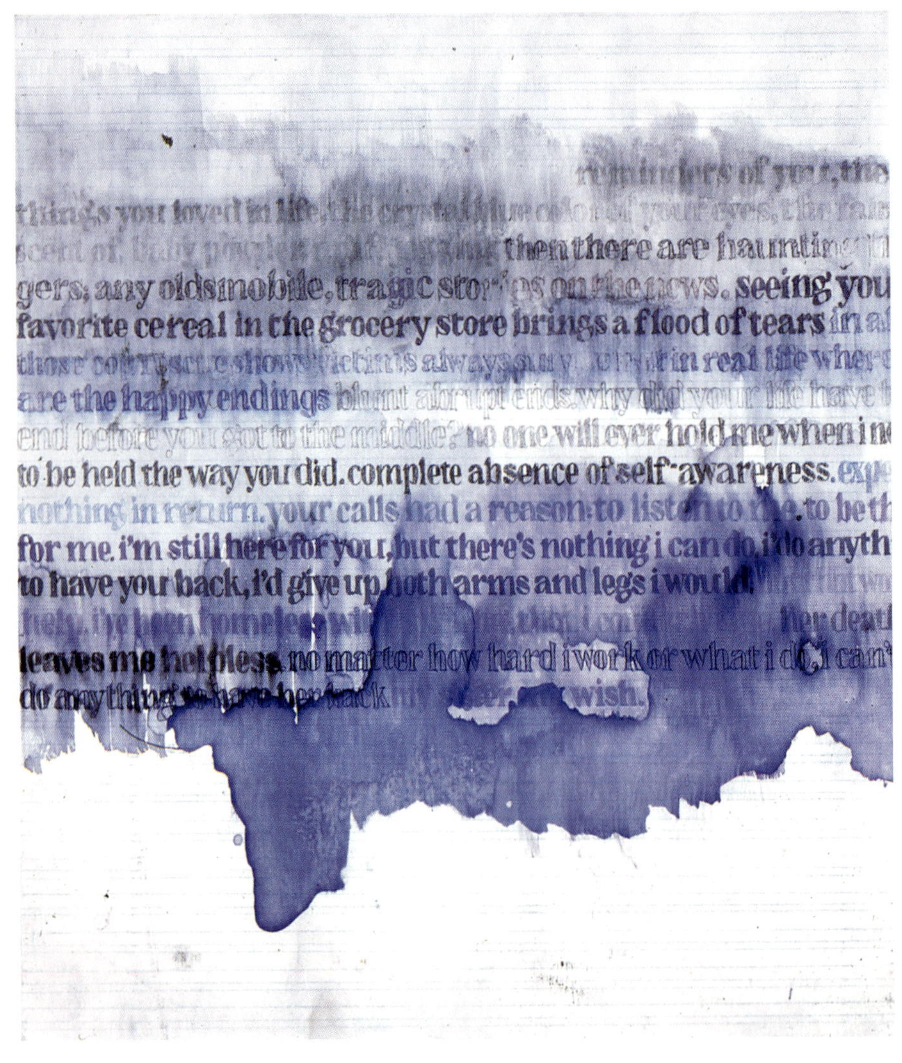
reminders of you, the things you loved in life, the crystal blue color of your eyes, the faint scent of baby powder and... then there are haunting triggers, any oldsmobile, tragic stories on the news. seeing your favorite cereal in the grocery store brings a flood of tears in all those courtroom show victims always... but in real life where are the happy endings blunt abrupt ends. why did your life have to end before you got to the middle? no one will ever hold me when i need to be held the way you did. complete absence of self-awareness. expect nothing in return. your calls had a reason to listen to me. to be there for me. i'm still here for you, but there's nothing i can do. i'd do anything to have your back, i'd give up both arms and legs i would. her death leaves me helpless. no matter how hard i work or what i do, i can't do anything to have her back... wish.

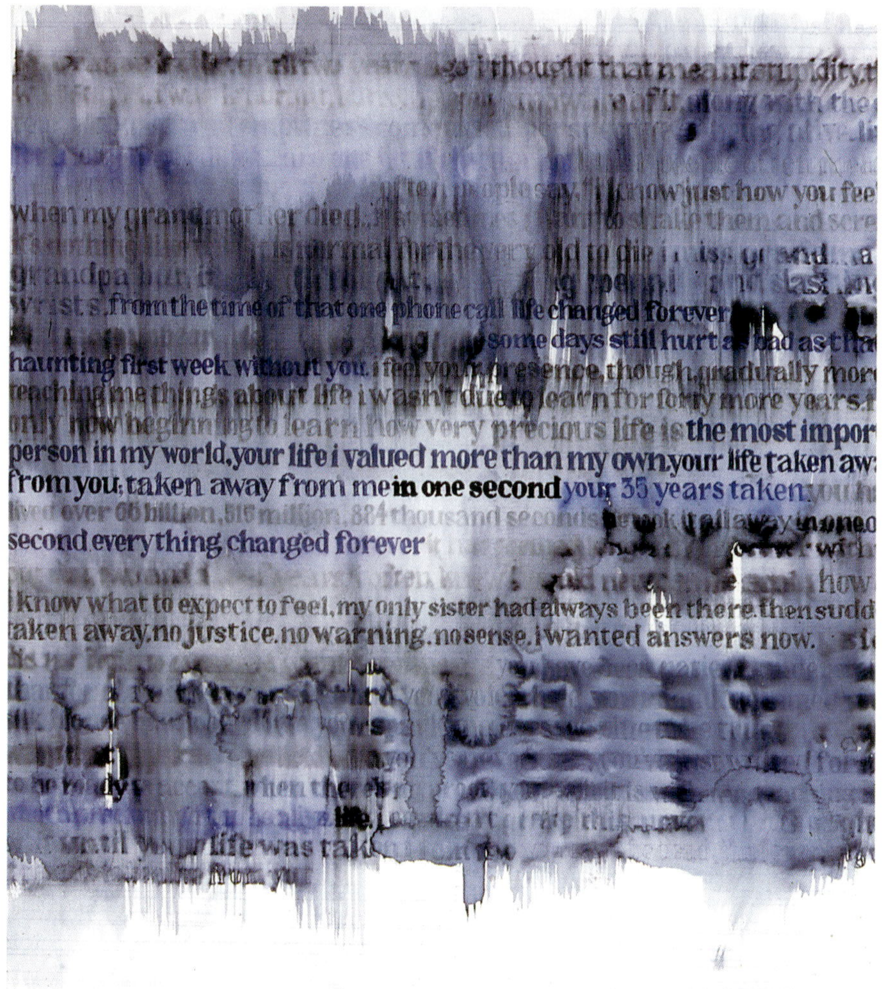
when my grandmother died. i wish... to die... is normal for the very old to die... grandpa but...
...from the time of that one phone call life changed forever...
...some days still hurt as bad as that
haunting first week without you. i feel your presence, though, gradually more
teaching me things about life i wasn't due to learn for forty more years. i
only now beginning to learn how very precious life is the most impor
person in my world, your life i valued more than my own. your life taken awa
from you. taken away from me in one second your 35 years taken you h
lived over 66 billion, 515 million, 884 thousand seconds he took it all away in one
second everything changed forever
i know what to expect to feel. my only sister had always been there. then sudd
taken away. no justice. no warning. no sense. i wanted answers now.
until your life was tak

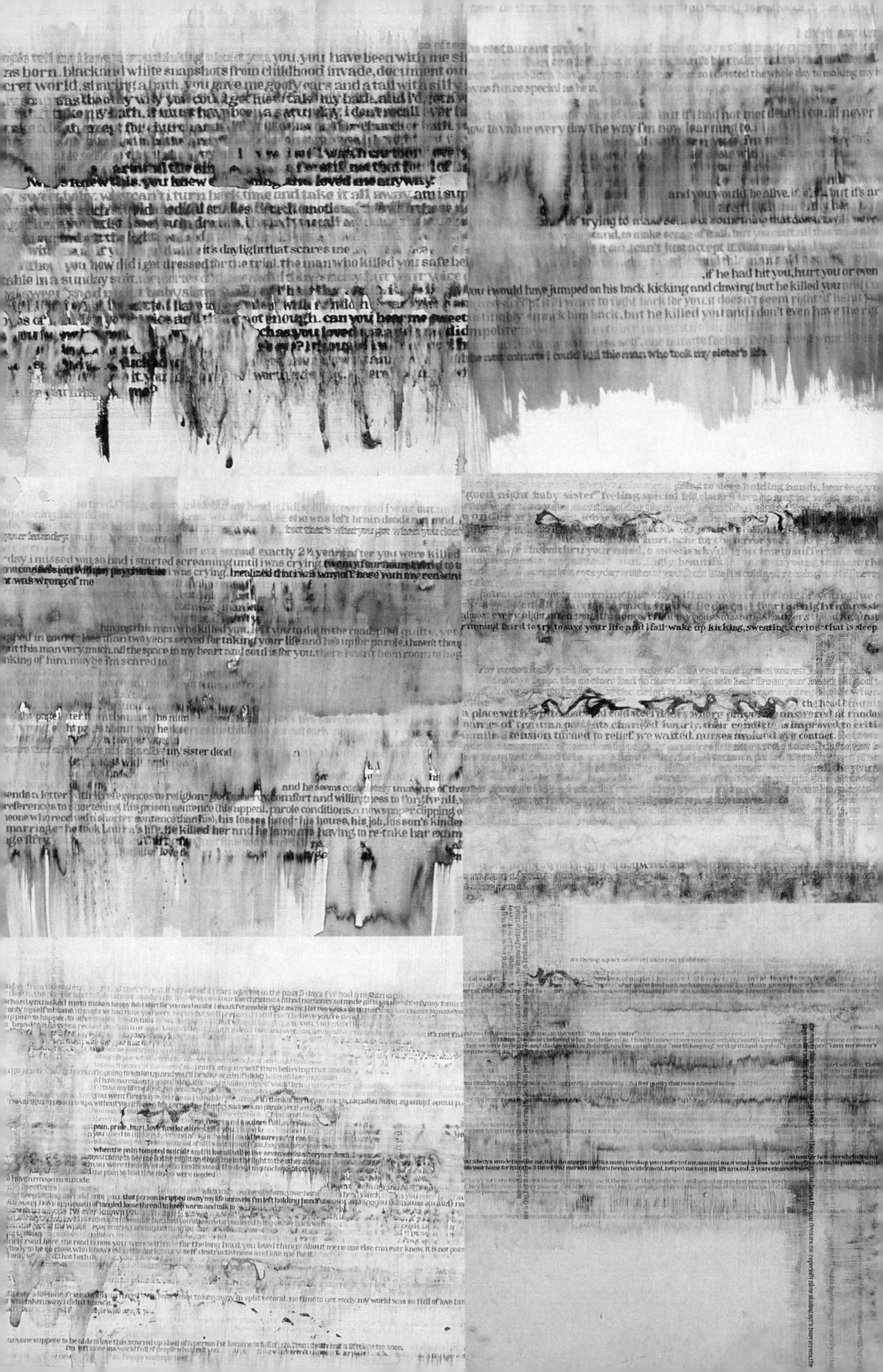

...ople tell me i have to stop thinking about you. you. you have been with me si...
as born. black and white snapshots from childhood invade. document ou...
cret world. starting a bath. you gave me goofy ears and a tail with silly...
...it was the only way you could get me to take my bath. and i'd get a w...
...make my bath. it must have been a saturday. i don't recall ever ha...
...take a bath except for church parties...

...you knew this. you knew e... ...you loved me anyway.
...sweet baby. why can't i turn back time and take it all away. am i sup...

...it's daylight that scares me...
...you how did i get dressed for the trial. the man who killed you safe be...
table in a sunday suit...
...not enough. can you hear me sweet...
...as you loved me...

...how to value every day the way i'm now learning to. i...

...and you would be alive. it...
...trying to make sense out of something that doesn't make...
...i can't just accept it that man...

...if he had hit you, hurt you or even...
...you i would have jumped on his back kicking and clawing but he killed you and i...
...punch him back. but he killed you and i don't even have the rig...

...the next minute i could kill this man who took my sister's life.

..."good night baby sister" feeling special big sister...

...so tired. i can't even make out my head is full. sitting over and i want out an...
...she was left brain dead and mad...
...hurt that's what you get when you don't...
your laundry...
...day i missed you so bad i started screaming until i was crying. twenty four hours later i to t...
...i was crying. i realized that i was wrong to be with my real sist...
...it was wrong of me

...having this man who killed you. left you to die in the road. pled guilty. yet...
...ed in court—less than two years served for taking your life and he's up for parole. i haven't thoug...
...this man very much. all the space in my heart and soul is for you. there hasn't been room to beg...
...nking of him. maybe i'm scared to.

...i see you alive. my sister dead

...and he seems completely unaware of the...
sends a letter with references to religion—god's mercy, comfort and willingness to forgive all. ...
references to shortening his prison sentence (his appeal, parole conditions, a newspaper clipping o...
...one who received a shorter sentence than his), his losses listed—his house, his job, his son's kinder...
marriage—he took Laura's life. he killed her and he laments having to re-take bar exam...
age fifty...

...every night, often i am in the ambulance, i'll try to save... smashing his doctors bend against...
running hard to try to save your life and i fall. wake up kicking, sweating, crying. that is sleep...

...the doctors had to shave your head to...
...in a place with bright lights and cold steel floors where privacy is answered at random...
...ranges of trauma patients changed hourly. their condition improved to criti...
...amilies' tension turned to relief. we waited. nurses avoided eye contact...

...richard you asked me to make me happy. fish short for you real maili i should've made it right away. i let two weeks go by other...
only myself to blame. i ought to have time you were so careful. well prepared. i still can't believe you're dead...
...suppose to happen to other people. anyways...
...broadcast there was a reunion...it is you. you can't d...

...i can't stop myself from believing this one day i...
...i have no reason to go on living. if it wasn't for myself i would bring...
...i take my life right away...
you went first...
...when the pain tempted suicide and i'd lost all faith...
...you were the only one who understood the despair, the darkness of living...
the pain so bad that the drugs were needed.

...pain, pride, hurt, love and fear...
...i have no reason to live...

...that person is ripped away my life unravels. i'm left holding hands...
...tangled loose thread to keep warm and talk to...

...lonely road here. the road to now you were within. for the long haul. you loved things about me no one else can ever know. it is not poss...
...to be so close. who knows...self destructiveness and love me for it...

...taken away in split second. no time to get ready. my world was so full of love...

...anyone suppose to be able to love this scarred up shell of a person i've become. so full of ache. from death i had a lifetime too soon.
i'm just alone in a world full of people who can't see you...

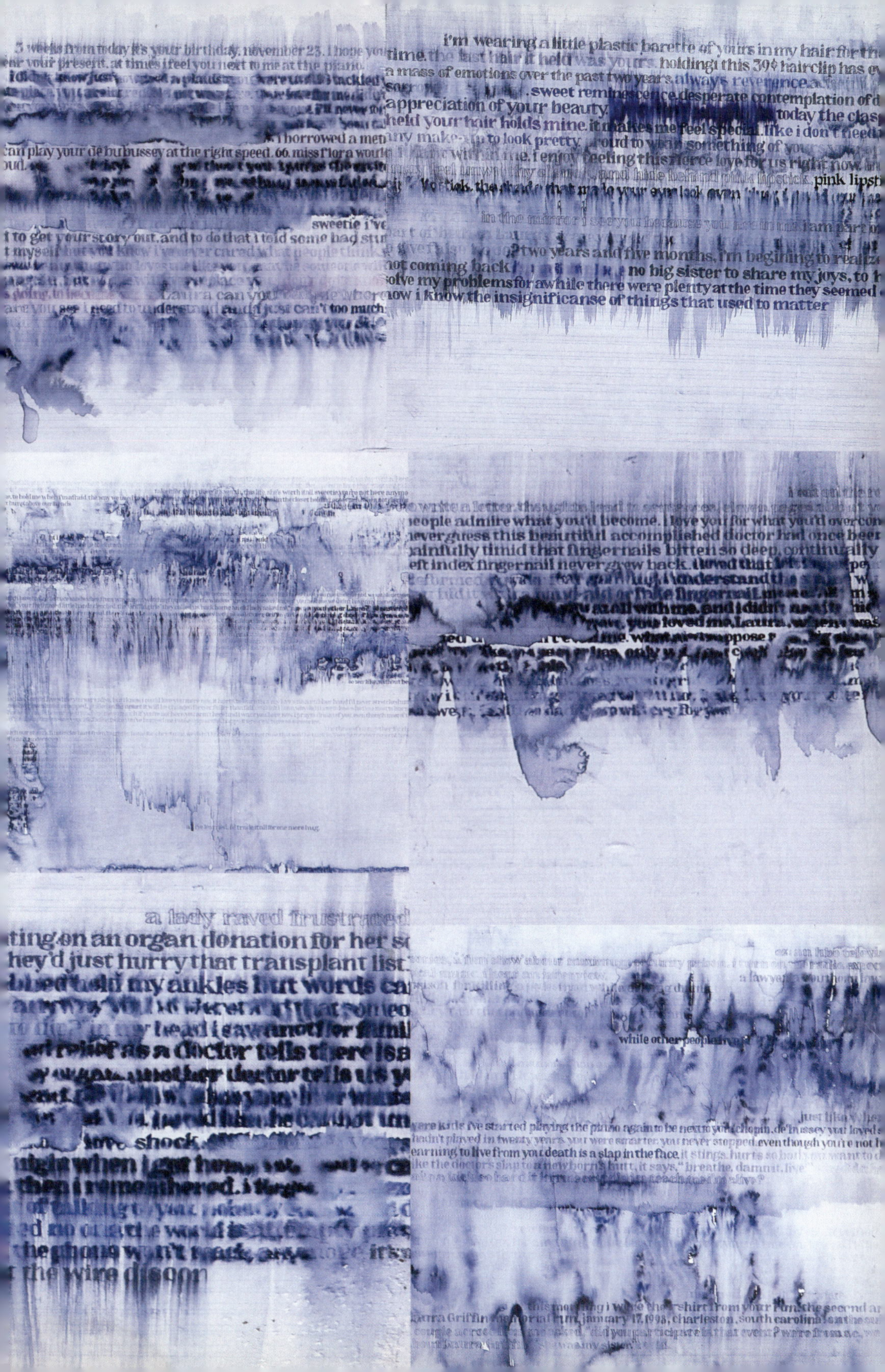

5 weeks from today it's your birthday. november 23. i hope you...
...your present. at times i feel your next to me at the piano...
...can play your debussey at the right speed. oh, miss flora would...

...i borrowed a me...
...

sweetie i've...
...to get your story out, and to do that i told some bad stu...
...myself but you know i never cared what people think...

Laura can you...
...are you... i need to understand and i just can't too much.

i'm wearing a little plastic barette of yours in my hair for the
time. the last hair it held was yours. holding this 39¢ hairclip has ev
a mass of emotions over the past two years. always revenge...
...sweet reminescence. desperate contemplation of d
appreciation of your beauty... today the clas
held your hair holds mine. it makes me feel special. like i don't need...
...to look pretty... proud to wear something of you...
...feeling this fierce love for us right now...
...pink lipstick. pink lipst...

in the mirror i see you because you are in me. i am part o...
...two years and five months. i'm beginning to realiz
not coming back... no big sister to share my joys, to h
solve my problems for awhile there were plenty at the time they seemed
now i know the insignificanse of things that used to matter

...to write a letter. the...
people admire what you't become. i love you for what you'd over com
neverguess this beautiful accomplished doctor had once bee
painfully timid that fingernails bitten so deep, continually
eft index fingernail nevergrew back. i loved that...
...understand th...
...fingernail...
...you fell in love with me, and i didn't want to thi
...you loved me. Laura, what...
...what...

a lady raved frustrated
...ting on an organ donation for her so
hey'd just hurry that transplant list.
...told my ankles hurt but words ca
...
...head i saw another famil
...relief as a doctor tells there is a
...another doctor tell us y
...
...love, shock...
...night when i got home...
then i remembered. i forgive...
...talking...
...the phone won't reach, an... hope it's...
...the wire disconn

while other people...

...were kids i've started playing the piano again to be near you. chopin, debussey you loved
hadn't played in twenty years. you were smarter. you never stopped. even though you're not h
earning to live from your death is a slap in the face. it stings. hurts so bad i don't want to d
...like the doctors slap to a newborn's butt, it says, " breathe, damnit, live...

...this morning i wore the shirt from your funk the second
Laura Griffin memorial fund, january 17, 1998, charleston, south carolina...

Ed Kashi

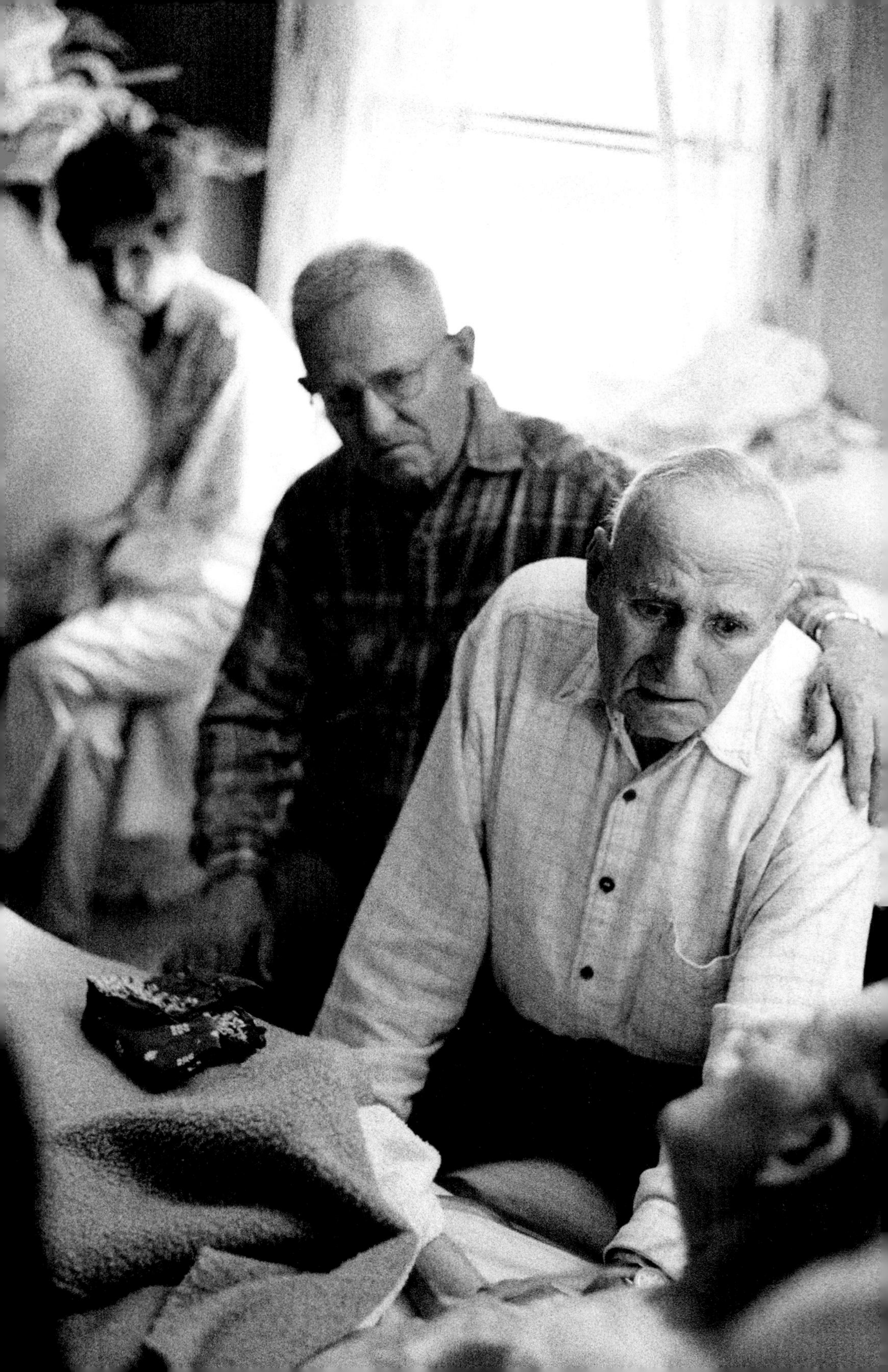

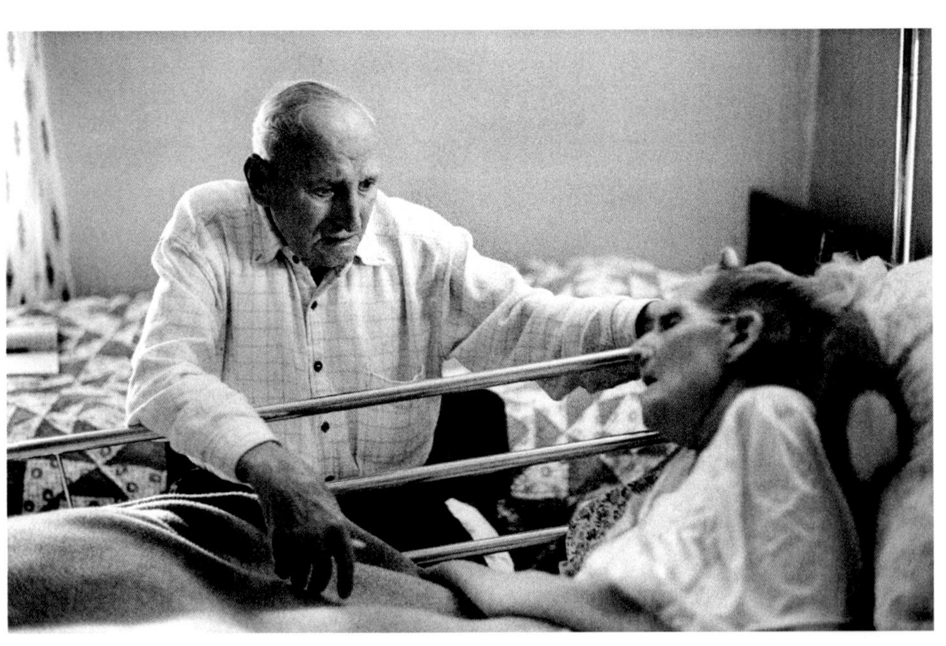

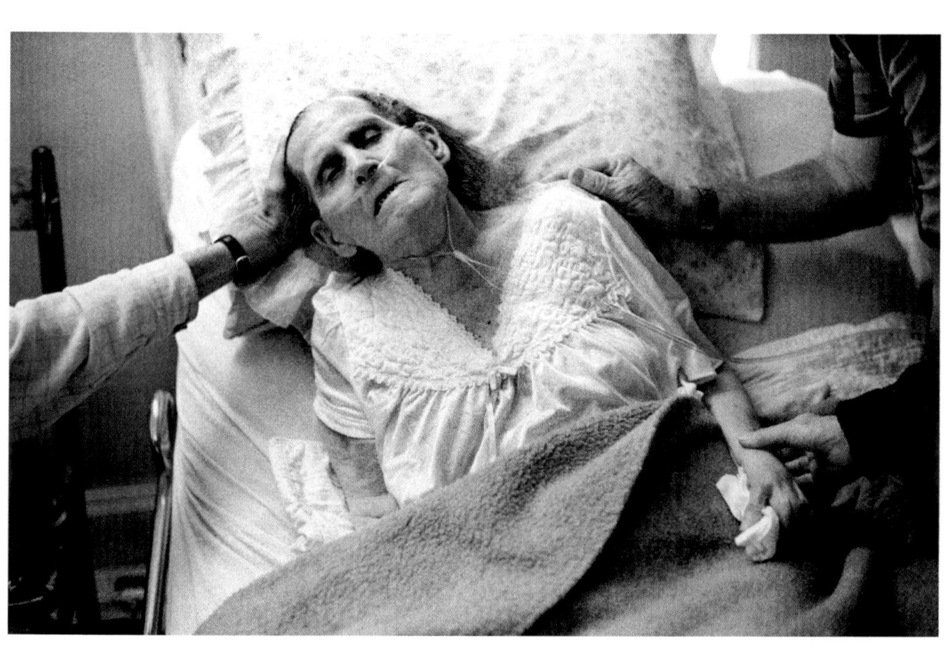

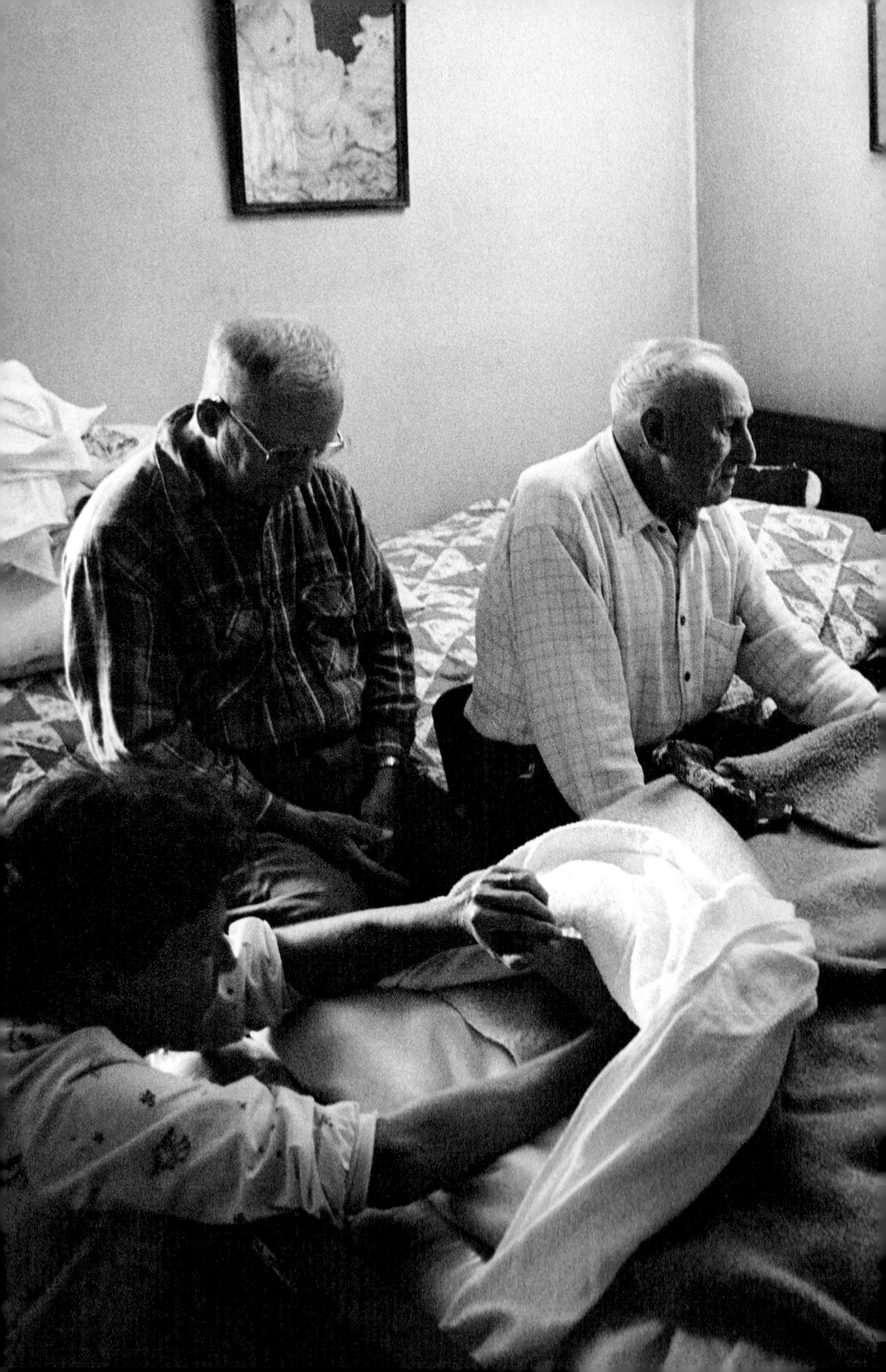

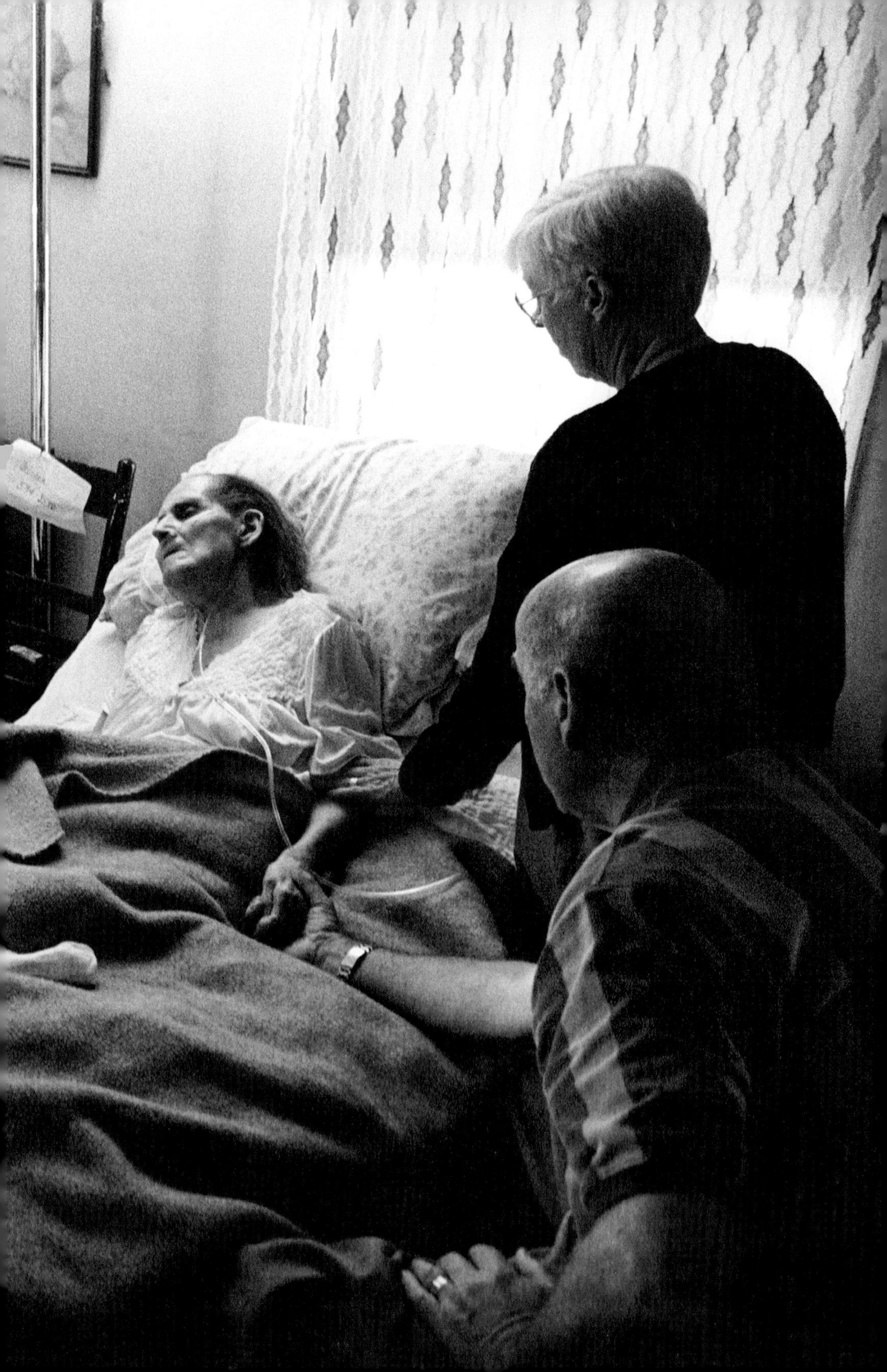

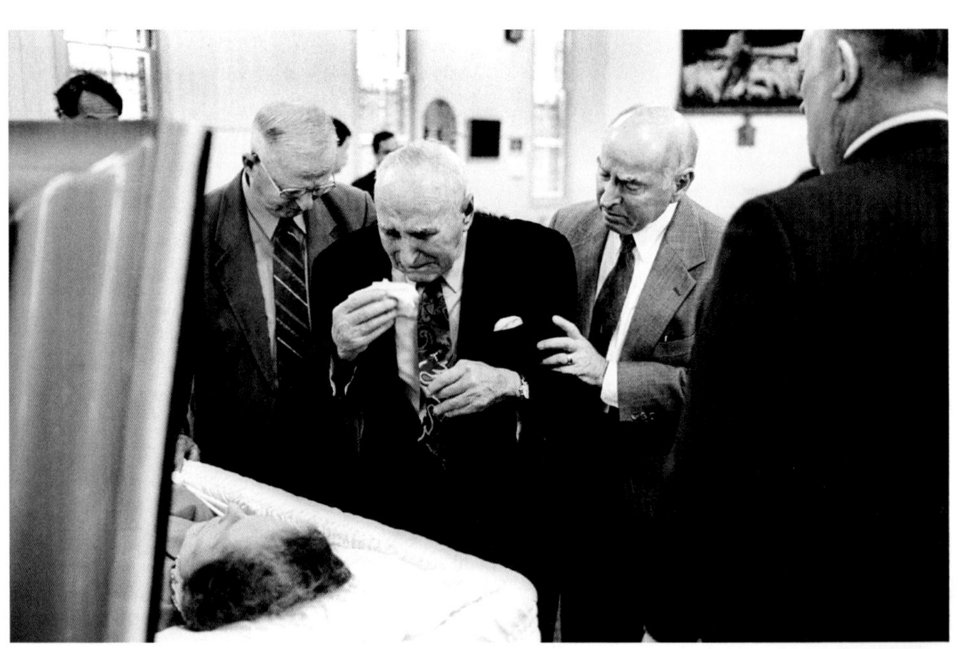

Last Good-bye

The drive to her house was quiet and tedious. The questions of what to expect or how to react went through my head. Visions of horrifying tubes and masks poked in her like a pin cushion and pale white limbs hanging off the bed while the rest of her body lies under a clean white sheet tortured my head.

I wondered what thoughts were jogging through my mother's head. I pictured what it would be like losing someone I grew up with. Someone who was my best friend, my sister, my date when I didn't have one. Someone who raised her glass at my wedding, and someone who almost was prouder of my children than I was. I never asked my mom what she was thinking during the five hours, over the course of the day, that we spent in the car. Some things are meant to be left alone.

I sat in the car while my mom slid the brownish red pigment over her lips according to the reflection in the mirror. She closed all her materials in her bag, and walked up the front steps to the open entrance. I followed shortly behind. An old Muslim man led us upstairs to Amy's room. My mom kissed two of Amy's former nurses who helped her through her struggle with cancer. As their embrace parted, Amy came into view sleeping for eternity, wrapped up like a baby. Right away the happy spirit I had remembered was replaced by the vision of the absence of life. I gasped and fell into tears. The bleeding emotion dripped into my palms as I left the room.

The scarf was draped over my head. In the Muslim religion this shows a form of self-respect, women are supposed to be completely covered. To me this unfamiliar drape signified the emptiness I felt in my heart and represented the lid that would encapsulate my feelings. Just as the knot was tightened in the cloth under my chin, men carried Amy out in a wooden box with suns and moons carved out of it. We all followed as they carried her to the mosque where prayers would be said, and then a drive to the cemetery.

We drove to a one-hundred-acre parcel that was purchased for a Muslim burial ground. Right in the middle was a mosque, painted in brilliant colors like metallic gold and mint green. They showed the beautiful round shape of the small, one-room building. There, Bawa was in a tomb under the ground. He is considered a religious figure to the Muslim people. Here is where the women watch from afar, as the men lower Amy into the ground. I slowly observed all the women standing on the hill. Some mourning in tears, some in reminiscing laughter. But neverthe-less mourning. The strong breeze blew my tears away from my eyes. I could hear a strange yet beautiful chant being sung by the hardworking men. She would have loved the weather on this day. Not too hot, not too cool, but sunny and breezy. It seemed like it was just for her. Looking around, I noticed that very few people are buried here compared to other cemeteries that I had been in. Each site has a story which every person knows in this close knit community. They buried Amy wrapped in a cloth, and laid her in the man-made hole which was supported by wooden planks. They placed her head on a pillow of dirt and turned her face toward the mosque so that she could see Bawa. Then every man took a shovel in hand. The sound of the shovel as they were inserted into the grainy dirt, made tears stream down my flushed cheeks. The dirt and rocks scraped together, leaving an echoing sound that carried through the wind and pierced my ears. This was the final good-bye. And with that, the men came to us on the hill and escorted us down to Amy's covered body. We all swept up some rocks and flagstone in our hands and placed it on top, like icing on a cake except not as sweet.

Up until now, I had been walked through the steps of death, but nothing that I have ever attended or talked about could have prepared me for this. Like many things in life, we are so quick to speak of them without experiencing. When we do finally get the chance to see what we have been speaking of, it is nothing like what our minds told us it would be. This held true in my last good-bye, and I'm sure in Amy's also.

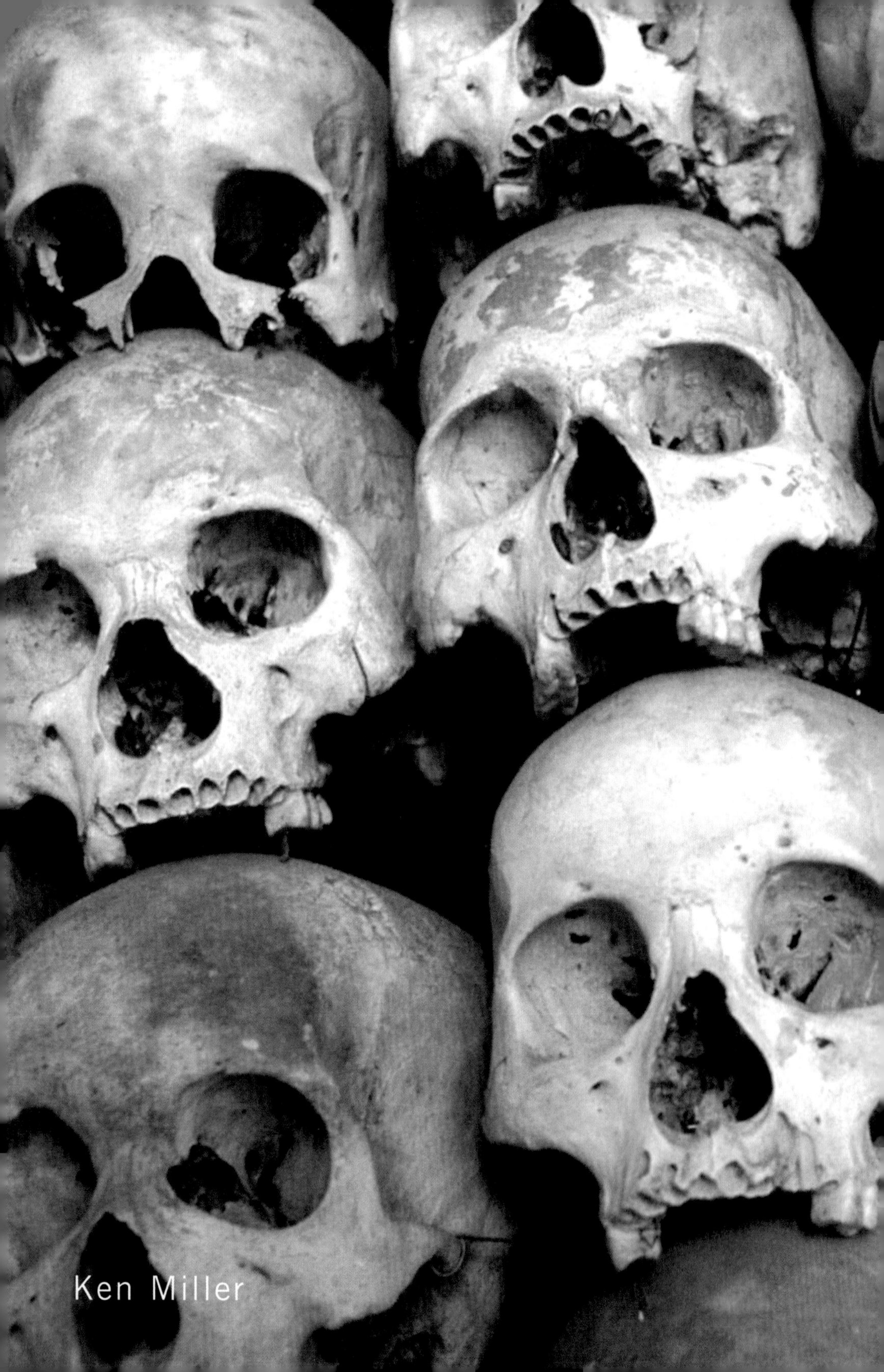
Ken Miller

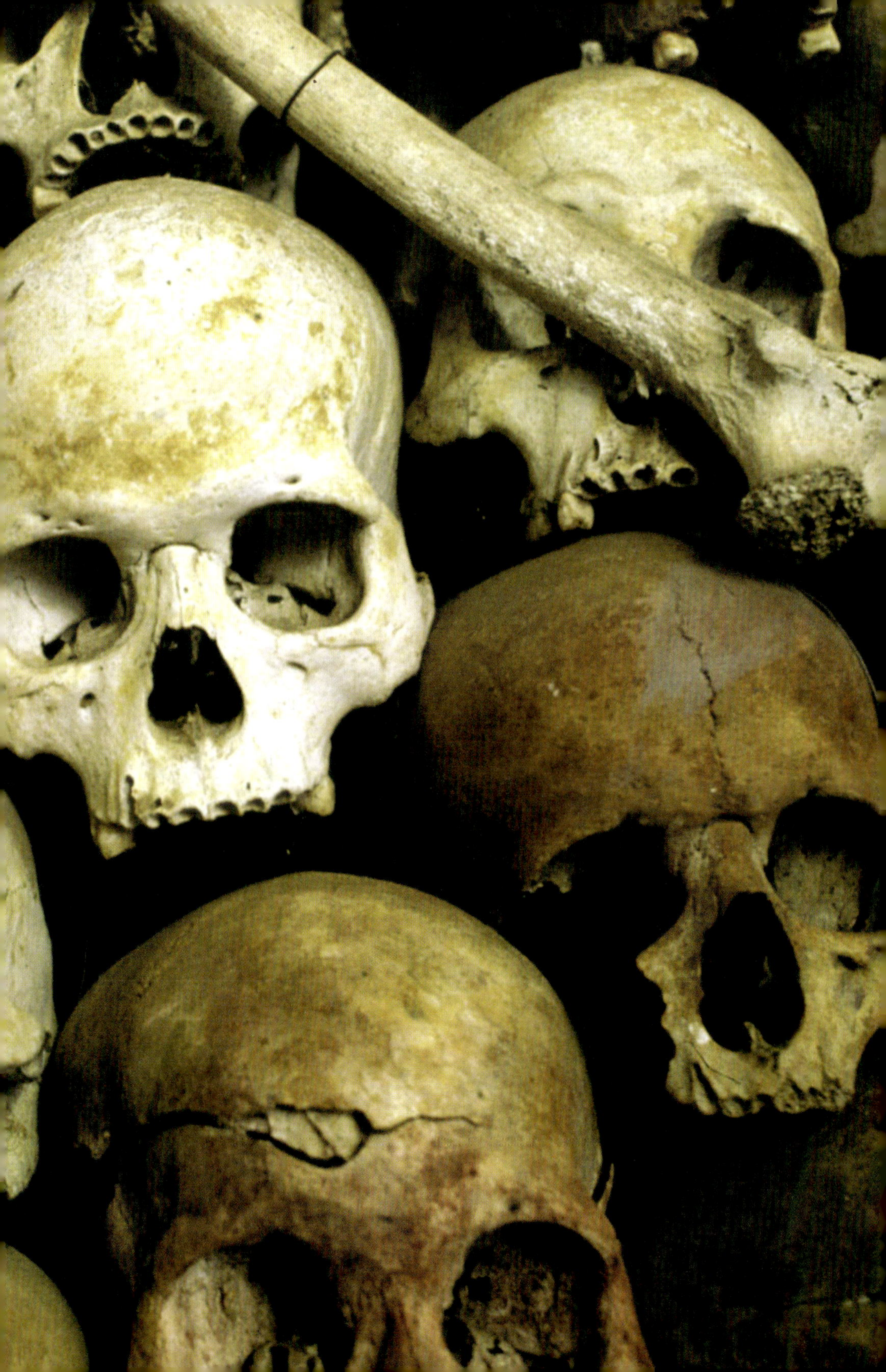

Harrell Fletcher

What do you want to have happen
to your body after you die?

I want my body to be buried without
a casket in the ground in the
country. I want my body to
decompose, to become compost.

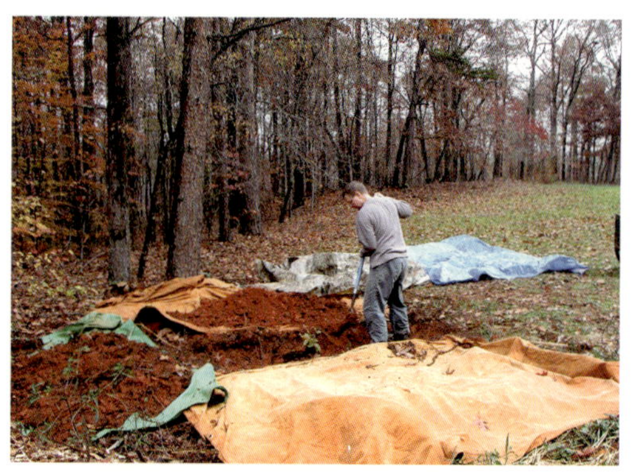

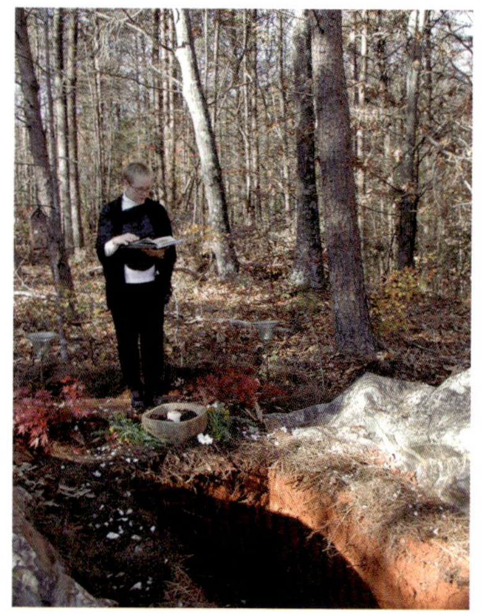

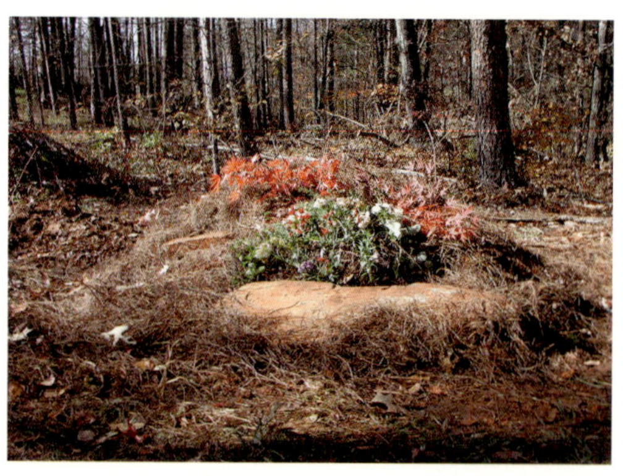

Kimberly Campbell

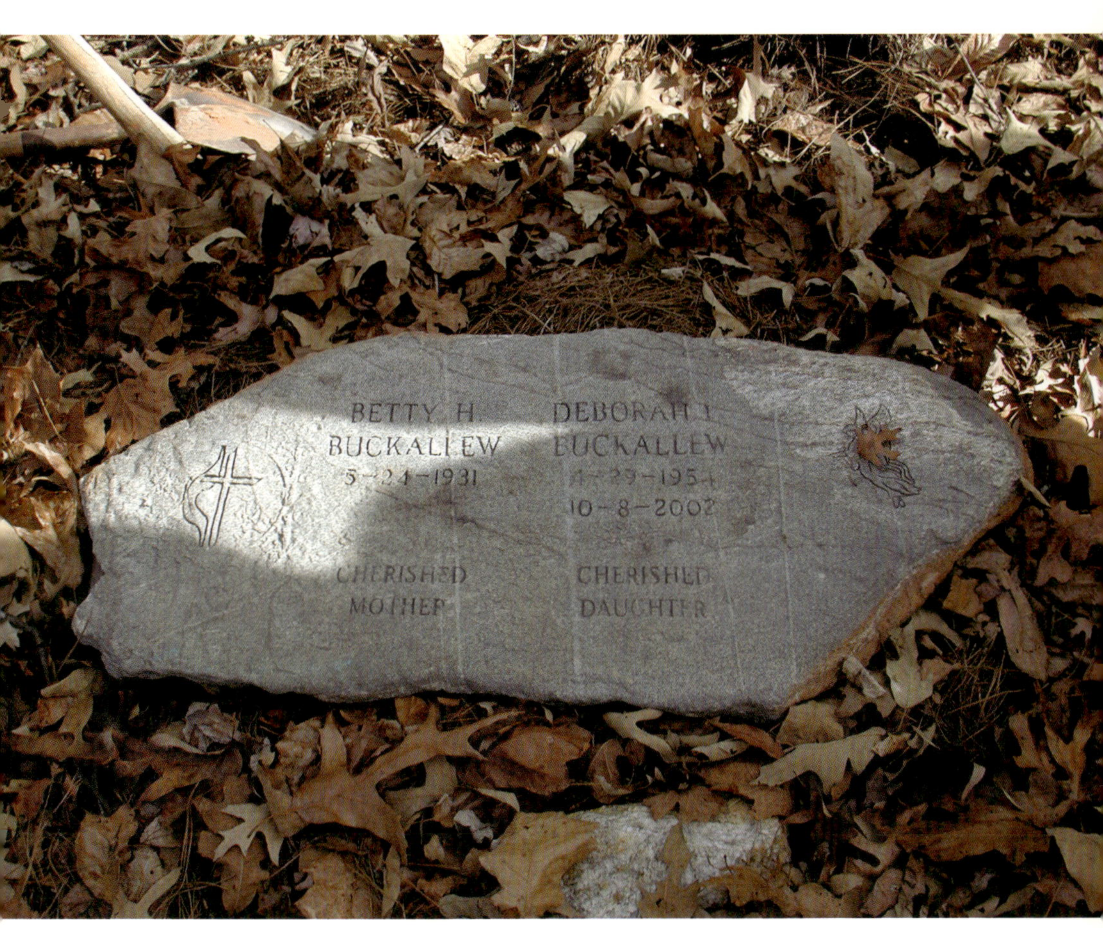

BETTY H.
BUCKALLEW
5-24-1931

DEBORAH L.
BUCKALLEW
4-29-1954
10-8-2002

CHERISHED
MOTHER

CHERISHED
DAUGHTER

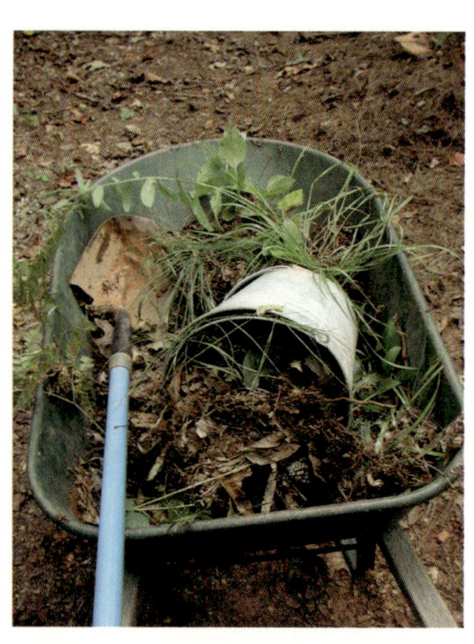

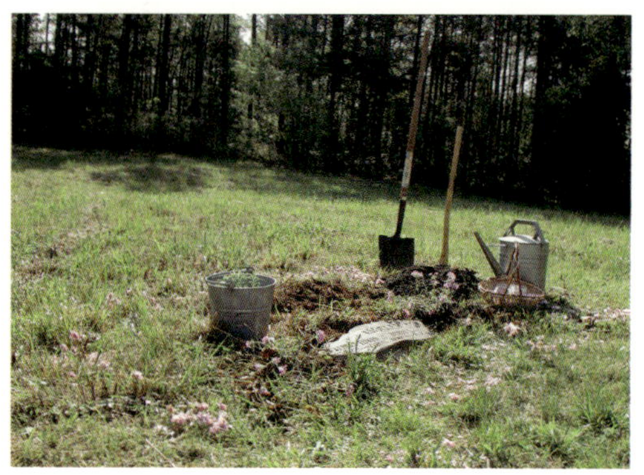

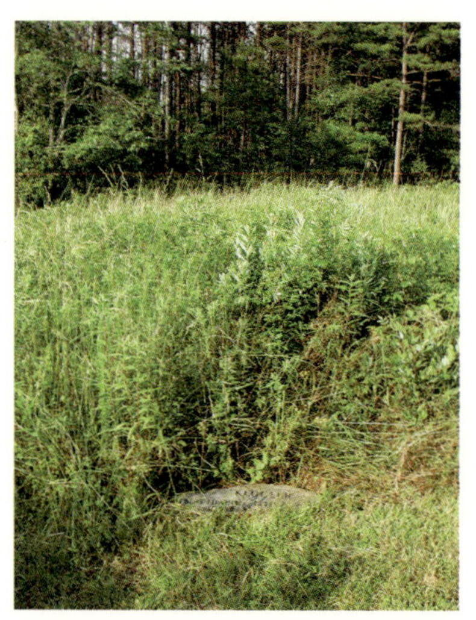

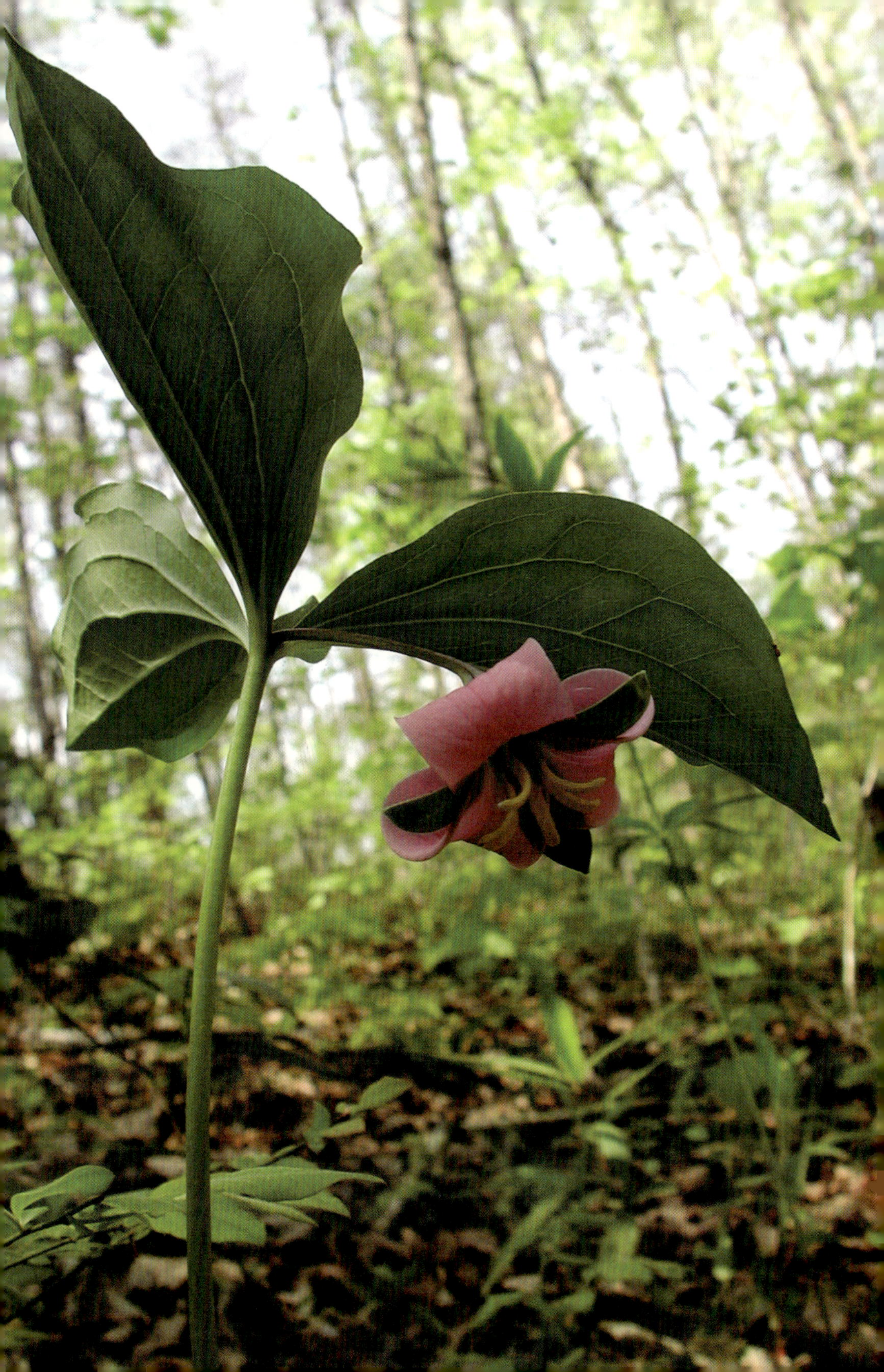

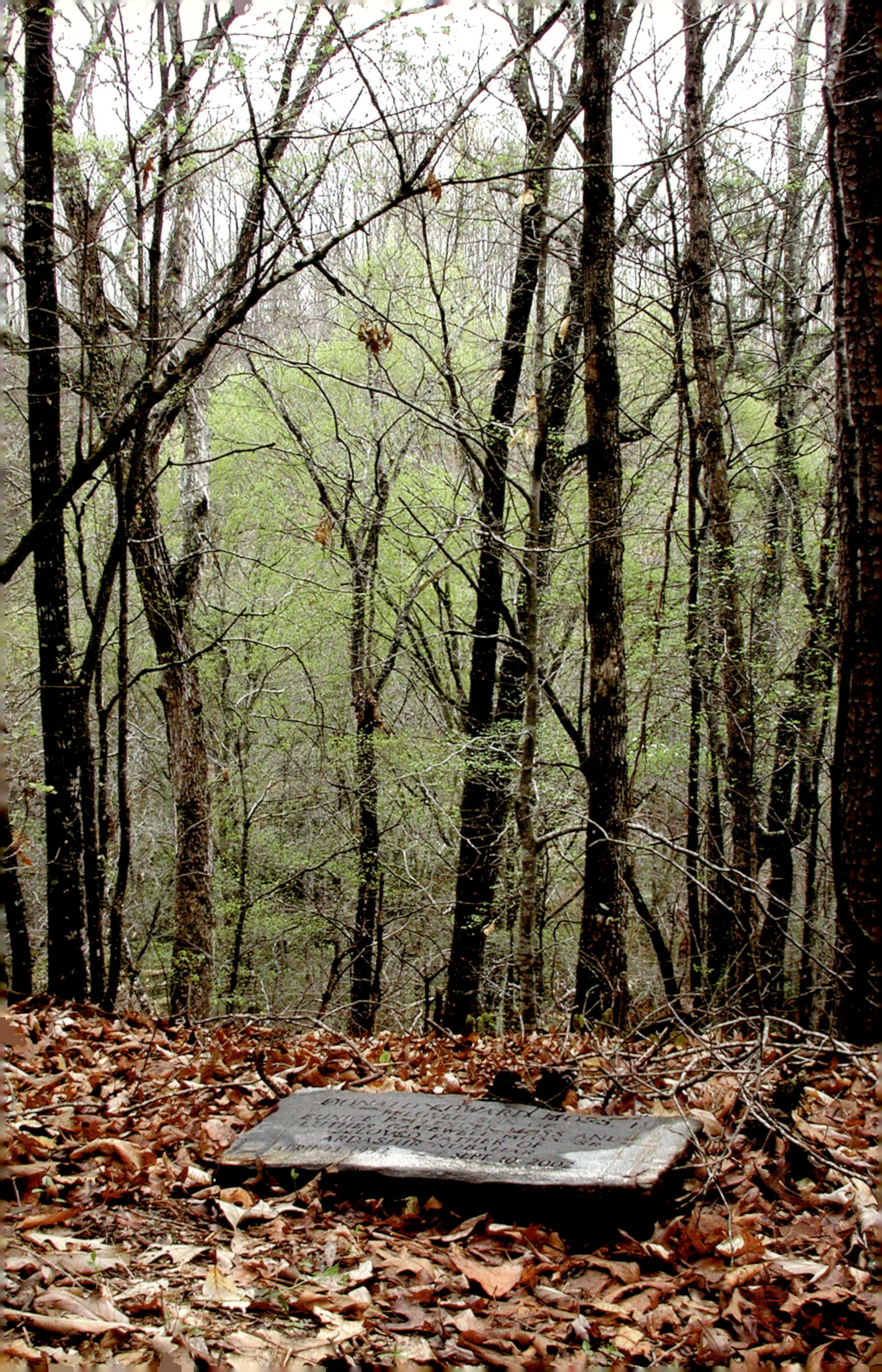

DONALD EDWARD HORST II
BELOVED BROTHERLESS AND
FUNKLE FAREWELL OF
BELOVED FATHER OF
ARDASHIR TOOBAR AR
SEPT 10 2002

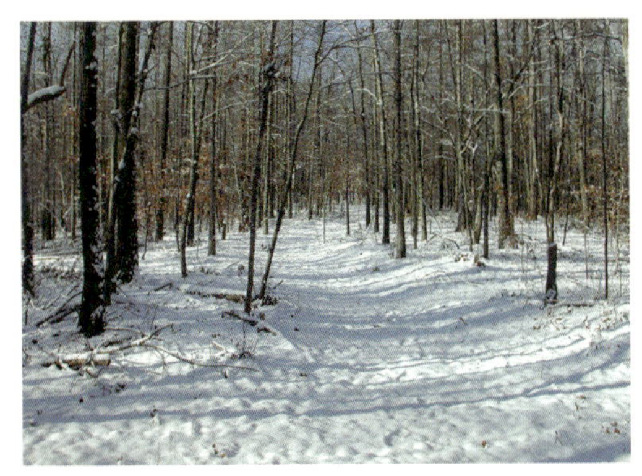

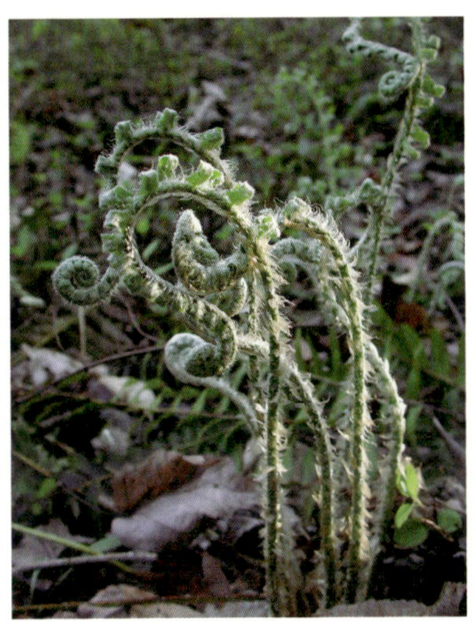

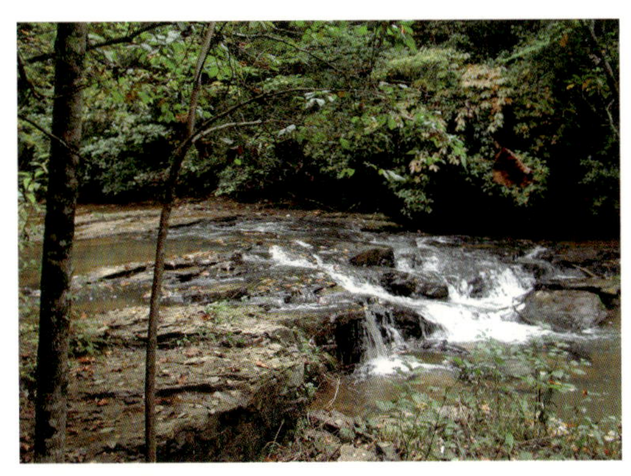

Erik Auerbach

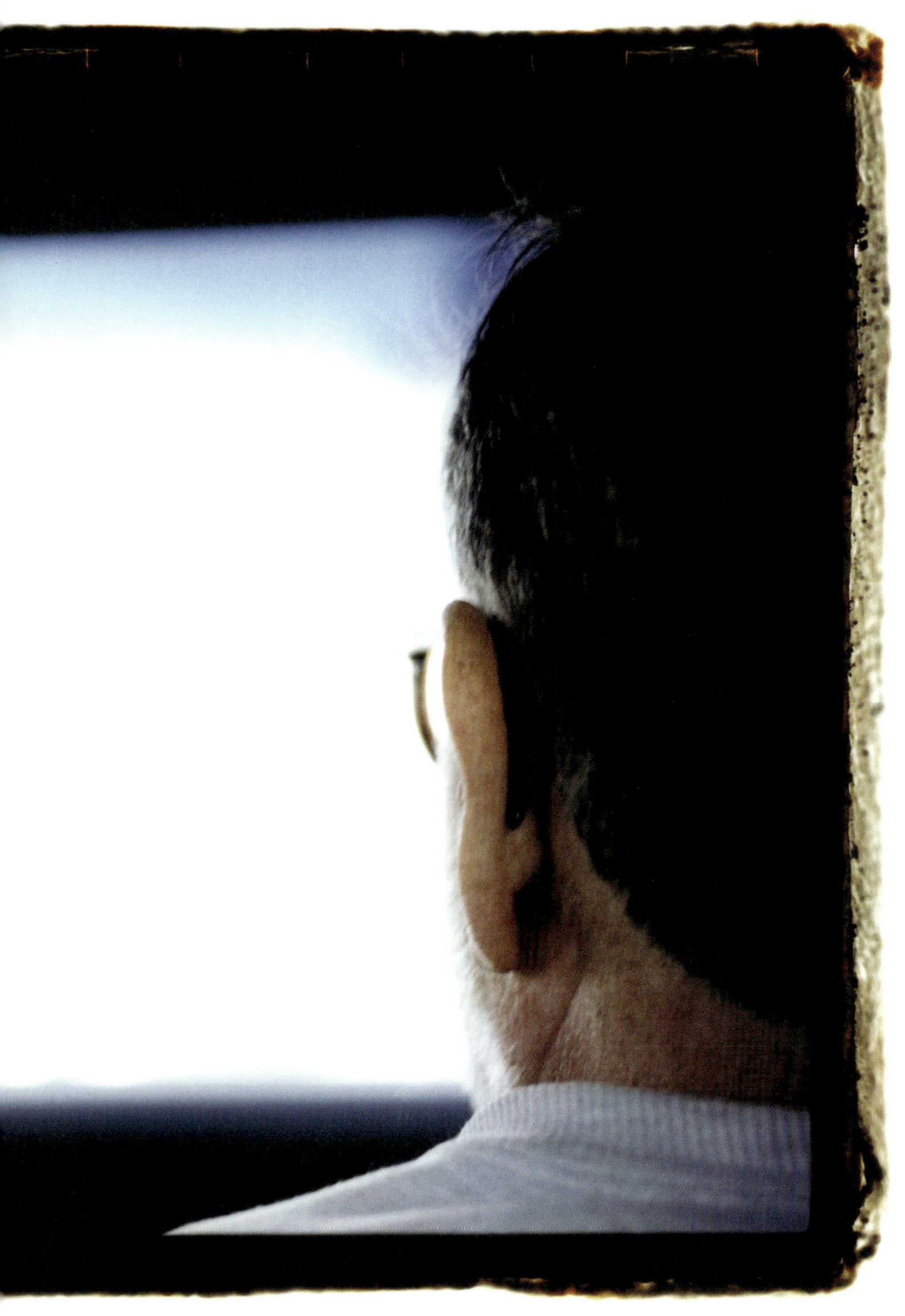

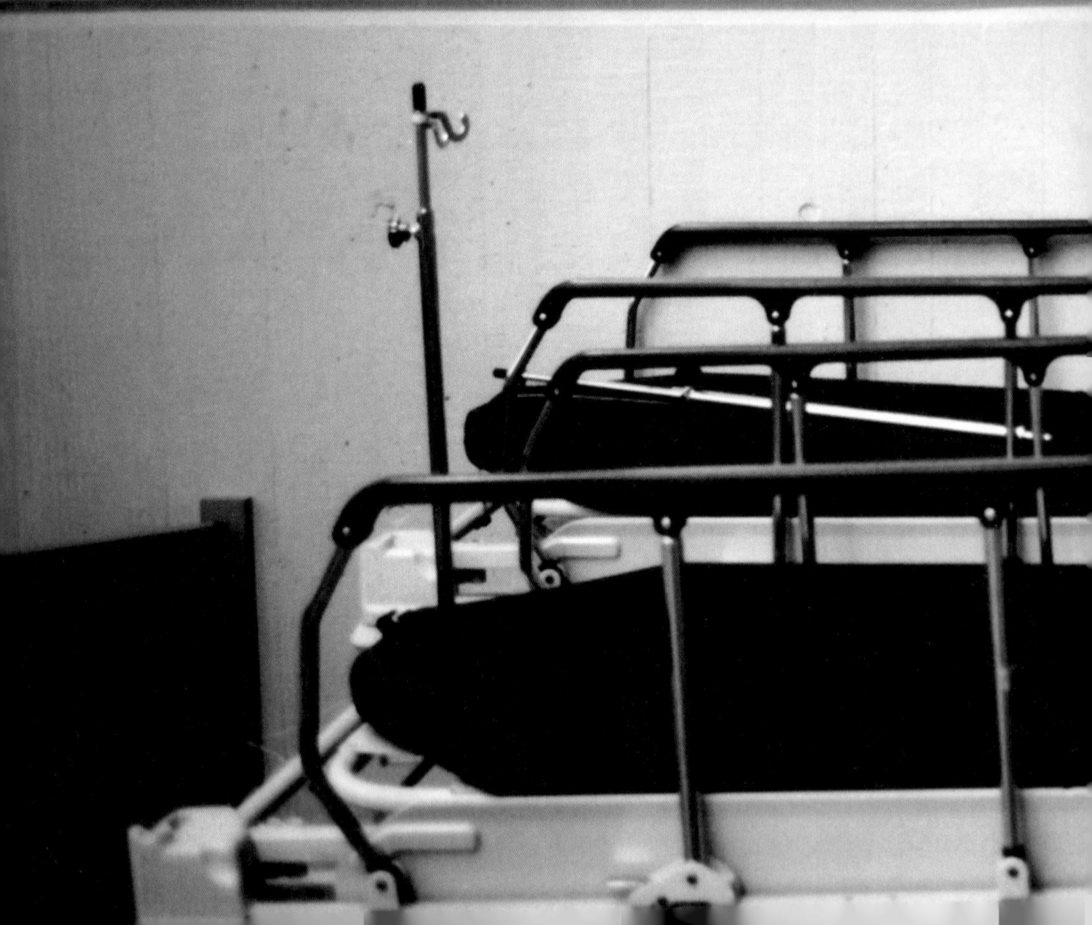

ELEVATOR T
HOSPITAL
ADMISSION

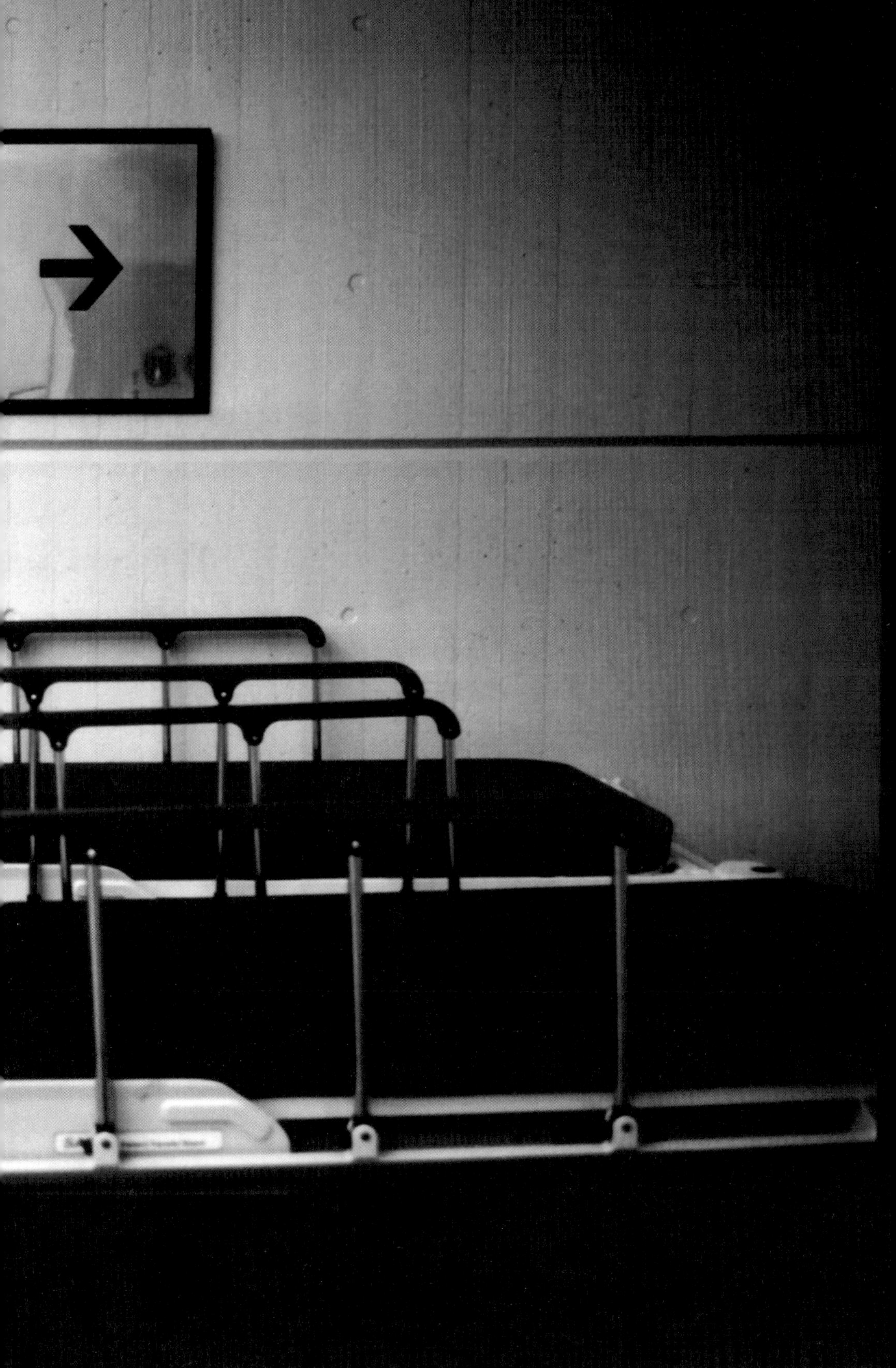

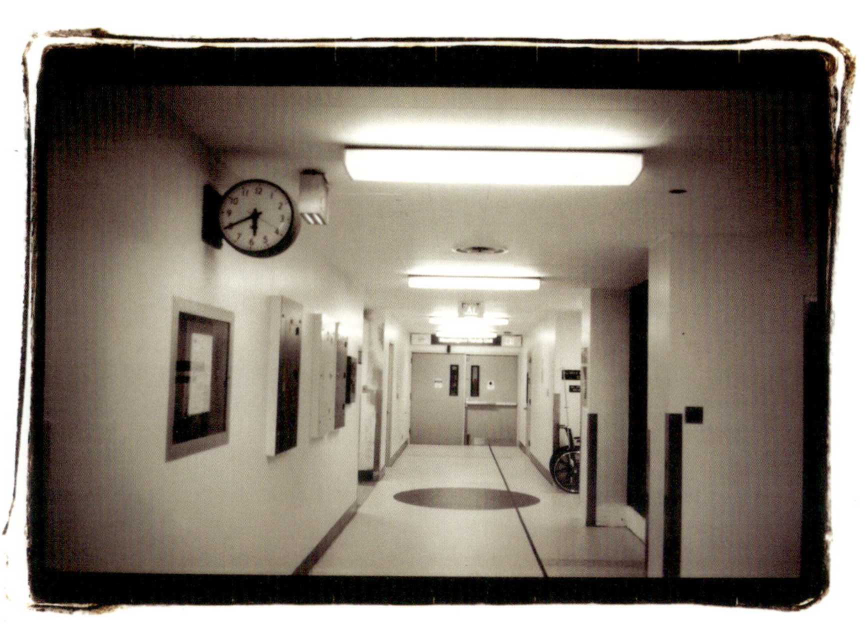

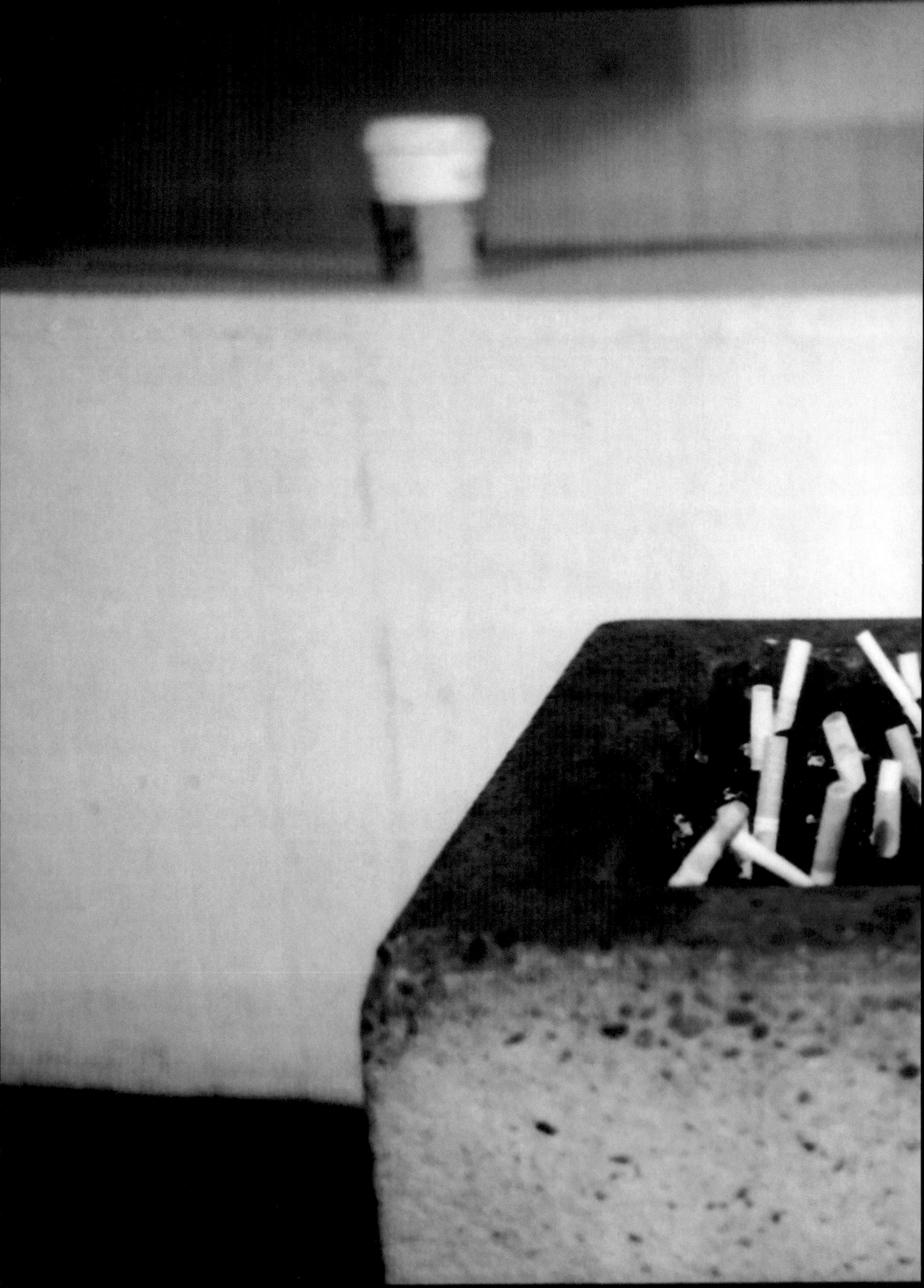

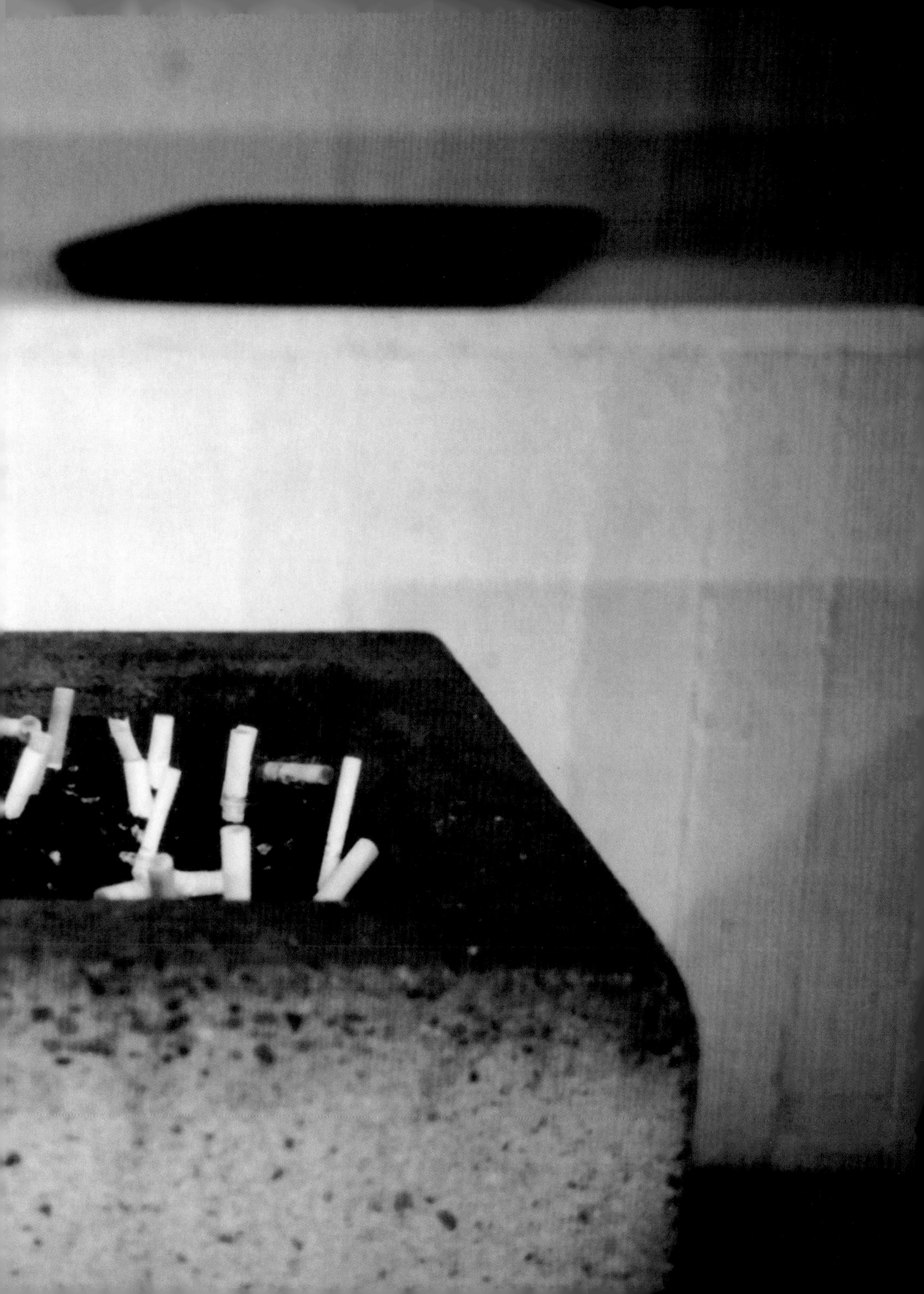

Inform

You Are

ation

Here

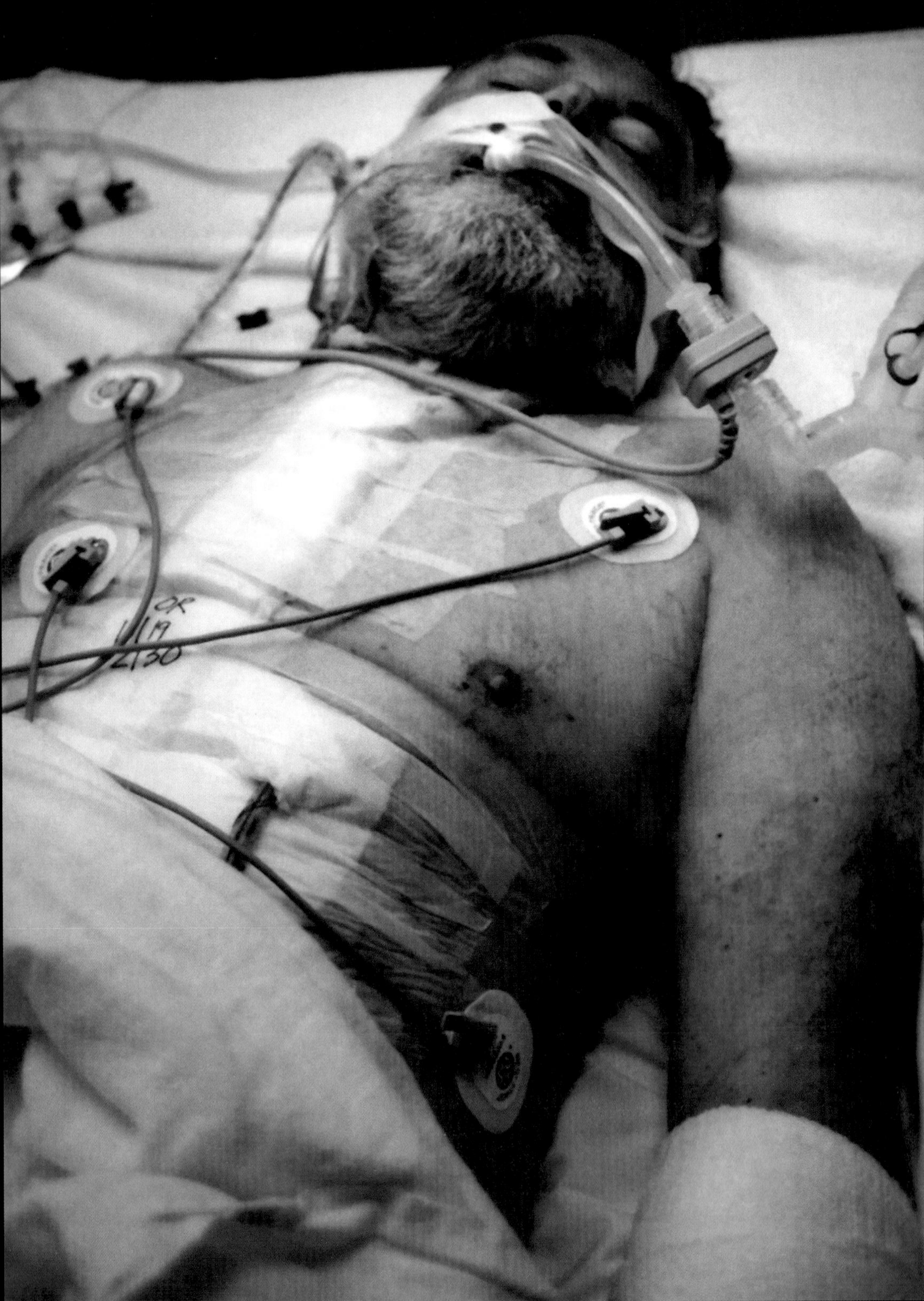

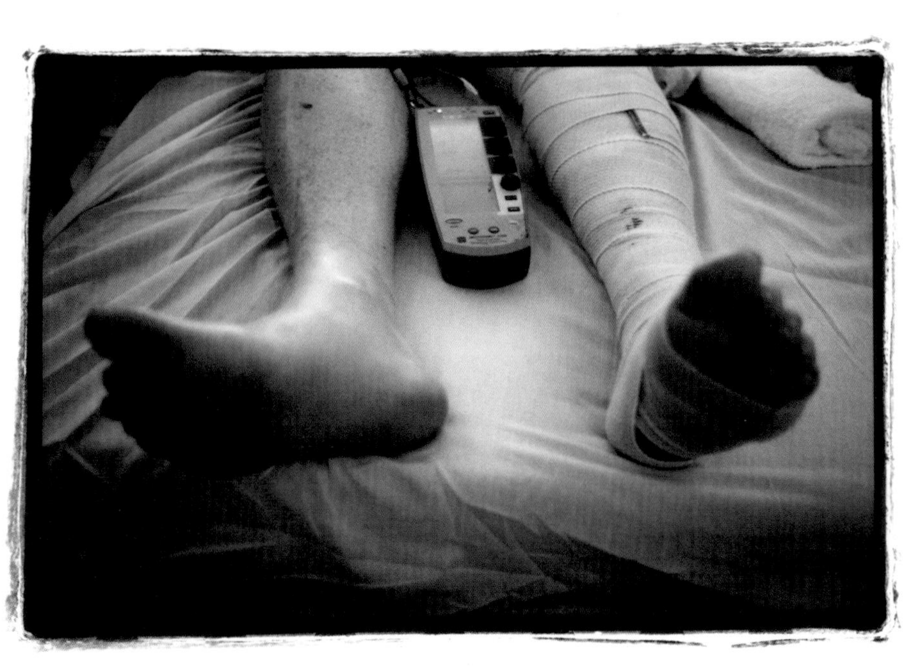

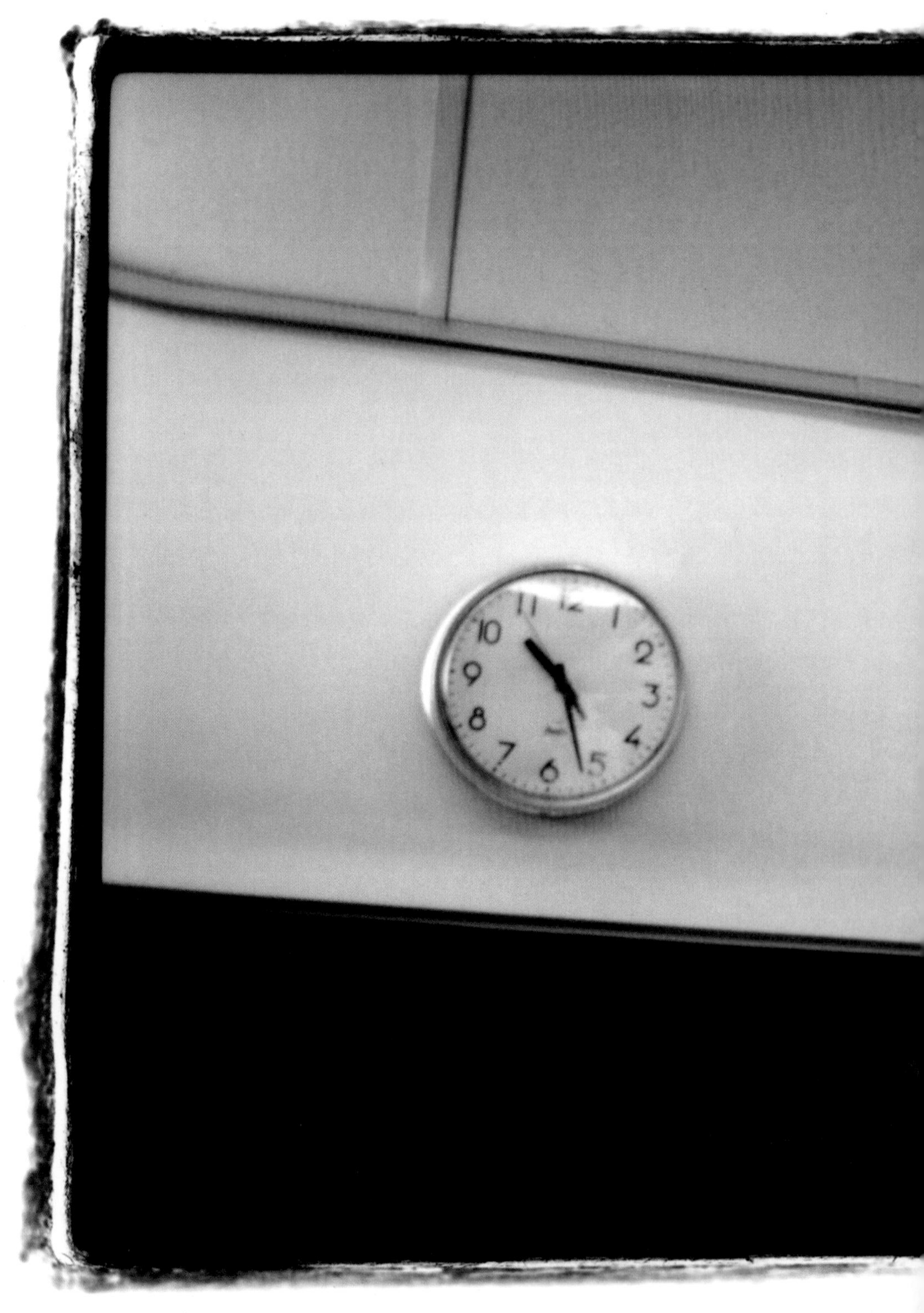

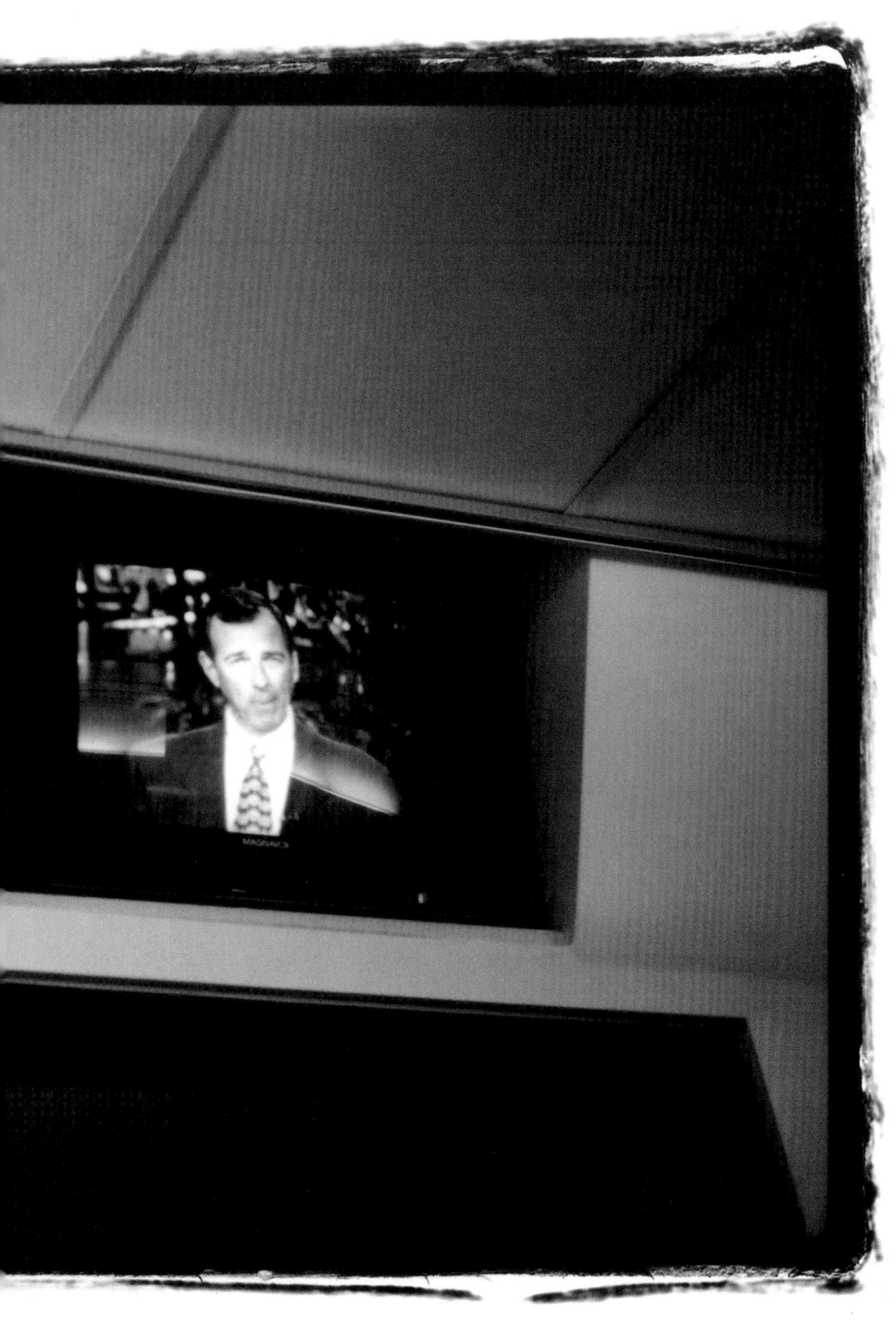

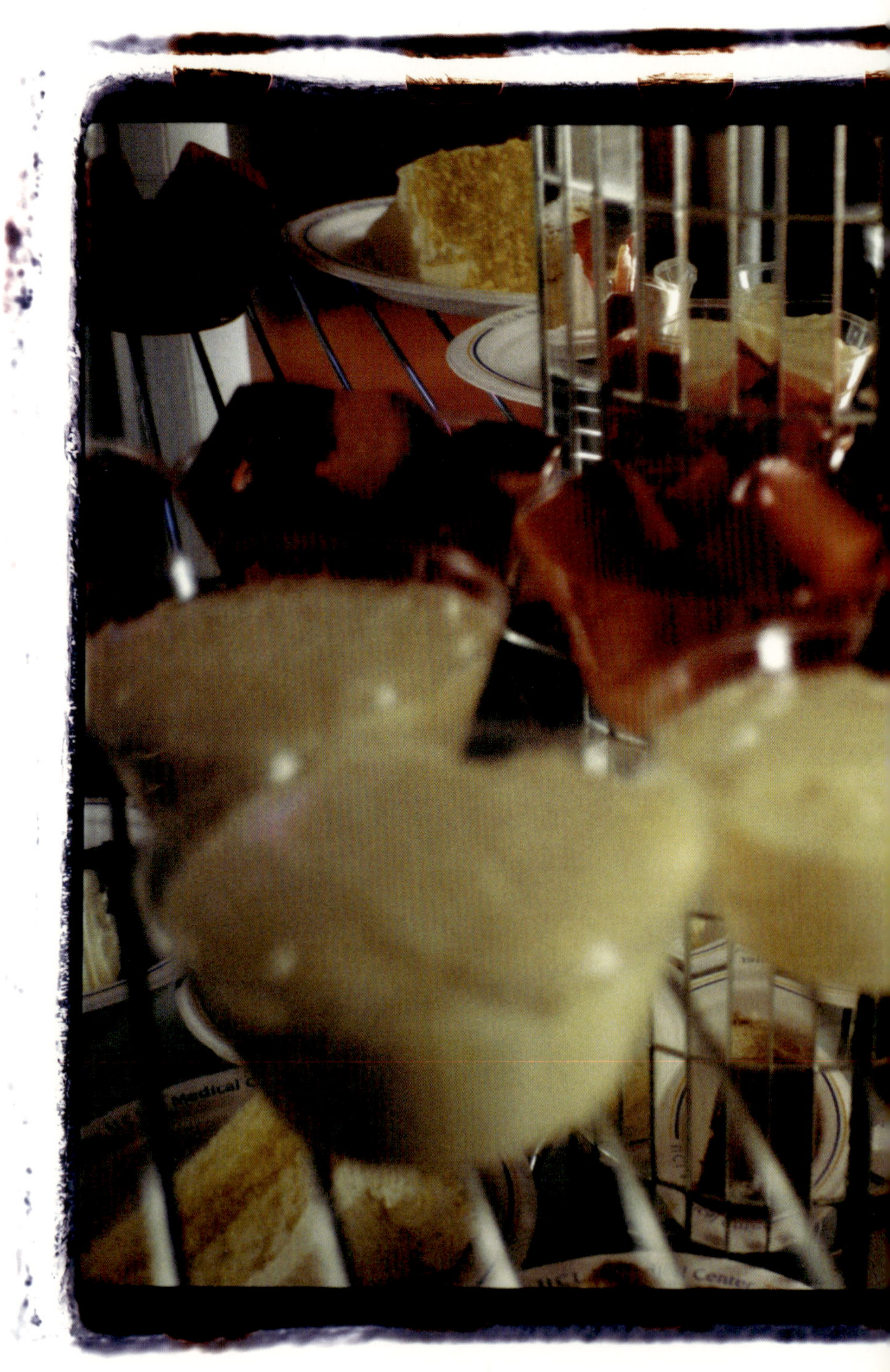

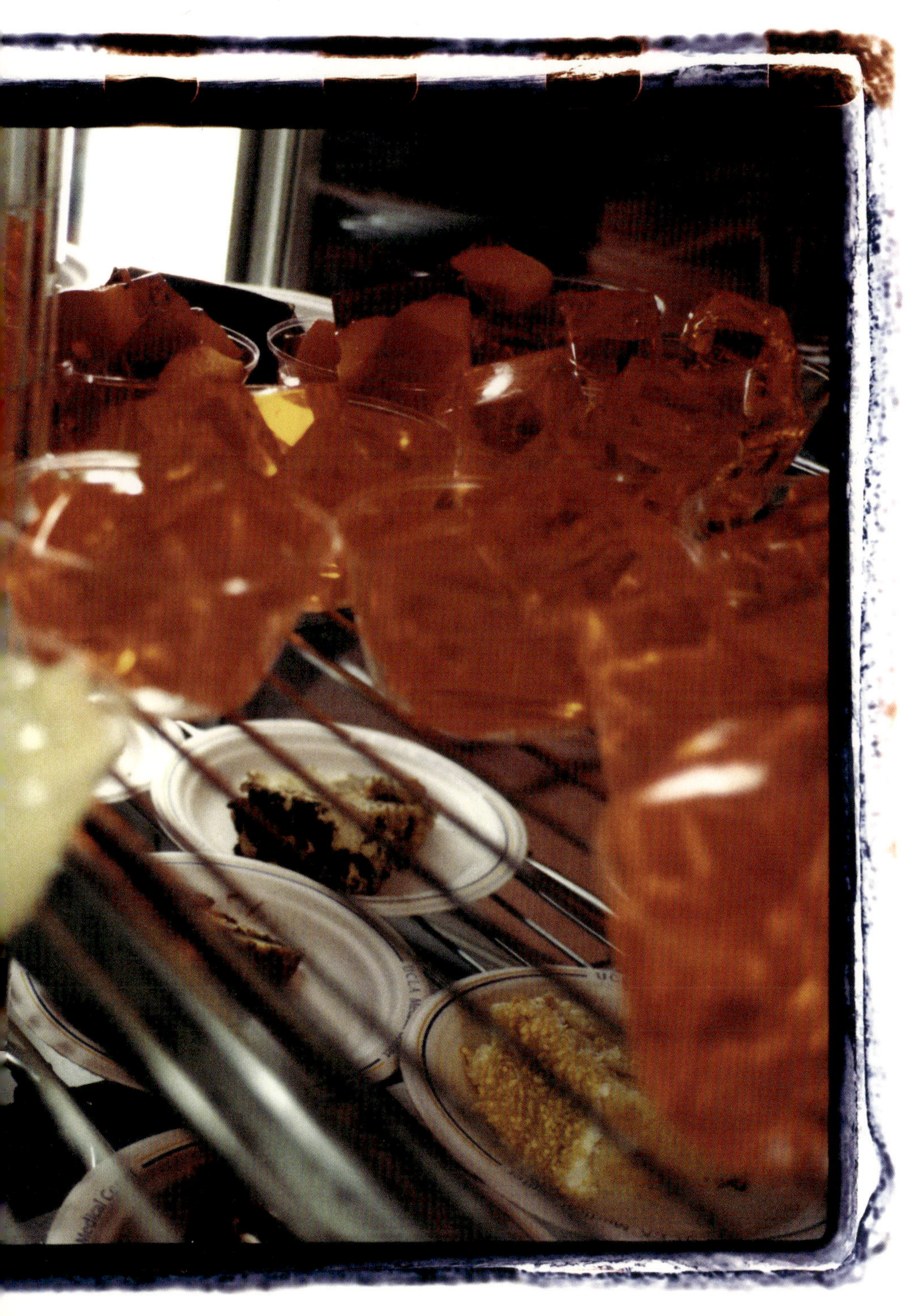

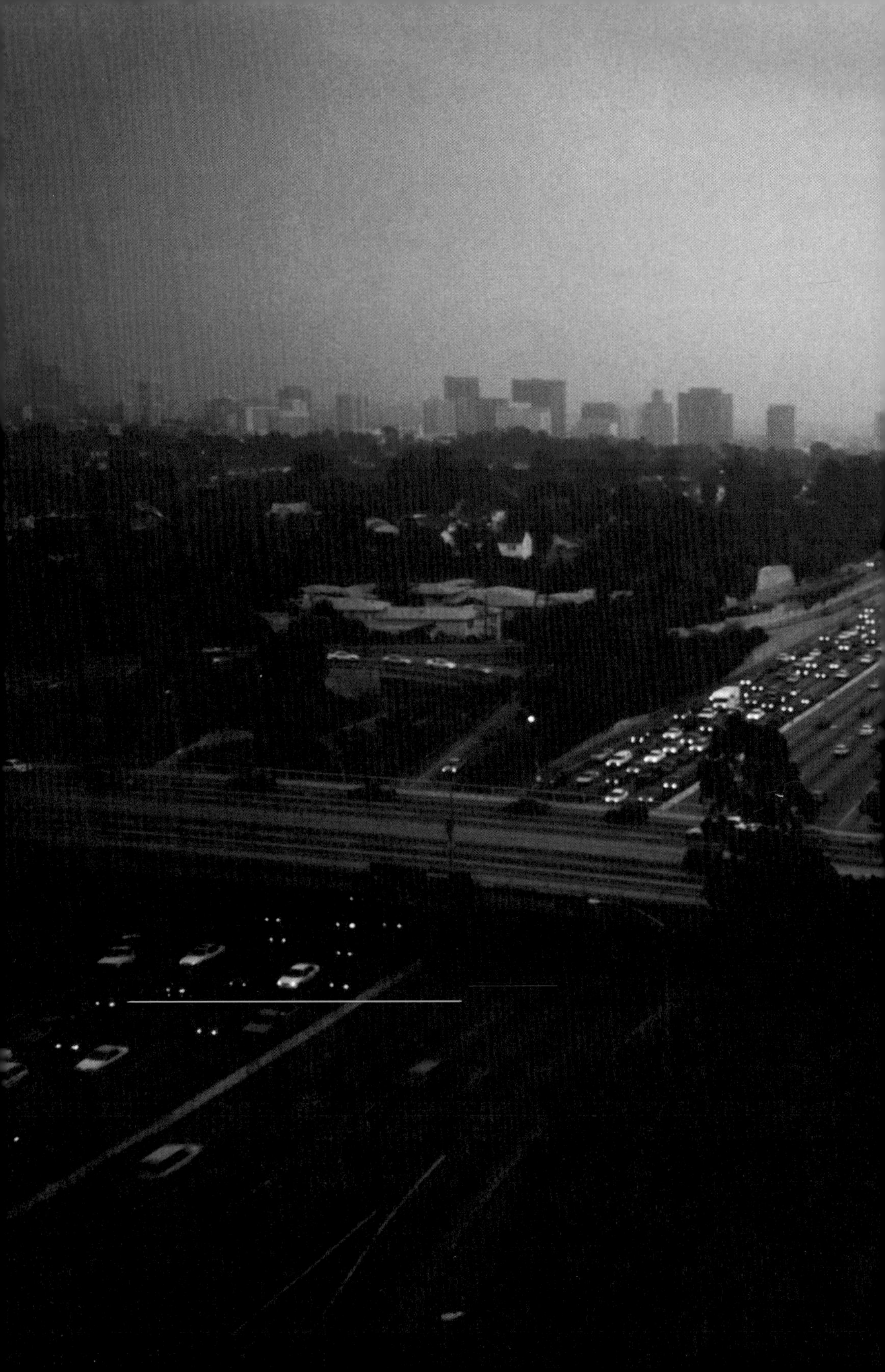

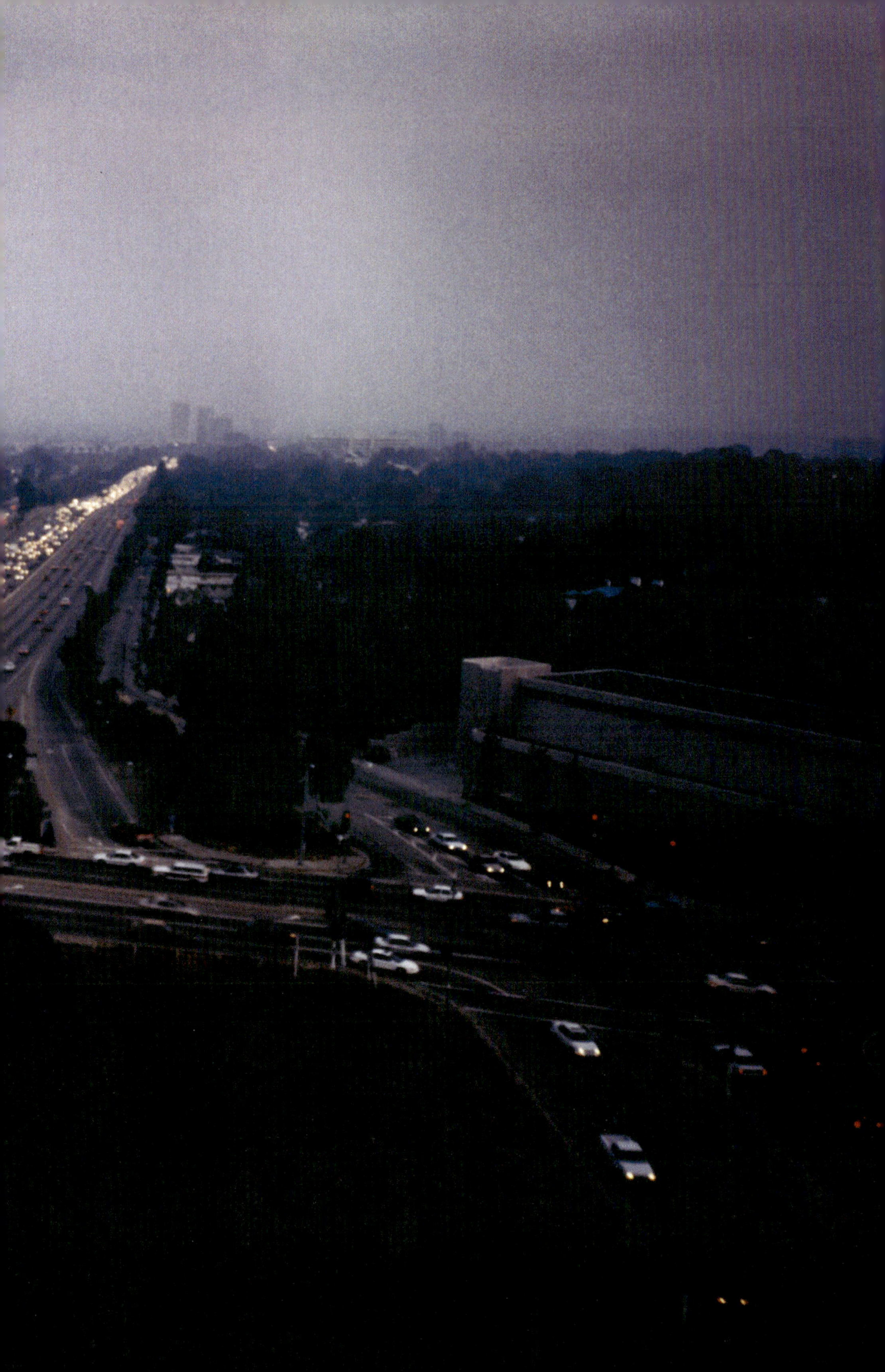

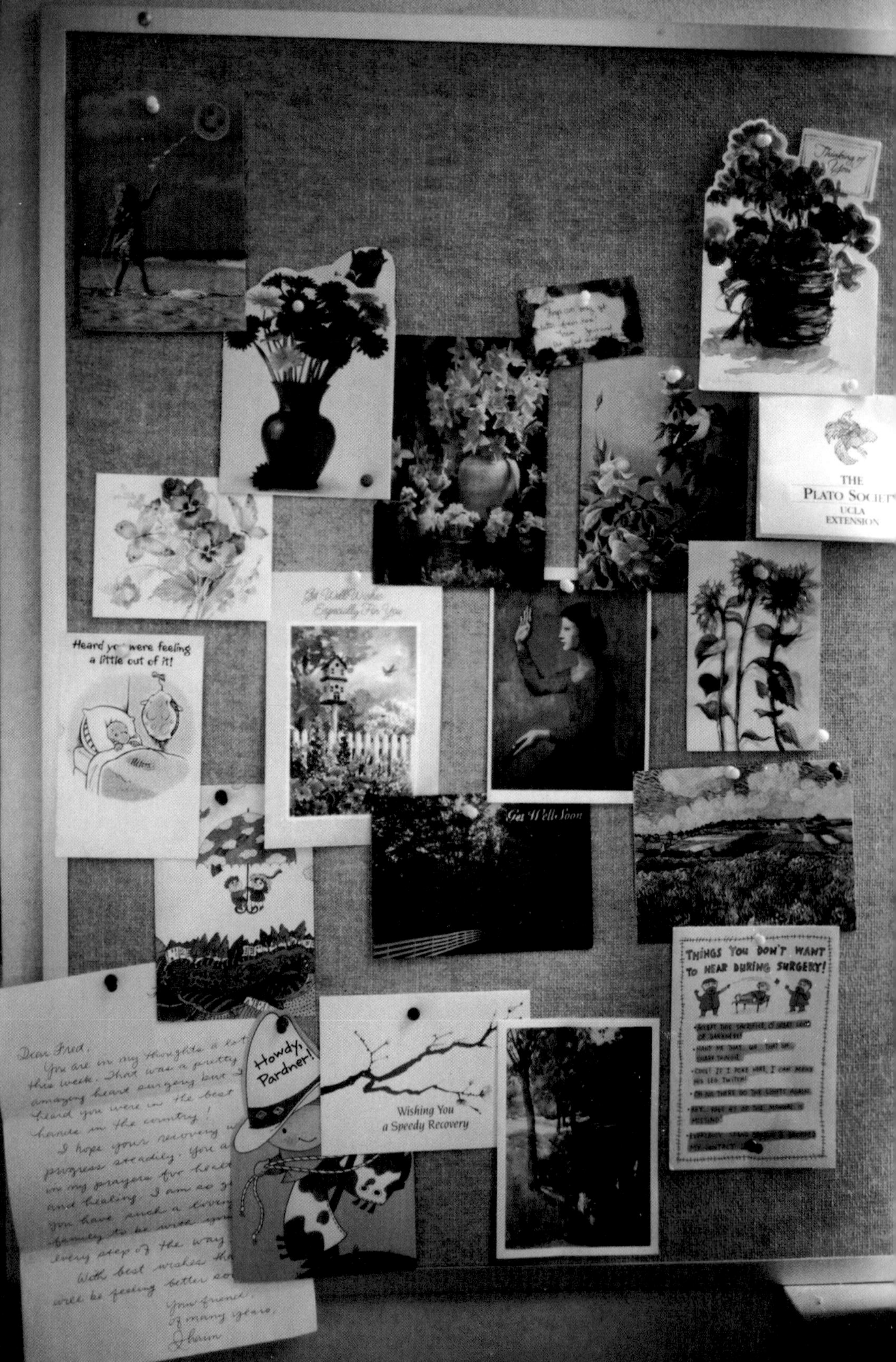

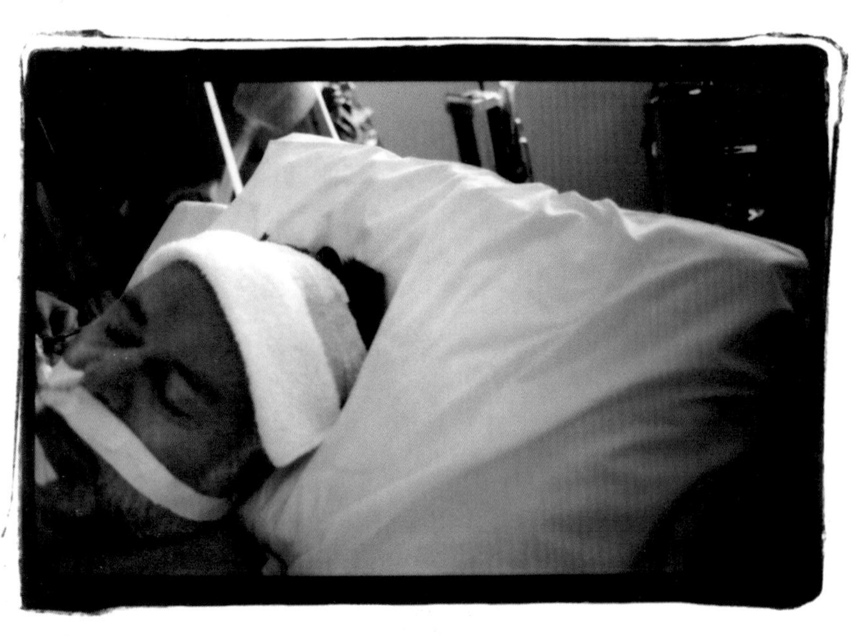

Mary Clare Griffin

Don? Mom calls out, her voice thick and muffled,
but as strong as it can be, like the last big wind
before the storm blows over and away.

Yes honey? He rushes in close.

Am I going?

Yes sweetheart, Dad cries out.

Then let me go. She turns away.

Her last words. Hear them again:

Don?

Yes honey.

Am I going?

Yes sweetheart.

Then let me go.

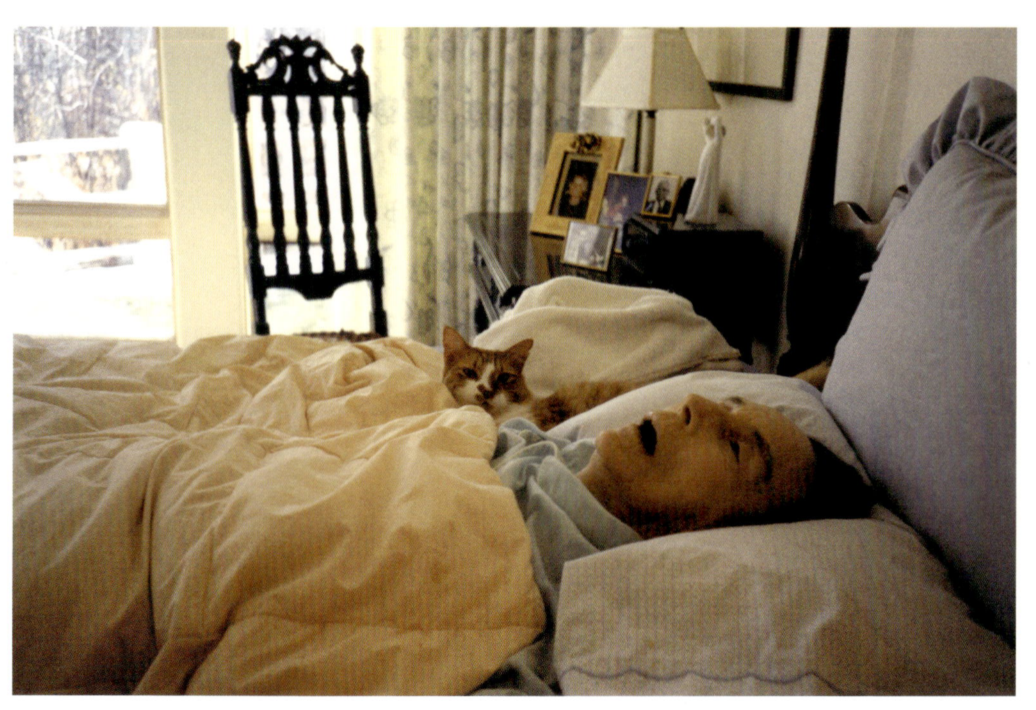

Remembering

Vicenta Ibarretxe Aritzmendi

Sidney Arnold

Carl F. Baumann

Cecile Berger (nee Elmalem)

Jack Cecil Berger

Betty Berle

George Robert Brockelt

Papa Carl

Bernard Carr

Lola Carr

Helen Cather

Virawong Changkasiri

Margarete Connolly

Facundo Cordova

Wilna "Grandma Billie" Coslor

Liz Cunningham

Don Fabricant

Dallas Footh

Helen Footh

Felton Geeter

Amy Goldberg

Herbert Goldberg

Janet Angela Baksh-Gomez

William Alan Gordon

Barbara Griffin

Laura Griffin

Nicholas Samuel Hale

Mary Jane Hoiles Hardie

Lisa Hargis

Eurnice Irene Hatchet

Seth Hennings

Irving Ira Herman

Jose Hernandez

Clara Olabarria Ibarretxe

Petra Olabarria Ibarretxe

Sara Lee James

Minerva Kerslake

Faith Griggs Knox

Connie Kohler

Isabelle Walker Kuehne

Bobbi Anne Lambrecht

Justin Craig Levine

Samuel Levine

Nathan Lichtman

Lurrean Loggins

Willy Loggins

Luke Miller

Lela Jo Johnson Moore

Noodle

Maxine Peters

Marquez Preston

Colleen Rowland

Kenneth Vieth Sampson

Alison Crocker Sanders

Dorothy Shepard

Anne Stuart

Mussa Toueg

Beatrice Luks Weiss

Biographies

Enrique Andrade was recently included in a traveling exhibition of Latino artists from California. He has collaborated on art projects with several community-based institutions, most recently with WORKS/San Jose and the California Historical Society. He is also the art mentor/art instructor at Continuum, an adult day health-care program for people with HIV/AIDS, and teaches at Creativity Explored, an art studio for people with disabilities in San Francisco.

Stefanie J. Atkinson is a photographer, video artist, and educator. Her video projects have examined various indigenous populations and religious ceremonies. Her most recent photographic work includes an independently commissioned black-and-white documentary of a woman's journey from diagnosis through various treatments and stages of recovery from breast cancer.

Amy Auerbach is a photographer who earned a BFA degree in photography from San Francisco State University. She recently received a fellowship award from the Society for Contemporary Photography in Kansas City. Her photographs have been exhibited nationally and can be seen locally at the SF MOMA Artist's Gallery.

Erik Auerbach is a photographer who earned a BFA degree in photography from San Francisco State University. His exhibitions include the Society for Contemporary Photography, Houston Center for Photography, San Francisco Camerawork Gallery, and Intersection for the Arts. He recently received The Friends of Photography/Calumet Emerging Photographer Award.

David Balluff is currently a graduate student in electronic arts. Prior to her death, his cat Noodle had traveled cross-country, and enjoyed backflips and flies.

Albert Baris is a funeral director with the Baris Funeral Home in New York. For more information visit www.baris.net.

John Baumann has been writing and creating theatre in San Francisco, California, since 1994. He has performed at The EXIT Theatre, ODC Theater, Dance Mission, The Marsh, the SF Fringe Festival, and other Bay Area venues. In 1999, John co-founded Right Brain Performancelab with polymath-artist Jennifer Gwirtz. Their performance pieces are a new-vaudeville blend of mime, dance, puppetry, story, and song.

Betty Benard was born in 1935 in Galveston, Texas. She has been creating art at Creativity Explored, an art studio for adults with disabilities, since 1991. She is a very versatile artist who usually works from memory and imagination. She enjoys depicting family gatherings—houses overflowing with people and flowers. Betty has exhibited frequently throughout the Bay Area and recently showed work in Japan.

Marco Berger was born in Casablanca, Morocco, in 1957. He grew up in New York City. He has been an elementary school teacher for nearly fifteen years. He currently lives in San Francisco with his wife and his daughter.

Kimberly Campbell is the founder and director of Memorial Ecosystems, an organization committed to environmentally and socially responsible death care. For more information visit www.memorialeco-systems.com

Suda Changkasiri holds a master of arts degree in industrial arts from San Francisco State University. She has taught art at Creativity Explored, an art studio for people with disabilities since 1999.

Alena Natalia Charow is fifteen years old. She grew up in New York City, and that is where she knew her grandparents. She currently lives in Moscow, Russia, with her parents, her sister, and her brother.

Peter Cordova was born in the Philippines in 1966. He has been working at Creativity Explored, an art studio for adults with disabilities, since 1996. Peter says he has a lot of memories of growing up in the Philippines and would like to go back. Gallery visitors often use the word "tribal" to describe his vivid human and animal forms. According to Peter, he "once saw a big wall with animals and people and then I mixed it all together and I draw from my imagination. If something doesn't work for me I have to use something else." Peter also takes an annual trip to Reno to indulge in gambling and the nightlife. He has a great love of dogs and hopes to soon have one of his own.

Amanda Coslor is dedicated to the creative process and honest expressions of personal life experiences as well as values. She is the co-founder of The Dancing Tree, an alliance of artists who facilitate, develop, perform, document, and publish the stories of underrepresented people from around the world. Amanda has degrees in anthropology and dance from Mills College, has been a practicing counselor in areas of sexual trauma and substance abuse, and is currently studying to be a midwife.

Patricia Coslor makes her home in Custer County, Nebraska, where she has time and space to paint. A former theatre costumer and fashion designer, she now devotes her time to watercolor painting. Her paintings have been published, and she has won awards for her work.

Harrell Fletcher has worked collaboratively and individually on interdisciplinary, site-specific projects exploring the dynamics of social spaces and communities. He has also developed a series of more personal and idiosyncratic pieces that take various forms—drawings, prints, writings, events, videos, and sculptural objects. He has exhibited both nationally and internationally.

Audrey Frank spends her days trying to figure out how things work.

Banira Giri is one of the most influential poets in Kathmandu and one of the few women writers to have established a reputation outside of Nepal. She has published several volumes of her poetry as well as novels. Her poem "Widowed Night: An Expression," was excerpted from her book, *From the Lake, Love,* by Himshikhar Publishers.

Jim Goldberg is an artist and writer who has been involved in long-term collaborations with mostly invisible or misrepresented groups of people, and has received numerous awards and grants for his work. He is currently working on two new book projects—one a fictional autobiography and the other on the immigrants of Greece. Jim is represented by Pace/MacGill Gallery in New York, the Stephen Wirtz Gallery in San Francisco, and by Magnum photo agency. His work is reprinted with the permission of the photographer. Originally published in *Hospice: A Photographic Inquiry,* 1996, Bullfinch Press/Little Brown and Company.

Wolf Gomez is a multimedia artist who grew up surrounded and influenced by the vibrant colors and cultural flavor of the Caribbean islands. Wolf has been a lead artist and youth mentor for Southern Exposure's Mission Voices Program. She has exhibited and is collected both nationally and internationally. Her mixed-media paintings explore the nuances inherent in building a home away from home.

Beth Griffin began her formal art training at the age of six, instructed by Mrs. Betty Byars who resided on Dead Man's Curve in Laurens, South Carolina. During Beth's second year of classes, at the age of seven, "Miss Betty" committed suicide by swallowing Red Devil Lye. Years went by and Beth did art. She did too many drugs. Which she finally kicked, with her sister Laura's help. Then her sister got killed. "The paintings in this book, the 'Laura Series,' spilled out of my soul, and when I'd start to cry, I just let myself cry on them—snot and all. This series, has given birth to every project I've done since then and in some way, keeps her with me."

Mary Clare Griffin entered Seminary soon after the publication of *Language Lessons for When Your Mom Dies* (1999, distributed by Greenleaf Books), where her theological degree focus has been on bereavement and grief/loss issues. Her mother's last words were excerpted from this publication with the author's permission. Mary also facilitates and leads workshops on estrangement and reconciliation, with a particular emphasis on healing fractured communication both at the end of life and in the mother/daughter dyad, as well as with other family relationships. She is currently writing another book, *Theological Anthropology: The Challenge of Being Human,* and can be reached via email at Maryclaremcg@aol.com

Lt. Col. Dave Grossman is a former Army Ranger and paratrooper. He has taught psychology and military science at West Point and Arkansas State University. His passage was excerpted, with the author's permission, from his book, *On Killing: The Psychological Cost of Learning to Kill in War and Society,* by Back Bay Books and Little, Brown and Company. For more information visit www.killology.com.

Jennifer Gwirtz creates choreography and conceptual performance work. In 1998 she co-founded Right Brain Performancelab with her husband, John Baumann. She has been performing in San Francisco since 1995, has facilitated workshops for The Field San Francisco and is a certified Pilates instructor. Jen has nearly finished her first book, *A Manual for A New World Ergonomy.* She and John live together in San Francisco with a house full of memories, stuffed animals, and many, many episodes of *Mystery Science Theater 3000.*

David Hale is fifteen years old, a freshman at Huntsville High in Huntsville, Alabama. He plays guitar and is interested in Russian and Slavic studies.

Marilyn Michlin Herman is a mother of three and recently lost her husband.

Mitchell Herman As I continue to learn about who I am, I realize the positive influence that my father had on my life. I now have to learn to cope with the loss of my beloved Dad. I miss him so much. At least I get comfort knowing that we had no unfinished business.

Todd Herman is a filmmaker and photographer. He is co-director of The Dancing Tree, an alliance of artists who facilitate, develop, perform, document, and publish the stories of underrepresented people around the world. He also co-directs the documentary film team Life Like Films. He has won numerous awards for his film and photography work and has exhibited nationally and internationally.

Jessica Herman-Goodson is a graphic designer who currently resides in Boulder, Colorado. A love of travel, exploring new places, and issues such as family and memory influence the art she creates. In addition to design, Jessica enjoys mixed media, art journaling, bookmaking, and jewelry design.

Camille Holvoet was born in 1952 in San Francisco. She has been working in Creativity Explored, an art studio for adults with disabilities, since 2001. She is known for her pastel drawings of luscious cakes, pies, and pastries as well as portraits of people she knows or remembers from the past. Camille says her work helps her deal with her anxieties. "It's part of my therapy."

Ed Kashi has dedicated his photographic career to documenting the social and political issues that define our times. His images have appeared in *National Geographic, The New York Times*

Magazine, Time, Fortune, Geo, Newsweek, and other domestic and international publications. His photographs have received numerous awards and have exhibited worldwide. His work is reprinted with the permission of the photographer. Originally published in *Aging in America: The Years Ahead* (2003 by PowerHouse Books), in collaboration with his wife, writer Julie Winokur. www.edkashi.com

Kelley Kerslake is a painter living in San Francisco, California. Her work continues to exhibit nationally. She is also the director of Access Arts, a non-profit arts organization for people with disabilities.

Jassim Mohammad Al Khafajy is 31 years old. He and his family live in Falluja, Iraq. He is an engineer, but now drives journalists between Jordan and Iraq. Jassim's photographs were excerpted from the series, "Iraq from Within: Photographs by Iraqi Civilians," *Daylight Magazine,* Issue 2 (2004), and represent the organization's first community arts initiative. Jassim Mohammad photographed within Falluja, documenting the mass graves of people who have died in the war there. Jassim also coordinated the distribution and collection of the cameras. This project could not have been completed without the assistance of Daniel Pepper and Sheryl Mendez. For more information, contact www.daylightmagazine.org. "I wish Americans at home could see what they do here in Iraq. I do not believe this new government is really Iraqis. Mr. Bush is a liar and his troops make trouble and steal everything. This is a small picture of our situation here."

Elizabeth Knox is the founder of Crossings: Caring for Our Own at Death, which is a home funeral care resource center. "We educate and encourage families and communities to take back the intimacy of after-death care— washing and dressing, home wakes, transporting the departed in one's own vehicle. Our work began as a result of the sudden death of my seven-year-old daughter. Nine years later, my mother crossed over. We had them both at home for three days after death before driving them to the crematory. We have helped hundreds of families do the same—be present to the grief and love and wonder of a home funeral."
Crossings: Caring for Our Own at Death
P.O. Box 721
Silver Spring, MD 20901
301-593-5451
www.crossings.net

E. Francis Kohler lives in San Francisco where he works at Creativity Explored, an art center for adults with developmental disabilities. He also makes documentaries that look at the lives of some of the artists who create there. Somewhat obsessed with classic movie monsters, one room in his flat is essentially a shrine to *Frankenstein's Monster, The Wolfman, The Creature from the Black Lagoon, King Kong,* etc. Francis is frequently making sounds/music for the outgoing messages on his answering machine.

Michele Kunard was born in 1951 and has been working at Creativity Explored, an art studio for adults with disabilities, since 1987. Michele often creates images of fish, birds, and animals. She has also painted a number of cathedrals, capturing the light through the windows and bell tower. She felt that they were a success. She hopes to continue to draw and paint, incorporating new images and techniques. Michele is also among the founding members of Theater Unlimited, a theater program for adults with disabilities.

Paula Levine is a Canadian American visual artist, living and working in the San Francisco Bay Area. She has worked in video since 1983 and has produced over twenty video works. Through experiments with narrative structures, her works reveal and question forces present within spheres of social experience, culture, and politics. Her work brings together public and private worlds, and acts as a kind of crossroads.

Richard Lichtman is a writer living in Richmond, California. He earned a PhD at Yale University in philosophy and a master's degree in psychology. Among his publications are *The Production of Desire: The Integration of Psychoanalysis into Marxist Theory, Essays in Critical Social Theory,* and *Dying in America.* Richard Lichtman currently offers workshops on death and dying. For more information contact rlichtman@earthlink.net

Michael Bernard Loggins was born in 1961 in San Francisco, California. He has been writing and drawing at Creativity Explored since 1984. His writing and art have exhibited at galleries in San Francisco, Los Angeles, and New York. His current book, *Fears of Your Life,* is available through Manic D Press. He likes to spend time at Ocean Beach and hang out at his girlfriend Hope's house.

Melanie MacKinnon loves pancakes, hugs, and the mountains. She currently resides in Boulder Colorado, with her daughter Maitreya (aka Pumpkin Love), and her honey, Mike. She haphazardly writes poetry from time to time, rarely likes to clean her house, and is consistently enchanted with life.

Ken Miller says that "One of the things that attracts me to using the camera as a way of seeing the world is watching the changes people go through. My first attempt at this was in the Haight Ashbury neighborhood of San Francisco. I began working with the street alcoholics, Nazi skinheads, and boarding care home residents back in 1982. By 1988 the street alcoholics began to die, the skinheads started on the road to the penitentiary, and I found myself working with the drug-addicted street prostitutes in San Francisco's Tenderloin. In just a few years I saw many of those women die as a result of AIDs. Prison, death, and intense suffering. My projects have always reflected change and impermanence."

Larry Miller and Mindy Zlotnick were foster parents for medically fragile babies for seven years in San Francisco. Larry is now studying to be a chaplain, and Mindy is teaching infant massage to parents of babies with disabilities.

Winifred L. Montgomery specializes in the manipulation of sharp and dangerous objects: molten glass, pointed words, adolescent minds.

Leroy Moore Jr., aka "black disabled man with a big mouth and high I.Q.," is a writer and disability activist living in Berkeley, California. He is executive director of Disability Activists for Minorities Organization, which specializes in advocacy/consultation for persons with disabilities. He is a member of the Molotov Mouths poetry group, and their book *Molotov Mouths,* is available through Manic D Press. www.leroymoore.com

Douglas Morris After the death of his lover of fifteen years, he left his job in the corporate sector. He took up his lover's work, working with developmentally disabled Deaf adults for the past nine years. Doug now teaches art at Creativity Explored and is an American Sign Language Interpreter. "Remembering my lover is important, but moving on with my life, although difficult, is more important."

Alise Murphy is a housewife and mother in training.

Pilar Olabarria holds an MA in conceptual art, an MFA in installation and performance art, and a postgraduate degree in art therapy. She is interested in mixed-media art, mostly installation and performance, and recently started painting with oils. Pilar has received numerous awards for her work. She currently teaches at Creativity Explored, Napa State Psychiatric Hospital, and Vacaville Correctional Medical Facility.

Sara O'Sullivan was born in 1966 in Sacramento, California. She has been creating art at Creativity Explored, an art studio for adults with disabilities, since 1991. Sara executes spontaneous drawings and paintings of people she knows, birds, and animals. She is an enthusiastic artist and always welcomes new ideas and projects.

Delaney Persons has taught ceramics to adults and high school students since 2002. She has also worked with terminally ill cancer patients at the University of Pennsylvania Hospital Cancer Center. She has seen many people die, and although another's passing is difficult to witness, she finds it just as beautiful as birth.

Brenda Rasmussen is the 44-year-old mother of Dallas and Peter. Following spiritual bliss, I am Brenda child of the universe. Blessings and love.

Jay Ruby is professor of anthropology at Temple University. He has published extensively in archaeology, popular music, film, television, and photography, and has been exploring the relationship between cultures and pictures for the past thirty years. His introduction is excerpted from *Secure the Shadow: Death and Photography in America,* 1995, MIT Press, Cambridge, Mass., with the author's permission.

Nakkali Rupta is a photographer living in San Francisco.

Zoë Ryan was born in Australia in 1995. She lives in San Francisco, California. Blessed with a strong will and shining optimism, Zoë's pursuits include circus arts, ballet, drawing, painting, songwriting, and attending the Burning Man Festival. While blessed with many friends and loved ones, she sorely misses her father, who recently passed away, and wishes he could come back and be with her, if only for one more hug, or a day at the beach.

Lori Sampson is a textile artist and bodyworker. She has had previous lives in the fashion and entertainment industries, and is currently pursuing a master's degree in body-centered psychotherapy at the California Institute of Integral Studies in San Francisco.

Susan Schwartzenberg is a visual artist/photographer. Her work ranges from the development of books and installations, to curated exhibitions and larger scale public works. Her themes include biography, memory, and studies of urban life and history. In 1998-99 she was a recipient of the Loeb Fellowship for Advanced Environmental Studies from Harvard University. Susan lives in San Francisco and holds a senior staff position at the Exploratorium. She has exhibited her work internationally.

Gordon Shepard is a visual artist who concentrates on circus and circus-related themes. Some of his inspiration comes from his life experiences, since he once was the featured clown with a small circus known as Big John Strong & Son many years ago. Gordon attends Creativity Explored in San Francisco, an art studio for adults with disabilities.

Noemi Sohn is a Filipino American poet, lecturer, and activist. Both her writing and activism address issues dealing with racial justice, ending violence against women, and disability rights.

Doug Stoddard is a San Francisco civil servant who spends his Saturday afternoons volunteering at Project Open Hand, an organization providing meals to people with AIDS or who are otherwise critically ill. His passions include San Francisco, his friends, and vodka martinis.

Cheryl Strayed's fiction and memoir have been published in *DoubleTake*, *Nerve*, and *The Sun*, among other magazines, and in several anthologies, including *The Best New American Voices* (2003) and twice in *The Best American Essays* (2000 and 2003). The recipient of many awards and residencies, she is a graduate of the MFA program in fiction writing at Syracuse University. Houghton Mifflin will publish her first novel, *TORCH,* in 2005.

Melissa Stuart is a young-at-heart middle-ager who loves family and exploring the essence of life and trying to capture this spirit in creative expressions. She loves to paint life, especially faces, bodies, animals, and nature. Her intention is to discover "what is" under all of our conditioning.

Larry Sultan is a photographer living in Northern California. His work has exhibited in galleries and museums both nationally and internationally, and he has won numerous grants and awards for his work. He currently teaches at the California College of Art.

Miria Toveg is from North Africa. She is an acupuncturist and herbalist who lives in Northern California with her family.

Elizabeth Westrate is the owner of Five Spot Films, a documentary production company in New York City. Elizabeth's photographs were printed with the filmmaker's permission and excerpted from her documentary film, *A Family Undertaking,* which follows several families as they forgo a typical mortuary funeral to care for their loved ones at home. To learn more about Elizabeth's films visit www.fivespotfilms.com.

Willy Whitefeather is an honorary chief of the Black Creek Cherokee of Florida, a teacher, healer, traveler, storyteller, river-rafter, and backwoods guide. He wishes to pass on a message of peace and hope to the young people of the world. Willy's *River Book for Kids* and *Outdoor Survival Handbook for Kids* are available from the National Book Network, 1-800-462-6420. His film, *HOPE* is available through Luna Media Productions, www.lunamedia.org

Katherine Wiemelt is a visual artist and designer who used to see beauty in things falling apart. Now she looks for beauty on the edges of discontent.

Index

Acknowledgments

I am especially grateful to Enrique Andrade, Stefanie J. Atkinson, Amy Auerbach, Erik Auerbach, David Balluff, Albert Baris, John Baumann, Betty Benard, Marco Berger, Susannah Bothe, Kimberly Campbell, Suda Changkasiri, Alena Natalia Charow, Creativity Explored, Peter Cordova, Amanda Coslor, Patricia Coslor, Harrell Fletcher, Taj Forer and *Daylight Magazine*, Steven Geeter, Banira Giri, Jim Goldberg, Wolf Gomez, Beth Griffin, Mary Clare Griffin, Lt. Col. Dave Grossman, Jen Gwirtz, David Hale, Jessica Herman-Goodson, Camille Holvoet, Ed Kashi, Kelley Kerslake, Jassim Mohammad Al Khafajy, Elizabeth Knox, E. Francis Kohler, Michele Kunard, Paula Levine, Richard Lichtman, Michael Bernard Loggins, Robert Margolis, Melanie MacKinnon, Ken Miller, Larry Miller, Winifred L. Montgomery, Leroy Moore, Douglas Morris, Alise Murphy, Rebecca Novick, Pilar Olabarria, Lidia Orloff, Sara O'Sullivan, Delaney Persons, Brenda Rasmussen, Jay Ruby, Carla Ruff, Nakkali Rupta, Zoë and Robin Ryan, Lori Sampson, Susan Schwartzenberg, Gordon Shepard, Noemi Sohn, Doug Stoddard, Cheryl Strayed, Melissa Stuart, Larry Sultan, Miria Toveg, Elizabeth Westrate, Willy Whitefeather, Katherine Wiemelt, and Mindy Zlotnick, for taking the time to contribute to this book, and for openly sharing the many intimacies and interpretations of your experiences with death and loss.

Thank you Tito Tealdo for your gentleness, strength, and competence in making an easy transition for my father and my family. Thank you Louraine "Nee Nee" Loggins for getting the photos to me as promised. Thank you Mindy Zlotnick for all your help, encouragement, and for a wonderful afternoon looking at pictures. Thank you Lee Miller for introducing me to Mindy. Thank you Miria Toveg for your love and for introducing me to Cheryl's work. Thank you Scott Idleman at Blink for your patience and thoroughness. Thank you Rupert Jenkins and the San Francisco Arts Commission Gallery for the opportunity to develop this book into an exhibit. Thank you Jennifer Joseph at Manic D Press for your expertise and for introducing me to Scott. And thank you Kate St.Clair for your impeccable work in copyediting and proofreading the manuscript.

An undying thank you to my mother, Marilyn Herman, and to my brothers, Mitchell and Scott Herman, for your trust, your understanding the necessity of this project, and your acceptance of the presence of my camera during Dad's passing. A deep and tender gratitude to my wife, Amanda Coslor, for your clear vision, your belief in my vision, the acuity of your editorial suggestions, and the solace you provide me. And finally, thank you, Dad, for always being there even when I thought you weren't. I love you and miss you.

Todd Herman

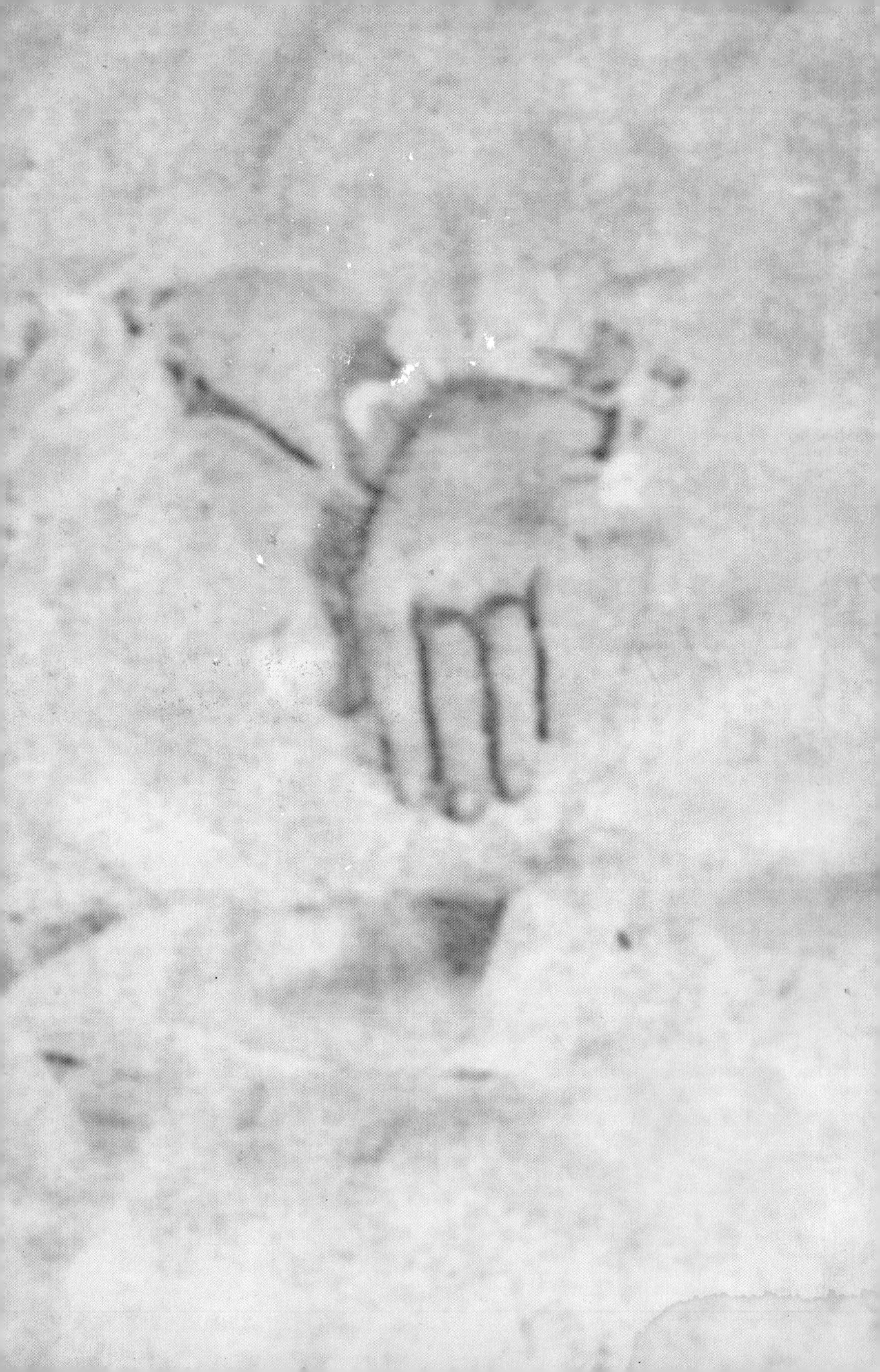